Einstein, Religion, Politics, and Literature

Connecting the Dots

Science, Religion, Wall Street, Obama, The Bible, Big Banks and Buddha:

The Institutional Matrices Of Our Lives

The Real-Time Essays and Short-Stories

by

Lonnie Hicks

Lonnie Hicks

December 2010

Foreword

This book examines the matrix of American institutions, their behaviour and values as they impact American society.

Often books address specific areas in society but the whole matrix of institutions at play upon individuals in society is neglected.

This book seeks to give readers, especially young readers, a sense of this matrix, as it informs and impacts daily life.
Only then can a society can be evaluated as harmful or beneficial to its citizens. Fragmented, non-interdisciplinary approaches leave the reader with fragmented, unintegrated views of the world.

Accordingly, the chapters in this book are wide-ranging in their topics but each focus upon a major institution and illuminate how the threads of this societal matrix cohere. I conclude we are at a critical juncture in American society and make concrete suggestions as to how we could proceed and solve real problems.

Book sections include essays on:
a. The Federal Reserve, Banks and Wall Street
b. Politics, the Obama Administration and the 2010 Elections
c. American Family Structure and its place in American Society
d. The Middle Class in America, the Poor and America's Future
e. The Role of the Internet and the Fight for Control of it.
f. American Literature and its underlying assumptions about human nature-Being an examination of the meaning of the quest to write the Great American Novel
g. An examination of the Bible as Literature and its underlying assumptions, history and political view
h. An examination of the assumptions of modern science, including scientific Theories from Newton to Quantum Mechanics, and beyond
i. A collection of short stories and vignettes from real people, which both records and illustrate The mind-set of Americans in This First Decade of the 21st Century
j. Story-Poems on the environment
k. The American Way of Romance, Humor and Wit

Note: A first consideration in looking at American institutions is to look the dominant financial structures in society and the role that they play in the matrix.

The United States, The Federal Reserve, The Banks & Wall Street

Updated: 12-12-10

Summary:

Updated: 10/22/10 What to do about the financial situation now.

Updated: 10/24/10 more detail on how all this works and more reasons why we hate Wall street and the banks.
Updated: 10/25/10 The Beautiful, the Ugly and the Unavoidable--Our Near Financial Future. Updated: 10-26-10 Who is Suing Who For What and I Have to Pay?
Updated: 10/28/10 Who Owns 40% of the American Economy?
Updated: 10/30/10 Reform the Global Banking System. Seriously, it can be done.
Updated: 11/30/10 But First A History of Banking in the United States. A Must Read
Updated: 12/7/10 What Does The History Of Banking Reveal To Us Today?
Updated: 12/12/10 Why is there no recession in China, India and the East?

It is a tall order to look the history of these institutions and their impact historically and currently on this country. But let's have a go nonetheless.

Let's start with first principles with some basic history and definitions:

First what is a bank and what is the history of banks?

Banks are generally conceded to have come in to existence as early as the 18th century BC. and often operated out of religious sites or temples which had guards, natural and unnatural which, it was thought, made them safer depositories of everything from cattle, to grains to credits. Their function was safekeeping and to avoid moving goods and gold along dangerous routes. Rather a "credit" was deposited one "bank" and cashed at another bank.

But I propose to look at modern banking in its relation to the rise of the nation state.

That jump-starts us to the 12th century where a confluence of several factors caused the re-emergence of banking as we know it to into Europe. Those factors were:

1- The expansion of trade and exploration

2- The Crusades

3- The launching of expanded warfare.

Trade was driven by new merchant and capitalist classes, whose profits from both trade and exploitation of other lands brought to Europe incredible new wealth and a lust for gold, salt, gunpowder, plunder and spices as key drivers in the whole process.

For the first time since ancient times medieval European princes could take new wealth, trade and plunder and parlay it, via war, into new conquests to protect and expand their interests both in and outside Europe.

Since taxation of an impoverished domestic population was not sustainable, this new wealth which banks controlled and this new merchant class offered vast new resources, and the Kings wanted to get their hands on it. So they compromised with the new middle merchant class to get it, giving up some political power in the process, and giving us essentially middle class democracy. Of course, these dynamics took centuries to work out but work out they did.

Banks played a key role in the early process especially the Templars, who are conceded to have created the first international banking system.

If a Lord or Duke was off on a crusade these Templar banks offered to keep safe his gold and previous plunder. Banks as fortified establishments inside huge, safe castles could offer that service for a fee and there was a network of such establishments (and the Knights Templar could offer just such a network,) it meant that a credit of gold at one end of the network could be cashed at the other end of the network without having to risk actually transporting gold and risking theft or plunder from highwaymen and thieving employees.

But the larger point is impoverished or aspiring European princes suddenly had new wealth from the merchant classes and they promptly sought to use that wealth to conquer other lands and the world itself, seeking new wealth, plunder, cheap labor, commodities and slaves.

Banks played a central role in financing these wars and still do as monarch, both democratic and non-democratic, seek financing in the form of taxes, loans, land confiscations and control of lucrative trade routes and commodities.

—

This is the central relationship between the modern state and banks. This remains the central relationship between the modern bank and the United States government.

Banks finance our wars in that the United States has 14 trillion in debt and much of it is owed to the banks of the United States, such that these wars would not be possible without the loans coming from the banks which buy US debt, bonds and other instruments.

Which banks? The ones we all know Wells Fargo, Chase, Citibank, B of A, and investment houses like Goldman Sachs. And the biggest bank of them all is the Federal Reserve Bank. And citizens, too, buy these treasury bonds. So we are all in it.

A closing point to be made here is that just as most Americans owe some bank loan money or otherwise, so does the United States Government owe the banks a lot of money and more depend upon these very same banks to pursue wars, pursue much of its domestic spending, and to pay most if not all of its debts. Taxes and arms sales are the United States governments other sources of revenue. Tax income for 2009 was only 2.7 trillion, arms sales maybe 200 billion, and the rest is borrowed or printed, So you see the picture.

Let's have a closer look at how this works tomorrow.

Oct 18, 2010
Well to understand a bank, think of it this way: you put into a bank your hard-earned 10 dollars and we now want to know what happens to that money. Here goes:

1-The happy dollar multiplies like Octo-mom and by magic becomes 100 dollars over night. That is to say banks are allowed to keep only 10 dollars on hand while loaning out 90 dollars. The assumption here is that most folks will not want their money at the same time and if more than expected do, the banks can get needed funds from the Federal Reserve at virtually zero interest rates (while charging us 4-6 percent.)

In a bank panic, as happened in 1929, this is called a run on the bank because the bank does not really have the 90 dollars. It has been loaned out to others who will not in fact be able to pay it back, in most cases, or have years to pay it back in a situation which calls for the bank to have all that cash on hand immediately. So the bank closes down, the depositors lose their life savings and the bank owners walk free.

But, aside from financial ruin here for the many, the important point to understand is that the 90 dollars was created out of thin air. It was not really there and most importantly was probably never there. It was money created out of thin air. But how do banks spend money they don't have?

—

6

First some losses can and will be covered by the FDIC, or re-insurers like AIG (remember them?) so banks feel free to gamble with depositors money.

2- Second, the Federal Reserve Bank which is, most people don't know, the chairs of the major banks in the United States. Yes, those same major banks in which we place our deposits. If any thing goes wrong these banks put on their federal reserve hats and borrow the money from the federal reserve system which in fact can just virtually order that the money be printed up and give it to the banks (to themselves) at zero interest rate. And you thought the US treasury had control over the money supply.

So banks have a kitty which includes trillions of dollars, depositor funds, free federal reserve dollars, Fanny Mae, Freddy Mac, Sally Mae, and FDIC insurance if things go wrong and in the end the tax payer's foot the bill for recurring financial debacles and no one goes to jail.

This is a system which produces boom and bust and periodic recessions and depressions, for a very real reason; it makes no financial sense whatsoever. Every once and a while the bubble bursts and the real losers are the taxpaying middle class who lose everything. The banks don't lose, you can bet.

I know, this is discouraging news. But this is how the system works. It is a game of musical chairs inside a bubble. Last one without a chair in the chair-parade is the hapless taxpayer every time.

But wait there is more bad news for the gloomy glutton. But let's save that for tomorrow.

Oct 19, 2010
Now what, you may ask, is the federal reserve any way? It is essentially the privately owned central bank for the United States. Other countries have them as well.
Taxation revenues are not enough for governments, we can see, to pay the bills, pay for wars, pay for citizen services, so governments, several centuries ago, and hit upon the idea of accessing other funds other ways. To wit:

1-To expedite borrowing from banks, the concept of the central bank was created (reserves for the Feds, to coin a phrase) such that borrowing could be centralized among the major banks in a given country. Those way governments could raise a lot of money quickly in this centralized system and get at citizen funds over and above direct taxes. This worked for while until the advent of fossil fuels.

2-With the advent of fossil fuels in the last 125 years, coupled with population growth on the planet which has exploded, this means that

—

governmental costs have also exploded. Such pressures also have meant wars over natural resources to feed these burgeoning populations. More people are alive today that in most of our history. 6.8 billion souls vs. a population plateau, which has existed at 2 billion souls for centuries. Earth's population is now projected to reach 9 billion by 2050--fossil fuels have made this unsustainable life style possible. Now this growth has its repercussions as I have described above and elsewhere.

In a word, our population growth rates will quickly outstrip the capacity of the planet to sustain such growth.

The manifestations of all this are easily seen: we are running out, or foreseeable, will run out of everything at this rate of growth.

But back to the banks. The current Federal Reserve system was created in 20th century to help finance all of the burgeoning needs. It was essentially a huge credit card system for Governments which needed more and more funds to meet the exploding needs of population and the related wars, for growth, to expand technology, for what can be easily seen as the most expensive and wasteful century in the history of the planet.

But such waste is, and was obviously, unsustainable.
Now the banks had government as their greatest borrower and, as we all know, if you owe the bank the bank owns you.

This is true of governments as well. But where is the money coming from that banks are lending to these governments? Mostly from our deposits in those banks, from "investments" in third world countries, from "printed" and manufactured dollars and arms sales. Thus, governments desperate to keep the ship afloat, access funds through direct taxation, through our own bank deposits and borrowing--all to keep this leaky vessel afloat.

The current "austerity" programs we are seeing all around the world, where Britain is looking at cutting everything, in France where cutbacks are creating riots, in Spain, Ireland, and Greece as well, are all debt driven political manifestations of bank debt owed by those governments.

He who rules debt, rules the world.

So you see this bank thing is no small thing at all. We are the Debt Driven Century spending and borrowing more and more money to prop up a financial system which is in dire need of serious reform.

See, told you only a gloom-glutton would like this installment.

But there are solutions. There always are.

Oct 20 2010

We pause in our exploration of banks to put out some solutions (to preserve our mental health) and then we will return to our main topic.

If, as I posit, that virtually all of the western world is in debt to the banks, who in turn got the money from depositors like us, from printed money and from third world markets and borrowing, what is to be done?

Conservative and radical right wing elites in virtually all of the western countries have seized upon this debt situation to demand cutbacks which is really using the debt situation to achieve right-wing political objectives.

This is the "a crisis is a terrible thing to waste" philosophy being used politically to demand the re-impoverishment of the middle classes in all of the countries of the west--to the benefit of the banks, the stock markets, and the super rich--because of the debt that is owed; we want to know to whom are these huge sums of money owed to?

The answer in the United States is Wall Street, huge hedge funds, the super rich investors, international banking interests and the like. There is not a shortage of money, rather it is its concentration in the hands of one percent of the population across all of the countries involved which constitute the problem.

Trillions of dollars exist in those hands as they put pressure on governments to dis-invest in their own middle classes, under so-called "austerity" programs under pain of not being able to borrow any more money from them in the future.

Right wingers in those countries are happy to oblige because it fits their political agenda.

These "bad economic times" is great cover to strike out at immigrants, at the middle classes, at minorities and at other historical enemies, under the guise of setting the economic house on a better footing.

This is false. In fact, it will quickly, within three years, bring on a second, more severe recession, probably a depression, in the entire west. We will also drag down China with us and the depression will be quickly world-wide in scope. After all, who will be buying all those Chinese products if the West's middle class population is jobless and homeless?

The financial engine of the world will grind to a halt, and worse:

1-We will enter a period of alternating deflation and inflation, permanent under classes in many countries, increasing concentration of wealth in

—

9

fewer and fewer hands, riots, increasing warfare as countries seek to gain resources to feed their populations.

2-New debtor laws with interest rates rising (30 percent even now on certain credit cards, which means bank debt can never be paid off) and a permanently indebted class comes into being. Only a banker could love this scenario.

3- Bankruptcy laws which were re-written in 2008 in the United States which gave the banks and credit card companies the right to seize 25% of a family income in bankruptcy proceedings for an extended period is a horrible example. This is a stark statement in law which creates a permanent debtor class.

So now what will happen and what are the solutions to all this? Can it be headed off before disaster strikes?

Well yes. Let's look at what likely scenarios might be which fall into two groups: constructive solutions and destructive solutions.

For today, let's looks at one or two of the constructive ones.

1-Restructure, default, renegotiation and forgiving of debt national or personal are the first possibilities.

It happens all the time. Argentina defaulted on its debts and now Argentina thrives despite claims that such default would ruin the country. The fact of the matter is that world-wide current debt cannot be sustained or paid back under current terms and the social costs are too high even if it could be paid back. (Note this is what is and will continue to happen to mortgage debt in the United States. (The money to pay it back is not there.)

Restructure is an obvious eventuality. Restructure loans national and individual. The issue is that no company or country ever savaged its middle class and quickly returned to prosperity. One cannot cut one's way to prosperity; especially cuts which benefit only the few.

Shared prosperity is the only modern model that has really worked.

Financial blood-letting and "cutbacks" is a financial fantasy born in the bankers" heart.

2-**Default** is the other obvious way to go. In fact, in the housing sector in the United States, this aspect is already under way. If the people, or countries for that matter, cannot pay the banker debt, they default.

Simple.

—

But what are the consequences of such a mass event financially? Default happens as anger at the system becomes overt, where trust in the system has eroded and citizens rise up and decide they will no longer play by the rules that the bankers themselves appear to have broken. The social fabric will be rent and there will be the need for some serious needle work along some other lines. But default is already happening--and needs to happen. It is inevitable. In fact, threaten the bankers with default and restructuring most times will happen.

Tomorrow we look at still other possibilities and ways out of the mess.

Oct 21, 2010
Loan modifications are on the table now, but there are problems with it . The banks actually make money on foreclosures since many of them also own the loan servicing providers. Any chance of a modification a year ago, therefore, was moot and in fact did not happen for most.

What has changed, as of today, is that banks, now can make money on foreclosures still by charging fees and costs to these loan servicing companies they own. They have added other sources of income since then as well. (Ever wonder where those pay-day loan companies suddenly sprang from? The banks figured out they could charge 20-30 to a hundred percent interest to poor people and many of the major banks finance these little enterprises and no one complains.)

So money pours in from pay-day operations, from foreclosures since the they own the loan servicing organizations, they can also make money on modifications now since the Feds, mainly HUD, is now offering loan and loss guarantees for modifications which meet the guidelines, (in California 31% of total expenses) On top of that, if default occurs anyway, after the loan modification, there is Sally and Fanny Mae plus FDIC, (the latter three institutions now owed, repeat, owned, by the Federal Government,) meaning our money will be funnelled to the banks via this route as well. And guess what, despite all this, the Federal Reserve is now also talking about a trillion more to buy "toxic" assets, there is still no credit coming forth to individuals and small businesses. The banks are taking the money and hoarding it, paying huge bonuses, and buying up small banks and the competition, *with our money*.

So the banks will do just fine, no matter what.

The homeowner has one weapon in his or her arsenal--walk away and default after living in the home mortgage-free for six months to a year.

The credit takes a hit but that may clear up in two years, but by then you have the cash saved up for essential needs, or declaring bankruptcy can forestall foreclosure altogether.

These are options not just for Americans, but for governments as well. We can expect to see more and more of this happening with governments as it becomes clear that most governments cannot, in fact repay their outstanding loans and face a population rebelling and rioting against "austerity" programs imposed by the banks on governments-cut backs which will, in fact, in two-three years, bring on yet another recession. Then the bitterness meter will have hit the roof, possibility endangering civil society itself. France is just the tip of the iceberg.

So destructive solutions will surface unless the monied classes realize that shared prosperity is best way to go, not hoarding gold and stacks of money in their vaults.

This realization is what saved the system in the great depression plus World War II. But elites today are not that smart. After all, the Marshall Plan was the attempt to re-build markets in Europe and Japan after war destroyed those economies. That was smart and it paid off in that these countries needed everything after the war and became crucial markets for American companies.

Now as I have mentioned in another blog, the best example of a constructive model is the German example. See my blog on "What America Must Do to Survive" on this site.
There are models and examples of solutions which are possible, constructive and within reach.

Moreover, as can be seen from this analysis, governments and government spending are not the problem, they are mere symptoms of issues that now face everyone, individuals and institutions.

Other constructive solutions I have proposed include:

1-Wall Street cannot be trusted with depositor's money, (remember Wall Street investment houses are now banks as well) so the thing to do is to deny these corrupt institutions their life-blood, our daily deposits, our 401k''s, our labor union pension funds, and city and state government deposits as well.

Money is the only language they understand. Don't continue to give them ours.

No real interest will be forthcoming and remember the system has not changed one wit, financial reform bill or no. A threat to take the money out will work.

—

Take the money and have it invested locally or insist with your union, your city, your state, or your employer that funds be invested locally with local banks, coops, savings and loans and the like. Jobs will return and this economy will recover. Individuals can do this right away. Lobbying with have to take place to get the rest done and perhaps a state referendum.

If not, pass the hat, get yourself a stick and a red bandana.

2- A second thing to do after dealing with the money funnel is to deal with political minions who are prisoners of monied classes. Start with the referendum, and statutory law.

More on that later.

Oct 24, 2010
But first let's take a closer look at the statement made above that banks make money out of thin air.

An example:
A deposit of 100 magically becomes 400 dollars in that banks take in the 100 dollars, and to meet reserve requirements, must keep, say, on hand 20 dollars. The remaining 80 dollars is lent out. The borrower takes the 80 dollars and deposits it into his or her bank and that bank does exactly the same thing--keeps 20% for reserves and loans out the rest.

Note there is something very odd about all this. To wit:

1-No new goods are being produced here, only money changing hands among banks.

2-This "multiplier" expands the money supply in what, to the very astute, can easily be seen as a gigantic ponzie scheme which will collapse periodically, domino-style, as exemplified in the 2008 wall street collapse. Even a few depositors demanding all of their money at the same time will cause the whole system to collapse, and it did.

3- The banks can take the risk because they have the Federal Reserve, the Government, FDIC and the tax payers and others to bail them out, as they were bailed out just this way.

4-Also we might ask what all of this money backed by anyway is.

Well, sit down for a second, shock might cause you to collapse. *This is all backed by nothing.*

Currency, this paper money we use, dollar bills and the like, used to be backed by silver or gold. That is, until 1971, you could take your dollar bill and go to the bank, or the government and demand a dollar in silver. They

—

13

were then called "silver certificates." Also for international trade there was also gold, in which nations could demand gold in the place of Ion's or paper currency. A nation was obligated to keep gold supplies in amounts matching the amount of paper currency in circulation. (This is what Fort Knox is supposed to be) Let's smile together.

In 1971 Nixon took the US off the gold and silver standards and the value of paper currency was allowed to float and its value then became whatever governments, individuals or countries thought it was worth or negotiated and/or agreed to.

Does this sound like a good idea to you? Me neither.

So paper money becomes subject to whatever the market will bear and becomes subject to the tender mercies of currency speculators with large sums of money to take advantage of fractions of a penny differences in currency values among countries to make even more money.

Governments sometimes step in and try to control the value of their currency, sometimes keeping it artificially low (China) as compared to other countries currencies so as to gain a trade advantage, namely exports. My goods are cheaper than your goods and my people, therefore, have jobs and your expensive goods don't sell and your people get no jobs and layoffs.

Finally, this paper currency is now severed from both gold and silver, has no actual goods of value representing its value, and can be artificially expanded and contracted by banks and countries, becomes the play thing of banks and wall street, thereby become purely financial transactions, not representing the production of actual goods and services and, artificially, become the economic engine of the world, where disaster is, and has been inevitable, periodic, devastating and recurring.

The clash over the currency and money and the quantity of currency or money in circulation is not an academic exercise. The struggle is between debtors and creditors. Anyone taking a look at economic history will quickly see that is the case.

Creditors loan me 100 dollars and if there is an expansion of the money supply there is inflation, too many dollars chasing too few goods (remember that from Econ 101? So it takes more dollars to buy the same 100 dollars worth of goods, say 105 dollars. The creditors, read here the banks, lose from their point of view, 5 dollars and get the loan paid back in cheaper dollars.

No, they would rather have a deflationary situation where there are fewer dollars in circulation so that those who have hoards of cash can buy up houses, loans and other items at less than their initial dollar cost. Say my

—

14

house was worth 100 last year but only 60 dollars now, who wins here? This is what is happening today and why. The banks are making money buying up our deflated assets, houses and bank accounts.

The banks win because they are the only ones with hoards of cash and can buy that house at 60 dollars not 100 dollars-cash. And if they don't have the cash they can borrow from the Federal Reserve to get the money with little or no risk in doing so.

Life aim's fair; never has been since the money system has looked like this.

So where are we? This last recession is not over, there's more to come.

But heads up we can get through this. But solutions have to wait for tomorrow--that is my way. A little suspense never hurt anyone.

Oct 25, 2010
There are several solutions on the table. Above some solutions have already been suggested. There are others in my blogs on Obama, and in the blog "What America Needs to Do To Survive."

Here is a quick summary, and then, I will add more about what to do with the national and the international banking situation.

1-We are headed for a new deep recession/depression where defaults and renegotiations will surely occur. This must be organized in a planful way. Individuals and governments must now start to insist that debts be forgiven or drastically altered to affordability levels, rather than insisting on repayments which is now decimating the middle class of the entire western world.

If these austerity measures continue there will be no one to lead us back to recovery because the middle class of America and Europe will not have the money to purchase the goods--if there are goods produced. Why? How can the goods get produced if the banks won't loan us our own money to buy the machines or invest in the economy? Rather we will see deflation in prices (we already have that) or rapid increases in interest rates or inflation. All of these are bad outcomes.

2-We need to be sure that large banks and investment houses never hold us over this kind of barrel again. We need to reform the financial systems of the western world (they are all now in it together protecting the money they got from the middle class in the first place.)

15

We should in most instances have to rebuild economies along the lines of the German example. A major reason Germany has survived the recession more or less intact is that it has a strong local, citizen-driven, community banking system. We need to follow that example in the western world. It a model that is sustainable.

3- We need to free ourselves from the monopoly banking and investment houses with a new model called "free banking." That is to say lets us treat these financial institutions as we do other enterprises, no bailouts, no Fanny and Freddie Mae (these are government bailouts in disguise) no quick fix loans from the Federal Reserve, no Dollar-Fiesta Handouts like in 2008. If they fail, they fail like any other business.

The Federal Reserve should put trillions into the Community Re-investment Act and bypass these characters altogether. (Look this act up. It is easy to see this act will be under attack in the new Congress because it is designed to do exactly what I am suggesting.)

4- To be taken seriously we should organize institutional power from cities, states, individuals, and pension funds and demand community investments of all kinds. Congress would love it since Congress represents mostly local communities. The banks would not support this for the sole reason it would cut into their profits and their investing in China.

5-Change the ERISA laws to accommodate these much-needed changes. If the Republicans like the free market so much lets administer some of that medicine to the banking system, to wall street, and the international profiteers.

Is all this possible? You bet. And it can start with each of us making the common sense decision to take our money out of a system which is exploiting us with our own money.

Make no mistake, change will happen and is already happening, people don't have the money to repay crooked loans made in a crooked monopoly system.

The only real issues are whether all this will happen in an orderly or a disorderly way.

I, for one, do not relish the disorderly way. That will be ugly.

Next time: Let's go down for more detail on all of this.

Oct 26, 2010
Speaking of disorderly I read in the papers that investors who got burned in the housing toxic assets caper are suing to get their monies back. This could tie things up for years and in effect, depress the housing market

—

16

along with this kind of legal action. This is disorderly. If the investors win large the banks could see their reserves depressed or be eliminated pre-emptively, even before a case came to final determination. Their story can and could be: "We can't lend out since we don't know what the legal liabilities might be." An already depressed economy becomes more depressed and life looks glum indeed. No loans for you and me and our money moves overseas.

If the banks win the legal cases expeditiously then the investors take the financial loss and won't invest in other worthy job-creating projects and guess who will then have to step in--our friend the Fed and then us tax payers take another round of unemployment perhaps or at least have to finance, in the end the Feed's efforts, either through a stagnant economy, continued joblessness or rising inflation. In all of this there are no actual goods being produced, merely money hounds exchanging dollars and balance sheet assets, toxic or other wise.

Golly gee.

Oct 28, 2010
A short note today: How much daily bad news can an optimist take? The note here is that in the last 35-40 years Wall Street firms, let's take Goldman Sachs, and has grown from 12 million in assets and 45 employees to the be mouth we know today.

How did that happen?
Wall street now receives over 5 trillion dollars a year of the American economies 13 trillion dollar economy-38 percent!
Why are we are sending that much money to them? We did not used to do this. So what happened we may ask?

How did wall street become the monster it is and too big to fail? That is the most important economic story of the last 30 years. America has essentially been looted of its basic production capacity and this has been replaced by a finance industry which is 40 percent of the entire economy and produces nothing except processing wealth from the middle class to its own coffers.

A society would have to be out of its mind to do this. This was all done with the promise that in 30 or forty years your money will be returned with interest. Except the 30 or forty years are now up and what happened? Sorry, not only was it not returned but 40% of our middle class wealth has disappeared and the explanation is "we told you investments are risky and you should have read the prospectus carefully."

Secondly what has occurred is that the enormous wealth is being used to a hostile takeover of our political systems and politicians, who could not and can not resist the bushels of money wall street funnels to them.

17

The substance of the republic is undermined. It reminds me of what happened in the Roman example: hoards of the poor in the cities, while the rich got richer-and that failed. This one will too.

But what to do about all of this? This financial debacle is not just an American failure, but this American failure is now global, most of Western society is involved.

A global problem now requires a global solution.

We now ask what that might be.

Oct 30, 2010
A global solution should first take a look at the current world finance and economic structure.

The current strategy is to dis-invest in the middle classes of Europe and the United States in order to pay trillions back to the monied classes is sure to end in default, renegotiation, re-structuring, modifications, and or forgiveness of debt.

If not we will get inflation, deflation, social unrest and general economic chaos with the rich building compounds, isolating themselves behind walls to protect their wealth while the rural and urban masses became poorer and more and more resentful.

Therefore, the issues go beyond the merely economic but reach the social, the political, and the geographic and basic resource allocations on a global scale.

Now in this blog we can start to look at what might work. The current WTO (World Trade Organization) attempts to allocate income based on trade. That in fact has been a methodology whereby wealth is transferred from the poor countries to the rich countries; where poor countries are stripped of their natural resources, their labor and these are consumed by the rich countries at highly favored trade agreements governed by the WTO.

The finance structure of all of this collapsed in 2008 revealing its weakness as a model for the future.

So what is to be the structure of the future? Mention this topic and people put a spooky finger to the wind and say "India and China will take over the world."

Let's have a look at that proposition. First China. China has tremendous economic growth rates of 5-15 percent and that is its strength. It has 1.3 billion people to feed everyday and that is its weakness.

18

Suppose you had 1.3 billion mouths to feed everyday? That is a tremendous burden. The US has 320 million or so as does Europe.

The Chinese will flatten out in resource allocations-coal, oil with population at about 2060 and replace the United States as the most voracious consumer of the planet's resources. This is bad news for China. Bad news because it is not sustainable.

The same argument can be made for India with its billion people.

Now Europe too, will die by demography since most European populations and that of the United States will disappear by 2060 or become distinct minorities in those nations. The demographic handwriting is on the wall.

Now what is missing in this financial scenario is the likely emergence of Africa. Africa has a 1.3 trillion dollar economy, 60 % of the world's arable land, a young population, 52 cities of a million or more (as many as Europe) and rising disposable income. Africa has infrastructure issues but has enormous resource wealth (the Chinese are investing heavily) cheap energy, land resources, an labor pool in which 75% of young people are getting at least an elementary school education (See the Mckinsey Global Institute's report on emerging Africa) and a finance structure which is decentralized (for now) and therefore, immune from central bank debacles. (Note however, centralization is being insisted upon by central banks from other countries.) But retail businesses are the basic businesses of the continent aside from the resources and extractive examples.

Add Africa to the mix and a path to sanity for global finance seems more possible.

A quick outline (we will do detail later) would state that the world financial stage must be protected from the predatory global banks. They merely suck the world dry and give nothing in return.

A more decentralized model is required, such as the German Community Bank system, and the Community Banking system in the United States. Re-instate the Glass-Steagall Act and get the investment houses out of the banking system once and for all. That is the path back to sanity.

Re-invigorate local and regional banks and let the Central and large banks live by the rules or die.

More on all of this later.

But for background one has to understand the real history and nature of banking in our own backyard--The United States. There we can see what our forbearers did to curtail the power of banks. They were seen a threat

—

from the very beginning in this country by none other than Thomas Jefferson who warned against them time and time again.

He said:

"Banking establishments are more dangerous than standing armies."

In fact the revolution was fought against England not over tea bags but over English banks who wanted control over currency in the new world. The colonies were printing their own currencies and prospering.

Battles over control of currency have occurred time and time again in our history as the banking industry sought to control finances, debt and the population. Now that battle has been rejoined as it was waged time and time again in American history.

A quick look at that history is now in order.

See this link below:
http://whatreallyhappened.com/WRHARTICLES/wildbankers.php

Then we will summarize key points tomorrow.

Dec 7, 2010
I have had questions of exactly how do banks control much of the economy and some of you have suggested that I have been too hard on them.

Perhaps.

But here is why they have been so powerful in American history and continue to be a threat to democracy and cannot be trusted with our money.

Think about it in the following examples:

1-If you make a million dollars today, by earning it or inheriting it, the first thing you do is take it to the bank. The bank now has your money to use anyway it sees fit and gives you a piece of paper every month telling you how much interest you are earning. But the fact is that your money has been loaned out to someone else who might take years to repay it.

2- The same example is true for individuals who put their monthly pay checks into banks, send off their 401k payments, etc, all landing into the banks bank accounts.

20

3-The same example is true for governments as well. They put money into those same banks. Banks have come to point where they have everyone's money to play with, with few controls or regulation over what they do with those funds.

One, in this, cannot underestimate the volatile situation where greed and large sums of someone else's money collide.

It *is always disastrous* for you and me.

But why, I have been asked, doesn't the government do something about this?

That is a good question best answered in the context of a current situation. There are two answers:

The chair of the Federal Reserve has announced the intent to put 600 billion new dollars into circulation thereby making dollars cheaper and thereby increasing our exports and thereby creating new American jobs.

The validity of this proposition aside, Bernanke has received a firestorm of criticism for doing this from the banking industry and wealthy individuals.

Why should this be so? See my above example, but this is the eternal battle between creditors and debtors. Creditors, the banks, want fewer dollars in circulation because that, makes the dollars they hold, worth more. The more dollars in circulation makes the dollars they hold worth less because more dollars with the same amount of goods equal inflation.

So the monied classes see this move as a direct threat to their wealth.

And this view is shared by the monied classes world wide--they all have the same interest in reducing the amount of money, in this case dollars, in circulation.

Now what is also important, but not generally discussed, is how these hostile reactions from the monied classes carries with it disguised threats and reveals thereby the true source of their power over the state and individuals.

The reaction they have can be measured in the price of gold. When it goes up, and it has, the monied classes are warning governments, individuals, politicians, corporations in the following way:

"If you support loose credit, more dollars in circulation, and don't back austerity programs we will simply take our money and put it into gold. We will take our ball and go home if you don't continue to let us win the game of stripping the middle classes of their wealth, wealth we got from them in the first place."

You will have no loans, no money for growth, industry will grind to a halt and there will be social unrest, perhaps revolution and modern society will become ugly. **This is the out and out threat** being enunciated her.

And it is no idle threat, They could do it and they did it in 2008 and panicked the US government into giving them 800 billion. This ploy works.

The debtor is obliged to do what the creditor wants him to do,(in this case the US government,) even if it means shooting the family dog--or in this case impoverish their own people and their own middle class.

In this only the politicians and the wealthy survive, everyone else, in the name of austerity, are obliged to help the wealthy protect the value of their dollars and their wealth. These are always the battle lines as societies have battled the banks and the wealthy for control all through history. The lesson is clear: Don't let a few people take over control of the people's wealth.

I know, astonishing. But this is the way things really work.

After all, it is an incredible act to punish your own people in these ways. Governments often will do it until the people revolt. (This is the true story of the reasons for the American revolution.)

Stories about "protecting the future for our kids," about "fiscal prudence," are smoke screens especially when we see the same happening to individuals in the foreclosure area, where families are paid small sums to clean up their own houses for the next occupants and then turn over the keys to the local sheriff's eviction squads operating as minions of the banks.

It doesn't get more stark than this.

Why and how does this kind of thing happen now, every day in America?

Jefferson's warnings about it echo down to us. Andrew Jackson's hatred of the First United States bank now make more sense. The crash of 1929 reverberates and we can see some of the causes behind it.

And now we face yet another, more global version of those same historical battles. It happened in Rome, and all down through history.

This time much depends upon the outcome since we are a global economy now.

So now we ask what is likely to be the outcome of this battle in our super global context and what is a stake and what are the remedies?

More tomorrow.

Dec 12, 2010
The global finance situation is as follows:

The western countries and the United States are busying decimating their middle classes at the behest of the banks and are, in essence, setting up their societies for long term recessions and or depression.

But note in the east, India and China, South Korea have not undergone any recession at all, and in fact, are still growing at 5-10% a year.

Why is this? Why are we in collapse and they are growing? The first and simple explanation--they have not allowed private capital and wealthy individuals to control their currencies. Their governments do.

What we are seeing is that when you have private banks (note here that the Federal Reserve is not federal at all, it is a private consortium of the most powerful banks in the country. They deliberately gave the organization that name to conceal it's private status.) It is an independent organization, despite the fact that the chair is chosen the president. What we have then is our currency being managed in the interest of those private interests, our huge banks. Clearly bad things happen when you have your financial structure organized this way.

This is not the case in India, China and the east. Governmental controls, which we had in this country until the last 30 years, have been dismantled and we see what occurs as a result.

In contrast the Chinese people, save 20% of their income, much of it factory workers sending money back home to the rural areas, and government control means that political leaders have to manage currency in the best interest of the mass of people or risk rebellion or revolution. It also means that currency is not seen as profit center by private interests, so costs are lower. You can't have big bank making billions of charging the population to use their own money and expect things to go well. They don't.

The governmental example has no profit motive built into the structure of currency management and governments tax just enough for governmental expenses and some savings. Plus, savings rates in China especially, are high, but the government does not try to make a profit off those savings. This was how the United States was organized early on, until the private banks came in and took over, got beaten back and then they took over

---

23

permanently about 100 years ago and we got the great depression as a result, wars, and boom and bust debacles.

In contrast again, note China today is not a warring nation partly because it does not have the profit motive so many of our bankers have in the profits that war brings.

True, China has rising inflation at 5% and the government can and will respond. The Chinese people don't want to pay half of their income on food as they have in the past.

But the point is that the government can be responsive. This is not possible with the currency is in the hands of the super-wealthy, the banks and wall street.

Second, under governmental control of the currency, the government can be responsive to global trends which move quickly and can manage its global finances strategically. The United States cannot do this.

The proof is in the pudding: China and India have prospered with their system and we have suffered near collapse under our system and are now decimating our own population to pay exorbitant debt back to banks and the rest of that crowd.

Politics in the Obama Age

Note: In this section we look at politics in America and its political institutions, beginning with an account of the rise of Barack Obama, his campaign for president, and his eventual election as the first African-American president.

The huge problems he and the republic face are explored and concrete suggestions are made as to what, I suggest, can and ought to be done to move the country back to the right track.

But, first let's have a look at the rise of Barack Obama, his background, and my predictions two years ago as to how he would govern and with what effectiveness before he took office and in the last two years.

Let's see if I was correct in those predictions.

Title: A Blog on Obama –His Election, His Administration: My Report Card January 2008- December 2010

Summary:

This is a blog done during the electoral campaign of Barack Obama and 100 days after; and it makes predictions about how he will govern and the issues America faces. It is continued here as I follow his presidency.

Also included are my proposed solutions to American problems. It was my attempt at prognostication and my current evaluations. Much of it became the book on Obama "The Obama Chronicles: Stories From the Heartland."

The book covers the reactions, ideas, comments and thoughts of many Americans during his campaign and now two years later.

Updated: 7/10: The Supreme Court Decision on Unlimited Campaign Spending--What Does It Really Mean? The Blog Goes On.

Updated: 7/1/10 Updated 7/13/10 Update: Bad to Worser

Updated: 9/27/10 So What To Do?

Updated: 10/12/10 The Blog Today is Not for the Faint of Heart--Why Spoil Your Morning?

Updated: 11/ 5/10 Update: And We Are Not Talking Figs or Fig-Leafs.- Can't Afford Them.

I am in the middle of this book about President Obama.

I am from Chicago. He is from Chicago as a politician.
He did his community work in the neighborhood where I grew up.
He was a senator from my old neighborhood of Hyde Park.
He currently lives in Hyde Park.
I went to school at Hyde Park High.
My dad still likes in Barack" s old senate district 13th.
Barrack's family is mixed. My family is mixed.
His great grand-mother on his mother's side was part Cherokee.
My great grand mother on my mother's side was part Cherokee.
Barack Obama stole my job and is currently impersonating me... (smile)

The book is about half way done and describes the Chicago
Obama moved to, the Chicago he learned his politics from, the Chicago
of my child hood.
I concentrate on the values, the Chicago values, he learned there and the
mid-west values of Kansas which his mother taught him.
He organized his campaign based on those values and won; I think the
presidency because of those values.
I spell them out.
Every person from the mid-west knows what they are:
They are not like NY values, or California varies, or the values of the
South-they are mid-western.

Let's have a look at Chicago and Barack Obama and those mid-west
values I make such a big deal over.

Well, what do you say about Obama?
He is the conjuring image, the prototype, the summation of all of the
American dilemmas.
Is he Black, is he white, why is race so important in America?
Where are your racial papers? Obama has none.
Is he for equality or is he the one saying you can make it in America if you
work hard. Don't you or do you need affirmative action?
Why bother with civil rights marches when you can be President and
write the civil rights laws?
He is the new generation that says the old hatreds are over.
We don't know and don't care about who is already dead and buried
in the cemetery.

He says he is against corruption and the corrupt politics in Washington, but he did come from Chicago. Did any of that rub off on him?

He is for peace and getting rid of Cowboy violence.

He embraces his former enemies and gives them jobs.

He reads to the children at night.

He writes home every night via the internet to millions of people who supported him.

He is the father for all the single women who now have a new man in the house that they can tell their children to look up to.

He is quiet, no drama Obama.

How do you write about a person that looks like that?

We Americans don't care.

Obama greatest strength it seems is that if we are going to have to stare at someone on TV for 4 or 8 years we chose him for all the reasons above.

He is slowly moving from the rank of politician to family member-guess whose photo is in the homes of millions of Americans, hanging up beside the photos of family members-Barack Obama.

Obama gets internalized, becomes family, The young boy who made his grandma proud.

How do you write about that?

Day Three:

The magnitude of the issues facing the new President is so large. The solutions now being discussed are not going to make a dent. The new President has to tell the American people what is not going to be good news.

The summary is as follows:

1-The American life style will have to be downsized. The consumption society is no longer sustainable. This means small houses, group living, exburgs, technological enclaves, green zones, young people pressed into national service, fewer college bound folks, young people leaving the country to take jobs in other countries-where the jobs will be; changing demographics-Americans are not replicating themselves- too few babies and that means other groups will gradually become the new Americans, ditto in all of Europe and Russia. They, too, are having declining populations and will see demographic changes in 50 years. Americans, the English, the Italians, the Russians, the French all are reproducing at rates below replacement levels. Others, immigrants will replace them in 50 years. That is why immigration is an issue all over the west. This is becoming evident.

Technological village life is coming, (no commutes needed here, less energy needed and cheaper, with college kids and young people providing much of the labor to a graying America whose age and life expectancies continue to increase-taxing the health care system for the next 30 years.

Well, what are to be the solutions?

Financial system: Devolve to local and regional banking structures. They still exist and pre-date the concentration of the last 30 years.

Political System: Devolve to more local control with technological innovations with labor being a combination of national service- youth and immigrants. Everyone wins.

Energy System: No real good solutions here--so many polluting sources. The best bet is to get rid of the cars, downscale dirty industries, reduce population-reduce the polluting population segments-but this will be prohibitively expensive and we will not likely succeed-carbon cap or no carbon cap.
At best, the energy jobs and technology will have to be conceived and built overseas and exported to the United States. We can't afford to revamp the energy system on our own. We are in debt 13 trillion dollars and frankly broke. What will happen is our kids will have to follow the jobs overseas and meantime, the government will default on the debt, restructure, and/or face rampant inflation. None of this is good.

The Political System:
Politics has become seized by the special interests and career politicians. No good solution. The system will decay or be revamped toward more local control. Let's hope it's done in a planful way. If not, it will be messy times in the republic with more and more poor people, a decimated middle class and returning vets who will not be able to get the health care they need or find jobs. That is why we must continue the two wars. You don't want all those vets back home and dissatisfied. The wars are an employment program not only for the vets but their families' back home dependent upon the military contracts and the companies they work for. Stop the wars and massive unemployment and depression occurs overnight.
All of that is bad news.

Housing:
Group housing for middle class kids: Poor and immigrant families already do it.

Fifth day Installment:
Obama is in St. Louis-recounting the first 100 days. Well what has happened is that people are content with the fact that he seems to be trying. His approval ratings are up to 63%; for the first time more people are saying that the country on the right track and the economy is tanking slower than expected.
Well, good, but not good enough.

The point is that Obama gets credit for trying. The man works hard. He is on TV tonight undoubtedly to remind people what he has gotten done. A bill izard of trillion dollar bills is coming as far the eye can see.
Well that might help but that is not his message overall. He knows none of this will work without the mobilization of the American people, especially the young and the college-educated. But he has not mobilized them and likely will not despite the fact that he knows they are the key to America's future.

What has to be done-and he won't say it-but you heard it here first:

1-The fifty percent of college graduates who can't get a job and have returned home to live in the basement have to be mobilized. They have to be given training, money to go to the small towns of America and help in the greening and revitalization of those small towns. That is the key to America's future. Other young people will have to migrate outside the country to where the jobs are. The corporations have done this seeking profit.

The aging middle class in this country is and has been abandoned. Our only hope over the next twenty years is to get some of our young people the technological skills to help those towns.
They have the time if we pay them to do it.
They can create the green jobs we need to revitalize small towns and then they will live there. Impossible? No. The fact is that this model already exists all over the world.
Most of the world's innovation is done in enclaves (Silicon Valley, Hong Kong, Singapore, and France.) The "innovation centers" attract the bright and the entrepreneurial and, in fact, drive the world's economies, These folks like to be close to one another. Make the small towns attractive-example the NC Charlotte-Greensboro area, the San Francisco area- all attract these individuals and their counterparts who drive the world economy.
What is the ultimate driver in all this is also in places like China- is cheap educated labor- ditto India.
So what are the pillars of both prosperity and economic recovery world-wide?
They are what they have always been; cheap labor, cheap energy, cheap food. That was the United States 40 years ago. Not now. No cheap energy, no cheap labor, and rising costs for food diverted to ethanol use to save Iowa farms.
But who has cheap food (self-sustaining small farms?) China does, India does.

Who has cheap energy? China does, India does partially because they use old technology and cheap labor. So here they come. Western societies are expensive, don't produce anything any more and are graying.

—

2-Devolution to simpler technologies is inevitable because our windmills and water power and computer power will be cheaper every 18 months, but alas, they are not enough alone.

And finally we will have to lose our total dependency on currency:

More likely have to depend upon neighbor barter systems to some extent. You help me harvest my crop and I will help you. Or we loan the harvester out as the community harvester. Re-introduce community co-ops on a massive scale.

Far-Fetched? Just you wait and see. People do this in small towns already and with young people back in the small towns to help many small towns could be placed back on an economically sound footing.

If we do not, then things can get rough.

In the United States there is only five days worth of food on the shelves. If that supply is disrupted people will spontaneously leave the cities and head for rural areas anyway. That is devolution of the disorderly type, and we don't want that.

Tomorrow: We need some more detail and what is to be done with those greedy wall street moguls?

Obama and the Media: His Future May Depend Upon the Media-True or False?

Selling the idea of Hope, and even Democracy, propounded by a black politician from corrupt Chicago was more than much of the media could stomach.

Media Storms and False Bluster:

For young people who paid attention to the press and media coverage of the election, the contentiousness, seemed at times overwhelming. The adult world appeared scary to some of them who were unsteadied by the vitriol which came pouring into living rooms across the nation. They watched the Daily Show where the political news came with a bit of humor instead.

But make no mistake this election was a media event-a media bonanza. "The right could raise hundreds of millions pitching "Obama is coming with his terrorists friends and he is not one of us" pitch;" the left had "lets take the country back and elect a black man—wouldn't that be special?" message.

Commentators and pundits whip-lashed listeners and watchers with daily atrocity stories to pump up ratings and to get candidate A to spend money in the media to counter the overnight claims of candidate B... Guess who getting rich-the media was.

—

Conservative media operations condemned Obama while making millions off politicians-Obama too, democrats and republicans-who bought air time, off drug and conservative groups who bought politicians to defend the status quote. The politicians had it easy: whip up the constituency and tell them to donate to your campaign, whip up the right or the left special interests and tell them to donate to your campaign, go on TV and help media with their ratings—so they make more money, some of which you expect to get back in donations.

It's all about money. for everyone involved. There are no virgins here. Obama raised more money but he got most of that money from the same conservative special interest media conglomerates and wall street which he condemned. He tried to raise money from small donations but it was not enough. Everyone got money from wall street and what a coincidence Wall Street got billions in bail out money.

It's all about money. Is that too cynical?

The tabloidization of media in the United States is rampant, driven in part by shrinking revenues in print media especially newspapers, TV, Radio, even the internet are all in cut back mode. A presidential election can represent 25% of the entire revenue for the year for some media outlets. Presidential and off year electoral campaigns are crucial to the bottom line. There is, however, less news, rather we get phony atrocity scare stories and gossip; we get reporters interviewing reporters both getting pay checks from the same boss conglomerate; the two then interview the politician who get donations from the same conglomerate. This makes no sense. We get distractions, reality shows, Jerry Springer-like amusements, so we don't interfere with the folks really running the important things which affect our lives.

Think: where were the media in examining the Iraq war, in examining the Bush torture sessions, civil liberties erosions, the environment?

They were all feeding from the Washington money trough while the middle class in the United States was being sold out, jobs sent overseas, while whole industries were being abandoned and being told all of this was good for America.

It wasn't. Wall street collapses, life savings disappear and the plan is keep it going after modest reforms.

The old Whoopi Goldberg quote is a good one—paraphrasing:

"You don't mind getting mugged in a bad neighborhood, all they get in your wallet; but don't go anywhere near Wall Street—they rob you of your life-savings and your future."

31

All of this is ongoing in the context of increasing tabloidization of media and segmentation into markets, conservative radio stations, liberal radio stations, print media, broadcast media all fragmented and segmented' all commanding audiences which never have to hear a dissenting view-audiences which can be prompted to send money and support to a candidate after their segment has been hyped by the fragmented media.

Cross over media-that is media which talks to a wide audience-is becoming more and rarer. More and more Americans are listening to fewer and fewer media and only to those individuals and media that agree with their political and social points of view. This is not compatible with Democracy which assumes a free press, that free speech results from exposure to a wide variety of points of view—an informed public.

Grab your hat. It's going to get rocky.

July 1, 2010
 Note that the Supreme Court has given the green light for unlimited spending by corporations and labor unions in presidential and other campaigns. This is really bad. But we can see why it occurred

Unlimited spending is good for corporations, it increases their influence in Washington; it is good for the politicians because they all take that money and spend a lot of it on media, conservative and liberal media-campaigns cost billions per year; it is good for the politicians because they can keep much of those donations and not really account for it. The loop holes are you can give or loan that money to other candidates that is the unspent portions of it. Wow. what a plan. Who is monitoring these items? No one.

So, rest assured. It is as bad as you suspect it is.
But all is not lost. See my blog on "What America Needs to Do to Survive" on my website and on this site.
What is not there is the suggestion that we take and convert part of the military budget and use it to train vets in green technology so that when they return they can make a living. Likely no. But it is an idea.
Also I had placed a blog item here entitled "Unemployment? Who Gains and Lessons We Should Be Learning From This Recession." My publisher made me take it down, pending publication. But if you want copy of the early chapters, let me know and I will email it along.

July 2, 2010
 The Financial Reform bill is near passage. (It has now passed) And it is severely lacking. It is a failure.
The banking system, wall street and the threat they pose to the American people remains in place.

—

It seems the politicians did not want to jeopardize campaign donations to them selves with a campaign year coming up this year.

The new consumer protection agency in the bill is tied up in hundreds of exceptions to its provisions and it has been placed under the control of a former Sachs Director as of this date. There is a hint there. (Elizabeth Warren has been given the role of advisor.)

The opportunity has been lost here and it won't come back. Financial reform will take another recession-depression and that will happen in 2012 when trillions of debt in the EU falls due. They don't have the money. "Belt-tightening" means you and I are out of luck. Anyway, who can afford a belt?

See my blog on this site entitled What America Needs to Do to Survive? for more details.

Sept 28, 2010

So we are in election season again; the Democrats and the Republicans-Tea-Party forces are now raising money to feed the media monkey once again seeking to convince us that things are either ok, will be ok if we just get rid of one party, or the opposite, if we just vote in the other party.

What we really have here is gang politics. all about jobs, money, politicians and special interest gangs looking to get or retain control over your wallet and my wallet.

We watch and feel unable to stop this slow-motioning mugging from occurring.

What to do?

This all sounds complicated; and this mystification is presented to breed a sense of frustration and to justify the continuation of the status quo.

Here are a few simple things I and others I have suggested elsewhere. (See the blog on "What America needs to do to survive") for more details.

The system as it now stands is a gigantic pyramid scheme based on money--our money being transferred to Wall street and corporations-the government is merely the middle man in all of this. They go there and regularly take those funds from us via government subsidies, tax loopholes, bailouts, special laws, policies which make for continuing high unemployment rates, continual war which keeps the war-profiteering companies in cash, graft, waste, and outright theft. Over a trillion dollars is missing in the so-called war effort. Missing. Unaccounted for.

What to do:

The first step is to shut down the money flows going to wall street by withdrawing funds from our 401k"s and investing them locally. (There will be no real interest gained there anyway) The same would be true for all bank accounts.

Put the funds in local co-ops, credit unions and local community controlled banks. Our money is the life blood of the system. We should withdraw that support.
Labor unions, pension plans, even payroll deduction plans, all ultimately end up on wall street. This funding source should be shut down.
On the legal side, the ERISA laws should be re-rewritten to facilitate this process. More on that later.

With as few as 100, 00 people participating this could bring the whole system up for review and change beyond reform.

Left wing millionaires and billionaires should be encouraged to take their funds out of wall street and put it into local community banks, co-ops and the like to rebuild devastated small towns and to fund an internal peace corp. to pay young people, now idle, to help in that effort.
Funds, too, will be needed to create local farming and food production. Self-sufficiency, sustainable planning is the core idea here.
Funds should be used to finance the technology enclaves I have proposed in another blog, to work with small town revitalization planners as well.
The city should not be neglected in this, but that is a more problematic situation. More on that later.
What to do: Part Two--Upcoming.
Buying American has become too expensive so we buy from China, because that is all we can afford, and mind you, males in this country have actually lost 5% of their income since 1997. NAFTA?
In fact there has been no real increase in income for Americans since 1968, (See article in Ramparts Magazine "The Last Christmas in America.")
In response, the single wage earning family had to become a two-wage earning family to survive, had to become a credit card using family and a "let's take money out of the equity in the house family to survive;" and to boot we all get blamed for "living above our means."
Ok, enough of this cheerful news. What to do you say?

We should look at solutions tomorrow, always tomorrow.

But for this election note that even if the House changes over Obama can use the veto, and that will give us what we currently have--state-mated politics, which means things continue on with that slopping sound continuing in the background--politicians, banks, wall street and the corporation types feeding at the public trough, slopping down our dollars to gamble with.
If they fail they can send the bill to us and the FDIC.
Or have the Federal Reserve once again buy up a new round of "toxic assets--now disguised as "quantitative easing."

So you see the blog today is not for the faint of heart.

But as I used to say to my students "Don't bring me a problem, unless you have some solutions attached."
So tomorrow I will follow my own advice.

Nov 5, 2010
This will be a short blog today because solutions are few. But let's take a look anyway.
First: The left and the right have to fix the economy. Now that means jobs but let's not get carried away with the "jobs" mantra. Our system has blinded us to real economics, in favor of finance economics. The jobs fixation is a good example. First this is a goal which is not attainable in the short run. American job recovery to pre-recession levels will take *five to fifteen years* at the current pace of new job development. We simply don't have the time to pursue a jobs strategy with millions of unemployed, and note that longer term unemployed are basically becoming not employable any more and need years of training to become so.
So what to do?

Economics and Jobs-What Should Be Done

Let's do the following exercise:

Question: If you had a job what would you do with the money?
Answer: I would pay the mortgage on my house and pay my bills.
 Solution: Give money directly to individuals to do this and skip the banks altogether via direct loan modifications, and direct write-downs of debt. It will happen any way via the default and foreclosure route.

So solve the problems directly.

The job route will take too long and present ideas around jobs will not bring back enough jobs anyway and will take years to achieve.

The second thing to do is to head off debt enslavement. This is the banks strategy. All debt, credit card debt as well, should be written down or eliminated. That is what the 600 billion should do.

See above for the first steps. (Sound far-fetched? Not at all. This already happening as foreclosures and bankruptcies will attest.

 The second step is to change the ERISA laws such that our pension monies and daily deposits do not go to wall street and the banks.

Everyone can do that.

—

35

There is no interest to be gained anyway (one percent) and keep the money locally and regionally, thereby depriving wall-street of its power. Everyone can close out a bank account and put it into a local co-op or credit union. I have written of this elsewhere on this site.
Think what 600 billion would accomplish with the above goals. A lot.

Then funds will be freed up and disposable income rises and the economy is given the boost it needs. But also organize and revitalize community and locally owned banks. This mess started because 30 years ago Americans starting sending their money to wall street (5 trillion a year now) and wall-street has taken those funds and gambled with them..

Title: What Does America Need To Do?

Right Now Solutions

Updated: Oct 22, 2010

Summary: An abundance of Warning and Caution:
Updated: June 15 2010 What about the BP oil spill?
Days after it was suggested here BP came up with 20 billion. Humm, but what next?
A blog on this in three days.
Updated: 6/ 20/10 What to do now after the spill?
Updated: 7/13/10 I Didn't Think Things Could Get Worse, But I Was Wrong.
Updated: 7/15/10 Right Now Today Solutions
Updated: 7/16/10 Who Has Destroyed American Prosperity? Special Insert
Updated: 8/12/10 So Where Are We Now?
Updated: 10/21/10 Take Your Money Out and Bring it Home.
Updated: 10/22/10 The German Example

The first area to look into is those pillars of American success I identified above: Cheap Labor, Cheap Energy, Cheap Food and a country filled with natural resources.

Special Insert: Who is killing these pillars and why?

The greatest negative influence on these three pillars of American prosperity in the last five years has been wall street and the major banks.
1-**Cheap Food**: The last nail in the Cheap food pillar was in 2008 when Goldman and other investment bankers entered the wheat market and bought long thereby inflating wheat prices from an historic 3 dollar level up to 15 dollars. This resulted in food riots around the world, since the United States supplies the bulk of the world's wheat. They are still there making billions off these artificial food shortages bringing food insecurity to millions, not only around the world but in the United States as well.
2-**Cheap Energy:** The same scenario is true for energy, especially oil. Wall street and the bankers drove the price of oil from 25 dollars a barrel to 125 dollars a barrel and the cost at the pump from 1.25 a gallon to nearly3-4 dollars currently. Our cheap energy price went up and has stayed up. Now these same two robber barons are poised to make money on the cap and trade market. Who is going to profit from cap and trade as a solution to the energy and pollution problems--the large banks and wall street?

37

3- **Cheap Labor:** Labor used to be cheap because the cost of living in the United States was low. A single wage-earner could support the family. 1968 was the last year in which real wages increased. Since then it has gone down meaning now the wife is working and the kids can't find a job at all, and on top of that, the kid is competing for a job with grandmother who is supporting the kids and the grandchildren. The college educated child can find no job. 50 percent of all college graduates come home after graduation, not finding a job. This kind of under-employment and unemployment is the bank and wall street way of keeping labor costs low. People will work for pennies to support their families.

Given this recent history we need to look at what are the other influences and the history of these pillars and then on to specifics on what needs to be done to solve these problems.

To the list I will now add, a decent birth rate or immigrant flow, small town and technical green enclave investment, income distribution reform, land distribution reforms, banking and financial reforms and a re-thinking of the purposes of an economy.

Cheap labor built this country, from the Chinese coming to lay the track for the railroads, to the Africans working the cotton in the South, to the immigrants from Europe who cleared the land in the west, who worked the factories, fought the wars and made America what it is today. Needless to say the labor scene is not the same today. Cheap labor has been outsourced to other countries.

The American middle class has not only been abandoned but 40% of American savings were taken from them and their homes, their major asset, are now selling for half the purchase price to those very same interests which took the savings and the land.

We are heading for a two class system, the rich and the poor. Certainly that is the pattern becoming evident in many of our cities.

In addition, there is the lack of labor, cheap or otherwise, which is the demographic issue. Americans are not having children, nor are Europeans; and the demographics are becoming clear: by 2060, some demographic studies show, the reproducing populations of Russia, Britain, France and Italy will, in essence, cease to exist and the traditional populations will be replaced by immigrants from other countries. The same trends are evident in the United States as well. Latin American birth rates outstrip those of Americans and demography become destiny, in a flice.

So, as we age in this country, we see a younger population replacing an older one, of a very different stripe. Our children will learn more Spanish in the short-run but English will have resurgence in the next generation. What is to be done in this context is now our challenge.

The first issue in the short run is the economy. The country will, and already has, in certain communities become a two-economy society. Why should I, nor can I, compete for basic living necessities with individuals earning 2-3 times more than I do?

—

A two-economy solution, whether created or defacto-realized seems inevitable. The rich will likely not be allowed to shop in the second economy where the price of necessities can be artificially raised in a so-called "free market." This solution creates a low-cost economy of necessities for those who provide the labor. This makes sense and many do this to survive anyway today. Thrift shops, discount stores, Walmarts all attest to the fact that the middle class cannot afford middle class and upper middle class prices. Devastatingly, 40 million Americans are now on food stamps and millions more on Medicaid. This is horrible.

The second pillar of revamping the labor force (the one above creates an economy which works for them) is to have that labor force become more self-sufficient and not be susceptible to being wiped out by Wall Street machinations and global trends in far away countries. This means the re-claiming of productive land and small towns where they can be supportive of a laboring population. Bartering, co-ops, low living costs, plus a land reform policy can make the country side more productive and sustainable especially in the context of greening these small towns to produce energy for re-sale to the grid.

Believe it or not Detroit is trying this approach. Tear the decrepit buildings down, down-size the city, allow for population loss, put in self-sufficient gardening and farming plots, bring in technological enclaves. This is an admission that the city model does not work, at least in Detroit.

Now you have idle workers in small towns all over the country. We can make those small towns productive with massive investments. How you say is that possible? More tomorrow.

Feb 18, 2010 - Survival Chapter Three

As I have stated elsewhere, our children, will not be able to afford the suburban home of the past.

In the cities they will be forced and are, already, living three to five a house or apartment. High unemployment will remain with us and a revamping of the economy from a service emphasis to a new high-tech, green emphasis will take time. What to do. Here are a few modest proposals about what to do with the labor force, idle out there and hurting.

1-Create a **massive internal peace corp.** Put people to work re-vamping small towns for their change-over to a more self-sustaining model. This includes local organic food stuffs, grown and consumed. Free up land for this purpose. People will grow gardens. Put money into green training and irrigation projects. Bring people languishing unproductively in the cities back into these very same small towns. Bring back and support local and regional banks and co-ops of various kinds, crops, loans, machinery, techno co-ops can work if local.

Remember what happens when we allow Wall Street to become our bankers? Take those same highly educated city grads, currently living five to an apartment, and give them money to go back home to their own small towns, or others to help set up the infrastructure need to fuel this internal peace corp. re-generation of America. Move people out of the cities with incentives to go back to the small town or the medium sized town. We have technology now where we don't need to congregate in cities to be productive, that was an industrial model where you needed the labor force close and available near ports and transportation hubs. We don't need this so much in this post industrial era. Has this model been tried? Sure. Dependent wage-earners in the city are an economic failure. We should admit it and go local and regional.

The poor won't be poor if they are given the means to access the basics of life. The middle class can revert to the community help model that is still in place in many small towns, and has been for centuries. After all, most of the world was a small town model until populations were forced into the cities to serve the needs of robber barons.

Now the second aspect of reform is to take the **technological enclaves** I have described and integrate them into what I have described above. I have noted that much of the information revolution is actually driven by a few high skilled enclaves around the world and by relatively few people. They are Silicon valley-like enclaves in California, China, Singapore, France, Germany, Hong-Kong etc. These enclaves are small towns where participants know one another and exchange ideas. This is the second model of small town regeneration. These **type two** small towns are to be in contact with **type one small towns** and can become training cadres for small town re-generation. How? Give them tax breaks to do so and guess what they will have at their disposal; cheap labor from the sources we identified above. That is what we need to do in the short run, town by town.

So we have a new source of cheap labor, idle now but can become productive again. Empty the cities get people out of what are inefficient enclaves and get them to places where the population can begin to benefit itself not a few hundred thousand rich souls who control city life.

Ah, not possible you say? The choice here is stark: Either we organize this new re-generation by planful means or it will occur in an unplanned way, which is to say people abandoning the cities and invading the country side looking for the means to survive. Be mindful here that any disaster of any meaningful proportions will initiate this process anyway and we will not have planned for it

A last stark fact: The average grocer has three days worth of food on the shelves. People will invade the country side looking for food and this will be the plan I just discussed being initiated the hard way. And that is ugly.

The collapse of centralized authority, unplanned, happened with the collapse of the Roman Empire, initiating the Dark Ages, and happened, in fact, in the bible as I have argued above, and happened with the collapse of Egyptian rule in Canaan. It happened with Katrina. Any breakdown from natural or man-made sources will create the pattern I describe above.

Feb 22, 2010 "What Does America Need To Survive?" Chapter 4
Have there been other examples of civilizations abandoning the city as unworkable; or central authority collapsing, of abandoning empire as unworkable? The Mayans abandoned pyramid building, the Greeks, the Babylonians, the French, the British, the Romans, countless examples. Most large scale centralized authority systems fall down. They are not generally pulled down. The most recent example is that of the Russians who abandoned their empire as unworkable.
It is part of a normal pattern.
So now to get to the detail: Include the army in the small town regeneration project, along with the young and the college-educated. Many of them have ties to these small towns and it would be a home coming. Have the technological enclaves close by with small towns providing labor in exchange for training. Isn't that what the Army does anyway? Focus efforts in regeneration on greening and self-sufficiency. These would be key. This would mean small truck farms, wind, solar and the techno-enclave would be in proximity: and, ultimately, able to produce energy for the gird.
Of course, there will be a fight over the land. Currently developers, banks, railroads, utilities and the US government own most of the land in the country. There would have to be a new land use policy. Survival is at stake. But the fight could be won because small states dominate in the US Senate and a deal could be struck because their states would benefit from such a plan.
Think of it. Most of the wasted resources in this country are utilized keeping the cities afloat. They are not economic, crime ridden, have no real products they produce, have teeming unemployment looming and bound to get worse and net resource wasters. They demand massive investments in transportation, food, energy and give little back in terms of long-term sustainability. Young people, the idle, the technologically advanced are better utilized on the country-side landscape. Just a thought. So cheap labor is possible to put back into the American equation. As I am fond of saying, this will happen well and planned or ill-planned and ugly.

Feb 26, 2010 "Survive"

The next item in tandem is **cheap energy**. Above we have mentioned wind and solar. We add to the list battery power, and nuclear power. There are ideas around the idea of clean coal and cheap oil, but we are better off looking at fuel substitutes that include vegetable oils and other grain based fuels. At the very least stockpiles ought to be created for the emergencies which will surely come in the future. But will all this be enough, timely and efficient in the face of climate change, aging populations, declining incomes, looming depression, and political paralysis?

Such timing is critical, the answer is unknown. However, we have no choice in the energy field; we must act as if we will succeed. The overall goal is clear; create a society which city and country-side produce net energy give-backs to the grid.

Friends of mine stated part of the problem succinctly, "Why re-build an outmoded infrastructure; build the new one directly."

On the energy level the task is a delicate one: We have to build the boat we are sailing to Europe on while sailing to Europe. The reason that this is even to be looked at is that you can do this if you build the boat as a series of rafts strung together. Those rafts are small towns. Seen this way, it is possible to accomplish the task. Of course there is not enough money in the world to re-build the old infrastructure, but a green infra-structure is possible under scenarios I outline below. That structure is cheaper in the long run, more competitive, locally controlled and has cheaper labor costs, as I have outlined above.

The next issue is **cheap food.** America has long been the bread basket of the world but that small-farmer model of production has long been replaced by big agriculture which now means genetic farming where corn itself has reduced strains available and most of them owned, repeat, owned by the Monsanto's of the world. It is illegal to grow the corn without their permission. And to boot Monsanto has created grain strains which can only be planted once.

This, of course, changes the cheap food equation. If grain seed and indeed water, and the very air can become private property then the house of cards will collapse. Clearly this system is not sustainable and is not viable as a public good.

Re-generation will have to be accompanied by a re-thinking of who owns food grains. Who owns water, land, air? It is instructive to even have to discuss these issues this way. What hath progress wrought?

How can food be re-democratized? It will have to be. Hungry people will find a way to feed their families and Monsanto and their patents will have to stand aside and let people grow what ever they want.

Now potential catalysts in all of this are returning veterans from our two wars. (War is a form of employment which is why it so easily becomes popular.)

These folks, having made sacrifices for the country will come home, assuming the wars end, will need jobs and there are none. They will need medical care, in a medical system which is broken. They will need re-training, in a country which is cutting college budgets. Something similar happened after World War One and those vets marched on Washington. It can happen again. These might when they and their families find they cannot make a living once back home. They are good candidates for re-generation projects where living costs will be lower and green re-training possible.

But the potential volatility of that issue remains. The two-economy solution will become more apparent with these veterans back home. After all we have an example of this with the military itself where the internal military economy runs on it own terms not those of the general American economy. So what then is the next issue to be solved? We need to look at small town economic models and their regional counterparts. Tomorrow.

Feb 27, 2010 "Survive"

The economic picture is glum, but things will sort themselves out well or badly. Let's concentrate on well. The first item many of you have mentioned is the issue of where will the money come from to institute many of the ideas I have outlined above. Bob mentioned the national debt, two wars, and a trillion dollar deficit. All true. The national debt is 12.4 trillion dollars and soon the interest payments against that debt will be the second largest item in the national budget.

What will happen? What can happen? Can we or our children pay this debt? No; not right now.

What will likely happen is either default or re-structuring. We owe the money to the Chinese and the Japanese and the banks mostly and we will likely simply restructure with all and create new lower payments. The Japanese and the Chinese will likely will agree, to the extent they can see their exports increase to us in our re-generation efforts here. They could get some debt funds paid back in that way, along with currency re-valuation in the Chinese example. And guess who will be in China, utilizing that cheap labor-US companies who can produce for the US market utilizing this foreign labor and also help create that green market back home as well. This has synergy. Sloppy synergy but yes synergy. Inevitable? No. But a logical path.

The two wars cost about 1 trillion a year and have to be wound down slowly so as to not exacerbate all those towns dependent upon military contracts in the United States and all those countries dependent upon US military bases abroad. (There are 745 such bases scattered around the world.) We are a war-dependent economy seeking to become a peace economy that will take time, say 20 years.

—

43

So the first step in economic re-generation will be the global changes described above from the perspective of the United States. We can't pay the debt and, in some cases, (bank debt) should not be paid. Besides we need the money for the internal changes above or we pay in internal disruptions from economic chaos if we don't act. Think 20 rolling Katrina's due to water shortages in one case, food shortages in another case, rising inflation which make the dollar worth a lot less, transportation breakdowns, terrorist attacks etc.

We are a fragile over-technologized society, and so interdependent that five airplanes can bring our economy to its knees. This is not good.
Now the small town answer here is, therefore, a good idea not only for economic reasons but for strict military reasons as well. Ninety-five percent of the people living on one percent of the land is a bad idea militarily. Disbursement is a better idea.
Now the mix we are talking about here is one of small-town, regional and yes some cities where cities make sense. But the basis of the American future has to be local, upgraded with technology, not massed populations in vulnerable cities. Re-generation is re-building America from the bottom up and abandoning top-down systems.
So how much time will this all take and what are the barriers?

Mar 1, 2010 "Survival"
A wise sage once said "What to do is easy, but the first step of what to do is the problem." The same is true here. The answer to the question of how long we have to accomplish certain critical first steps is functions of how long will the first steps take. And what are those first steps? Here we go:

The country has to be put on a disaster footing, whether that disaster is any of the calamities I have described above or some one not yet conceived. Here is what I think we have to do, over what time line, with what human power sources and at what cost:
1-Just as we have voting booths and places in every community in the United States we must do the same for the regeneration effort. We will need in an emergency, power, medical, housing food, water, and energy and ways to move people efficiently. We partially have this in place with F.E.M.A but I would not bet my life on their help, would you?

The first scenario is the three to--five day survival period. In a disaster we want people to be self-sufficient and be able to survive for at least three-to five days after an event or in general:
--That is every home must have five days of food, non-perishable (remember, we assume no power will be available)
--Each home must have or access to five days of clean water
--Each home must have access to an emergency medical kit
--Each home must have a shortwave radio kit or access to same

---

--Each home must have a fuel generation kit, assuming gasoline supplies will quickly become depleted

--Each home must have access to the ability to produce heat or fire

--Each home must have a tent for temporary shelter if necessary.

--Each home must have seed grains for a vegetable garden (yes, let's think ahead)

--Each home must have a 12 volt battery, an auto battery will do and, add two bicycles, and a crowbar and rope.

--Each block must have a disaster warden, someone who would get training in the above items and their use; a paid position.

Right now some homes have these items, most don't. Some communities have their processes in place, some don't.

Shopping list item one for the state and federal government: Have our re-generation work force, (remember these folks?) create "Survival Support Kits" on every block in America. Kit production will provide jobs; make survivability a real option for Americans not only for natural disasters but other kinds of slow degeneration from economic collapse as well.

These kits will be on every block, or within walking distance and supplement those home supplies I have described above. Why all this effort? The worse thing you can have is millions of people in the cities on the move after five days looking for food or trying to escape the chaos of the cities.

There are massive issues with this kind of movement. You want folks to hunker down in place and survive for at least five days to ten days until state or federal efforts can be mounted.

Hunkering down also makes security for these communities easier, rather than dealing with a scattered population on the move.

The details of how you get fuel without gasoline I will spare you but survivalists know them well.

How much will this effort cost? Unknown, but my guess is each kit and its mobile container will cost in materials about 750 dollars. Labor costs would be about 500 per kit, transportation, training and placement and after support: about 2,500 dollars per kit for the first year. Let's add contingency costs and the kit total is 5,000 per unit. How many units? Let's say a million units installed in each of five years: 25 billion total.

Of course there are other costs as well. All we have here is survival day's one through five. But what about after the five to ten day period I have postulated. More on that tomorrow.

All of the above effort gets us five to ten days of sufficing, mostly in the city. Beyond the ten-day mark there is a lot more to do. Moreover, what I have described above is mostly related to the cities. The country side effort is presumed to be in place from the other efforts described above and will have similar outlines as the city effort except that the Army, state and federal forces will lead that effort.

After ten days cities will be out of food and masses of individuals will head toward the country-side to escape what will be an increasingly chaotic and dangerous city environment; people use guns to get what they need, looting, dogs running in packs, sanitation issues erupt right away. Terrible. These patterns of behavior are not uncommon; we see them in every prolonged disaster or emergency.

Most of these ideas work in fire, earthquake, terrorist action, drought, power failure, water issues etc. They are not great for nuclear war. There all bets are off.

Now in the country side you have to have in place before the above disasters or slowly degenerating circumstances (the latter is more likely) reception centers to receive the city dwellers. Housing, kits, medical attention, sustainability planning all will have to be done before hand. The kits I speak of have to be along major exit routes and highways out of the urban areas and final destination points have to be marked out before hand to handle millions of people.

Food stuffs, water purification, temporary governmental functioning, security issues, communication, transportation and mobility-- all issues that this country has not acted upon and may have to. A slow moving degeneration of our financial systems in the easiest to deal with. But think back to October 1929. The collapse of the stock market put millions on the road looking for food and work. Then most people had country cousins who grew food. Today this is not the case today. This can happen again and we have done nothing to anticipate or prepare.

What will a truly national or even regional effort look like? We build that infrastructure block by block, city by city, region by region focusing our effort based on what areas, cities or regions have the best sustainability components and spend money in those areas which do not. The hives are put to work creating sustainability for the have-nots.

But details and costs loom here. How can this be done in the next twenty years-an arbitrary time period, but one I think is the last window we have to have gotten much of this in place.

We create hubs, local and regional until a national network is in place. The jobs it will create will help. The products, all aligned with sustainability and green goals give the country a future in the global economy, and we come out if it stronger militarily and mentally.

But as always the question is what comes first, who does it, how much will it cost and how effective will this effort be?

—

46

March 3, 2010 "Survival"

The mounting of a national effort encompassing a local, regional and country-wide effort will take twenty years. It will involve a simultaneous re-vamping of the American economy and political structure such that local self-sufficiency to the maximum degree possible is built into the new system. Our issues with infra-structure, energy, power, food etc are all based upon the assumption that the present system will be in place when clearly the present system needs to be totally re-conceptualized. The maxim is that with every complex system at some point there simply isn't enough brain power at the top to manage systems when they reach a certain size, no matter how much technology we throw at it.

The dream that we could automate our way to a well run system is a dream. It happens over and over again with empires, cities and even small regions. People run systems best who are close to the production of its basic outlines.

What if I were President? What would I do? Well the American people, and others in other countries, do not really believe that life can change from what it currently is. We are paralyzed into complacency, feel powerless to change anything and not sure if we really want to see much change. As one of my students said, "Will I still be able to still play piano?"

Now the first thing I would do is to shake up the situation with new Federal law that would place in each American home the basic needs I have outlined above for the first line of defense in the event of an emergency in American cities. Each home or block would receive one of the kits I describe at a cost of five hundred per kit.

This is the "wake-up call" approach. Things have to be shaken up. Kick the mule to get his attention. This is a signal that we as Americans are vulnerable to various emergencies and must make preparations. I would bill it as the first steps toward local control and de-centralization, away from centralized banks and financial systems to more local ones, to more local political and social control, to a more self-sufficient country; re-building America from the bottom up and creating new self-sufficiency green and smart jobs. This is true re-organization and cheaper by far than the current centralized system which mostly benefit, life-time politicians, lobbyists and the rich.

   That is America's future if America is going to survive and compete in the global economy of the future. If this is not done the current situation where the top five percent of the population has control over more wealth that the bottom ninety-five percent will create social unrest of enormous proportions and a re-alignment will occur through the messy method and social unrest, rather than through the ways I am proposing here. Let's hope we all come to our senses.

Update June 15, 2010

An interesting question here is how do the re-generation principles above match up with an actual emergency, such as the BP oil spill? The above was written before the spill but it provides an example of what is happening and how, if a re-generation plan had been in place, things would be different.

First we have a spill, the largest in American history which will contaminate over 1/3 of the Gulf of Mexico, is an environmental disaster, will affect the livelihood of thousands along the coast and inland as well, among some the poorest states in the Union. Unemployment, damaged tourism, and decay will be with the regions for years.

And to boot we are treated to a scene where politicians parade across our TV screens promising relief but delivering none, in it mainly to get their faces on TV and hoping thereby to get re-elected, no FEMA springs into action, and payments have to come from BP and meantime how are people going to feed themselves, and make boat and house payments? A mess.

Now under re-generation, first of all, BP would be required to click a computer screen and transfer a few billion dollars directly to local banks who where the individuals involved could draw upon. This would take a few minutes. Right now they are sending checks after a claims process.

But we have no local banks. Besides the politicians want credit for relief because that means votes for them. Too quick relief and they become irrelevant.

Local banking structures that have the house note and the boat note could and would be in place under regeneration. There is no substitute for a local person who knows each individual in the community and their needs. If BP didn't transfer the money then the Federal Reserve or the Federal government should or under re-generation would be required to. It is a down payment on ultimate claims but people in emergency need money now, not later. Have I mentioned local co-ops. They are even better than local banks but many don't have the electronic transfer technology to handle some transactions and don't hold the mortgages and boat notes. Credit unions are also good choices, but same problem. We have to build these under re-generation.

Second, given what is a slow moving disaster a livelihood for millions has now been destroyed. Where will they find work? Many, as was the case with Katrina will abandon the old jobs and livelihood and we will see decay, boarded up business and migration. Under re-generation a self-sufficient plan would be in place to have those unemployed be employed locally in techno and small town enclaves and available for disaster relief. There would have been a plan B. There is no plan B now in place in the Gulf and

—

there was no plan B; and there is no plan B even being planned for the Hurricane season upcoming.

Hurricane season. Boy is there a need for plan B. When the winds arrive what hopes for a return to normalcy might be dashed and millions will be in need or at least on the move.

Are we preparing? Nope. The states say we have no money. The Fed says BP is going to pay, BP is going to say hey, and the people responsible for rig safety are registered in the Marshall Islands and can't be touched. A court battle will take years and people will be long discouraged or gone and nobody will in the end take responsibility.

The moral of this tale is clear: Communities have to plan for self-sufficiency against man-made and natural disasters. Plan for food, energy, and the labor force to rebuild or sustain what is in place. The large entities, the government, BP etc can't and don't have an interest in helping. It is not profitable for the oil company to give away too much money, and is useful to the politicians only in as much as they can get votes out of it for the next election. After that they move on to the next photo op.

We have to think that the self-sufficient frontier societies of 150 years ago have to be wedded to the techno-innovations of today to keep this country going and for it to thrive. Be sure to write your congress person.

Jun 20, 2010

Now that BP has come up with 20 billion the first interesting point is that it could not deliver the funds directly or quickly to the people who need it. No, they gave the money to the US government. Be prepared for a long wait while the state and local politicians hop a plane to Washington to see if they can get their hands on that money and control of it's distribution so as to dole it out to friends, supporters who can help them get re-elected while the people in the gulf deplete their life savings, go into debt, search for other work, prepare for cleanup which might last years, contemplate that 1/3 of the gulf being poisoned, while the marshlands affected by the spill die and make the land areas more vulnerable to hurricanes just months away.

Things ain't going so swell.

So what to do?

First get the money out of the US hands to local banks and /or co-ops formed by the communities themselves, composed of the members of that community. (A pipe dream I know) But some people have formed communities and they ought to be encouraged.

—

Secondly, a regional disaster recovery plan ought to be instituted following the steps I have outlined above. (Has anyone heard from FEMA lately?)

We ought to be hiring the unemployed and the skilled to go down to institute the plan on a regional basis. First we need to implement the short term emergency plan I outlined about while simultaneously instituting the long term plans I identified. Note here the ability of residents in the area to earn a livelihood from the Gulf may be affected for many years. A new plan for the small towns in the area has to be created So what is to be the new self-sustaining model for the area? Obviously the last plan of depending upon the sea and tourism didn't work so well.

I like the idea of desalination of the sea, solar power and water power from the Gulf. Make the hurricanes pay from them selves by harnessing the wind to produce electricity. Just a thought. Here would be cheap energy, cheap labor and we could introduce elements of cheap food.

Will this happen? Only God knows, but I would not take odds on it.

Jul 13, 2010
We had a score card on what is needed to turn America around, avoid disaster, and save our widows and orphans. So how are things going?

1- The Gulf: Not so good. We have delay after delay and we have not only one disaster but many. The Hurricane season is now, to peak in September. Are we prepared? No.

Citizens still don't have the money they need to survive not to mention repairs to their lives and cities and even if that hurdle was surpassed there is the matter of fishing and livelihoods all gone for the time being. BP is borrowing money and trying to sell assets because of the spill and that means no new or on-going help from them.

The marshlands are gone. This is a slow moving disaster, but, a sure one.

Are housing, diseases, schools, state finances, rebuilding efforts kicking in or likely? Nope.

Score card F

2- The new Financial Reform bill coming through the Senate is a bust. It does not change much and the current wall-street depression will happen again. Why because the European Union has trillions is debt due in 2012 and no way to pay it So do we. That means trouble for you and me because American banks and other central banks will pay themselves first, and bring us the bill. We, as taxpayers, are last in the queue. So. we are looking at no loans, likely inflation, and more austerity programs and lay-

---

offs and unemployment? "You folks," the mantra will go, "have to tighten your belts."

Who can afford a belt?

Score Card Financial: F

If you don't want to be cheered up any further, skip the next section because things get worse.

3-Unemployment: Millions are now on tender hooks waiting for Senators demanding payoffs for their states for supporting the unemployment extension; meantime the unemployed suffer, many times after having spent life-*time paying unemployment insurance.* Some one please explain what happened to all the excess funds in the unemployment funds, both state and national? Spent. That's what.

Now the cruel aspect this unemployment season is that wall street, and the banks take our money (remember we deposit money in their banks everyday and they took that money and gambled it, lost part of it, took the profits after hedging our funds, made millions, and greed upon greed, took 40% of the values of our middle class homes and 40% of our 401k and now benefit from this employment cycle because cheap labor is back--five applicants for each job, depressed wages, and those with jobs work long hours knowing that there are five people who will take that no- raise, reduced benefit, position they currently have.

Lets be clear: Who does unemployment benefit and who has the money to buy up our de-valued assets at pennies on the dollar--the same folks who took those assets, and used our own money against us, and if there are any losses in all of this, they can simply use government funds to get paid for those losses--if you are a bank--getting paid with money that was is our money again-essentially we are covering banking losses incurred using our money in the first place. The FDIC will collapse. No one can cover the trillions in losses here.

I told you this would be depressing.

So despite all of this can be done? Well there are some critical things, but now you should have a headache, I do, and need some sleep.

Tomorrow. Hint: A solution is not to put another gang in charge to take their turn at feeding at our trough-meaning Republicans.

Jul 15, 2010

Hello all. What is to be done? Well can't do it all today but here are some quick effective items. These are things which may seem unconnected but are not:

1- First the power of the banks and wall street derive directly from us citizens and the fact that each day we give them our money to play with and gamble with. The first step is doing not to do that.

a. Move your money from the big four banks to a local bank, co-op or credit union. That keeps it local and denies the beast the money-food it uses against you.

b. Everyday you give money to wall street through your 401k. Don't do that. Keep yourself liquid; keep the cash. There is not going to be any interest on your money for years anyway. Keep it at home. It denies the beast the money it uses against you.

c. Create your own local bank (that is what a coop is.) Your money stays home and is safe. No Wells Fargo, No Bank America, No Citbank, No Chase. (Note all of our local banks are dying.) Revive them and make them work for you. If you haven't guessed by now it is all about your money, put a lock on your wallet.

d. Make sure your retirement money if it still there is not being used against you. Insist the local union, or government change the Erisa laws so that you or your communities keep the loans local and the money local. Better still insist that the people taking your money and investing it in wall street invest it locally to produce jobs and green technology. I hate to say it but unions are heavy investors in wall street. They should not be doing that. Tell to local union and city council they should be investing that money at home. There are no interest rates increases for the foreseeable future anyway. If they had done that at Katrina or in the BP Oil spill the problems would have a solution, a local solution, local funds, money invested at home to directly benefit the communities where those funds came from in the first place. And don't forget to help local poor communities. If you don't" the poor and formerly middle class will be on the streets knocking at your door looking to feed their families too.

These are actions you can do, you can control and would be effective.

Tomorrow: What to do about all those politicians and parties which also want your cash?

Aug 12, 2010

So are things better yet? Sadly no. But if only a few hundred thousand Americans followed the above advice change would occur. Wall Street and the Banks would feel that pinch, so tight is the system, that a few billion

—

would likely threaten their bloated money needs. And, they would scramble in the next year or two to get money from the feds, like before, or up their fees. But, we would be gone local with our money. So a trap can be laid and set.

Now, to be clear, this is the single best thing to do to change things--redirect your money locally.

Secondly, I am asked are Republicans better than Democrats since the former support local control. (Big laughter here) These Republicans are not talking about local control and self-sufficiency in my meaning. They are talking about their local control over you and your money. They are the same folks in bed with the Banks and Wall street. Are the Democrats better? Nope. We have to stop drinking the cool aid which makes us fail to see that they are all in it together, spending our money and squandering the future of our children. Go to the mirror and slap yourself three times and say "I must not think that the future lies with giving my money to any politician, Banker, or Wall street." (Yes Virginia, wall street counts on getting your unemployment check deposited regularly) So you are the golden goose.

Stop getting et.

So let us think on these things for the future. Tomorrow I will outline Plan C. Plans A and B have been outlined above but we need too, a Plan C.

Sept 27, 2010
Here at the brink of the next election, what to do you may ask. The answer is clear; talk to local townspeople about implementing the above. Start a local dollar pool and co-op (like a local investment club) and meet in homes to get it started. The election is important. I won't tell you who to vote for because all of that is less important than taking control of our own future.

So what you may ask is plan C?

The first step is to make an analysis of what resources are available in your community to do the things outlined above, available land for self-sufficiency uses, available local capital, technical investment capital, available labour pools, political strategies, union supports for withdrawing money form banks and wall street and insisting that it be invested locally.

Investigate the Community Reinvestment Act and apply for funds for your community--which is the purpose of that act in the first place and billions are available. (These funds come directly from the Federal Reserve.)

Identify the goal as "Local Investment With Local Funds" and call a meeting to discuss the problems and local steps for your community while

---

53

also seeking outside funds to aid in the development of those local institutions which will be needed.

You want in the end local foodstuffs, locally grown, local financing, and local labor and energy sources. You can do it in a city but it is difficult. (We all should look at how successful Detroit is in this.) But movement toward self-sufficiency is a good goal for every town, no matter to what degree that might be possible.

You probably have some ideas of your own, if you think about it.

Let's talk again later this week.

Oct 21, 2010
What can be done is to tell city hall to take the money out of the major banks and invest it locally or demand that the major banks invest it locally and that all mortgages be retained locally, We are talking billions of dollars. The same should be said to the labor unions. What are they doing sending our money to wall street any way? That worked our real well didn't it? It's our money: we should take steps to control how it is spent.

Now the state: letters and emails should go out to state governments to add stipulations to wall street investment contracts that state funds be invested in the state or at least that state generated dollars have a portion reinvested in the state. This already exists with banks in the Community Reinvestment Act and has been in place for years. Its precepts should be expanded and extended.

This is very doable. A companion piece ought to be a referendum which places these ideas before the state and have them embedded in law. If done I guarantee you that the banks will do modifications and promote jobs and this country will move toward a sustainable recovery. It is your money. Don't give it away every payroll deduction and check to those who can't be trusted to protect middle class interests.

This is possible.

Oct 22, 2010
Now I have several emails asking how this re-distribution of banking dollars will actually work. The answer, I think, lies in the German example. Germany will, this year, post a 3 percent growth in GNP (Gross National Product) and will likely loan 150 billion to bail out Greece. Germany has bounced back from the recession and is doing well.

Why is this?

The main reasons are, in my view, lies with the German community banking system where communities directly invest in local banks and in

---

54

many cases, own them. A second factor is that German workers, their middle class, sit on the boards of many corporations. A third factor is that the Germans did not decimate their manufacturing base the way other countries did. Finally, Germans save and hoard cash. It is their cultural way.

Add these factors together and what we have seen is that despite the near collapse of the German National Banking system and a German TARP of billions paid out by German taxpayers to save the National Banks, Germany has come through all of that just fine.

The reason is, I believe, are the factors identified above. We can do this in this country. Community banking, local investment, aligned with some of the other suggestions I have made above will work, if perused vigorously, But that is a big if.

Let us hope.

Title: The 2010 Elections-What Do They Mean?

Updated Dec 2, 2010
Summary: Here we go. There will be no turns in Washington for the next two years because noses will be growing longer and longer.
Updated: Nov 5, 2010-"There Will Be No Jobs Soon"
Updated: Nov 6, 2010 "Now Let Me Get This Straight--Give 600 Billion to the Banks?" Who Thought This Was A Good Idea?
Update: Dec 2, 2010 Bullocks Anyone?

Nov 3, 2010

Here we are the day after the elections and the pundits are out in force spinning the results. The Republicans are planning a January trip to Washington to put an end to debt, government spending, the health care bill, and all things Obama.

The Democrats are pointing to silver linings, doing "mi culpa" and basically saying that "we did some good things" but secretly happy that they don't have to take heat before the 2012 presidential election when the big money gets back in play.

This is not to minimize the results of the elections for both, but the fact remains that both sides have sold out to wall-street, the banks, and the corporations.

So nothing will change except the increasing impoverishment of the middle classes, a deepening recession, unto a depression, huge banks playing blackjack with depositor's money and a volatile angry, American politics where little is actually accomplished; thereby maintaining an entrenchment of the status quo. And this is precisely the outcome which benefits wall street.

No change or loans for us thank you very much.

The banks are taking our money, (add to this 600 billion from the Federal Reserve) and using it to cover their own toxic assets, increase our debt to them, and trying to reduce the value of the dollar to raid the central banks of other countries, buy up their real estate and other assets with these cheaper dollars. It will ignite a currency war.

But meantime back home. here are a few important items of note which will have an immediate impact in the next few months.

Let's see what the deeper meanings underlie, not only the election, but the next 60 days.

1-This election essentially involved the loss of 35 or so blue dog democrat seats in mostly red states. Therefore, there is a resetting the clock back to the pre-Obama period. These blue dog democrats were way right of the centre of the party and now what has occurred is the democrats have a much more left party caucus pressing Obama from the left. There will be fewer moderate republicans to please, because they are gone from the party so now there is a clarification of the battle lines for 2012.

Moreover, since 55% of the electorate did not show up for these mid-terms, things will look very different when the mass of these voters show up in that presidential year in 2012. Both parties know this and the next two years are a waiting period as they both try to appear busy.

2- Secondly the Tea-Party people will, even before January, have to witness the current republican establishment face several critical dilemmas:

A. The Federal Debt ceiling has expired. The current Republicans have to decide whether to let the government come to a halt, ala Newt Gingrich in 1994, and risk immediate public anger and probably face Tea-Party pressure to let it happen. They will, if unwise, let the ceiling expire and government come to a halt pretending they are the new more tea-party republican party and to hell with the public; they look conservative and responsible.

They could decide to extend last years budget which would require no debt ceiling legislation; or increase the debt limit of the republic, up to perhaps over 15 trillion dollars-this would have to be done by early spring--or do it with some fancy accounting tricks, or they could steal the money from the social security trust fund which they have done in the past to pay for wars.

But these are unavoidable dilemmas, so expect an avoidance in an off the books accounting gambit to hide an increase in the debt ceiling.

What will also likely happen is an extension of the current budget until after January when the Tea-Party people show up. But they will show up angry because the Republican establishment essentially voted to keep the current deficit budget and spending going.

The current Republican establishment could whack off huge chunks of the current budget in the next 60 days (not likely) like social security, the pentagon budget, health care, the poor; but where would such cuts come from in the amount of money to make a real difference? No where, that's where. Expect a freeze to keep up appearances.

Also, if possible, expect the Republicans to punt to the Tea-Party people who come in January--if they cannot get Obama to join with them in a secret pact agreement about what to cut.

3-Then there are the Bush Tax Cuts which expire December 31, 2010. What to do about that? Ignore it, extend the deadline, or cut a deal with Obama to have all tax cuts extended?

At issue here is that among the tax cuts is the Alternative Minimum Tax cuts which benefit the middle class. If the cuts are not extended it will end that tax cut for the middle classes who will scream bloody murder, even as they might like to see the tax cuts for the rich expire.

Complicated huh.

So you can see what the horse-trading is likely to be. My prediction: all tax cuts will be extended--the Democrats to protect the middle class and the Republicans to protect the rich.

Then there is the health care bill and its implementation aspects, some of which have to be decided in committee. This is ugly, but any hearings will also make it clear that the bill has lot in it which benefits the middle class and to air that would help the democrats and Obama. So we will see a lot of general talk, seeking to keep resentment going, but few real changes.

And then there is the unemployment extension for the 99 month people. Congress left town without doing anything about that and the deadline to do so is here in November. December is urgent. If they don't act you'll have a chunk of people upset, and unemployed for the holidays; not to mention the loss of consumer purchasing power to help the economy recover. The Republicans and TP people will have to wear Scrooge Hats around Christmas time if they don't act.

The Economy: Here we are at the economy. What can the Dems and Reps do about the economy in the next sixty days? Not much. The ideological lines of demarcation are so rigid there is little room for compromise. The Dems will claim slow progress and the Reps will claim the Dems made the unemployment mess and both of their noses will grow longer and longer.

Finally, to boot, the Tea-Party people will be looking over Republican shoulders in the next 60 days making their views known about what to do about the above items, and being ideological purists that they are, they will come to town angry no matter what the Republican establishment types do.

So the scene is set.

So what is likely to happen in the next two years? The Republicans will overplay their hands and subpoena everyone, threaten to shut down the government, back off of massive cuts, especially in the military (too many republican votes there, back off social security, too many republican votes

---

there etc) all the while claiming massive victories for the benefit of the back home crowd.

In the end only Wall-street and the banks will in fact, be left standing dusting off their check books for the 2012 elections to make sure that nothing in Washington changes-once again.

This blog is not for the faint of heart.

Nov. 5, 2010
Just a quick note today to be amplified tomorrow. All the talk today is of the economy and of jobs.
   The truth is that "putting America back to work" is a flawed strategy. Think of it this way. At the present rate of job accretion, it will take five to fifteen years to recover the 11 million jobs lost since the recession began.

It will not happen. It takes a 100 thousand jobs a month just to keep pace with population growth and 150 thousand jobs is minor compared to the need.

Add to this the fact that the long term unemployed are not employable and may have to be given re-training which will cost billions we don't have. Add this to the returning vets who need jobs, housing etc whose medical costs are high in an already aging population; add to this that many of the jobs created are low-paying service jobs and you have a bleak outlook on jobs.

Jobs will not happen- and that is the real problem--especially if you understand the real unemployment and underemployment rate is 17%.

So what to do? For a short answer see my blog on this site on "A Report Card On Obama" and a companion blog on this site called "What America Needs to do to Survive." See the Nov 5th entry where this discussion begins.

More detail tomorrow.

Nov 6, 2010
Obama and company recognize the fact that jobs will not be coming back. So what to do while pretending that they will?

The current strategy apparently is to float the 600 billion onto the currency market, allowing the dollar to dip in value, thereby, increasing the demand for cheaper American goods and thereby increase American exports and thereby increase American jobs.

Sound convoluted?

Well that's because it is.

The announcement that his trip to India (now underway) with 200 American tycoons in tow, will result in 50 thousand new jobs is to put window dressing on the problem. Yet, true, it is a start.

What has to be done I have identified in Obama blog on this site.

The problem is simple:
Consumers, who propel 70% of the American economy, are debt ridden, and like good soldiers some are trying to pay down the Debt That Has No End. They will default in increasingly massive numbers. (Already happening.)
What has to be done is to lower or forgive that debt or put money in their pockets by direct dollars--that would have been a better use of the 600 billion-- rather than the round-about-give-to-the-banks-first strategy. They will simply spend it over seas and not put a dime into America.

Gloomy? Well yes. But not if people take off the blinders and see what is occurring. Things have changed. What we do, therefore, has to change also.

The old strategies will not work.
So we have to look to new ones.

I have a few, modest suggestions. Tomorrow.

Dec 2, 2010
Time is short today so first lets list some solutions and come back tomorrow for the detail.

1-The military budget is 60% of the total federal budget. It has to be cut because that is where the money is. 10% cut = 100 billion

2-The top 1% of the population has 35% of the wealth and half the tax rates of the rest of us. Tax their stock market holdings 15% along with capital and dividend income. 15% revenue= 1.8 trillion

3- Increase the current cap on social security and Medicare taxes to include the wealthy. The current system has no tax on people earning above 110k per year and is a free ride for the wealthy. Best guess is 2.3 billion inflow.

4-Have a tax payroll holiday for the middle classes thereby putting money in their pocket, increase the home mortgage deduction, and declare a moratorium on foreclosures. Outflow approximately 2 trillion.

60

5-Put the 600 billion into mortgage relief, greening and insulating American homes. Remember winter is coming and oil prices are rising. There will be demand to keep warm. It will be a long winter with high prices and cold voters, otherwise. Dollar return on this investment is two dollars for every dollar invested =1.2 trillion

That is the flavor of some of the suggestions and any three of them will eliminate the so-called deficit. (Net of all of them is 1.3 trillion against a deficit of 1.2 trillion. No more deficit.

There is no need to go after social security. That program has no deficit. No need to go after the middle class at all.
The money on wall street is our money and they should have to give it back.

These are just preliminary but achievable in a short period of time, absent political stagnation. I know that is a big if, but a solution is a solution even if blocked.

Let's hope our leaders get some bull apparatus and act.

Title: Nose Measuring Politics-A Proposal

 Politics these days has such a crazy-quilt aspect to it, it is difficult to figure out what is going on.
The Blue Dog democrats lost whose very existence made people wonder if the democrats were Dogs or Donkeys. I say they are Donkey-Dogs.

Similarly, the Republicans have become confused with being a mighty elephant on the one hand, or a tea bag at the bottom of my tea cup on the other.

This is symbol discombobulation such that bipartisan may mean us poor voters might have to contemplate a tea sipping elephant (an ugly thought) but I might pay money to see that elephant attempt the act with that trunk; talk about a pinkie.

Or, we might have to contemplate a huge blue donkey with a tiny dog's head.

This is too much like falling into the rabbit hole and what is needed here, therefore, is brain-clearing simple measures of who is who in Congress now, and simple measures of who can be believed and who is yet another girlie boy and boylie girl out to line their own pockets while giving us Cheshire Cat smiles of reassurance that things will be ok as long as some Republican or Democrat is defeated in the next election.

So what and whom is to be believed here? If we don't have some measure of truth it will be a long two years.

I propose the following modest remedies:

Each Monday all of the Congress people, the President, the Supreme Court the bureaucrats, everyone will be required to undergo full body scans and pat-downs under the Capital Rotunda. (Now there would surely be some ugly cellulite and some huge Rotunda's in that group--but let's be careful to not show this at breakfast time though.)

Now bear with me here because this would inject some much needed humility into our governing leaders and at the same time probably get the airport version of the electronic full-body-grope rescinded.

In fact, there ought to be a law that no votes can be taken on anything that Congress people themselves have not been directly subjected to themselves. That would cool their legal ardour such that the rest of us can get some peace from their ceaseless attempts to protect us and make

---

things better in the country while failing to make things better in this country.

Secondly, each Monday of the week, all of our leaders ought to have their noses measured. (This is the infallible Pinocchio Test) The electronic grope machine might be adjusted to tilt upward a little and accomplish this nicely, and, we would have an objective mendacity measure.

A centimeter's growth of any nose would constitute a recall and that individual or individuals would be considered to have been voted off the island and sent home. This makes sense to me, I saw it on television, so it must be ok and it must be true.

Third, all body scans of our leaders ought to be made public and shown in the Congressional Record, and any one found to have 100 dollars bills concealed anywhere ought to get the nose treatment identified above and be forced to bend over each morning, turn around and look through their legs-preferably naked, while being scanned.

That would be huge punishment.

Delicious.

Now this "experience life as we experience life" methodology might also have a sobering and beneficial effect on American life.

Congress, all of them, have to fly economy, drive their own cars in traffic like we do, watch bad TV, (no private screening rooms anymore) eat bad food, pay for their own stamps, have all of their face book friends turn on them, and the greatest indignity of all--have to pay for their own meals instead of having lobbyists pay for their meals, their hotels, their golf games, their libraries after they leave office, and have their pensions cut after they leave--well you get the idea.

Worth a shot, don't you think?

Title: Deficit Cutting: Myths:

Facts: What Is True?

Updated 12-10/10
Summary: A look at the facts and myths about:
Social Security-is the fund going broke? Medicare: Will Its Cost Bankrupt Us?
The Military Budget: Is It Really 60% of the Total Budget?
Social Programs: How Much Do They Really Cost?
Deficit: What Is To Be Done? Updated 11-30-10-So Where Is The Money?
Updated: 12/1/10 "If You Want Money for the Deficit, You Have To Go Where the Money Is."
Updated: 12/3/10 "Now Let me get this straight: My pension will help fund the European Bailout of Ireland, Greece, Spain?
Updated: 12/10/10 So who is going to be taxed again?

In this blog I was just trying to find out the facts about these items in a period where "deficit-cutting" and "big government" blare out of my TV, pages in the press, and among friends who opine right and left on these matters.

So I thought I would do a little investigation myself. In the coming few days I will share with you what I found out.

MYTH: Social Security causing part of our deficit and is going broke.

FACTS: First a quote from a New York Times article from the chief actuary manager of the fund (Mr. Goss) and a second quote from the Director of the Congressional Office of the Budget.

Mr. Goss is talking about the state of fund based on 2009 figures and projections and the proceeds from the funds investments in treasury securities.

"In a year like this, the paper gains from the interest earned on the securities will more than cover the difference between what it takes in and pays out."

"Mr. Goss, the actuary, emphasized that even the $29 billion shortfall projected for this year was small, relative to the roughly $700 billion that would flow in and out of the system. The system, he added, has a balance of about $2.5 trillion that will take decades to deplete. Mr. Goss said that large cushion could start to grow again if the economy recovers briskly."

—

"Indeed, the Congressional Budget Office's projection shows the ravages of the recession easing in the next few years, with small surpluses reappearing briefly in 2014 and 2015."

See the link below for the full article.

http://www.nytimes.com/2010/03/25/business/economy/25social.html
For those who are numbers junkies, like me, should also take a look an article which details the Federal Budget for 2010, and for 2011. See link below:
http://topics.nytimes.com/top/reference/timestopics/subjects/f/federal _budget_us/index.html?inline=nyt-classifier
The Deficit Commission Plan comes out December 1, 2010 and is not likely to have the 14 votes necessary for a vote in the House of Representatives. Meantime, many groups have their own ideas for deficit management. Here is a link detailing some of those plans. We will then evaluate the whole lot afterward. Meantime a link:

http://www.nytimes.com/2010/11/29/us/politics/29fiscal.html?_r=1&ref =federal_budget_us

Home work.

Come back tomorrow and we will begin to sort all of this out.

Nov 30, 2010
Truth Telling About Social Security

First the question is does Social Security contribute to the deficit?

Answer no.

The program has a 2.5 trillion dollar surplus at the present time. So why would the Deficit commission target one of the few programs which has a surplus and money available to operate out to 2037?

It makes no sense. So why is it on the chopping block?

Well, first let us have a look at where this tremendous surplus money comes from.

Answer:

It comes from you and me. Every pay check a sum is deducted from our paychecks for our social security retirement and those funds are placed in the social security trust fund and much of it is invested with the idea of increasing its total amount so that it will be there when we are ready to retire. That is the story put out there. But it is true?

—

65

So, like good investigators we want to know the truth and to find out the truth in America you have to follow the prime rule of thumb:

Follow the money because there lays the truth.

The truth is that the 2.5 trillion has been raided by the federal government, mainly to pay for wars the country could not afford (remember Iraq and Afghanistan?) for bank bailouts, (remember instituting the Bush Tax Cuts which we could not afford?) Remember the lost jobs, the lost manufacturing base, and the Wall-Street bail outs? How can a country afford all of this in a little less than a decade?

Answer: We, the people, could afford it because we saved up each month. But the money was taken from yours and my retirement funds, social security monies, yours and my pension funds (remember we are also putting money in that pot too, yours and my taxes, yours and my daily deposits in the banks, yours and my Medicare taxes, yours and my unemployment funds, at an actual taxation rate of 53%--all this ultimately ending up in the hands of the banks, the corporations, and wall street who were taxed at 16% and was used by them to generate obscene profits overseas and/or obscene losses which ended up having to be paid for by raiding our retirement funds to cover such losses and monies wasted in endless and permanent wars and other boondoggles.

I don't mind government spending, at least you get something back for that money after the monied classes have deducted their deductions, loop holes and subsidies benefits which, while only a pittance, is better than the alternatives of no benefits at all.

But what did we get back for the purloining of our money by the corporations--jobs and profits exported overseas. What did we get back for the purloining of our money by wall street--economic collapse and bank gambling, lost values in our homes, in our 401k.s, almost permanent unemployment, and now a threat to our pension funds (remember this is our money too, deducted every paycheck,) low or no pensions, foreclosures, impossible credit card debt and to boot, in all this, we are told it is our fault and we have to learn to tighten our belts.

I don't know about you but this doesn't seem right.

Well that is because it isn't.

More tomorrow.

But first a glance at borrowing from the Social Security Fund since 2002. This borrowing was clearly seen coming and predicted. Here is one prediction. After we will see if the prediction came true. But first the prediction:

—

1998:Testimony by Alan Greenspan with Senator Hollings saying:
"We owe Social Security 736 billion right this minute."

In 2002 actual borrowing from the fund: 165.4 billion
2003-projected--164 billion
2004-projected--180.6 billion
2005-projected--203.8 billion
2006-projected--226.1 billion
2007-projected--247.9 billion
2008-projected--268. billion

Total projected borrowing: 1.11 trillion from the fund.

Source:

**http://demopedia.democraticunderground.com/discuss/duboard.php?
az=show_mesg&forum=102&topic_id=17321&mesg_id=18550**

Now how much did we actually borrow and how much exactly is left in the
fund in cash. (Actual income for the social security trust fund in 2009 was
about 700 billion and outlays are about 520 billion.)

And what about the unemployment trust fund. What is the story there?

That tomorrow.

But the point is that someone here loses big, because the banks, the
government, the corporations got the money and can't or won't pay it back
to us and therefore all of the talk about cutting social security. Why:
because the funds on paper are 2.5 trillion but some of that the cash is
long gone and what is left in the fund is a lot of iou's-to us and the banks
and wall street can't or don't want to pay it back.

But exactly, again, how much real cash is left for the boomers you and I?

It difficult to find out this piece of information.

What does all this mean and what is to be done?

Hint: There are solutions.

Hint: You can't look at a government debt and a government budget like
the family budget. It is not like the family budget. Don't fall for that false
analogy.
In our family budget we cannot print money in the basement--the
government can (or more accurately, the Federal Reserve, the banks can;)

—

we cannot raid our neighbors for resources, the government and our banks can.

We can't create taxes. The government can.

Well, you get the idea. There is no real analogy between one's home budget and the processes which underlie the budget of an entire country. So ignore politicians we try to tell you they are the same. They are not.

So what then you ask is to be done?

Tomorrow.

Dec 1, 2010
Busy day today so let's cut to the chase and identify what will really cure the deficit. We will post here an outline and in the coming days go to detail on some of them.

But first what will not work:

1-Cutting down the middle class and driving it to poverty will not work obviously and will likely in a year or two create a huge rebellion once people realize what has happened to them. A likely trigger will be the Republican discussion of eliminating the home mortgage deduction. This will do it. Not only have Americans seen their homes lose 40% value but the elimination of that deduction will increase their taxes by thousands of dollars, and put even old ladies in the streets in outrage.

Moreover, the consequences of this kind of action will be:

Lower revenues (taxes) for states, cities and localities, lower purchasing power for an economy which is 70% middle class consumer driven; higher defaults, foreclosures, rising health care costs because people will drop health insurance and flood the emergency rooms for health care. Impoverishing the middle class, therefore, is not a good idea and helps no one.

2-Cutting back government spending or attacking the deficit in dollar amounts large enough to make a difference, is a pipe dream.

You might as well shut down the entire government, and move us all to third world status. Government spending is the one area that the middle class gets something back for its taxes.
We get nothing back from the banks and wall street,. We, not them, fuel the economy of this country. 70% of the GNP comes from the middle classes and we pay the taxes--yet the profits go to the banks and wall street and the corporations. **The middle class provides the only real**

———

money in the entire system. The rest of the institutions in the United States suck on that teat.

3-Cutting the military budget substantially, while desirable and possible since we spend 60% of the government's budget on the military, the fact is that will take years to accomplish and since the military is so entwined in our economy it has become yet another institution too big to fail and so many Americans depend upon military largess to survive--but that budget has to be cut anyway, but it has to be done gradually and with perhaps an initial 10% cut to start things off. (This has already been proposed by Gates, but he wants to "re-invest" those savings back into the military, therefore, it is not a real cut. I say lets take a real cut.)

4-Economic growth as a way of reducing or eliminating the deficit, (jobs and exports) is too slow to avoid disaster. We will all be in rags before the jobs return and that will take at least five years.

What can be done then? Let's start with a simple idea. There is not a shortage of money to be used to eliminate the deficit. The problem is that 35% of our money is in the hands of 1% of the population-the so-called market.

Solution: Get our money back.

I like Richard Woof's ideas about taking the income of all individuals with more than a million dollars invested in the stock market and apply a additional 15% tax rate. They keep 85% and this will eliminate the deficit over night. Really. It would.
  What is astounding is that the so-called deficit commission has not even brought this up. Why? The two chairs of the commission and most members of that commission represent those same wall-street-banks interests. So no surprise this is not included in possible solutions.
(See Richard Wolff's ideas on this)

The mess wall-street has made we are going to have to pay for while wall street proceeds forward, "fully recovered" from any of the effects of the recession and notice that every announcement that the unemployment rate has gone up is greeted by a rise on wall street. Why. Because middle class assets become cheaper and the unemployed default and foreclosures become available cheap. Meantime the big bonus payments have returned.

The American people will catch on sooner or later to all of this and there will be hell to pay.

When you want to reduce or eliminate deficits at home or in government you have to go where the money and the money is in the hands of these monied classes who in the last thirty years have gotten rich off the rest of

—

us and now it is time they pay that money back. They have gotten rich off the American credit card and our loans to them-(yes we loan them our money every time we make a deposit.)

But who are these folks and how much would be really made available if we did this?

More details tomorrow.

Dec 3, 2010
But the problem is not just an American problem. We are a part of the global finance system. Just out is the revelation that during the finance crisis of 2008 and continuing, the Federal Reserve bank loaned over *9 trillion dollars* to itself, to banks foreign banks and domestic, to cover their losses.

That is 9 **trillion dollars**, not counting the 600 billion now coming over the horizon!

Where did this money come from, remembering the entire yearly output of the American economy in one year is only 13 trillion.

For comparison a billion seconds is 32 years: a trillion seconds is 32,000 years. So a trillion is a very large burrito.

Why did this happen and where did this 9 trillion dollars come from?

Answer: The banks used partly our funds, our pension monies, our daily deposits and the Fed simply printed the rest. Understand this is how the system works.

But the real news here is that the 9 trillion was essentially used to cover the fraudulent investments wall street had sold to investors foreign and domestic. A good part of it was to pay foreign banks back that might have collapsed once it was known that such investments were worthless. The US essentially had to take our money to cover up that fraud and lost gamble and their selling fraudulent assets to these foreign banks.

Meantime, companies like Goldman Sachs, had seen this coming and essentially took out re-insurance and took short positions on all of this, even as they sold these worthless assets to others and reaped huge profits in doing so.

AIG the major re-insurer, Fanny and Freddie Mac, FDIC, the American tax payer took the losses, and the banks took the profits. This is welfare for the rich.

And the story does not end here.

70

The domino rolled right across the ocean to the European Common Market where the bail outs of Ireland, Greece, Portugal, and Spain now loom.

Austerity programs will not solve anything there.

In fact, the European Central Bank does not have the money for the bailouts, up to a trillion dollars, and will not have anything like what it will need if Italy goes belly up--which it will.

In fact, the ECM will have to get part of the money it needs, not just from Germany and France or England, but from American taxpayers.

The Germans will give much but there is a limit since their taxpayers will revolt at some point if they are made to suffer to bail out others.

So how you ask will all this get done? It will get done by borrowing money from the managers of those huge pension funds which exist at the Federal, State and Local Level in the United States and else where and the Federal Reserve buying ECM bonds. This, again, is our pension monies and deposit monies and the accumulated profits wall street has from the so-called recession.

The American taxpayer actually is helping to fund banks all over the world--foreign and domestic--with our pensions, taxes, social security funds, unemployment insurance funds etc.

This will be the second bubble to hit in 2012. All of this is not sustainable as currently constructed.

But the chief aspect of this which is not sustainable is that the profits cannot continue to be grabbed by the few. The entire system has to be re-constituted to produce prosperity for the many not just the few.

Actually, that is the European Common Market's underlying principle. The strong help the weak. We have to learn that trick here in the United States by ensuring that the strong don't use our money to prevent this bedrock principle of shared prosperity from being implemented, which they have succeeded in doing in the last 30 years.

Ok, now that you are cheered up there is a need for a hot toddy or something.

Tomorrow we go to detail.

Dec 10, 2010
Forgot to mention that the new tax deal is not so great.
More detail on this next week but the facts are:

1-That the lowest earners have their taxes go up not down, or neutral

2- The longest term unemployed are left out of the deal entirely (the 99 month people)

3- The Estate Tax exempts those earning five and 10 million per couple, per year, thereby increasing the deficits of every state in the union.

4-Social security, unemployment, and disability incomes remain taxed. (This is double taxation, these earnings are taxed when taken out of our paychecks and taxed again when we use these funds. Note capital gains and dividend income remain taxes only at the 15% percent level while the rest of our income is taxed at the 21% level.

The democrats are right to revolt against job-killing tax breaks for the rich.

Yet Americans seem to be unaware of all this and still seem to believe that our system is better than the rest of the world. Huh?

But what to do? That is the question.

Note: The family is intricately related to both society and politics. This is a blog entry which has a look at what their relations are and how they intersect which our political institutions, in my view.

Title: Politics, the Family, Birth Position, And Political Values

Updated:10/9/10

Summary: There have been several books on the issue of whether a child's birth position in the family pre-shapes their values, political views and attitudes in general. We take a look at these ideas adding to the mix the factors of family structure. Let's see what a discussion of this set of factors bring.
Updated: 10/4/10 The Dominant Father-Passive Mother Family Structure
Updated: 10/7/10 Dominant? Who's Dominant? Both of Us Can't Be Dominant? Right?
Updated: 10/8/10 Why Do We Have A Dominate-Father Family Structure in the First Place? Updated: 10/9/10 So What About the Benevolent Father Family Structure?

Oct 1, 2010
The obvious first point here is that everyone is born and most of us are born into a family, or perhaps orphaned at an early age, and if we survive, grow up with or without siblings. Also, most of us grow up inside a family structure of some kind, or at the least with significant adults providing supports, love, direction and succour.

The next logical question is how do the circumstances of our rearing affect us, our values, our beliefs, and our political and social views?

I propose to discuss the given structure of a family and relate that structure , to the birth position and sex of the child in that family structure and to that child's social, political and world views.

A tall order indeed; one which will likely fail- but well worth the journey, in my view.

But first we need to identify what family structures are posited.

We could identify many but the ones I propose are:

1-The single mother family

73

2-The single father family

3-The dominant father-passive mother family structure

4-The dominant mother-passive father family structure

5- The father-mother competitive family structure

6- The absent mother and the absent father family structure (not the orphaned structure)

7- Divorced and Separated Families

8- Blended Families

9- Interracial Families

10- Intercultural Families

11- Other structures. (Oldest male child, oldest female child, youngest male or female) Gay families, Lesbian families

12 Minority families

13-Culturally Dominant families (or white families in the US.

(These typologies alone can provoke responses, indeed, are instructive in themselves.

I will direct my discussion to the impact of these structures on:

1-The oldest male and female child

2-The middle male and female child

3- The younger male and female children

A second set of variables will be what is the impact of these structures apt to be on the child's notion of:

1-Freedom

2-Love

3-Justice-Equality

4-The family itself

5-Society and Politics

6-The State

7- World views

A through look into all of this cannot be done in a single blog (a book is coming) I am hoping discussion and feedback can sharpen that proposed book.

So lets start out here and see what we come up with in the coming days.

I believe a good look at important issues to start one's day is as important as a good breakfast. Let's have toast.

Oct 4, 2010
First we want to define a few terms. I will start with the dominant-father passive mother family structure.

The father is, in this structure, the dominant member of the family. He is expected to provide for the family, sits at the head of the table, represents the family and, needless to say makes most of the important decisions in the family. While mother may or may not discipline the kids, the dominant father is often presented to the kids as the ultimate dispenser of rewards and punishment.

This is a common family structure one which is probably most common in the world, reinforced by the Christian bible, by Islam, and by most other religions. God in most religions, if there is a God, is usually male, stern and requires obedience.

Passive here does not necessarily mean the wife or partner is totally passive, although some are. But that passivity can exhibit a hidden strong reaction to the dominance of the father figure. Mothers can react to this dominance by fighting against it all the while playing the passive role. Mother might subvert the "authority" of the father by developing secret pacts and relationships with the kids. She might say "be good or I will tell your dad but if you do what I want you to do I will not tell him."

In a word Mother steals the kids, keeps secrets with them and dominates their emotional life while dominant dad works and, over time, slowly

---

75

retreats from the family, her and the kids because he is gradually entrapped in his role and is now dominant, but becomes the emotionally isolated, closed, father who has no real relationship with the children except as the bringer of fear and critiques. Often he looks at the kids as disloyal and unappreciative of his efforts and the wife becomes the one who "spoils" them. She does and there is a reason for it. Alliances matter in this family.

These are common observations, often commented upon by others.

Some times DD will try to form his own emotional alliance with a girl child in the family to thwart the alliances the mother is constructing. The young girl becomes "daddy's girl" due to the attentions of the father and may come to hold mother in open contempt because the young girl is given the impression that she is more important to dad than mom and simultaneously the young girl holds mom in contempt for the reason that mom appears passive and weak to the young girl, who makes a secret vow "I will never become like mom." In extreme cases the young girl sees her self as the "wife" figure or the most important person in the family aside from dad himself. She becomes aggressive and self-regarding and all this might also bring her in conflict with her siblings who notice all this.

If the alliance is with oldest male child then similar patterns emerge. However, there are some differences with the oldest male child which we will explore later.

So essentially what you have here is a family often at war and often split internally. If dad's dominance is never challenged you have the peace of a family where dominance is never challenged and all seems well, quiet and peaceful, but, underneath, there is seething anger among everyone, which is not allowed to come out in the open.

Now what we want to know is what kinds of attitudes emerge from these two variations on the dominant family in the male and female child along the variables I have identified above?

Who says families are dull? Lots of drama going on there--but keep in mind so goes the family so goes the nation and vice-versa. Family dynamics determine how a culture or a country interacts with its citizens and with other cultures and countries in the world.

Let's have a closer look in the coming days.

Oct, 7, 2010

The oldest child (male or female) is usually given more attention than siblings (except maybe the youngest sibling) and has a dilemma. Let's take the case of the oldest male child. This child will seek to become like dad. But "dad-ness" involves dominance as a birthright and the females are expected to defer to that dominance.

But the male child is also dominated by the father figure setting into motion an inner conflict. The male might challenge the father, and at the same time view the females in the family as less than equal to himself, the oldest male child.

Smarting from fatherly dominance the oldest male child might seek an alliance with the mother in which case conflict with dad emerges and grows and can become intense, with the father making it known that an alliance with the females is not approved by him. In order to avoid that conflict the son may form a secret alliance with mom all the while maintaining at least the appearance of a close alliance with dad as well. This is a tricky trick to maintain and mistrust often occurs and suspicions of hidden alliances. Or the oldest son could retreat from all of this and emotionally abandon the family with friends or retreat inwardly to other things.

If the son and the father do form a close relationship then the two will have bonds around the interests of the father, and "male things." This alliance is seen by siblings and this becomes yet another aspect of the family structure where unstated conflicts are present

Now with this structure in place the father-dominated male child learns some lessons:

1-Freedom is the unchallenged right of males to act. The females of the household are not actors; they cannot initiate action without the father's approval. This notion of freedom dovetails with American culture where the United States behaves in the world with a notion that we have an untrammelled right to act, without restraint, upon all other countries in the world. Freedom becomes power over others and it is learned in the home.

2-A variant of this is, of course, male-bonding social organizations, fraternities, and the like. But this also engenders male-female splits in society creating this tribal split along gender lines and the two sexes, over-time know less and less about each other, especially in our times when women are in the work force and many come to see themselves chaffing under this male dominant family structure. This also creates yet another

—

77

layer of tension in the family. Bad economic times can cause this structure to facture and a high divorce rate occurs in this structure.

Of course, bad economic times might cause this family as well to become closer in order to survive. In the short run this can be good. But come the "good times" again the old tensions will re-emerge unless the couple learns the ways of peace during this "bad time" cooperation period.

Now another point to be made here is that this structure can and does change and is not being judged as all bad. There are many positives also at play. Some personalities are suited to this structure and things can go quite well. But later in life tensions may erupt even after a seemingly tranquil childhood when the male child seeks to act upon his childhood influences as he seeks to find a female willing to play mom's passive role, this can prove to be difficult.

But there are other factors at play which generate this family structure which are in fact, seen by some, as positive. "Maleness" and the need for a warrior mentality and military service can be functional in a young man who can, thereby, prove to his dad that he is worthy, and a man. The military gives the male child an affinity for male sacrifice for the family and also for his country. The latter often becomes, for the father and the male child, a proving ground and a bonding experience for each.   Self-sacrifice for the country, military strife and American attitudes of domination toward other cultures are a comfortable fit for young men from this family structure. And we do need these traits, at least many think so, in order for the population to rise to the needs of war. This is not new.

But underneath, remains the idea that the male child wants to be dominant like dad and may in his youth be a bully, a super male, and might rise up and confront the father early or his late teens-often in the context of protecting mom and the kids. This will not be tolerated and the son will then find military service very attractive as a way of exiting from this kind of strife with the father.

More tomorrow.

Oct 8. 2010
Now we ask, once we see the negatives of the structure, lets have another closer look at the positives briefly mentioned above.

The dominant father feels that he is making huge sacrifices for the family, denies himself even the softer aspects of marriage and its emotional comforts, and that translates very easily into sacrifice for ones country, state. town or village or even for God.

There are tremendous reinforcements for this attitude by nations who have a need for young men and women willing to make life and death sacrifices for the country. And, as we have seen, even the conflicts inside this family structure, seen from the point of view of a warring country, are not negative but positive when seen from the point of view of a country which needs to go to war occasionally, or has continual wars of expansion.

Young men are often eager to go and want to exit this family structure, often fuelled by the idea that the military life is a rite of male passage to manhood, encouraged by both father and society, even religion. The interpretation of a powerful, angry God, note, is a close approximation of the angry, powerful father figure in the home.

Mom, too, has to prepare the male child for military service which might end in his death.

So to be clear, if we see this family structure in historical terms, many if not most warring nations produce this structure, encourage it and welcome it. So do many religions. So do many social structures.

Why?

Because it is functional for many nations. And, it has been around for many thousands of years. From the Romans, the early Israelites, Christians, the Greeks, show many examples of the all powerful father dominated family structure, women, slaves and other conquered peoples all in the same family structure. This is the Roman example.

Of course, a society which is at war or threatened, can utilize that threat to insist upon obedience as a virtue to ensure the survival of the nation.

So there is a relationship between a country's history, social mores and the family structures it produces.

Now we can ask how many families in the United States exhibit this structure? We have partially explored the reinforcing and interlocking aspects of its generation. Now we want to know how many.

Approximately, (a guess) 45%. How do we know? One survey found that approximately 45% of Americans see God as an angry, revengeful God

---

who is involved in our everyday lives. This, is of course, not a scientific answer to the question but it is reasonable to assume that a family belief in a God of that nature will likely correlate to the father-dominant family structure we have posited.

Now keep in mind a father-dominant figure in the home that, to the children and the wife, looks, acts and feels like the Christian God of the old testament, can be scary.

So what we want to do next time is to return to look at the how all of this affects the children and the wife, and the father as we continue our exploration of the 7 variables identified above.

Things are getting complicated. But things human usually are.

A last point to make is that a warring nation does form and even distort family structures to meet the exigencies of war itself. The population has to be ready for war and since obedience in an military context is essential for success in war this family structure is consistent with those kinds of national needs.

So these lessons are first learned at home and accounts in part for the prevalence of this family structure throughout most of history.

A country of pacifists is soon conquered.

Oct 9, 2010
But the dominant-father structure is not the only structure we can observe in society.

If we take current religious ideas about the nature and involvement of God in our lives, that survey found that:

1-25% of Americans believe God is benevolent and not directly involved in our daily lives.

2-23% believe that God is distant and removed from our daily lives

3-15% believe that God is critical but removed from directly influencing our daily lives.

4- Only 2% of Americans see themselves as atheists.

So most people profess a belief in God and have notions of what personality and penchants that God might have.

Now for a country to survive, internal family strife cannot be universal, although some societies have tried to create the totally military society, preparing young men for war from an early age and positing glory and victory in war as the highest ideal young men can aspire to. It is easy to see how those same societies would want the family structure to compliment, indeed generate such young men.

So family structure matters in states which see themselves as under threat or who have frequent wars.

But what of the 25% in the American survey that see God as benevolent; as kind? I suspect there is a close correlation between this belief and new testament Christians who see in those pages a kind and benevolent God. Jesus counselled to seek the divine within, rejected the rebel role for one more pacifist in nature.

This is a God of kindness and mercy-yet is still God.

So we ask how this is reflected in the family structure currently and historically..

Let's look at the dominant but benevolent father- mother counsellor family structure.

Here the father is dominant but mother is a counselor, often consulted and somewhat more of a partner in family matters. Often the two will cooperate, and even divide family duties between them. She makes decisions or takes initiatives in areas related to the home, church, the children and the couple's social life.

This is a more of a cooperative model, yet underneath the father in cases of conflict usually prevails especially in areas where he has assumed control; money, jobs, ultimate decisions about the kids, career and where the family lives.

The two are more community minded in this model and more plugged into activities outside the home. So how do they fare in society and historically?

—

81

For a link to an article on these four views of God, see below.

**http://iphone.usatoday.com/News/2086728/full/;jsessionid=F90E869B
73EE7A5126C0EAE103FBEF67.wap1**

Lets have a closer look at this benevolent structure tomorrow.

Title: The Middle Class, The Poor and America's Future

Summary: This looks at why American politics has the contours that it exhibits. It asks the question what political stances do the poor, the middle class and the rich take in our political system and why.
Second, a comparison with European political systems is made looking at these same class groups and the similarities and differences we see there and why.
Updated: Nov 29 2010- The Middle Class Holocaust Coming.

In the recent mid-term elections in the United States political debate excluded two enormous topics of obvious import: the two wars in Iraq and Afghanistan and the plight of the poor and middle classes in the United States.

The economy was discussed but not its real impacts on real people now short of resources and whose life chances are declining. Rather, we were treated to debates about tax cuts, deficit reductions, "big government" and "socialism."

Why should these discussions take on these contours?

We will have a look at the middle classes and the working poor in the American political landscape and how they place themselves in the political spectrum and why.

We shall also compare that to the multi-party system and the coalition patterns extent in Europe. There we find distinctly different political patterns and outcomes. How do the two systems compare and why and with what political outcomes.

Let's start with a quote from two European scholars who ask the questions; do political coalitions between the middle class and the working poor explain the nature of political structures in Europe? Why are there no coalitions between the poor and the middle class in the United States?

The scholars Iversen and Soskice are quoted from a paper given by Phillip Manow in Seoul, Korea in March of 2007 gives us some clues as to why such coalitions exist in Europe but not in the United States.

83

See link below.

http://www.korea.ac.kr/~kwon/Conf/Manow.pdf

Here is a longish quote from that paper.

"Iversen and Soskice start from the basic observation that in multi-party systems the left is in government more often whereas the right more often governs in two-party systems. Why is this so?

In a multi-party system the lower and the middle classes together can tax the rich and share the revenue. In a two party system the middle class can either vote for a centre-left party or a centre-right party. If the left governs, the middle class has to fear that the left government will tax both the upper and the middle class for the exclusive benefit of the lower class. If a right party governs, the middle and upper class will not be taxed and redistribution will be marginal. Therefore, in a two-party system the middle class has the choice either to be taxed and to receive no benefits, or not to be taxed and to receive no benefits. Obviously, it would prefer then not to be taxed.

From this simple and highly stylized account it is clear that the middle class will more often vote together with the lower class in multi-party systems – or to be more precise: middle class parties will more often enter into coalitions with lower class parties in multi-party systems than in two party systems.2"

Underlying this analysis is a stark premise: Politics is about money and resources--who gets what, when, where and how.

Another premise, equally important and less apparent, seems to be that prosperity must be shared for a culture to flourish. A peaceful means to accomplish this must be identified and institutionalized. Otherwise, the rich will greedily absorb a disproportionate share of everything, refuse to give it up, and the society ultimately is thrown into riots, anger, social dislocations, revolution and all things bad and not so incidentally, the destruction of the middle class.

Well lets see how these principles do and do not apply to America, especially since at this critical juncture, these are precisely the questions which our country now confronts, even as political discourse ignores them altogether--if we take the last election as an indicator.

Next time. Who is getting what, when, where, why, and how in the United States.

Nov 29, 2010
I make the argument that the systematic attack on the middle class in this country involving so-called deficit cut backs, privatizing social security,

cutting Medicare, cutting education spending, cutting wages, contemplating millions of unemployed indefinitely, also constitute opportunities. There are now opportunities for the middle class, in seeing itself becoming lower middle class, to begin to see and form a coalition with the working poor classes and to see it has common interests with even the current poor.

From this an ethos of common prosperity can emerge and the country can get back on the right track again.

Having most wealth the hands of the rich is an unsustainable idea.

This opportunity for the middle class to finally see that all the money in this country is money they themselves supply to Wall Street institutions who translate those funds into political power which has been used to ransack that very same middle class--taking from them in just three years, their home values, their savings, their jobs--and their futures even unto retirement--all under the guise of deficit reduction. This is a middle class holocaust.

This is and will become even more devastating. It in fact, it turns America into a true welfare state: The rich controlling most wealth in a Neo-Dickens world where most will have to depend upon alms from a government controlled by those very same rich classes.

http://www.nytimes.com/2010/12/05/us/politics/05states.html?ref=tod ayspaper

Fish are having trouble identifying water.

More tomorrow- where we will focus on "deficit reduction" and the agenda behind it.

Dec 4, 2010
Actually I started another blog on deficit reduction on this site. Refer to that blog.

—

Note: The internet has become a part our lives. The question is how does it impact our political values?. Currently there is very much a question surrounding its potential and actual impact by political and governmental forces in undermining the freedoms in societies around the world. I have chosen internet dating sites as a way of starting that conversation and in the process put light on how the internet as a whole works-much of it alarming.
Importantly, many Americans seem unaware of the dangers the internet poses when used by forces seeking to control its citizens seeking access to information.

Title: Internet Dating Sites: Love Found or Money Scams?

Updated 11/21/10

Summary: This is the beginning of a series looking at this phenomenon in American Society Updated: 9/22/10 GPS Sucks
Updated: 9/23/10 It Is Far Worse Than You Think Update: 9/24/10 My Way of Picking a Date is Better Than Your Way of Picking a Date
Updated: 9/28/10 Now the US government might want to be able to see who you talk to on Face Book
Updated: 9/30/10 "Are You Real or Are You a Computer?
Updated: Are You The Computer to Whom I Am Talking?
Updated: 10-9/10 There is such a thing as too much information about you floating around. Updated: 10/11/10 So What Happened to Dating Sites in 2007?
Updated: 11-16-10 Dating and Chatting by Cell phone? Not so safe, apparently

In discussing internet dating sites the proposal here has several aspects:
1- What is the profile of dating sites; how many are there, and how do they operate as businesses?
2- Who owns these sites, who invest in them, and what has been their history?
3- What kinds of information do they collect, in what detail, and who uses the information; who has access to that information and who can buy it?

86

4-   What has been the experience of various population groups in using these sites?
5-   What are the pros-cons, successes and dangers of these internet phenomena which by conservative estimates involves tens of millions of individuals each day?
6-   How do these sites fit in with social networking sites such as Face book, My Space and other sites?

Finally I propose to step back and take a look at how these sites and others sites on the internet fit into what I term the Data Harvesting Society.

What is apparent is that many of the sites on the internet irrespective of their outward stated purposes really exist to make money off the data that their subscribers and non-subscribers provide. This data exists forever in their servers and may, and is sold, to other institutions at a price—institutions which may include the government, employers, foreign entities, advertising agencies and the like.

What started out it seems to me, to be a race to gain access to the desires, needs and habits of the American consumer has mushroomed into virtually transforming American society into the Surveillance Society where virtually all of the major institutions in society have access to the most detailed information on Americans--all of this for sale and used for purposes no one really knows or reveals.

It is not easy to get information on all of this and all consumers and citizens have are vague promises that their information will never be sold or disclosed. That promise may or may not be true or kept; but more importantly, what is lacking is information and disclosure about these institutions and what information they currently collect and what uses that information is being used for. There is very little information, very little cooperation, and virtually no transparency.

I conclude with the proposition that all of this bodes ill for American society-especially when it is so easily used in political, social and economic battles and other purposes too nefarious to detail.

This is a long list, I know. But it is a list which must be looked at and surprising few have been willing to take a close look at its implications.

I am reminded of a comment of a friend:
"I realized I was placing my most intimate thoughts, identifying my friends, my tastes, their tastes, onto a computer screen, turning all this over to a computer run by people I don't know, who will and

can use that information for purposes I may or may not approve of and in some cases I pay them a subscribers fee on top of it. That's crazy."|

Sept 19, 2010
Scope

Well, the first question is how many of these sites are there and how many people participate and to what degree?

The scope, if the publicity blurbs are to be believed, is staggering. The top ten sites according to one site "The Top 10 Online Dating Sites of 2010" have the following information on the top ten sites.

1- Match.com claims 25 million members
2- Chemistry claims 15 million members
3- Perfect Match claims 7 million
4- EHarmony claims 7 million
5- SeniorPeopleMeet 1.5 million
6- SingleParentMeet 900k
7- Love and Seek 1.3 (Christian Site)
8- Zoosk (International Site), 6 million
9- Spark 2 million
10-Friend Finder 3 million

This is 68.7 million members, and assuming an average member-ship fee of 20-25 dollars a month, the total dollar revenue might be as much as 1.7 billion among these top leaders alone. Add to these social networks, Face Book and My Space and the "Adult" sites total membership for all might be 150 million for the paid sites and revenue up to 3.7 billion dollars per year.

Membership, including the social networks (Face book claims 500 million alone) (obviously some of these are duplicated memberships) and we see that Americans are participating in on-line sites at very high rates--150 million is my best guesstimate at this point.

Now the question which arises first is are these sites effective in producing the relationships their subscribers are seeking, and what kinds of information is solicited from prospective members and how is that information used, and by whom?

More on this tomorrow, but one pattern does emerge. The more popular on-line dating sites demand much more information from

---

their subscribers than the less popular sites--one estimate is that subscribers end up answering more that 233 questions about themselves and their prospective friends, mates or lovers.
That is a lot of information being handed out. There is little protest as members are told this is to enhance their chances of success and is a protection for them in that more information is provided to them about prospective suitors. The obvious is that all this information is a direct benefit to site managers in soliciting advertising dollars from third parties. After all, they have more information to offer. Smaller sites cannot demand so much info and therefore are less successful competitors.
Tomorrow let's take a look at this information mountain and how it is used.

Sept 20, 2010
The demand for detail about members, or consumers is driven by the "personalized" advertising model. That is each consumer is presented with Taylor-made appeals based on tracking that consumers interests (with or without their permission) as they surf the net, or from the very information they may voluntarily provide for other purposes.
Google and Amazon are the leaders in this. Go to a web page on a Google search and you will find advertisements taylor-made to your interests. How does Google know my interests? Because Google has been tracking you on the web even after you leave the Google site–wherever you go.
Amazon is more restricted. They track what products you look at and make recommendations. But it is all there.
Now an extreme of all this on internet dating sites is that programs exist to track your movements through your cell phone such that you can be sold products as you window shop, or you can be told that a person of the characteristics you desire is two blocks away from you.
So GPS is now at play.

Given hard times and recession, these sites and these tactics are enjoying a boom.
Individuals, singles especially, find it difficult to find time to date and often cannot afford expensive outings. These sites offer a social life, albeit all on line, at comparatively inexpensive rates. Moreover, since marriage gets postponed during recession times, the period of single-hood has been expanding and is now extended even longer because of the financial costs of dating and marriage.

—

So we have an explosion of digital relationships-which are not face to face and all on a computer screen.

But, let's get back to the data aspect. Tomorrow.

Sept 22, 2010

Well, as some of you have pointed out, the GPS thing is truly shocking. Not only because you're friendly cell phone is beaming your shopping location back to advertisers but is, as well, tracking you. Where ever you go.

Repeat. Where ever you go.

And guess who is knee-deep in all this. Apparently Google. See below this article from the NY Times where we see Google and GPS location companies are fighting over who gets to control this technology. (This is much like seeing two bullies fighting over who gets to pick your bones.)

Here is the quote from the NY Times article:

"The value of the data surpasses the placing of ads on phones. It also allows companies to make inferences about a phone owner's wealth, lifestyle and shopping preferences, which is also sought by marketers.

"We learn pretty interesting things, for instance who prefers Wal-Mart over **Target**, or **Walgreens** over **CVS**, who is split, which stores they will travel to get to," said Thaddeus Fulford-Jones, chief of Lobately, a location analytics company."

"The two companies are fighting for the lead in the nascent but promising business of location-based data that uses GPS or Wife signals to locate phone users. These services not only direct people to businesses, but collect information about where people are. That is valuable information that lets marketers direct advertising to people where and when they are most likely to buy.

ROY FURCHGOTT

Published: September 15, 2010

http://www.nytimes.com/2010/09/16/technology/16phone.html?ref=glo bal_positioning_system

Now the phone companies tell you that the chip in the phone can be turned off, but guess what? They can override this feature and locate you anyway.

And, given the Patriot Act, the Government and others can, without permission, or a court order intercede this same data. Now note on your cell phone you may have text messages, bank data, medical data and a host of other information. Plus, the thing might give you brain cancer. All in all, a not a good deal for the consumer.

Now who, do we imagine, might want to also purchase this data? The internet-dating sites, of course.

They can use the data to verify the data presented on their sites and use that data to assure subscribers that their sites have verified the information in profiles. And, you can have that verified information, they tell you, for an additional charge in the "premium" upgrade.

My own info being sold back to me.

Consumers? They don't like it? What are they going to do-sue? Don't think so. After all bad stuff might come out and who has the money to sue Goggle anyway. No, this is the first step toward the Black-Mail Society.

Shut up or we will tell what we know about you.

Depressing? You bet.

See below a link to a NYTimes article of Sept 20, 2010 which details the mushrooming lawsuits in this area.

http://www.nytimes.com/2010/09/21/technology/21cookie.html?pagew anted=2&ref=technology&src=me

But, the story does not end here. More later.

Sept 23rd, 2010
But you say "I am not a member of any internet-dating site so I don't have the problem."

Not necessarily.

A visit to a site most times offers the consumer a "free membership" or a "no credit card needed" claim.

But one most often has to enter an email address.

This is the first step.

Most sites, dating and non-dating sites demand an email address.

Why?

Because an email address can and is sold to third party individuals for nice fees. An email address gives the site a count of who visits the site even if they do not join the site. An email address allows the site to place a cookie on your computer. An email address is the source of spam. An email address is gold to any web site. Often, that is all that is needed for a site to make money--or a cookie.

Cookie?

If you don't know what a cookie is we should take the time here to look at what I call the "Cookie Monster" industry.

Here is how it works. Every time you go to a site, unless you expressly forbid it, the site places a "cookie" on your computer. The claim is that this is done to make your return visits more "convenient" for you. The actual purpose is to get inside your desktop or laptop and to track your subsequent visits. Cookies are little notes on your computer and many are more than just little notes, some seek to invade your computer and send information back to the site about what you have there on your computer, your visits to competitor sites and god forbid other information you might have on your computer.

You have to expressly deny these cookies and most times if you do you can be denied access to a given site. Your bank places cookies, Amazon, Google, all of them do this.

With cookies, hackers can use these same cookies to send you back a virus, spy ware, worms and god knows what. They can send it to you and to any one in your contact list as well. So the thing spreads.

That is why I call the thing a "cookie monster" The one browser which allows you to get rid of cookies easily is Flock. But guess what, Google just took it over from Fire fox. Cookie Monster just got "et" by a bigger cookie monster.

To make matters worse in all of this, companies, and their secret friends--hackers--can now send along a cookie just by your going to the site and nothing else and even if you don't open an attachment, a hacker can send along a virus just by having your cursor briefly go over an attachment without even opening it.

Even those innocent looking "I like it" thumbs up buttons on Face Book and elsewhere are not so innocent. Clicking on them gives advertisers and site managers access to information about everything you like and also access to the likes, tastes and habits of all your friends on Face book.

Nothing is as it seems it seems.

So the outlook is gloomy. Yes it is-right now--until people wake up to what is happening--and they are. The lawsuits are coming thick and fast.

So that is why many companies are trying to stay ahead of the game by moving their operations to the cell phone, or even reducing their presence on the net. (More on that later)

But a last word of doom here (this seems to be a theme) is that these issues go way beyond dating sites and now international governments are also getting heavily involved.

Remember, around the world the internet is seen as an American invention (actually it was done at CERN. (Yes, that same CERN) to help scientists around the world to work together in planning the project and to stay in communication.

But later in this blog we should look at how most governments in the world want to control the internet, not only because it offers tremendous ways of controlling the citizens through an information net, but also because many nations see it as a American plot to destabilize their countries. Think tweets sent from Twitter during the Iranian election process. Control of information sent, gathered, analysed is now used as a weapon of war. Let's hope dissenters have never done a profile anywhere or posted their email addresses or own a cell phone. Not likely huh?

So now you see the problem.

What to do?

Sept 24, 2010
What to do is maybe premature. Let's look first at the central issue: Do these sites work in terms of matching people with their perfect mates?

No one knows for sure. But one thing is clear, despite the claims of perfect matches, the divorce rate in the United States has not gone down. So what ever is going on the impact of these sites remains in question.

But let's have a closer look at who is running some of the most popular sites, their claims and their documentation for results.

e-Harmony comes to mind. Their advertising is everywhere and smiling happy couples hit our TV screens with dulling regularity.

Those behind E-Harmony are psychologists who use algorithms (essentially personality tests) to steer subscribers toward that perfect mate, subscribers who pay upwards of 60 dollars a month for the help. E-Harmony claimed at one point to be responsible for 2 percent of all US marriages but there is no way to verify this claim. Moreover, the site does not allow you to go fishing for a mate, candidates are chosen for you after answering almost 260 questions. The heart of this process is of course is the test and the algorithms behind it.

The rub here though is that no one is allowed to see the algorithm behind the test to see if it is valid or not.

E-Harmony's competitors claim that without peer review of the assumptions in the test no scientific claims can or should be made. Besides, critics say, the site scrupulously separates subscribers by race and gender preferences. (Is this changing?)

"E" claims over twenty million people have filled out its survey and that raises the interesting question of who gets to see that data and who does e-Harmony share that data with? Despite claims of privacy there is precious little information here about what actually happens to that data.

What we can see emerging is a pattern where if e-Harmony does share that data with, say advertisers, us Americans can be pitched with ads that

—

reach our innermost desires- for love and a partner- these basic human desires with the help of these sites can be used against us, or at the very least used to sell us say "Brawny" tissues."

These are what I term "Psycho Controls" in which sex, desires for love, children, babies, wealth whatever are sold to the highest bidders; where data about this may be sold indeed to develop psychological profiles a government might find useful in controlling its citizens.

If these institutions know what buttons to push because they are being given the data to tell them which ones to push, by us, most of us will respond and do respond. So, does advertising work and why it works, based upon what data, becomes a central question in American society. And the answers are not particularly pretty. (Take a look at your medicine cabinet if you think you are unaffected by advertising.)

While dating sites may fight over which methodology is best, the central question of how the data they are collecting is used or sold is largely ignored.

But do sites that allow subscribers to pick their own dates do better?

Let's take a look tomorrow.

Sept 28, 2010
But before taking a look at this issue, the news today indicated that the Obama Administration stated its intent to seek legislation to wire-tap the internet including Face Book, My Space, cell phones, Skye and other telecommunication-related technologies.

The rationale is that terrorist use these sites and law enforcement must be able to track them there to protect us.
Interestingly, when Saudi Arabia and China wanted control over the internet in their countries Google, and Blackberry complained that this was be an infringement upon the principles of a free society and constituted surveillance. Well here we are in the United States at that very same point. Presumptively, we can be survielled until the last known terrorist is apprehended. The home, the office, and the internet now become "electronic ankle bracelets" on each and every member of the population.

Scary indeed.

Now of course, this will extend to the dating sites as well. So be aware.

Now our last question was whether these dating sites actually work in the case of those sites where the subscriber is allowed to browse for h/her own dates and mates.

Good information is difficult to come by. Searching reveals that the internet is swamped by articles and phony news articles which have many stories of success. But there is no way to verify such claims in the aggregate and few negative stories actually exist out there as a counterbalance.

How much sites contribute to marriage and beyond, however, must be balanced off with the facts we know such as: 60-70 percent of people meet and marry their future partners face-to-face at work (50%), at church, school or childhood friends. Then add those who never marry at all and the odds of finding a mate on the net are pretty small.

If all that is true, we want then to have a look at the actual experience of some who have tried their luck.

That tomorrow.

Meantime:

See the NYTimes article on this on the Obama initiative:

http://bits.blogs.nytimes.com/2010/09/28/internet-wiretapping-proposal-met-with-ilence/?scp=2&sq=government%20privacy&st=cse

The Electronic Frontier Foundation sounded the alarm on its website:

"These proposals are the most frightening we've seen in a long time. The first is a bill called the "Combating Online Infringement and Counterfeits Act," which would give the Justice Department new powers to censor websites accused of aiding "piracy." The second is an Obama Administration proposal that would end online privacy as we know it by requiring all Internet communication service providers -- from Face book to Skype to your webmail provider -- to rebuild their systems to give the government backdoor access to all of your private Internet communications."

Website Link:
http://action.eff.org/site/MessageViewer

**http://action.eff.org/site/MessageViewer?em_id=13241.0&dlv_id=2686
2**

That tomorrow.

Sept 30, 2010

On those sites where a match in chosen for you, data is scarce on how successful those matches are. Some may end up in meaningful friendships, or dates or marriages, or long lasting relationships and marriages. There is no way to know for sure what happens.

But we do know some things. When subscribers are given a cafeteria like assortment of possible partners to choose from, or create a shopping list of their desirable traits in a mate, a new kind of syndrome sets in.

In real life one meets a limited number of people. But on the internet you can, on the screen at least, meet hundreds. The individual tends to sense an abundance of choices and becomes picky and even rude. Notes, winks, and flirtations can go unanswered, or ignored, or worse responded to impolitely.

Too many choices can breed a certain arrogance, especially when you realize that the 80-20 rule applies. That is 80 percent of the subscribers end up being attracted to the most desirable 20 percent of the subscribers. That is to say since most of the subscribers are looking for the same and similar traits the 20 percent having the experience of being pursued and the 80 percent have the experience of not being the ones pursued. But individual subscribers cannot see this on their screens. They see only the people they are in contact with.

Moreover, since academics and psychologists are the ones using this data subscribers are actually paying for their research costs, providing the funds to do the research which otherwise might not be available.

Now interestingly, a subscriber is, most times, conversing with a computer monitor which may or may not have a picture and you in fact may conversing with computer generated messengers. Sites in fact, have an interest in having customers continue to seek that mate since they continue to collect the fees if the process is more drawn out. For example: You have situations where thousands of males and females are seeking dates with members of the 20 percent who are long gone, dated out, married or otherwise disengaged.

How is a subscriber to know and it is clear that the site has no real interest in saying so since a continuation of the monthly fee is in their interest.

An attractive picture can be one obtained from almost any source and the messages and little notes can be computer generated and most sites demand that all messages and notes go through the site-no direct personal information allowed. The rationale given is that this protects the subscriber from stalkers. A legitimate concern to be sure.

However, one also must note, there is no stalker danger where the subscriber is fictitious or does not even exist or is long gone-and who would know?

So nothing is simple here. And the hapless subscriber cannot know who or what he or she is really dealing with on the other end of the note. It might be a person, hired a minimum wage, but it is not the person in the picture. At some point a subscriber after months of trolling, can get a note saying the person has taken their profile down or cancelled their subscription, leaving the hapless subscriber out of luck and with perhaps months of subscription fees. A suggestion for an actual meeting is a acid test and the 20 per center ceases to communicate.

If an actual meeting does occur you may be looking at a person 20 years older than the site photo and who may have grossly exaggerated her or her allure-and you are out months of subscribers fees and then at some point realize you have been scammed, or if, naive, simply think you have been unlucky.

Next time lets look deeper into this question of how do you know if you are being scammed and save time lunching with Gordo.

Oct 2, 2010

Another aspect to all of this is most sites will send you data which supposedly show how many people are interested in you, requests may come in from so-called "buddies"; or phony replies to your requests to communicate.

A second aspect (which I have blogged about) is Google and Face book advertisements. (See my Google blog) where a server can send you phony data on all aspects of your subscription-phony hits. After all, how would you know.? (This is no idle sentence. I tested over 20 sites testing these ideas.

More later

Oct 5, 2010

Note: The bill which would demand that online sites like Face book, Google and the rest, create unencrypted versions to allow governmental access has been postponed due to thousands of emails going out to the

Senate committee dealing with it.

But, but , but the word is that they will take it up after the election.

Now I was discussing a major underlying issue on ads, dating sites and access to the internet.

What we essentially have with advertisements on the web, dating sites, Google, most sites, is that we pay money for a service which cannot be independently verified as having been delivered. What we get back is numbers on a page which say that our ads have appeared on so many web pages, or x number of people have responded to our profile or blurb. Or we may see numbers on the computer screen that x number of people have visited our web site (Google Analytics) but have no independent way of verifying those numbers on the screen.

98

If I pay to get my car fixed would I be satisfied with getting numbers on a computer screen?

Any number can be generated by a computer and placed before the subscriber. So, we in fact, don't know.

But how to investigate this? How do we know we are getting what we paid for?

It turns out that is not so easy to verify, especially when a lot of the communication involved is one-way. They write you but you can't easily write back or get in touch.

Banks, brick and mortar stores with websites, investment houses, dating sites, Google, all offer predominately one way communications. Google basically says, "Hey its free so don't bother us."

Let's look again later at communication digital style.

Oct 9. 2010

So what we have here is a model for how companies have figured out how to make money on the internet.

1-Give them information that they cannot verify but charge them for it.

2-Identify what they like (profiles) and sell that information to third parties (this is the institutionalization of spam)

3- Do not provide any real customer service because that is costly and dangerous, and since folks might catch on, make communication difficult.

4- In the case of online book sales (my problem) don't provide a way for any author to verify what actual books sales are and tell them that it takes three months to get paid.

Added together, these factors are a scam, a money pyramid scheme.

5- Use information provided you by subscribers or web surfers to identify their secret desires and use that information to sell them more products and services.

6- Use information provided by these folks to provide "free" services but utilize that info and sells to third parties or gives it away to government entities or employers since this will cut way back on complaints.

What are you going to do complain--to whom? They are all in it together.

So entities like Face book are utilized by everyone like ex girl friends or boy friends to out you, to tell your friends what an awful person you are and to boot you can't delete them as friends or easily delete your face book profile. (Even if you do the data remains in their servers)

Humm, this feels ugly. To boot you now have a friendship network which is not real but digital and littered with enemies posing as friends, who can very easily send info about you (true or false) to everyone who matters to you, even your employer, girlfriend, boyfriend, your mother and your dog.

—

Cheered up yet?
Let's try again tomorrow.

Oct 11, 2010
Don't have much time today but I will indicate a topic for tomorrow. I
wanted to know who owns these sites I had noticed a sea-change in their
nature in 2007-2008. They exploded. So who ultimately is reaping the
profits and how does it work?
I have covered this partially above but there is a darker story here (who
can resist a juicy dark story?)
My view about that sea change can be summed up in two words:
Penthouse and Comcast.

Update: Nov 21, 2010
Note: On cell phone dangers, and incidentally cordless phones as well,
may be dangerous: see the NY Times article of Nov 13, 2010 "Should You
Be Snuggling With Your Cell phone?"
Cell phone manufacturers have now taken to include warnings on the
Phone and other brands, apparently fearing law suits. This is no idle, not to
worry about kind of thing. The lawyers know it and such warnings are
now routinely included the fine print of cell phone manufactures. Yes, the
Phone too.
Apparently the phones should be turned off when not in use, and kept
away from the body and of course, the ear. The danger is more
pronounced for the young, even those who do not use the phones and are
merely exposed to their radiation by a sibling, or parent can suffer. Golly.

So what to do?
More later

Note: American literature has been examined in many varied ways. I take a look at American literature seeking to understand its broad themes and specifically the political values we see embedded in the writings of major authors, but focusing specifically on one the most influential work in all of American history, the bible. Literature, I argue is part of the institutional matrix which has been a battle ground over the issues of what kind of country we want America to be.

But, first I tackle the pre-eminent American art form-the novel-asking the question what are the values and history of the intent to write the great American novel and underlying literary and human values we often see exhibited in the novel form.

American Literature and the Craft of Writing
the Great American Novel

Prologue: The Word

If I make a word
it is first sculpted from letters
on the page,
a canvass across which
letters skate
from margin to margin transforming
into meaning and sentence
which give us art, science, poetry
and civilization.

This is created from an arbitrary entity,
the scratchings we call letters
which in turn form yet another
mysterious entity we call the alphabet.

What manner of miracle is this?
All of civilization is born from
these scribbled scratchings?

So if each letter is an imaginary entity,
an arbitrary symbol we made up

which has no meaning by itself
and lives inside another arbitrary entity
we call the alphabet
what we may properly ask
is going on here?

Meaning here is deriving from an arbitrary nothingness
arbitrarily created from arbitrary letters
by virtue of common agreement around
what words will mean?

Ponder this:
we too, as individuals are letter unique
and, in our variety, form a kind of human alphabet.

What we all mean and can mean to each other
therefore depends upon the words we form
in our families and communities; our human alphabets.

So, one word letters such as "I" are too self-regarding
and are narcissistic anomalies
not true words at all.

Better words have more syllables than that
and have enabled us to form social sentences
more complex
which we can use for good or ill
peace or war, love or hate.

So watch your words and sentences
don't swing them recklessly in a crowded room
you'll put somebody's mind out
or create genius.

Big responsibility this
especially for us poets.

So in the end
in mass society
you and I are a single letter
but combined create all there is.

———

You can take that
as the first
and last
Word;
and by the way
arbitrary letters
are electrons at the sub-atomic level
and they combine to make molecules
and ultimately the greatest meaning of all:
The Universe.

Title: How to Write the Great American Novel

Updated: 6/7/2010

Summary: (Newly edited and typo-cleansed.) Humm, upcoming chapters on:
1. Scene Development--added 5/13/2010
2. Character Development--added 5/14/2010
3. Prep and Research
4. Narration
5. Tense Management-Page Turning Tricks
6. Publishing
7. The Curse of Chapter Three Added June 7, 2010
8. Writing Reading and Breathing added 5/17/10
Are novelists expert liars and should we be encouraging this?

First: A Summary of Initial Steps

Chapter One

1.First, you should read the dictionary, cover to cover. Build that vocabulary. Without it, you are hamstrung.

2. Live a full life; that way you have something to write about. If you feel you have nothing to write about, write about having nothing to write about. If you feel stupid and talent-less, write about it sincerely.

3. Learn to be brutally honest. Self-deception is boring.

4- Write really short pieces-first no more than a page. It teaches you editing, conciseness, and is great discipline.

5- Write only if you can't stop writing. It must be a need and you must be driven.

6- Learn a discipline or a subject matter, and master it. And then move on to the next subject.

7-Listen to book radio to get a sense of how others write.
Listen to the words, syntax, and choice of words. There will be a quiz.

8- Write things with a beginning, middle and an end.

9- Don't listen to other's telling you that you will fail; ever.

10- Learn to evaluate your own writing. Hint: If it doesn't make your hair stand up then it won't make anyone else's either.

"How To Write The Great American Novel"

Chapter Two

1- Above I noted the importance of reading the dictionary-- make that the unabridged dictionary--and get one, if you can, that has an audio component such that you can hear the pronunciation of the words. Words have definition and they also have music. Knowing the music is just as important as knowing the lyrics.
Prose and poetry both benefit if the writer is aware of the many aspects of the word.
But words are made up of letters, and an alphabet. (See several of my poems which illustrate the aspects of letters as the building blocks of words. The "G" seems to wave doesn't it? So notice the shapes of these little sculptures, which is what they are.

Second, words have definitions, definitions which have a history which is dynamic. Read the history of a word; it's historical to modern uses. There is an entire education is just reading through to the third, fourth or fifth definitions of a given word you encounter in a good dictionary.

The many possible meanings of a word are the writer's depth.
Day dream about the new words. Use them in your head, until you make them yours and then the next step beyond that is to make those letters and words into ideas.

Let's take an example, (always take a big important word, because you then become used to big ideas) although have you ever wondered what "the" means?

Note: back to the word. Let's take Death. What does it mean? Or Happiness? What does it mean? Look these two up in the dictionary. You be surprised at what they mean and have meant in the past.
Let's take happiness. It comes from the word "hap." The root meaning of Happiness is lucky.
Hapless means to be unlucky. See the point?

Now let's play; and introduce an idea.

Humm, "Death sits contemplating suicide." This is interesting idea. Most times all you have for a poem or a book even is the first sentence. Try it on for size and start writing. (My poem "The Death of Me" began just that way with a single sentence and I was dragged kicking and screaming into the poem and its ending surprised me.
Another example: Death said to Happiness--"You are just a lucky fellow, nothing more." Lot's of possibilities here.
You can get a novel out of this. How? Well, let's see. Johnny Death pursues his enemy Happy Jones and Jones has fantastic luck in evading Death all through the book. Happy wakes up from a dream, from a coma, his luck has run out and death makes the claim that no one is happy to the point of avoiding him forever. Is this a comment on life, on history, individual and collective? Maybe. Maybe it is just fun to play around with the definitions of words as a starting point of writing. Humm- that would make a good novel, even mythic. That is how Lilith was born from "Asunder."--from a single sentence.

"How To Write The Great American Novel"

Chapter Three

The second point: lead a full life.

Courage in life means courage on paper and having developed character in real life makes for a great novelist. Take chances, don't be afraid to fail and you'll soon develop lots of character.
So what is character and what is courage? See my poem on this: www.poemhunter.com search on Lonnie Hicks.

The basic requirement in terms of living is simple: always ask why and don't take anybody's word for anything unless you have felt in it your DNA.

That makes part of what makes a great writer.
Always ask: "Says who?" Have the courage of one's convictions, and note: notions of who's right and wrong are irrelevant to what life is all about. We live in a time when blame is what things are about and left brain logic rules. But there is no creativity there and you need that to be a great writer.

Example: Everything you do creates a path in the brain. The brain becomes wired to responding to the same stimulus in the same way. That is what a habit is. But, if you train the brains to always ask why then you create a new path-way after every experience and this called creativity. Ask why about every damn thing and have the courage to keep that stance even if it irritates people. You are creating a new brain with every "why."

Second, have courage to say "even if I am wrong that is not the point. So I am wrong. You in insisting it is all about right and wrong are a clunk head and not in keeping with the genius of the human species." Think about it this way: some of our ancestors said "we have to leave Africa because the climate is changing." The nay-sayers said "Are you nuts? How do you know what is out there? We could all die. Let's stay put and ask the local god to save us. We must have done something wrong."

No America, no Rome, no Marco Polo, no Greeks because cultural discovery depends upon a willingness to expose oneself to ideas we don't currently hold. The greatness of Rome and Greece was that the Roman empire welcomed all people, left them alone, demanded tribute, but everyone was welcome who didn't make trouble and there was that little matter of slaves, true. But the point in that the Roman empire was built on exposure to other cultures, stealing their ideas, and trade and tribute plus a dash of ruthlessness. Now the point though is that they learned from their exposures. They went from a tribal group in Italy to world power because of it. Alexander the Great had his generals intermarry with the conquered. The mixing gave the Greeks new ways of looking at the world and Greek culture dominated the ancient world. They were the masters of the "why." You should be too.

So live life, give a hug, a smile, have an open mind; don't be a coward. (See my poem on this at www.poemhunter.com.on this.

Now how can you live life to the fullest given the above? Don't need to do much really. You don't have to go on Safari in Africa to have something to

---

write about. You can take the inexpensive route and get started to working on the internal life first.

First, take 25 deep breaths each hour and the brain gets oxygenated and you become a changed person. Deep inhales, deep exhales.

Don't believe it? Try it.

This is called many different things in many different cultures: meditation, primal therapy, relaxation, bio-rhythms etc. But what happens is the same; you grow.

Ok, try it and let me know what happens. But you have to have courage to keep it up and don't get scared if you start to get angry, fearful, cry, laugh etc. It is you becoming the best you. Humm, and don't do it alone you will likely need help and some coaching.

"How To Write The Great American Novel"

Chapter Four

Now, the next item is learning to write concisely, with a beginning, middle and end. Many of life's stories don't have a beginning, middle or ending and this is what makes story-writing difficult. But we are artists and are not about following life, we seek to lead life. You, reader, can practice writing these one pagers and I invite you to send to me your one-page novels. Doesn't have to be good. See item three above. It is practice. So lets see how a one page novel would go. First, we need an opening line, inspiration, or an idea. We can simply take big ideas from the dictionary and use two of them as starting points for our one page novel. Humm, let's take Love and Devotion. What does the dictionary say they mean? Our novel can center around the differences between the two.

See "Sideline Powdering" on this site to see a poem on this subject. But, what about our novel?

Example:
Elina loves me with a burning hot fire and she kisses possessively. Everything about her tells me she is passion, the flaming star and her need to love me is evident, hot and immeasurable. Loryn loves me shyly, with a steady flame that I suspect will last forever. Luckily, these are two ways of loving in the dictionary gives us something to work with. The one page plot is that these two potential mates reveal their two relative values in a situation where my life is at stake.

The one-pager is: I am hanging on a cliff and my passionate love is overwhelmed by the prospect of my falling over that cliff and emotion takes her over. My steady devoted love is free from emotion enough to think and save me.

A possible point here is that Romeo and Juliet loved too passionately and their flame ended in tragedy. Love of this kind may have its costs. Steady devotion has a more level head and the lovers survive to look down the years. That is a one-page novel. Have a narrator contrast two couples. One couple lives and the other dies.
Interesting novel idea huh?

Let's do the one pager. But first let's do a quick summary of what we have thus far learned which will enable us to take on this task.
1- We will have started reading the dictionary. You just have to read three pages a day; choose two words to work with and daydream about the meanings you find there. Three words are too many, just two. Why? Because most humans are two-variable thinkers and can only hold two variables in our head--good, evil, up, down etc. That is why triangle love relationships are something most people have trouble with.
A rare person can hold in their head three variables say up, down and sideways. If you can do that it makes you smarter than most. Einstein could do four and this was the basis of the theory of relativity. But since you and I are not Einstein we have to walk before we can run.

Now item two was to work on yourself if you cannot go on Safari or some other great adventure. Internal experience is just as valid as external Safari-going. I suggested breathing and now taking daily health seriously. A good working mind is best for being a great author, evidence to the contrary notwithstanding. Now you don't need this if you are a politician; its not expected.
Now health: do that walk. do in-place exercises, find out what your body responds to and take supplements to offset the poor water, the poor diet, and the antibiotic-filled meats. Well you get it. If you haven't done step two, go back to step one and only then show up back here. We want everyone to start at the same place for the one-pagers.
How long do you have to do steps one and two before you get back here? Not long. Say a week. You will not be ready to write one-pager, but, it might cement the habits involved.

Ok, let's write something.

———

Remember; beginning, middle and end.

Three opening lines:
"I lie still. I know I'm dead."
She was blunt: "I don't love you."
"It was the end of the world."
Now each of these opening lines can make a great one page novel. Here's how. People ask me where do the ideas for novels, or poems or essays come from. The three opening lines above came from words in the dictionary; death, love, and world.
Now, let's do one-pager number one.
Opening third of the one-pager:
"I lie still. I know I'm dead."
Detail points:
Am I in a casket, in heaven, on a hospital bed, in a traffic accident, after a place crash, in a coma, dreaming? How about a surprise point: I am an unborn fetus.
You decide; choose one of the above and you can do that in a few paragraphs.
Now I am at the pivot point in the one-pager and have chosen my story path. I am an unborn fetus. Why? I am a sucker for irony. "I am dead, now means, I am unborn. Humm, the situation is I am not dead but getting ready to be born, but was I dead before? If not, why was I an unborn baby thinking about it? Did I have a previous existence?
That is the second third of our one-pager. And now for the big finish. How to create an ending that will be interesting and won't seem hackneyed. Here's mine. Describe the birth. "I felt myself being pushed down a warm tunnel. I could hear voices and I was worried because I had a tube in my mouth and was having trouble breathing. (Keeps the journey going for a paragraph or so.)
The ending: "When my eyes adjusted to the light they gave me to the woman they called my mother. I was startled to realize that I knew her face."
Now this is an ending. It leaves questions and is a surprise and raises a lot of questions on a lot of levels. Welcome to art.
You take the other two above and try your hand. Don't be shy. Failure only occurs if you get chicken and don't try.
Send them along to me and I will give each a two sentence evaluation. I have to get some exercise out of this too, you know. LOL

"How To Write The Great American Novel"

Chapter Five

Hope to hear from those of you who haven't tried the one-pager yet.
Now, in writing this one-pager or anything for fun or publication, you have a relationship between several elements.
Here are the ones I keep in mind.
a. The physical space on the page
b. The letters which make up the words
c. The sounds of the words, if you sound them out in your head
d. The writer
e. The reader
f. Time, place and space factors
g. The Take Away

Now what do all of the items above mean? Well, I am not going to tell you--yet. You have to make your first attempt to do the one-pager first. Then I will blab. But not until then.
While waiting for your missive here are a few other random notes to contemplate:

a. The English language has maybe 400,000-750,000 words. (Someone correct me please.) The permutations, in terms of word and meaning combinations, are, for practical purposes, infinite. So the dictionary approach gives you infinite plot lines and relationships. You could practically choose two or three words at random from the dictionary and conceive a plot line from them. (Something to try? Sure why not, especially since you can now do a one-pager around them) This is not even mentioning the differing meanings of these two or three words which add a richness to your writing.

b. Music. Words are sounds. In writing you should either write aloud in your head, or read out loud what you have written at some point. Why? Because, if not, you just have words but no music. You have to train your self to write with music. Music, (the actual sounds of the words) make the lyrics go down better.
Let's do an example of this and some of the other things mentioned above. Let's take the typical editor-sanitized sentence and then apply "the Hicks method of writing greatness" and see if there is anything to what I have been saying. The sentence is: "He walked to the door, put his hand on the door knob and opened the door." How many editors have you heard say:

"You walked him to the door but you did not have him open the door and go through the door."

This editorial style is killing, declarative, a verbal ghetto style and one I have a problem with. (My rebellion is exemplified in the last sentence.) If we are to write creatively we must pass through our eighth grade English teacher gauntlet and not make her into a fetishist religion. (Shakespeare invented over 2,500 words in his day that did not exist before--not to mention all the words he contracted) (i.e., invented and pruned) to make the meter and beat count at the end of the sentence. Don't get me wrong. I love Shakespeare--see my Story-Poem "Politics" where I imitate his style because I love that style so. But alas, he is still dead and we must force ourselves to move on.

Now back to our tortured, declarative sentence. Can this sentence be saved? It's virtues are several: it is clear, it has information, it is descriptive, but damn bland and it is what journalists do everyday. We here, are not journalists. We aspire to be artists do we not?

So ok, let's do ER on that sentence.

Well, first there in no music. The sentence is boring. As a novelist, you must learn to understand you have the reader on loan. Blow it with a dull sentence and the fickle reader will bail on you like a humming bird on to the next flower. Mentally at first, but too many of these in a row, and you will find yourself face down on the bedside reading table. (Did these sentences have music?)

Now for some music in our sentence. "He walked to the door, his hand trembling, and opened it onto a too bright light." Now was that better? The sentence has a little more flow to it now, it has some mystery, some emotion, and some context. It is not perfect but it is better to my ear. Yours?

Sentence construction: Life has five, maybe six senses--sight, sound, taste, smell, touch and the sixth sense. Now there are only five topics in all of literature and in all sentences; mind, body, soul, spirit, heart. These are the only topics in all of humanity. (An exaggeration, I admit, but humor me for a while here.)

So of all of these, ideally, could be in every sentence or at least in every other sentence. In our sentence what senses were being used, described, or utilized? You, reader, what do you tend to remember from your experiences in life; the visual, the sounds, the tastes, the smells, touch? We are all different because we sense the world in different combinations and with different intensities of the senses we have. Think of what you remember about an experience; ask a friend who was there what senses they remember from an experience you both shared. These differences give you a different writing style, coupled with the over-arching five

(MBSSH) See above.

Now we have the contents of a sentence above. Let's see if me, Mr. Smarty Pants, got all that in my sentence. (And I promise you I wrote that sentence without thinking about MBSSH or SSTST.

Well there is sight, (the door is seen;) sound implied, touch; no smell, no taste. We have body, some mystery, and at least, heart from the big five. Compare to the first sentence. With follow-on sentences you can weave a tapestry and a story which engages our senses and our sensibilities-which, he said, is the point of writing in the first place. This little experiment worked out luckily. Otherwise I would have had to go the blackboard and write out "I will not be overly pedantic" two times.

"How To Write The Great American Novel"

Chapter Six

This Blog will be interrupted today because I have to go out for about an hour to save the world. But here's some things to ponder. Note items a. and b. above. Words on the page.

How to depict loneliness on the page?

How about:

It
feels
like
falling.

This "representational" idea in another example.

　　　　"The Point"
Why do poets and authors
never seem to be able
to arrive at the
main point-
ever?

Here the canvass and the meaning are in sync. This is to remind that the page matters in this way and many others. You should practice with other emotions or ideas of your own, while I am away from this page. Don't cheat. Really try it. I will be watching.
Be back in a little while.

———

OK, here we go; the world is safe for one more day. Now where were we? The page is where we do our work and one should think of it as a canvass where, words, music, emotions, ideas, spirit come alive and mix to create something that did not exist in that space before. Mull that for a while. Meantime I want to concentrate for a moment on the issue of words.

Words, of course, are our coin in trade; and we have to be aware at all times that each word matters. Each word matters. So we are going to do something with words, involving a novel. So lets take our one-pager and try to make it into a novel. First a novel to be novel, must be new, or original, among many other definitions you will find in that big thick dictionary.

Also, novel in my usage means all of the MBSSH and SSTST. This is, of course, a complex enterprise, involving all of the senses, some of the great themes in literature, Death, love, God, mankind, womankind etc. that kind of stuff. And, this is expressed in words, and of course, and in characters as they encounter MBSSH and SSTST. This is a more rich, written environment, a more rich emotional journey etc. All this is easy to say and damn difficult to do.

Now finally; write for the ages. Who will read and be interested in my last sentence 400 years from now? Again, easy to say, hard to do, but let's take a quick example here to distinguish fast-food writing from writing for the ages. After all this is all about "Writing the Great American Novel" which will have relevancy years from now.
So let's just take it one sentence at a time. First "fast food" sentencing. "I feel like really depressed today." Not bad; you have some the things above in that sentence. Now what about the ages? "I feel really depressed today like everyone I know on my block. What does "like" in this sentence really mean and everyone on the block creates a much more meaningful context than my individual woes.
See my poem on this page "Feel Like a Simile Sometimes." This is not "smile," this is "Simile" the part of speech. This poem is intended to comment not only on one person's feelings or depression, but upon an age which feels like a Simile, "like" something but not the real thing. The ending is mysterious. Can you figure out what it means? Now the point here is one cannot write only for oneself absent any empathy for others. In the end who cares about your woes but you and yours, unless it is attached to" higher meanings, eras, ideas or contexts? The lesson here is avoid the pronoun prison IIIIIIIIIIIIIIIII is not relevant if it relates to only you and makes you a pronoun prisoner behind pronoun bars. (The capital "I" does

———

look like prison bars don't they?) See my poem on this; "Pronoun Prisoner."
Homework. See you tomorrow.

Above we said the page is the canvas and smarty pants here gave as an example above describing loneliness as downward sloping words on the page. Now that is great for a poem you say but what about a novel? How do you describe loneliness in a novel using words? Well first see the poem on this site called "The Aquifer." It has short sentences and short lines and plunges down the page. See at www.poemhunter.com (Search on Lonnie Hicks) other examples such as "Love Remains," and Kisses Unrelinquished."

Now for the prose example: "I feel like a simile sometimes," she said. "Like a train that can't loco mote, can't get down the tracks, you know;: I feel, you know, dead like the moon, but pretty; I ah, am depressed, sometimes, not all the time, but some of the time."

Well here the language on the page is disjointed, run-on and is in danger of the editor's knife. Fight back. Don't let them stab that canvass! That is how people talk when emotional; not particularly eloquent. But it does raise the question, why can't I write those sentences with a space between the lines, indicating silences. Blank space equals silence and real life has those. But the canvass can't be used that way because it costs more money to publish so artistic intent in quietly smothered the crib. Now don't get me wrong, this is no rant against the needs of an editor or a publisher; rather it is asking why not? And the answer makes sense, but keep to the habit of asking why. Keep that brain athletic.

Now here is a phrase to ponder: "Who told you that you were never to be betrayed or lied to in life?" Now this is interesting unstated proposition that much of literature (and indeed life assumes, perhaps irrationally.) Think about it; God gets betrayed and lied to every day, but we operate as though this should not ever happen to us. So much of literature is based on this irrational premise for character motivation. You can discover other motivational examples extent in literature, (can you say Shakespeare,) that have this unstated premise as a base. These precepts are what we need to examine if we are to remain in print for longer than the impulse buy. You can think of other precepts; we fish cannot see the water around us, and never ask why.

With one part of our heads we know human beings lie and betray (including ourselves) but we act shocked when it happens to us just as

———
115

though we have lived on another planet from those who lied or betrayed us. When we get over irrational shock we get to more interesting layers of human motivation and can make our characters more interesting. She betrayed him but he forgave her. She betrayed him and he vowed revenge. Now you say, hey people behave this way; some want revenge. True, but is that what writing the great American novel about? Some for sure are about that, but the commonplace is not what we are about here, we want to move the emotional frontiers just a wee bit further down the road. Who says revenge is the normal response? What if the person refused to do that? What then would be the story line; and just maybe, you have in writing that novel another way, opened new doors for your self and your readers.

Now, of course, doing this in a merely contrarian modality will get us no where; that is merely taking the opposite tack of whatever is on the table. No, I mean here really taking non-revenge reactions seriously and explore what those different reactions might be. What could they be? Well indifference, love, forgiveness, deflection, diffusion, displacement etc. Indeed, if you lived in a society where mistresses are ok, or multiple spouses are acceptable, what would your reaction be? In a novel you would have a more interesting character, but more importantly, you have a more interesting writer, who, in writing the character, explores and perhaps expands his or her own boundaries and potentialities. Ok, let's take a rest from the high-fluting and get back down to earth. But the point here is that new ways of being human are as often discovered on the page as in action in the world.

We have covered the words, the senses involved, the canvass etc. Now let's get on to the music. My favorite.

"How To Write The Great American Novel"

Chapter Seven

What is meant by music? Best to take an example: "Cobblestones are his tears, his monuments."
What do we have here as an opening line?
First, this is a very powerfully constructed line. "Cobblestones" as a word conjures up visions of colonial times, London streets; old town is various cities etc. Cobblestones are rounded and appear in many areas of the world.

Second, "Cobblestones are his tears..." Cobblestones are not "like" tears. Cobblestones "are" his tears. There is a lot here to examine. Not, cobblestones "were" his tears in the past tense, relegating the action to some past undefined period; but cobblestones are his tears. We have achieved immediacy here; urgency is lent to this phrase. We like that. We also have avoided the metaphor or simile if you like, because we are making a statement to the reader of immediacy and of essence. Why take metaphor when you can have the real thing? Cobblestones are real, metaphors are not.

This is more powerful statement. No "like." Now who is the mysterious "he" and why are we making the huge statement that cobblestones are his tears? Tears? Tears from what? And the comma? Why are we using a comma here? We are using the comma to get the reader to pause and think about what we just said. Secondly, this sentence has a beginning, middle and end; the comma is our mid-point, our middle. We pause, we take a breath, to allow the reader to think about it and we create a beat in our music, in the emotional journey we have introduced. Six syllables here, six beats, emotion rising; tears, old cities, now we pause.

The last clause is "his monuments." Cobblestones all over the world are really "his" tears, and, moreover, his "monuments." Who is this person? Our reality and perception of cobblestones had been utterly transformed and changed. The things we walk on are someone's tears, indeed someone's monuments. Can't ever see cobblestones the same way again because of a single sentence and we have the huge sense now invoked here of walking upon someone's tears.

All this is powerful stuff for six words. The sentence has a powerful opening, mystery, emotion, music, and a dramatic ending with middle and a beginning. That's what we want.

Second sentence: "I hear ragged air flapping over his garments as he falls--her face before him."

Well we are beginning to see that someone, him perhaps, is falling; and falling fast because the garments are flapping. Not falling as in a faint but probably falling from a great height. My, this is ominous. Her face is before him. There is possibly some love affair involving her. Is he falling alone? Is she falling too? Was he pushed? Is this a suicide?

All this is better portrayed on a canvass. Falling is better evoked thus:

"I hear
ragged air
flapping
over his garments

---

as he falls--
her face before him."

The imagery, the emotion, here is becoming clear and the music is sad music. You start to feel something is about to happen.

Third sentence: "She gave him water: clothed him."
Here we see something of the relationship between the mysterious "him" and her. She succored him, helped him. Was he sick, had he been injured? Was she a nurse? Why is he falling?

Fourth sentence: "His gnarled heart sang for her."
My God, his heart is gnarled. What does that mean; shriveled, disfigured, tortured? This is getting darker.

Fifth sentence: "His flight down, swan death down, because of her;"
Well we are at the middle. He is indeed falling "swan death down" implying he jumped. And it was because of her. Why would he do that? She gave him water? What has precipitated this death leap?
Sixth sentence: "the church bells rung for her in his tall tower pedestal."
Note these clauses are getting shorter because this fall is real time, there is not a lot of time left for him in "swan death down." We are told that he rung the church bells for her. Was she getting married and he had to ring the bell and that was too much for him and he decided to take his life because of this? What is this tall tower pedestal? Astute readers are getting ahead of me here guessing that the leaper is Quasimodo from Victor Hugo's "The Hunchback of Notre Dame."

Seventh sentence: "How much love is it in downward death to have love's name on your breath?"
Sad, sad. Indeed how much love is this? Sadder still is for human kindness and perhaps pity be taken for true unrequited love. (Pardon my irony here, but that is what this piece is about.)

Eighth sentence: "How much love it is for love's one glance be enough your life to forfeit."
Note this is not a question. It is a statement about the nature of Quasimodo's love. One glance.

Ninth sentence to the end of the paragraph:

"Quasimodo breathed his love in earthward flight; before crash his heart surely burst as he called her name-Esmeralda, Esmeralda; he then felt her

———

118

kiss once more before shattering land. All sufficed for what then came: Cobblestone Tears; Love's Remains." I still tear up when reading this line.

Well, I won't go through all of the exegesis here but "Love's Remains" becomes the image of cobblestones around the world, because they are Quasimodo's tears and his remains. You have to spare a tear for him; and try not to step on the stones.
This is actually a poem of mine called "Love's Remains," down-loadable, along with many others at www.poemhunter.com. and on this site. Search on Lonnie Hicks. There are over 470 items there.

"How To Write The Great American Novel"

Chapter Eight

Now we have to ask the question aren't there many different kinds of "music" to be heard in writing? Isn't there such a thing a "voice" or writing style, or even genres of writing types?

Well there certainly is. No one can be an expert in all of the various styles or claim any one style is superior to others. So then how does the novelist decide what music to play in a novel? Well we have a modest example in "Lilith." Lilith is a biblical character so I decided to write the book in what I conceive as biblical prose style; a bit more formal and appropriate for stories that were going to have lot of pronouncements from on high. The bible is still the best selling book in the world and the most goggled as well. There is a reason for that. Its style is remarkable; and in many parts poetic. So I choose to do Lilith that way, of course, adding my own deficiencies to the mix.
But, there are other reasons for writing the book. The secret can now be revealed: The Bible on the mythic level is the great American Novel and its music is the music not only of our culture but in Islam as well, in Judaism, in Christianity too. This is undeniable.

So what am I doing? I have, with "Lilith," tried to write only another chapter in the Great American novel and connect that to the great literary and social dialogues which have dominated our history from biblical days. The Bible is not just a religious document. It, old and new testaments and all the commentaries are also literary documents. How could I resist messing around in those waters? So I did. And I did so my way with my version of the biblical stories, biblical history and myths.
So what is that music? There are many ideas about the bibles" music, its

poetry and origins. I decided that my way of doing that style would be what came up and what came natural to me; that is mid sentence rhyming prose along with the points I have made above about writing. Remember "Lilith" is "historical fiction" and where my novelist rubber meets the road. See what you think about how well I have succeeded.

Now other examples of music and the choice to use what music. My view is that a good piece or sentence must be and sound authentic, even as different characters speak in a given scene in a book. That is a lot of chord changes, if you catch my drift; and it is what makes novel writing difficult and is what makes novel-writers schizoid. You must not only authentically represent on paper ideas different than your own, legitimately, but represent people you don't even like and moreover, have to be able to write their music, most of the time many of them on the same page, or at least, in the same book. This is beginning to sound like a heavy responsibility. Let stop here for a headache break.

The great themes in American history have antecedents in the bible. They range from the questions around slavery, women's rights, the role of kings, the Golden Rule, equality; freedom, justice, the moral life, and the moral life-style are all in the dialogues in the bible, seen as a work of literature of mythic proportions.
Let's see: Around 1200 BC a remarkable confluence of ideas emerged in both the East and the West where essentially religious and secular ideas underwent enormous change. The religious ideas from Confucianism to Hinduism to Islamic notions could be expressed in the simple maxim "Do unto others as you would have them do unto you."

Why this occurred is complicated. The genesis came from a change in circumstances among many nations of the world. The old kingly and Pharaoh systems where the Pharaoh was divine and the nation's fortunes depended upon his ministrations to the God or Gods fell into disbelief from the Mayans to the Egyptians before and after that date.
The populations of the world had grown to such an extent that kings needed to put thousands of soldiers into the field to triumph in war and that meant tribute, plunder, taxes, money and a greater dependence upon citizen soldiers, or slave soldiers. An elite cadre of kings" men with chariots could not stay the field with massed armies of infantry.

This was a massive change in the balance of power during this 1200 BC period where citizens were able to negotiate with kings around taxes, rights, equality, freedom, justice. Before kings did not need these folks since wars were small in terms of resources needed. In other cases, kings

———

120

could not sustain puppet states and these simply fell down and native populations revolted or filled in the void. This happened to the early Israelites. They were Canaanite vassals ruled over by puppet Canaanite overlords who were in turned ruled by Egypt.

Now these trends affected the Jewish fathers in that as they sought to establish a new religion among the Canaanite pagans in Canaan and start a new society based on equality and freedom and a new single God-Yahweh.

Peculiarly, the native religions initially had to be compromised with in terms of their Gods and the new Hebrew God. Powerful among these was the female Goddess Asherah who Canaanite women were reluctant to give up since Asherah was the patroness of childbirth and of women. The compromise did not last and the Hebrew fathers sought to prohibit her worship ultimately. Note that Asherahs" symbol was a stake or pole or tree and one of her symbols was the serpent as was true in Egypt as well. Notice that, in the garden of Eden, the tree is forbidden and the serpent is portrayed as an evil presence. This all has less to do with Satan in my view, (Satan is seldom mentioned in the Old Testament) but with the attempt to suppress worship of Asherah and a moral judgment upon things Egyptian. But, note for a time, she was seen as the wife or a consort of Yahweh.1

See these Nova videos on this topic:
http://video.pbs.org/video/1051895565/feature/67
13 13 13 13 The Bible"s Buried Secrets (NOVA PBS) NOVA The Bible's Buried Secrets Part 5 of 6

It took hundreds of years for the new Israelites to overcome worship of the old Gods and accept the new single god. And note further, all through the Old Testament the hostility to Asherah is evident for these reasons and others. But the strain in relation to the rights of women did not go away. It was not until 1972 that the Jewish fathers allowed female Rabbis.

A second point; Thomas Jefferson analyzed the bible taking out all references to miracles and the supernatural and wrote down the ethical and political precepts he found there. American political structures are based upon political and ethical premises originating in the bible, especially the new testament; and remember this was an enlightenment writer.

The bible in its various permutations give us, then, the priesthood of all believers of Martin Luther; all men are equal before God, where notions of

---

121

equality and justice come forth as moral precepts in this period.

Paul champions Thecla in the attempts to have her killed for choosing chastity along with Roman women of noble origins in Rome. The female lions in the arena refuse to kill Thecla; indeed protected her. Thecla travels with Paul and baptizes herself since she could not get a male to do it. True or untrue, the mythic life of the equality of women was nurtured and heard and understood by millions in the ancient world.

Jesus in his sermon preaches that the meek and scribes shall inherit the earth and did in fact, scandalously give women prominent roles in his ministry. The equality of all is Andrew Jackson democracy and Jeffersonian democracy which ennobles the militia citizen solider and the plain man.

Lucifer, in the bible, is the protagonist of city-building, wealth, power, cosmetics, alcohol, war and the Tower of Babel. All of the seven sins are not just sins of individual lapses. They represent this battle for human souls in the bible, between God and Lucifer, and is, in fact, a battle between the sinful city and the salt of the earth, the meek and the mild, between the Mammon's of Wall street and the good people of main street. Now, note here, the bible is stating not what causes good and evil but what life-style is conducive to good versus evil. And, if we read carefully, we are also given an explanation of the origins of human nature. This, too, is rooted in the differing social structures.

City-people, are wage-slaves, actual slaves, and are easily dominated and or led astray. Self-sufficiency, on the land, in small democratic communities, are the basis of the moral life and this is a life that God champions in the Old Testament and in the New Testament as well This view is also present in Islam. This is the view embedded in the US Constitution where the rural versus urban is the axis of much of American politics.

It is no accident that Islamic extremists see technologized America as the Great Satan and themselves as innocents. All of these themes, and more, are present in the bible and under-grid the Great American Experiment in Democracy.

Remember these implicit ideas emanating from the bible were also a factor in the toppling of the Roman empire which was, too, seen as the great Satan state by early Christians.

So all that said, what then are the great themes in American life and by extension in the great American Novel?

Notes:
1. Did God Have a Wife?: Archaeology and Folk Religion in Ancient Israel, (Eerdmans, ISBN 0-8028-2852-3, 2005), is a book by Syro-Palestinian archaeologist and biblical scholar William G. Dever (Professor Emeritus of Near Eastern Archeology and Anthropology at the University of Arizona). "Did God Have a Wife?" was intended as a popular work making available to the general public the evidence long known to archaeologists and scholars regarding ancient Israelite religion: namely that the Israelite god (Yahweh) had a consort, that her name was Asherah, and that she was part of the Canaanite pantheon.

I take Lilith as the wife and consort of God, and the name-sake of the Lilith preceding Eve in the Garden of Eden in my novel of that name. Note, also, that the biblical Solomon's wife is called Lilith as well. My goal in this is to re-introduce major themes and developments in consciousness in the bible and mythic history with Lilith as my protagonist.

"How To Write The Great American Novel"

Chapter Nine

Well I have some emails that challenge my assertion that the bible is the great American novel and demanding my first born as atonement for that transgression. I cannot do that today, but Monday I will try. For now, lets drop a few hints:

1-Who settled America and why?
2-What is the relationship between Jeffersonian democracy and the priesthood of all believers?
3- Who is Thecla?
4- What was the real underlying argument between God and Lucifer-- over not good versus bad but, what lifestyle produced good and bad.
5-Why did God reject Abel's offering and reject Cain's?
Back at this on Monday. But first a little more on the premises in the Lilith book and a small commercial.

Note for Teachers:
("The Gospel According to Lilith" also has an audio book which utilizes an historical fiction format to attract and hold student interest in the great issues in American literature.
The author, Lonnie Hicks, has written a novel which makes the argument that the bible, seen as an historical and literary work, contains many

seminal, antecedent themes found in American literature, and, in American history, society and politics.

Utilizing a cross-disciplinary in approach, the audio book and study guide challenges the student to think differently about the bible and argues that the bible is one of the great pieces of American literature.

The Nova PBS special "The Bible's Buried Secrets" gives us convincing archaeological data to support the idea that the early Israelites were egalitarian, freedom-loving and determined to create a religion and society without domination. The social structures they considered essential to this goal, are embedded were closely emulated, by none other that Thomas Jefferson, who put ideas around the importance of small egalitarian communities directly into his writings.

Notions of equality, justice and freedom are all in the bible and have animated much of western literature down the centuries even as the religious content of the old and new testaments have obscured this point.

However, new archaeological evidence, recently unearthed in Israel, indicate that the early writers of the bible were not invaders in Canaan, but were likely Canaanites serfs and slaves, who created a new egalitarian society once their Egyptian overlords collapsed in what is modern day Israel.

The importance of these new discoveries cannot be underestimated.

Our traditional view of the bible must be re-considered in light of these new discoveries as well in the context of the bible as a work of literature.

That is what "The Gospel According to Lilith" achieves. This historical fiction novel, introduces the student to the new bible- the bible as a literary work. With Lilith as a narrator, the student is taken on a journey looking at the bible as a document which produced many themes directly relevant and influential American literature and social history.)

So we can see that, indeed, there are similar themes in American History which converge with themes in the bible. The one I would like to concentrate on at this point is the biblical theory of human nature comparing that to the one many attribute to the founding fathers of America. Much has been made of the assertion that the latter created a government which assumed human nature was selfish, apt to pursue over-weaning power and aggressive.

Therefore, so the theory goes, they created a political system with "checks and balances" to curb the negative tendencies in human nature. The quick retort here is does this theory not apply to the founding fathers themselves, the revolutionary soldiers who fought that war for much higher goals than greed, and power mongering? Obviously not. This is a misreading of the motives and intent of the founding fathers.

It is the cable news version of the founding fathers and what their motives where. They, like the biblical founders, saw human nature as existing in an evolving, contextual milieu with outcomes much influenced by social structures and context. People in small communities will display a much more positive "human nature" that those in say, cities.
Human nature is malleable and subject to heavy influences from the environment. Human nature is adaptable. Both the biblical founders and the American founders had this view.
Moreover, common sense tells us this is true. How did we get wrapped up with the negative view that human nature is fixed, evil and aggrandizing? Well, no space here to go into detail, but the short answer is that historians have given us a pathological version of human history and ignored the eons of human cooperation which has existed over these same periods. We get a chronology of wars, brutality, kings and slavery and greed. But what were the common people doing these periods, or is this, again, the cable news version of history? Most people stuck together, and cooperated with one another to survive--unless thrust or coerced to the front to fight the kings wars. So context matters and who is telling the story of human nature and human events matters too.

Now we come to the literary issue: We want to know what is, in the novel, the author's view of human nature in terms of character, and character development in a given piece? Interesting question, but one that can become very obvious if you are an author writing a novel. What is human nature in our novels? What theory is evident there? Humm, scary isn't it? Now you can write a novel where by your own hand you depict human nature, through your characters. Are they two-variable cut outs, antagonist and protagonist, good and evil, bad or good etc? This is not only character depiction; it carries with it a notion of human nature. People can be described as good or bad and that is what you write? No, let's not do that. It perpetuates some pretty horrific stereo-types we should as artists, avoid. Are characters determined by their circumstances, fate-bound, unable to change their circumstances and doomed? This does not ring true, but Greek tragedy has that ring doesn't it, not to mention certain of Shakespeare's works?

As my grandmother used to say: "be clear children, are you raising slaves or freedom fighters", implying you had a choice in molding human nature, if

---

125

not behaviour. In fact, human adaptability is the hallmark of human nature. Here we have a creature that has shown incredible adaptability, settling in every climate, endured every hardship and thrived on this planet; now threatened by the ossification of "institutions" that prevent that very adaptability which has been the hallmark of the species very survival and longevity.

So a writer has a responsibility that a journalist does not have--to show human nature and its potentials not to perpetuate negative theories of human nature, first, which are not true, and even if they were do not forward the progress of the human race if we perpetuate them. And that is what a true artist will seek to do--seek that vision of human beings that is beneficial to the future of human beings.

So, mister smarty pants, you say, what does that character development look like which won't end up with a false rosy picture of human beings and human nature? What will these characters look like? Well, I made my attempt in the Lilith book. God develops; he transforms himself even in the old testament. First, he tries again in the Garden with two versions of genesis; he apologizes to Noah after the flood, lifts restrictions on alcohol and tries to bargain with his creations. Finally he decided to come down to Earth in the form of Christ, in the new testament and try again to make things work. God grows and initiates at least three entirely different convents with his creatures. He adapts. So does Lucifer. So does Lilith. What is emphasized in the novel is transmogrification. The nature of God is malleable--despite his reputation for being rigid. What he is rigid about is the context of living. He rejects Cain's gift of grain and accepts the gift of Abel because Cain's gift represents a life-style connecting with cities and settled agriculture which God disfavours preferring a gift of a lamb from Abel which represents the pastoral life. Pastoral life, God argues through much of the old testament and the new testament, is a better, more sustainable life style than the sinful life of the cities, kings and priests. After all the Jesus that sacked the temple, was a country boy and hated what he saw happening in the temple in the city. This rigid stance softens later but all of Christianity in the early church was small town people meeting in each others homes not in grand cathedrals in the cities.

"How To Write The Great American Novel"

Chapter Ten

Let's have a look at the malleable argument from yesterday in the context of America's founding, the novel, and the bible. What it means, in my view,

---

126

is that human beings respond to the circumstances they find themselves in and adapt. This first aspect of the malleable idea, in the case of both the bible and American founders, relates to the fact that both groups felt that contexts must be created to guide humans toward positive behavior. This is not to ignore the negative aspects of human behavior. They are to be taken very seriously and placed in a context where they too can be controlled. This is where the checks and balances in the US constitution come in. Humankind cannot be trusted with power, and absolute power corrupts absolutely; but this too is because of the malleability factor. Jefferson sought to embed the positive context of the citizen farmer, self-sufficient, close to the land in American political institutions. To his mind this was a model he considered sustainable for humankind; he put it into the Constitution in terms of protecting small rural communities. Cites are a context where people give up their wills to kings, bosses, corporations and crooks proving that bad environments can create bad people. Cities, both Jefferson and the biblical fathers thought, create trouble. Whether this is really true or not is, of course, another story.

Archaeological evidence now available indicate that the Israelites were Canaanites themselves, who at the collapse of Egyptian puppet Canaanite rulers introduced egalitarianism into Canaanite societies and reformed themselves as a new society with a single God. The animus against cities was aimed at the example of both Egypt and Egypt's puppet Canaanite rulers in Canaan. This was a country side revolutionary movement which rejected what they had seen as the outcome of Egyptian top down, centralized Pharaoh systems and similar systems all over the known world at about 1,200 BC.

Cities have given us, in their thinking, hierarchy, over-weaning power, war, slavery and greed in this view. True cities have given us intellectual growth, progress and even science. But the Jeffersonian and the biblical scholar would say the city is an inherently unsustainable model of humankind. They also have bred the capacity to destroy the planet. A small community, independent, close to the land, is sustainable. Face to face daily relationships is the best model for humankind and humans existed in these kinds of relationships for millennia. This precept also under grids, Greek ideas about democracy.

Curiously, models to green the planet and make every house a net grid contributor have this same model in mind.

Good and evil in terms of their generation, therefore, are strongly contextual.

Now next in this malleable story is the factor, obvious to many, is that individuals have the capacity to overcome their contextual contexts. One person in prison overcomes that circumstance and rehabilitates themselves. Some poor kids are defeated by poverty; some overcome the impoverished background and prosper. Some people in evil circumstances resist and do not succumb.

This is an important point because the capacity of human beings to supersede and transform themselves above their circumstances is also a feature of the malleability model we are here describing and key to biblical and American thinking. Malleability not only means susceptible to being heavily influenced by the circumstances one may find oneself in, it also means the ability to transform oneself beyond that circumstance. This is a crucial point.

This is what is being discussed in the bible, and in American history. Human beings, say in a religious context, can transform themselves and their circumstances through faith, faith in God, faith in Buddha, thought or meditation and human free will. God makes this point over and over again. The ability of the human animal to supersede circumstances both individual and group is the real hallmark of human history.

This is true of both science and religious theory, which we normally think as polar opposites in their views on this. The proposition here is that transformation is the normal state of human kind, indeed all worlds, religious or scientific. The American dream is a dream based on the belief that peasants could land here with nothing and by dent of hard work, God, luck or mayhem against the native dwellers, transform their lives and themselves. Jews, Christians, Islamic and other religious faiths believe exactly the same thing except the medium of transmogrification is faith, inner journeying, or by cognitive means. God in the bible says we have the free will to do so despite the temptations of the devil. So transformation is the key element in human efforts. But how exactly does this work?

Einstein tells us that E-mc2. This is remarkable primarily because it describes both human things, physical things and the nature of the universe we live in. And, Quantum mechanics gives us the exact same view of the transformative nature of the world and the universe at the sub-atomic level. Ok, that was a lot to absorb in one sentence. Let's unpack the ideas here.

First, E=mc2 is saying that energy can be transformed into matter and the process is exponential and ultimately mysterious. Science does not have a clue why this is the case. They believe it because they can manipulate it but no one of them has even actually seen an atom. No Christian has ever claimed to have actually seen God. Folks leaving Africa had never seen Europe did they? So what is the basis for action in these cases? You can fill in the blanks: faith, belief in the ability to transform ones circumstances, dumb luck and boldness. But the important point here is over-looked. Our universe is one where transformations are normal,(we fish don't see this water) and it is miraculous. How is it that a shift of one electron from one orbit to another transforms matter and we get water and hydrogen separated out, two different substances. Now that is mysterious. But there is more; any electron anywhere in our entire universe is in contact with its opposite charged electron no matter where it is in any other part of the universe. The entire universe at the sub-atomic level is in touch with itself at the sub-atomic level.

Welcome to quantum mechanics. This is a remarkable finding, because the transformations taking place in this construct are also talking place within us as humans and, more pointedly, in our human brains which, by definition, are a part of this same universe of transforming electron activity and probably explains why human beings can transform and supersede their circumstances and move from lower brain stem activity and develop, as we have, higher brain functions. In short, this has made possible our moving from our ape origins to the human development path. Embedded in this process is greatest mystery of all--the nature and genesis in the human mind of what we generally call the Idea. No one knows what an idea is but we all have them. We know that the brain and ideas are connected to the entire physical universe and is a major the driver of human activity and in my view, the engine which has allowed for human transformations. You can't get to Europe from Africa if you don't get the idea first.

So here is a conclusion to ponder: science, the bible, the great religions and thought systems say exactly the same thing--humans, both group and individual, can transform themselves and their circumstances by processes some call faith in God, by a natural transformative process the scientists say, by introspection and connection others say.
Therefore, the malleability of human beings is the ability to become what they are not today is at play in both the social and the scientific orders and in the physical world as well. To be clear: there is no conflict between the ideas of the modern scientist and the religious person. Einstein agreed, Darwin agreed, Newton agreed, modern quantum mechanics agrees.

So now we look a little closer at this remarkable constantly transforming world we live in. Matter transforms to energy, solids to gas and back again. We light a fire and view it to be unremarkable that wood can be

---

129

transformed into gases. We do not see the incredible statement that represents about the world we live in.

Now we want to lay out the steps we have covered. There is first the interconnection of all things in our world, both within our selves and in the physical universe as well. It is no accident that Christ said that we can find God by looking within and undergoing a transformative process or conversion which could be a form of liberation even under Roman rule. That inner divine spark, that capacity to connect to what is not oneself, becomes transformative and is exactly corroborated and agreed to by scientists who work at the sub-atomic level and at the level of black holes in the larger universe.

Transformative processes and capacities begin with the premise of universal connection of all things religious and scientific and, these transformations occur regularly and routinely.

Next we look at the outcomes of these transformations. I am dealing with here the issue of exchanges at the boundaries of these transformative processes. What is meant here is that as man approaches God the bedrock premise is and has to be that humankind has only a very limited capacity to understand what is present at this transformative process boundary. We can be changed by faith, by science, by observation of the natural world, by tinkering in the natural world, but our capacity to understand it is limited as we reach the boundaries of our own ability to absorb transformative changes. This is the argument of the founders of all religions. Humans can only understand so much because they are humans. Scientists say the same thing. We can understand black holes as possible windows onto other universes but we can never know those other universes. We can understand that dark matter and energy make up most of the universe but never be able to step outside and really understand the processes at work.

Why because to take a simple example; we humans are like fish. We swim in water and cannot jump out on land and take a cruise in the RV. We fish maybe can evolve to that point but to expect to be able to do that wily-nilly is absurd. We are fish and barely understand the boundary between our fish world and the thin layer above us which is an air-breathing world above the water we swim in. We can tinker at the boundary between the two worlds but fish are not oxen.

So what is this tinkering in science? The greatest experiment in human history at boundary tinkering is happening at CERN, Switzerland, where scientists are literally shooting protons into the nucleus of atoms at light speed hoping, by measuring the particle fallout, to see if any missing particles can be discerned. Why, because if there are, it means there is

---

another universe they have gone into. There is no question but at the sub-atomic level particles and electrons pop into and out of existence. The CERN effort is trying to discern where to they pop to; fish sticking a straw up above water to see what the world of air is like.

So what does all of this mumbo-jumbo have to do with literature and novel-writing you say? Well here are the take-away points. To put pen to paper is to participate in the above described transformative process because our ideas in doing so are directly connected to all points in this universe. The imagination is literally taking, through some mysterious process, things which do not or did no exist seconds ago and bringing them in to existence, here and now on paper. This process is taken for granted but it is of stupendous importance. Therefore, the human beings we can imagine on paper are, and can be and have been transforming for everyone living on the planet; take the idea of Freedom for example. A simple idea changed the world. That is the mission of the novelist to describe this transformation process in the characters who populate our minds and our pages.

Thanks for your patience in allowing me to get through this part of the Blog. Now back to the nuts and bolts of writing that novel-tomorrow.

"How To Write The Great American Novel"

Chapter Eleven

So where are we? A little summary here. Transformations and transformative qualities are the hallmark of the universe on the large cosmic level, are the hallmark of the sub-atomic level as well. In fact the only stable element on the periodic table is lead. The rest of the elements can and do constantly loose elections, gain electrons and disappear God knows where. Constant change at the sub-atomic level is also the rule.

Now on the human level we have to start to imagine that the instrument of transformation in human beings is the human brain. Our brain is a neural network with about a trillion cells. It transforms itself, and the connections it makes internally, interacting with external and internal stimuli constantly. And, in doing so, is constantly is changing, is constantly remaking the world we perceive and live in. Now that was a mouthful. Here is the bottom line: our perceptions of the world and the reality we all share is different and that difference is a function of the synaptic connections which we have grown based upon how we have used our individual brains over time.

Therefore, it is true that each of us has the capacity to make and remake, evolve, and change our individual realities to the extent that the human brain is involved. This is not so strange a statement. One day life is hopeless, the next day life is wonderful. How did that happen? Did the world change? No, you interacting with your brain changed. And that is what we are talking about here. That change and transforming capability allows individual "A" to get up new energy, change, and act in the world, while individual "b", without such a change, is still under the covers at home complaining about the state of the world. Brain transformations involving attitudes, ideas, thoughts (and by extension our reality and the realities of others) are so common that we take them for granted.

So how does this daily miracle happen? Is it brain chemistry, is the brain some kind of reality-shifting organ which we don't really understand. Yes, and we don't know much about it. We still in the 21st century don't know what an idea is and where it comes from or even where it goes. We can track activity in the brain but we don't have a clue what the thing is we are tracking.

So now that I have bludgeoned you with my transformation thesis lets novelize. "The latter word "novelize" illustrates my point exactly. I have never written the word "novelize" in my life. I don't know where the idea came from to write that word. I don't even know what reality "novelize" relates to. But the miracle here is that this invention of a new word, plopping it down into reality here on this page, is communicated between two brains, yours and mine. More, the invention of a new word, say something really big like "equality" can and has changed the world we live it. So it is no small item to discuss here. And it is no small item for a novelist to be concerned with as s/he writes that novel.

Now lets move to the next item on our list (remember that list we started with?) Let me refresh our brains memory (couldn't resist, sorry.)

Here are the ones I keep in mind.
a. The physical space on the page
b. The letters which make up the words
c. The sounds of the words, if you sound them out in your head
d. The writer
e. The reader
f. Time, place and space factors
g. The Take Away

We have covered physical space on the page. See my poem "Key-Board Lover" at poemhunter.com for another example of this point.

We have looked at words carefully with the exegesis of "Love's Remains" above.

We have looked at style issues and the music in a sentence or book, using my book "The Gospel of Lilith" as an example.

We have talked about the writer, you to some extent, and made recommendations on what it takes to sustain writing from health, to head, to heart.

We have just finished looking at historical factors which influence writing the great American novel, noting that our time, in America, is not a blank slate and has a history with a great piece of literature called the bible, which has to be reckoned with.
Now we will move to themes. Of course, the American story has not been a static one. Our mold did not end with biblical themes we have outlined above. American culture grew and changed. What has been the broad outlines of the changes we can identify in American literature? Have they outstripped the ones we have examined emanating from the bible? If there have been unique themes in American literature what has been their genesis and typology? Ah, something for tomorrow.

"How To Write The Great American Novel"

Chapter Twelve

Here we look at item "F" above; the themes in our examination of the American landscape, comparing these themes to those found in the bible have, of course, been impacted in the American example, by time, place and space factors. American history has ameliorated biblical themes and we now turn to have a look at the specific American version of those themes.

First, the United States, in many respects, represents a culmination of themes regarding justice, morality, freedom, equality long extent in the world. This country was, and still is, regarded as the "new world;" a place where there is chance to escape the stultification of countries and places ruled by tyrants, war-lords, murderers and killers. America, from early on, became the place of opportunity, a place where anything was possible, where one could come and get land, grow rich and be whatever you wanted to be.

This is the American myth structure. Now, the context and secret of this American offering was evident from the beginning; this "new world" had as its base, three pillars of what was to be its secrets of success. But first let us do context. Remember context? We need to understand the American context and then we can see how the themes in American history rolled out.

These crucial contextual items include the following:

1- America was born and matured as a frontier society which shaped and molded a rampant individualism on the mythic level. One man could as an individual was, and needed to be, as self-reliant as possible and, in being so, could change the world and create wealth with his/her bare hands on the frontier. This unbounded optimism still exists and was alive and well until George Bush killed it during his Presidency.

But this frontier aspect of the American experience also helped to form the America character. Rants against welfare mothers, Reagan democrats, and public poverty in the face of massive private wealth all attest to the sub-strata view that the individual is responsible for his or her plight and should not be given help of any kind. Rugged individualism for the rich, and massive dependent poverty for the poor. All of this remains in place psychologically even as the frontier closed over a hundred years ago; a view functional in a frontier society, not so in a wage slave society.

2- The pillars of this young American society included four other elements:

a. Isolation from Europe giving the new republic time to mature without getting smothered in its crib by jealous European nations.
b. Cheap labor and massive amounts of land taken from the native American population. Cheap labor was, of course, blacks taken from Africa and immigrants from the continent who cleared the land, farmed it, only to have it taken from them 150 years later by big Agriculture, developers and Washington taxes. The story of America, is in this regard, is the story of cheap labor. After all the nation's capital building itself was built by slaves.
c. Second and third pillars are cheap energy, (oil and coal) and cheap food round out the American pantheon of gifts that any nation needs to prosper. Everything else in American society, is and was built upon these pillars. It

is only recently that the cheap energy pillar has fallen away. And right away we see the result. Cheap labor has gone and now lives in India and China. That other cheap energy (coal, gas) now threatens the planet with green house gases. And cheap food is still in place but being genetically altered and stuffed with antibiotics. Cheap, but poisonous food, is a bad idea.

So this is the American context and how does all this play out?
1. The individual is seen to be free, mobile and most came here to get their own plot of land, worship as they pleased and to enjoy the benefits of liberty. But from these noble aims, we can see getting rich easily becomes greed, rampant individualism easily becomes public poverty and an "I have mine, not you go get yours mentality", mobility becomes freedom of the road, not political freedom. We are a republic, not a democracy; and by the way you immigrants, blacks and women are not included in this freedom thing.
All of American history can be seen, (exaggerated of course) as the outs who were excluded at the beginning of the country clamouring to get in. It has taken 200 years and the process is not yet complete.

So the American additions to the biblical themes have been evident. But the basic conversation was set in the bible So looking at Twain, Faulkner, Moby Dick, The Grapes of Wrath--choose your great American writer or work--and you will see these themes and factors at play; a dialogue which under-grids the entire American society and continues to be played out in the daily newspapers. Moby Dick and Thoreau illustrate attitudes toward nature. Twain looks at slavery, "Grapes" talks about that cheap food and how it is produced and the disenfranchisement of people from the land by big agriculture and their transplantations into city-bound wage-slaves. These issues are also discussed in the bible and the early writers of the bible made clear their point of view and that view has been bore out to some extent in American history.

So here you are now getting ready to write that great American novel. Hopefully, you come to the enterprise much better grounded in the conversations that have come before you and with a better understanding of why some writers have been considered seminal or great. The answer is they have pushed that American dialogue further and illuminated some small new aspect of this American story.

Now you may say "that's great. But I just want to do a simple little mystery novel here and get rich. I don't have any of the high-fluting goals in my writing that you allude to."

Yes, how very American.
That is fine. But if you want to write the great American novel, then try to take the above seriously. If not, this Blog will be a book soon, in about a month, in an expanded version--perhaps I can persuade you with more detail in that book. Let me know if you want a pre-copy. I would welcome feed-back to make it a better book than it was a Blog.

Ah, this being Friday I am halting the Blog for the weekend to respond to emails some of you have sent and to take into consideration many of your ideas (thanks for sending them along, by the way-(-www.lonnie@lonniehicks.com)

Note on editing:

How do you edit? Always edit. Let a piece sit you thought was so great and come back to it a day later. That is when some of the best work can be done.

Here is what I do, (everyone has their own style.)

--I take out all of the "and's" and basically put in semi-colons. "Ands" break up the flow of a sentence.

--I check for the music in a sentence. I like mid-sentence rhyming loose or close and vowel rhyming; this enhances flow.

--I make sure every sentence is worthy of my pen.

--I check tenses and make sure that tenses don't undermine the sentence. For example "he walked to the door and then he opened it."

Take out the "and" and the "then" replace with a period. Secondly make it present tense where possible. "He walks to the door; he opens it." Seemingly small but the action is more immediate in my edited sentence and a little more drama there too. See "Asunder" for dramatic writing. I edited that piece like a movie shot in a single long scene. In fact I think it has just about four sentences before the finish.

A page-turner is "created" art unless the piece falls out of you perfect already. Few of us can do that. All pieces can be improved.

Of course typos, etc and then originality. Have I said something here new, original, could I even invent a concept here and follow its logic. Could I invent a new word or concept of words? Shakespeare did.

For example I did a series of pieces taking words and put "un" in front of them: "The unexamined" "Unloved" Unhappy. Note here that changing a word in this way creates a whole new word-world. Unlove is not the opposite of love. So what then is it? See my several pieces experimenting with the "un" development. I think an entirely new aspect of language may lie there.(Please don't say "uncola" I have heard that joke.)

May 13, /2010 Note on Music.

Note on Music: Some have asked what is meant by music. Music in a sentence or paragraph may vary but the music I like includes the following example.

"He was his own best friend and now best friend was telling him to move on; telling him to let it all alone."

Now if you can move the action and have music too, that is good. It falls easier on the reader's ear if you have both elements. But what you say exactly is the music? Answer, it is subtle but it is vowel music.

Let's take a closer look:

1-"Best friend and best friend" is repetition music, just like many lyrics in a song repeat. It has a beat six beats ending in the first friend, "And not best friend" in the second clause." Note six beats in clause one and four beats in clause two. This equals ten beats. Note this is not just the famous 10 beat set, (Shakespeare used it lot) but ten beats matches the breathing cycle of human breathing as one reads, inhaling five, exhaling five. Moreover, it may match the beats of the human heart. A lot here huh?

I promise you I did this sentence spontaneously. Poetic training, training the mind, and hence the writing, to think in beats and music.

Now the second aspect of music in this sentence: "was telling him...." has both the music of repetition of a lyric but also rough rhyming between

---

"friend" and "him." "Telling is repeated in the last clause and the sentence ends with 14 beats and ends with a rough rhyming between "move on" and "all alone."

Now some readers will not hear this music at all. But no matter. The point is that the writer if s/he has the music in him or her does. It is on the page and the reader will find the sentence pleasing, even if he/she does not recognize the music that is there.

That is why so many writers also write poetry. The poetic ear keeps the brain working and imbues prose with another layer of interest.

SCENE DEVELOPMENT

Of all scenes none is more important, perhaps, that the first scene which is part of the first page, the first paragraph, and the first sentence.

This has to accomplish a lot for the author: catch the reader's attention, set the tone of the book, its initial impressions to the reader, begin the story in a riveting way and get the reader to paragraph two and perhaps introduce the reader to the main characters in the story.

That is a lot.

The opening line in fact, if an inspired one, can not only start a novel but make the entire novel revolve around that opening line.

Now if we look at the one page novels we did above we see that indeed they can be outlines for entire novels, or the beginning of a novel. Starting is always difficult.

So let's take a real example and then a fictitious one.

"The Gospel According to Lilith" begins with the line:

"Among the heavenly spires, upon the highest balcony, Lord watched Lucifer conduct the Worship of the Universe services for all the heavenly hosts."

Now the intent here was a combination of shock, awe, and to generate curiosity.

"Heavenly spires" asks the question: "Where are we? Are we in heaven? Is this novel going to take place in heaven.? Lords watches, invites the question is this God and then the answer comes: Lucifer is conducting worship services. Now this was Lucifer's role prior to his fall from grace but not many folks are aware.

What has been accomplished with this first sentence? We have set the scene, introduced two of the three main characters of the novel, described a novel scene, heaven itself, and introduced God himself into the story line.

It could be better but sometimes you have to choose, scene-setting or character or story introduction.

"This cannot be." he thought to himself.
We now want to know what cannot be. And the story is off and running at this point. God is speaker and he is angry about something. That something is the heart of the book--the betrayal of God by his wife, and the sequellia of that act is the content of the entire book, set up in the first three sentences; and I make it the seminal act in all of *human history*--God reacting to this betrayal. The entire book flows from there.

A second opening sentence is the one we used above; "I lie still, I must be dead."

Now this is not a novel and this is a made up sentence. But could it be a novel? What is set up in this sentence? The follow-on one-pager creates a scenario where a new born recognizes his mother as a familiar face from birth.

What novel can we write from this opening and did it accomplish the tasks we identified above: scene, characters, interest, and reader involvement?. A novel could be done from this where the mystery here at birth is never solved and the main character spends the novel trying to figure it all out. He goes to sooth-sayers, mystics, doctors and finally at some point at the museum the face of his mother appears on an Egyptian hieroglyph. There the story takes off into another direction. But the point is a novel can be born from a single sentence.

But as they say the opening sentence or scene is but the first step over the cliff.

Next time: What do I do after those first two incredible chapters?

CHARACTER DEVELOPMENT

How to develop characters after we have identified them. They exist but they also interact with other characters. Here is what I do. I often think of my characters as archetypes taken from dictionary definitions. Death, Love, Betrayal. These are already defined for me and I can extract their behaviors and points of view from the very definitions given me by the dictionary. Love for example has over 12 definitions. Which one will I use to describing my character's motivation in the novel?

Secondly characters for me often come from the poetry. I tend to write poetry which are mini-stories with main characters in them. The are portraits of individuals or circumstances-and many of them are taken from stories real people have shared with me.

So over time I have built up a library of "characters" which I can use in novels and stories. Now I have characters, (real people) outlines, (my poems tend to be one-page novels) motivation and context.

Next of course you need a story and have an idea of how these characters will interact in the story.

I'll not deal with story yet because interactions, for me will dictate the story. I have a rule for my characters, they must be real and authentic. This is achieved since many of my stories are based on real people. But also characters which will hold the reader's interest for 250 pages should not be stereotypes. Of course this is done all the time. Mystery novels, romance novels operate from a formula but we aspire to more don't we? So what to do about characters interacting in our story?

I have one rule--characters must be given genuine not phony points of view. In "Gospel" I take Lucifer's point of view seriously and explore it in the novel as he interacts with God and Lilith. We want to know what his thinking is and was. it makes for more interesting reading and it might uncover heretofore unknown aspects of, in this case the bible.

And that is exactly what happened. I wanted to know what is the real dispute between God and Lucifer all about. I started the dispute with the betrayal but beyond that there was much more, which is explored in the book.

So characters have to come alive on the page by being real actors and real people. "Evil incarnate" is a stereotype.

Writing, Reading and Breathing

If we step back a moment we have three unstated characters in every book, the writer, the reader and the experience of reading the book. This relationship, in order to be satisfying, beyond the normal aspects of story, character etc., has the aspect of being a human experience. Let's not be vague here. Beats and heat-beats have their own rhythms and the normal breathing pattern has about five on the exhale and five in the inhale. The writer, in writing, can break up that pattern. Poetry can do this rather naturally, For suspense and danger we, in life, naturally bate our breath, or hold it. A sentence can encourage the reader to do this by its construction, contributing to the sense of suspense. Short sentences can mean short breathing patterns. But go beyond that and the reader will need to take a breath or pause to catch her/his breath.

A flow of breaths as in a sensuous poem will create a flowing, relaxed breathing pattern with perhaps, deeper breaths being taken. This oxygenates the brain and the reader may feel the mild euphoria this might entail. Similarly shorter breath can create a sense of panting.

All of this an example of how writing can create breathing patterns in the reader and an author must be aware of all this and write to that experience.

Let's take an example: She moved with such easy grace, the flowing was not noticeable because her eyes riveted you in place.

Seven beats to the word grace: the breathing here has been interrupted before the normal ten. Something here is arresting our attention. "Noticeable" ends the ninth beat. Our breathing is now becoming more normal because we held up the breathing pattern with only seven in the first clause. The last clause ending with "place" is ten beats--back to the normal breathing pattern.

The reading of the passage by the reader, creates a breathing pattern that matches what is being said in the passage. Writer and reader are in concert and breathing patterns created by the writing match the content of the passage and any meaning the author seeks to impart.

Pacing is important in all of this from the phrase level, to the sentence level, to the paragraph and the page and chapter. The same principles apply.,

---

Well, that was pretty flighty. Next time more.

The Curse of Chapter Three

Most writers can do one to three chapters. But what to say after you have said hello? We have captured our reader's interest and the pages have been turned. But right about chapter three the beady eyes of the reader are upon you. Do you have a second act?

Much depends upon chapter three. So what do you do? First lets analyze chapter three. Working hard, you have set your scene, introduced your characters, set your story line in motion and now what?

Well, lets explore the possibilities:

1. Go into detail on one of the main characters and others. This introduces something new to the reader and keeps them locked in that chair for a while.

2-Change the time period, back-flashes etc

3-Change the dialogue, from exterior to interior. Jolt the reader.

5- Start what seems like a totally unrelated story.

6- Add some sex. This almost always works.

7- Have a violent scene, for this that like that kind of catharsis.

8- Start telling the story backwards. Create confusion and hopefully interest.

The list is endless and of course, depends upon your characters and your story.

Some people outline an entire book before writing but that can limit you when the time comes to fill in the detail and limits the actions of your characters. You might want to have them have the freedom to be spontaneous beneath your pen.

Now if you have a formula story going this won't be much of a problem, motivation is set: good wins our over evil.

But note here, for example, that this did not and would not have worked out in the "Lilith" book. At the end of the book Lucifer is winning. This was faithful to what actually happens in the bible. That is how the story is told there as well, to God's frustration.

Chapter three therefore, launches the true beginning of the book. Our opening two chapters are merely a literary device. Chapter three is fess up time and demands that we be real in our story. Most readers have one arm lofted above the bedside reading table ready to dump you if chapter three fails. No pressure, just wanting you to know.

Next time: Are novelists expert liars and should we be encouraging this?

Hint: that is one reason I tend toward writing about real people.

Title: How to Write The Great American Novel
Part Two

Updated: Oct 11, 2010

Summary: This is part two of an essay on writing the great American novel. Part one appears in another blog on this site.
Update: 10-1-10 "So if I write seeking to depict reality, what then is the nature of reality?
Update: 10-11-10 "Alice Lives in Harlem?"

Sept 29, 2010
How shall I tell my Story?

So we ask are we as writers writing from imagination, from experience, from some ideology or point of view, from human strengths and weaknesses? Upon what canvass?

Now with a novel you have several choices. You can write first person.

The story is being told from one person's point of view and that person is depicting what everyone else thinks and does. But the issue here is how do we know the report of this first person is true, accurate or tells the whole story? We don't.

We can tell the story from the point of view of some sort of narrator, omniscient or not omniscient. This person may have a God-like ability to

---

read everyone's mind in the story and is a reliable reporter of what is really going on in the story. Or not.

We can tell the story where each person is telling their view of what is going on and the reader is left to figure out how all of the these pieces fit together or not fit together.

We can tell the story interactively, that is, we don't know what the characters think and we judge them by their actions and reactions to one another as the story unfolds. Their actions define them not their words.

We can tell the story in the past, in the present or in the future or a combination of all three.

We can mix and match all of the above.

Deciding how to tell the story is often the crucial first step in story writing and there are pros and cons with each choice. Let's look at these pros and cons in the coming days-seeking to understand in choosing the consequences of each choice.

Oct 1, 2010
Now interestingly, if we base our choice on visions of reality that modern physics theories project, we get some interesting answers to these questions.

For example, Einstein, if he were to comment on this question, might say:

1-Since the past, the present and the future all exist at the same time then our story-telling should reflect this perspective. And since time and space is relative to the position and speed of the observer, then we might guess Einstein would choose a fluid time perspective for his story and his characters and we would have the same story being told from the point of view of all the different characters. But, the story would likely be different for each character because each occupies a different time and space in the story.

Sort of interesting huh?

A science fiction story might take this tack but add the aspect of multiple dimensions into the mix. Time travel, dimensions, black holes, and multiples of one's self do show up often in science fiction stories and come

---

directly more or less from string theory and multiverse theories of how the universe works.

Now this discussion becomes even more relevant if the ask the question should the author seek to depict some kind of reality and if so what is the nature of that reality if we include real world ideas real about how the universe works.

So depicting reality may be a legitimate goal rooted in modern theories of how the universe works. Now it gets interesting.

Now, we wonder, what would be the story construction if we take quantum mechanics as the true nature of the universe? Now that would be more than interesting.

Let's take a look tomorrow.

Oct 11, 2010
So what would our story telling be like of we sought to depict reality utilizing the precepts of quantum mechanics theoretical physics? (See my blog on this "Einstein" to get a quick look at the precepts of quantum mechanics.

Here is how it might go:

1-Since in QM the world is constantly changing, electrons are literally popping in and out of existence, this produces a fluid story line where characters are not only constantly changing but each character might undergo drastic changes which a single novel, often not explained.

2- We would have characters who impact one another (quantum entanglement) following the theory that all the universe, (our universe of characters too) are connected. If this is so and the basic nature of reality then all characters, whether close by or not are impacted by all others characters and their actions.

This would stretch across time as well and we would have inter-generational novels which tell how each character has been formed and is impacted by his or her family history. This. has of course, been done. This is to say that individuals are not individual but are the product of the impact of many other individuals, living and dead.

(I like this one but obviously it takes a tremendous amount of work)

Now let look at dimensional theory, (there are multiple dimensions to the universe)

Again this has been done a lot in science fiction but let's focus on the reality aspects of this:

1-In a novel, the imagination can and has created entirely new worlds, with totally different realities and different cultures, strange ideas and different ways of relating. We then want to know how does an imaginary world, or a novel created solely in our imagination, impact the actual behavior of our characters?

We have a lot of freedom here because we can introduce entirely new way of being and entirely new idea. Think about "Alice in Wonderland."
Now that is truly another dimension or perhaps another world. Think about fairy tales. What rules do these imaginary worlds, where pigs talk, and bears live in cottages and eat porridge follow?

So you can see that there is a theory of physics which actually considers even these flights of imagination entirely possible. Modern physics says that Alice in Wonderland or something quite similar, in a multiverse universe.

Humm, which ones of these realities you or I might choose, depends upon several factors. Let's look at what those factors might be in the coming days.

After all, that is the basic decision. How jarring it might be to tell an "Alice in Wonderland" story but set in 1920 America? You can do it but it would require a lot of work and set up.

If you did it on another planet, that might make the story-telling a lot easier.

You get the point. Let's visit Alice and these other worlds tomorrow.

Note: What follows here is an excerpt from my novel, "The Gospel According to Lilith" which, I think serves as an example of what I believe, constitute and attempt at great novel writing. Whether I have succeeded or not is for the reader to decide.

But, more importantly, the chapters serve as a bridge for the reader to look at the most influential book in American history, the bible. I examine the bible as a document, looking at it roots, from the earliest biblical days tracking its influence on American life and literature to the modern day.

Title: The Gospel According

to Lilith

BOOK ONE

TRANSMORGRIFICATION

An Original Novel
By
Lonnie Hicks

Chapter 1

Among the heavenly spires, upon the highest balcony, Lord watched Lucifer conduct the Worship of the Universe Services for all the heavenly hosts.

"This cannot be." he thought to himself. He felt a slow-moving anger build within him.

"How could this happen, yet escape my eye?" he said to his minister who appeared beside him. "How can all of you sit at my table and not know? Someone knew, someone must have guessed, and, yet, none who sat with me—none counseled me in this the most evil betrayal of all betrayals."

He cried out in anguish and faces looked up from all over the realm knowing that Lord was angry and justice was to be meted out to one or many. They tensed, waiting, knowing that anyone of them could fall dead and no one would know the offense or the difference.

"See him," Lord said still looking down at Lucifer whose beauty was undeniable. "I made him my most beautiful angel. I raised him on high. I made Lilith the most beautiful woman in the entire universe and this is how they repay me—with treachery?"

"He bewitches her and she becomes pregnant with his child?"

"This is all done in my very bed in the night?" He turned to the minister. "So you say she is with child and that child is his?" Lord said suddenly.

"Yes," my Lord, "it is so."

"You say she confesses such?"

"She did my Lord."

"Bring her to me. I would hear her. Bring her to me. I need to see her, hear her response, see if she will offer me false regrets or perhaps a plea of how she was deceived, or bewitched."

The minister stirred to leave, heart pounding, unsure if his part was beginning to be perceived by Lord—who would guess in time that he, the minister must have known of the liaison, but did not convey that truth to Lord. As he traversed from the throne room, he feared he might be struck down before he reached the door.

Down each step from Lord's throne, was a step into his own hell for surely the wife would betray him to Lord, if pressed, to save her own soul.

He was lost in the end.

"All this," he thought, "would have consequences far beyond a simple tryst and that this would ignite, among all in heaven, far reverberations. There would be here," he thought, "fatal sin, inexpugnable, wide-ranging and irremediable; and possibly war."

———

The minister survived the last step emerging out into Angel Air where the hosts were completing Worship Services.

In the pulpit, Lucifer was mesmerizing. He was magnificent. There was no denying that. His arms were outstretched in flowing robes as he told the angels to rise up in praise of Lord. They all took their wings and made them rise above their heads and move slowly up and down in a rhythm with his words, "Lord is good. Lord is great. Lord is on high." The minister Raphael could see how Lilith could be bewitched by him-everyone was. His heart went out to her.

He swept by angels and Cherubs, certain that his mission would not end to the good.

He found Lilith in her apartments red-eyed from crying, eyes which grew wide at his entrance, guessing, he guessed, why he had come. She crossed her arms around her stomach instinctively, he guessed, as a protective move. She was clearly pregnant.

He said "Lord demands your presence."

She nodded. "I understand." she said.

She roused herself robotically and prepared to leave. Even sad and crying, Raphael marveled--she was a beautiful woman. She was the most beautiful woman in the Universe. How could any not love her?

Chapter 2

Lilth's trek to Lord's spire was seen by thousands who looked upon her and looked away, fearing to look at her—least that act be noticed by those who could then report she had been looked upon favorably—and then, make this known to Lord, where interpretations could be made that, in looking at her, their loyalty could be questioned.

Lilith moved slowly thinking it was true; she owed much to Lord. He had given her beauty above all others, had elevated her above all others and made her his wife, making her immortal and almost his equal.

She knew his wrath would be severe. It would mean her reduction from her elevation—an elevation many had previously thought undeserved from the first instance. He would punish Lucifer as well. And she wondered about the child. What of the child?

Lord, at Lucifer's installation as Minister of the Universal Service, praised him mightily.

"I am, today, appointing Lucifer, whom I have favored to be Leader of Worship in the entire Universe. I have granted him the gifts, of beauty and grace. I have given him the power to inspire and the greatest gift of all—immortality."

"I have placed him on this high ground because he has found favor with me. He will lead you in the Celestial Rites, in the Universal Sacraments and, mind you, these are no mere routines. Without this inducement of my Spirit in the service all becomes dull ritual and does not cleanse the soul; and uncleanness, we see the contamination of the Spirit and some will fall--fail to make the Holy stance and become shadows whose dull lights, bring the dark, and bring to many, even angels among us, to the fall. Lucifer, I now name you 'Morning Light'."

"Here me now, Cherubim, elevate your dreams and aspirations to levels which, by my hand, you Lucifer,

now possess. I give you him to imitate. Follow his example such that you might rise as well to the highest highs."

Lilith was hesitant because she remembered that Lord had broken the rule of Strict Equality in taking one among them, no two, Lucifer and her—raised them up for others to admire—but, in doing so, made them a target for envy.

She spoke out loud to herself rehearsing what she would say to Lord.

"My Lord, am I to convey in this my gratitude or my remorse, because in being high, I have only earned my own isolation; I sought to cling to the only other who understood my plight, Lucifer. We were attracted to one another, enveloped in praise of you, but drawing, also, remonstrance's from others. We were two children caught between shinning much for parents' sake only to earn the envy of all the siblings."

"You are wise, Lord," she thought to herself. "Surely you understand, indeed foresaw, this circumstance. Surely, Lord you knew we, your creations, would be attracted to one another in our mutual need. So, Lord how can it be that in this, I or we, must have all the sin; can you not share in this as well--because in creating us, these events progressed and were inevitable? Can you relieve and, perhaps even eschew, the sufferings which surely your wrath might bring?"

"Bring to your heart forgiveness in this Lord," she said out loud, "for surely that way lay the peace." Her step was livelier now buoyed by this new ready defense. She drew closer to Lord's chamber. Her new thoughts, to her, seemed to make her prospects more bearable and her heart gained strength feeling there might now commence a reconciliation, not a condemnation; a negotiation, not blame; an opportunity there for redemption—hers and Lucifer's. Things might be mended back to whole again-if she could make Lord understand.

She neared the chamber door, still thinking, "How could I not love him; it was fate set in motion by Lord himself."

She entered and Lord surveyed her deliberately with Raphael at his side. Lord's mood to Lilith was one of anger mixed with agitation.

He did not speak but stood merely looking at her. Then, slowly he drew his clothing aside and sat upon his throne. Raphael took his place beside him.

Finally, he spoke not looking at her. His light was so great Lilith could barely look at him.

"All my love was gathered in you, Lilith. I took you out from among the Cherubim and pronounced you to be on high, scarcely a whiff from my own status. I loved you with the deepest fire within me. No soul gave more, Lilith, than was given you. No heart pounded greater than this heart pounded for you."

Lord paused. The tension was almost unbearable. All of heaven seemed to hold its breath. "And now, word comes to me that this was not truly reciprocated by you. While accepting my gifts you secretly stomped upon them, besmirched them, indeed transported them to another, giving to him what I had given to you; twisting all that is precious, tainting it to something clandestine, dark and betrayal-ridden, pursued in the night as I lay sleeping!"

Lord paused.

"Tortured, I in these moments, bled for you Lilith, from these wounds inflicted. First my thoughts were to find fault within myself. I did an inventory of where my own shortcomings might lie. I wondered what I had done to facilitate this happenstance."

"I cannot Lord..." Lilith began but he stopped her with a raised hand.

"No, I will have my say, I need to have this pain, to make fully visible to you my wounded entrails; to make them visible for all to discern."

"Oath betrayed," he continued, "if that were not enough, there is to this even darker news. What can be
the shade darker than darkest night? What is worse than this?" Lord stood; his hands clasped together, a great sadness in his eyes, as he wept. He cried a wailing cry.

"A child, Lilith?" he asked? "Here adds a three-fold foment, a new offense which is dagger sharp in my heart. A child is spawned of this dreadful match-a child. A child, whose heart, whose lungs, whose very existence conjures in me forever, images of the coupling, the sexual seed. The very face of betrayal is now alive, inside you, coming into the world. A deeper cut is made on the wound; a new affront is made visible here. I see inside you the fatal scar which will not heal. I am clubbed to my knees."

Lord stood mute for a long moment.

"A child, Lilith, no doubt conceived in the love meant for me--a child whose very existence will be testimony to my cuckold!"

"Tell me of it," Lord said suddenly his eyes continuing to tear, "tell me though I might die from the hearing. Tell me that I might understand not only the act but, as well, the circumstance. Tell me that I might feel and see what was in those fair nights destined to be me with you, in our bed, destined to be my child, not his. Tell me straight away, I have the need to know even if every word will be a rapier to my soul."

Lilith hesitated.

"Tell me!" he commanded."

"Lord..." she began.

"I must know." Lord said slowly,

While she paced before him, Lilith began sputtering and said, "Lord he was too beautiful and I sought most times to avoid his eyes because to look at him was to take me too close to feelings I sought to throw over-board. I am sure he was the same. I had to go to Service, and like the others, I looked upon him, and to do so Lord was to fall. My eyes would, once fixed upon him, could not look away. I was transported. I floated. Even while seated, he drew me with his spirit and his words. He was your emissary Lord, and I, like the others, were filled with his praise of you, his words were spoken so beautifully. The combination was over-powering." She paused.

"Go on." Lord said.

"One day I walked at Sermon's end, meaning to return to my apartments, but suddenly he was there, by my side. I looked at him startled, looking back to the pulpit to see if he was still there, but, no, he was there beside me. I froze at his booming voice, that sublime presence."

"He said to me beautiful words, Lord. He said I want to touch you in your violets and blues and indigos, and, I know I should not. I long to be with you he said."

"I have had no other thought," he said, "I have watched you sleep, Lord at your side; I could not resist coming each night to be near and hear your heart beat."

"Was that you? I asked him, Lord."

He said, "Yes."

Lilith was quiet for a moment and bowed her head as she remembered that conversation. "I thought it was a dream, but I knew it was his face. It had been him. And I, too, could feel him upon me those nights. I could feel his caress down my spine, all the while laying there in bed with you Lord, yet he came to me again and again and lay with me irrespective."

—

153

"I asked him if was him in the dream and he said, 'It was me'."
Later I said to him, "Lucifer, do you not know that I have this baby within? Are you aware?"

He said, "I had guessed and I am of the view we both should go to Lord and say we are in love and have the subterfuge to an end."

"I cannot," I told him. "It would crash down all the heavens. No, we must take the time to think it through, as to the best way to surface the news; for we must fully understand the moment of all this and what can be the foreseeable consequence."

"I do see," Lucifer said. "I'll agree to a wait but no more than two days. I'll not have fear guide us in this; we have little to apologize for except love moved us to bad judgment."

"Indeed," Lilith said, "bad judgment-is all it is, and it happened in a dream."

"But events transpired to overcome that plan." Lilith said. "Lord, you found out it seems before the two days expired." She paused. "I now stand ready to confront what I have done and make what amends I can."

Lord looked at her and finally spoke, "Do you love him?"

Lilith did not speak.

"I said do you love him?"

Lilith said, as she looked into Lord's eyes and saw the pain therein, "Yes I do, Lord. I am helpless not to, he has my heart, my soul and try as I may to resist, I cannot expel him; now the child makes that doubly difficult. In this Lord, my will is powerless," she paused. "I am lost."

"So you are lost, you say? But Lilith," Lord said leaning toward her, "I have given you and he the will to resist. Yet you say to me that my gift to you does not exist? Surely you know that your helpless claim cannot subsist in a loss of will? You have been given that from me forever. Give me another explanation for that one does not ring true. I am your Lord, responsible for your very being. No one knows better than I, your tendencies and capabilities."

"There is more to this, I suspect," Lord said smoldering "than that which you have thus far given me."

He leaned close to her face again. Lilith blanched, fearing Lord's explosive temperament.

———

154

"What more, Sire, can I cite? I am honest with me as I can. He seems to me not resistible and him, me. What is this "more" of which you speak?"

Lord spoke slowly, each word measured. "I am of the suspicion that you have not run to him, but rather, away from me. I am of the suspicion that you enjoy the pleasures of pride as much as that of love; but the final end is that you and he covet not only Love's Sweets but perhaps more; an entire kingdom, which has now a potential heir within your loins."
Lord paused and then continued, "Star-crossed lovers merit reprieve but none, I say to you, will be forthcoming for rebels and revolutionaries. Here before me plain to see is not only the seed of suspicion but the seed of a new dynasty, one which clearly, is designed to replace me."
Lilith, dumb-founded, could not speak.
"Leave me now, I will ponder these thoughts in my private, and see where they lead. I need now to think of larger things."

Chapter 3

Lilith went to Lucifer and he gave his thoughts.
"That did not go well, I see. He gained details and the details changed his whole view. We are no longer star-crossed lovers but pretenders to his throne. Lord will now eschew thoughts of forgiveness and treat us as rebels. You and I, and the baby, are the greatest possible threat, and, he will act swiftly as he must, because to linger would be, in his mind, disastrous."
"We must act. We must gather the Cherubim whom we can trust and plan for what surely will be an attack. You and the child must be given over to a safe place for the goal in all of this, from Lord's view, will be to take the child from you."
"Take the child?" Lilith asked, "What do you mean?"
Lucifer looked at her sadly. "I mean that he will likely not want to see the child survive."
Lilith touched her stomach aghast. "You mean kill the child?"
"I fear," Lucifer said simply, "or least we must be aware that he, or one of his minions, might attempt to do so. So your sequestration is critical in this. You must not be taken at all costs."
"Now," Lucifer said "let's go off to the garden spot and speak with those who might cast their lot with us, who understand the gravity of what we have before us."

Lucifer and Lilith moved under cover of veil and scarf after having sent word to key Cherubim leaders that they should meet on a matter of critical urgency.

In a flice, Lucifer stood before the small group of fifteen, "As many of you know Lilith and I have a situation. We fell in love, we were unable to turn our heads from one another, and that love, I am reporting here, was consummated and Lilith is with child."

There was a hush and then an audible gasp from the group, "With child?"

"My!"

"Lord will be furious, does he know?"

"He knows," Lucifer said. "Lilith told him hours ago and he has taken a different view. He does not view this as an affair of the heart. He believes that it is a part of a plot, a plot to over-thrown him and that it is his kingdom we want—to supplant him and place ourselves on the throne with our child as heir. Lilith is persuaded that he will not relent in this view. This presents, Lucifer said, "ultimate danger not only to us, but as well, to all of you."

"To us?" one in the group cried, "Why us?"

"I have not told Lilith this until now, but I have gotten word that he now regards all of you, and any those associated with us, as suspect and his plan is to smite one and all and your families as well."

Lucifer paused as his words sank it. "I am sorry to have brought this onto your shoulders. But, I don't know what to do. My first thought is to sequester Lilith and the child to safety somewhere, but beyond that, I also hear that Lord is ordering his closest guards to arms and plans to demand that all the Cherubim proclaim their loyalties to him, or to Lilith and me. He is not allowing any middle ground or time to ponder. Those that hesitate at the question will be killed."

Another in the back of the group spoke. "It's true, my wife has been summoned. I did not know what it was about."

"And mine too," another said.

"My son," said another.

There was the slow track of recognition as they all realized that some among them had been targeted and family members had already been summoned.

Lucifer said, "I am not asking you to make decisions now, but time is running in my view. We must summon those of you who plan to join us, combine all our powers and take up arms to protect ourselves. Lilith and I have the powers of Heaven with us, and, if necessary, we can defend ourselves against Lord's hosts and defend others as well."

That said, the night-shade came and all departed agreeing to meet in the early morning and report what responses there might be or rumors.

Lucifer and Lilith lay that night to contemplate how future events might transpire and what fate might fetch for their unborn child.

Lilith said in that quiet time, "I am for you in this, but I fear for the child."

Lucifer responded, "I will not back-step one wit for, if this is what we must do to preserve the child, then, so be it. If we must take up arms and provide the defense, so be it. If war it must be, then war it shall be, because there is no higher cause than that of defending those you love."

Lilith offered, "But are we right in this Lucifer, will the end be peace or destruction, and, if the latter, who then the winner? What if it is only a desolated world our baby seed will inherit?"

"I am not sure of what lies beyond these words we utter in the dead of night," Lucifer said, "the future is often shaded. But, if I take this single candle, if it will be all I have-the only beacon against this night- then, this small illumine will have to suffice."

Chapter 4

Before morning the reassembled group went to the garden to count the ones who would take up arms with Lilith and Lucifer, and, to retake from Lord their missing family members. Word had spread that hundreds were gone, taken by Lord who had chosen the women and the young, apparently thinking that they would more easily reveal intelligence as to who the plotters were.

There was anger in this Cherubim group at this—many had brought their thunder sticks, fire bolts and spears clambering in the meeting to storm Lord's castle and take back their kin; to declare that a new kingdom be proclaimed where Lord would be taken down, forced to reform and recognize the rights of Cherubim.

Lucifer stood before them and stated that a plan such as that "would only decimate our meager ranks. Rather," he said, "no, we have not the strength for a frontal assault. We must wait to gather strength and add numbers to our ranks and choose a spot and way of our own choosing for the assault. Gather now our brethren in this; come to, by morn, the high spot near the pulpit such that we can speak again and plan."

With that, and murmuring, the group dispersed and Lucifer looked at Lilith saying "You know what this means—he'll know we are gathering, he probably has already been told by someone from this very group; and headlong now we all rush to warring; all creation bates it's breath as to what will be this outcome."

"I agree," Lilith said simply.

The presence of arms in the ranks that next day underwent inspection by Lucifer who had to gauge what strength lay among his battalions. He had a battalion of higher angels and a battalion of arch-angels, Cherubim, Ranklings, Soarlings and others who stood before Lucifer and Lilith, eyes open, some bulging, all showing fear—the fear of the unknown, of rebellion, death and mayhem, of going up against Lord.

"None know," Lucifer said, "and I can not tell you the outcome, other than we must fight and get our families back."

Gathered then as one, they mustered to the planning of the initial battle scene which was to attack the arsenals, where the sun-bursts lay, deadly weapons, which could spew deadly radiation across whole galaxies. Several of these could take the battle to Lords' forces but only Lilith and Lucifer and Lord could trigger these weapons so great a force was needed to set them off.

Lucifer said, "We must first take them from Lord's arsenal because deprived of that explosive force might force Lord to early negotiate and spare us all a fiery death."

Lord gained word of Lucifer and Lilt's plan confirming his worse suspicions and this sealed the antagonism and hardened his heart. He told his ranks, "All the rebels must be killed." The word went out among Lord's battalions that all the rebels must be killed, and the cataclysm exponentiated.

"I will show all who rebel against the kingdom, the ingrates who conspire, that vengeance is mine and that my righteous wrath is great." He spoke to his assembled hosts charging them with battle plans, the first of which was to protect and guard the sun-bursts sequestered in the arsenal.

And, so it was, too, that Lucifer's hosts—banners waving--rode, in war's fever, pushing back both fear and common sense, supplanting them with glory dreams and ideologies- promising promises. The red robes of Lucifer's sermon garb became the flags of the battalions, some others yellow stripes; some merged these to give the assemblage color and inspiration.

They marched to music made by members of the heavenly choir; they were singing inspirational songs
offering encouragement and said, "Think of your families and your children."

Lord's wards, two-thirds to Lucifer's one third, felt confident of their numerical superiority. Raphael said "At best, this "war" will be over in a day."

Their mood was uplifted since Lord rode with them at the head in full view of all the hosts. Lord had his chariot and stomping steeds that mounted the arsenal hill standing there snorting magnificently. Lord fingered their reins.

He spoke aside to his general who said "Their numbers are puny most Lord; we shall no have difficulty in running them through. We only await your word in this and we will down upon them and they will run Lord, they will not resist. Tell us now when to bolt and we will all be home by tomorrow."

Lord peered down among them seeking Lucifer, finding him sitting a winged horse seemingly calm. The general said from his own look "he seems confident Lord--almost complacent."

"Let's then," Lord said, "offer him, in this, some discouragement."

With that and a wave of his hand the general sent the signal down the ranks to drive a wedge with the chariots to break through the middle line of Lucifer's infantry, which, the General thought, would fold rather than hold, and once split, the general would take advantage of his superior numbers, would take down Lucifer's divided troops in small groups.

The down-hill race had begun with Lord's charioteers plunging into Lucifer's ranks in the middle and, immediately, the center of Lucifer's infantry line broke retreating allowing Lord's charioteers to enter at the center. But five ranks in, to Lord's astonishment, Lucifer swept down with his own charioteers on the flanks and had Lord's charioteers surrounded on all three sides; a trap Lucifer devised, had been sprung. Every horse was speared and wounded, went down, as chariots, charioteers and horses from Lord's ranks floundered on the ground.

The chariot men—not used infantry combat—were no match for Lucifer's infantry forces now reinforced with even more infantrymen. Meanwhile, Lucifer dispatched more infantry from the rear to prevent Lord's charioteers from being reinforced while Lord looked on as his finest fought bravely but finally succumbed.

The shrieking of men, horses baying, lives ebbing, banners down, some limply waving, painted the scene where heaven's hosts took the look of a red hell, of red blood flowing.

There were some who stumbled blinded by lance or spear, by blood from head wounds; some wandered, mumbling incoherently. All in the gathering dusk faded from view underneath the gloaming.

Later, Lord sat in his Council of State; his ministers were glum and sour. Lord said, "This Lucifer has the faculties given him by me. I shall not again underestimate his use of these. Make me now a single plan to prevent the sun-bursts from falling into his hands. We meet here again in

---

an hour to see what you have contrived and, mind you gentlemen, failure this time is not an option. If we visit defeat again, I will spell for each and every one a consequence which will not be liked."

The next day Lord's Angel Hosts assembled at the launching point and Lord surveyed their ranks and spoke, "I have given you the high assignment to protect our people down below as they seek to secure the sun-burst beams. Your job is to swoop low, drop your maiming hooks and swoop up again to cause mayhem in their ranks and then release the Swooping Prey back down among them as human bombs." Lord raised his hand and said, "Fail me not. Fail me not."

The Angel Hosts flew high, each carrying a Prey, a tiny demon cherub, who would swoop down aiming
toward the eyes of the enemy, thereby blinding them.
As thousands of Angels lofted, surveying the field, seeking Lucifer's hosts and spotting them, made Lord to know they were in place, awaiting his word to attack.

Meanwhile, Lucifer muttered to himself that "This is not a good development." This was a surprise because Lucifer had no aerial counterpart to challenge the Angel squads of Lord. He murmured to his general, "Do we have anything to counter this, we are exposed to attack from above and must need, therefore, to hunker down and take the blows?"

The general was glum and only said, "We have nothing, Lucifer, and must pray the damage is minimal."

Lucifer's forces arrayed themselves on the ground and moved to close positions, one to the other, each spreading his shield or wing to cover one another against the diving demons, who sought to split the seam between the covering wings and shields and find the eye of its holder.

The battle started. Immediately there were screams as the demons smashed irises and blood spurted from the unlucky targets; Lucifer, despondent, saw his ranks waver and his hosts break and run, fleeing. He knew he would likely face the wrath Lord would muster for he was, indeed, a vengeful Lord.

But from the air came a trumpet sound and looking up Lucifer could see Lilith at the head of new hosts who came rushing in on a tremendous cloud, around her thousands of her personal hosts and Cheribums, who she had been busy in recruitment. This sight for Lucifer was a welcome one. Lilith flying above was the picture of a fierce woman warrior crashing down upon Lord's angel hosts and cherub demons—her angels counter-attacking, spewing cloud-gasses which enveloped the Prey, blinded them.

Eyes aflame from the cloud-gas, the demons shrieked and sank to the ground there crushed by shield, sword and lance.

Other hosts fell from the sky as Lilt's hosts shot cloud-darts which, just head-size, enveloped shoulders and face, and then the scream, as the demon hosts clasped both hands to face, cried for Lord, and began the deadly plummet to surface ground where, amid gathering shields, Lucifer's hosts again swarmed over them.

Once grounded, the fate of Lord's flying demons was sealed. Demon Prey were up-tossed from the mayhem; severed Angel limbs and angel parts lay aground; de-feathered wings and screams, bloody hearts lay strewn all upon the battlefield, signaling a rout.

Silence then; deafening, as both groups paused to intake the final scene where Lilith floating just above the ground, her hosts all around, saw shock on the faces of Lord's hosts, dismayed at the outcome before them.

But Lucifer looked to his recruits; thousands were blind meandering, crying out, and asking for comforting. The battle was won but at great cost.

The battle was won to Lilt's credit but, it also entailed many losses to Lucifer's minions. No new battle could be waged soon by them. Lucifer took his place beside Lilith surveying Lord's form on the far hill. He stood still and then turned away. Lucifer knew there would be another battle line drawn and that one would have a different outcome.

He and Lilith embraced as the hosts cheered. She took his face into her hands, planting a kiss. Lucifer said "I understand this is one battle and many more will have to be before we can declare victory. But know in all of this I stand with you for all eternity, for we have been given the gift of immortality, and shall live together for best or ill, for all time. I pledge here now my hearth and kin to stand with you now and to the very end."

Lucifer cried softly holding her, feeling that seed within her, and said, "All my effort and purpose is growing inside you and my equal pledge is to love and honor you. We have this mold cast, have set ourselves upon this path; have by this primordial scene fixed our future. We cannot go back, or mollify what destiny has
planned for us. If this then is the primordial fork, then let it be that we shall play out our part, not retreat or soft wield our deep felt commitments and sentiments."

The hosts rose in one voice "Hosanna, Hosanna," they all voiced as one.

"We now bury our dead," Lucifer said, "and pray them on to peace and prepare ourselves for the next onslaught."

Lord, too, made vows of his future intent. "It was she," he said to his lieutenant, "turned the battle with her treachery, it was she who came to manifest how far she has gone into treasonous treason; it was she who wielded the spear which pierced my heart on that battlefield; it was she who rallied my enemies, turned my Angels against me and clambered down to destroy the loyal angels."

"I shall mark this day the beginning of time when fatal sin came to this kingdom. I shall this day mark the forked road--one fork leading to my kingdom—the other to sin and treachery. Here a new history begins and I shall judge all by these new standards. In this new era, all is will and no will, chose or eschew, chose which road beckons you. Mercy shall not visit those who diverge from the righteous path; rather, blood shall be their destiny and I shall visit upon them a terrible judgment and cast them into fiery hells where they shall burn forever."

Here, Lord. issued the first decree, for in the kingdom, previously, there had never been treason and hence no need for decrees. But, here now, was a new era beginning and all knew Lord's new terrible wrath now commenced and new decrees would be placed upon them. Loyalty and obedience to the word was now the primary order.

That night in his Throne Room, Lord sat his head awry—in his mind recasting the day's events, reliving the horrible sights he had seen from his hill-top perch; mindful, so mindful, that he must prevail next time or lose all he possessed.

"But how best to defeat them," he mused aloud as he thrust himself up from the throne and began to pace, "to accomplish that task? Am I to don the warrior-cloak while still grieving grievous loss? How can my mind clear if my heart chokes off in my chest? What is my prize of gold or kingdom if my soul dies quietly in the infirmary pierced asunder?"

"Even now I have her face before me: Lilith," he said, "how could you abandon me? How could you not love me for all I am is in you? I gave you immortality so that I could always be with you. I feasted in my heart of hearts each moment near you. Betrayal is crime true, but the greater loss is not to be able to be near you; the former is mere effrontery, the latter is murder most supreme—mine."

"This is murder which does not allow death, the death without the dying, an eternal damnation, a carving out of my being— from all existence—until I stand here now a hollow hulk, speaking, breathing, talking, commanding, but my essence has been exorcised. And that, as all

---

can surmise, is true murder done without the dying." Pausing, Lord said, "These two shall, in due time, clamor down to the gates of hell begging to be let in, once my wrath is upon them."

At light Lord woke amassing his resolve, conjuring the plan for the day's assault knowing his scheme, if executed well, would crush the rebellion and rebels; all would be thrown down the Pit of Wells to fiery hell, to their final end. He would start again with new, loyal, hosts, with a new ethos and would again grant kindness without regard or thought to its consequence. He had made Lilith and Lucifer powerful, close to himself in their majesty, and now he faced them combined against him. He would not make that mistake again.

He spoke to his assembled hosts, "We, today, will cast off yesterday and face this new sunrise and, I say to you, I guarantee that this day all, unto the last one of them, shall fall; that the last unto the last of them shall drop their treacherous shields, flee, or be destroyed; that one and all of them shall break before my judgment, be captured and thrown down the Pit; that each and every one of them shall recompense the heavenly balance sheet."

A roar went up among them and Lord sensed a refreshment of their faith and resolve. "Now mark these times," he said "newly minted, for all creation is now re-born, a new time not so innocent, is upon us, one which has been marked by this stain—a stain which must be expunged, a debt to be paid."

Another roar echoed and each rank made its bow pledging to Lord a victory for one and all.

The field where the battle was to begin was on a softly rolling plain with seven rising hills, where each detachment could rise to the fight, but, before hand, each battalion was hidden from each other behind a hill's crest. It made surprise easier for both sides but more difficult to see how the battle progressed since, in this scene, there were many skirmishes but no one single, large, battle scene. It was terrain made for tactics and maneuvers, not massed pitched battles.

Lucifer surveyed it all, Lilith as his side. She said, "This is not the ground I would have chosen because my aerials cannot hit the mass, but must swoop down upon fragmented groupings, thus, losing the element of efficiency. This day will then be long and nothing can be counted as done until all the small battles have been counted, and even then re-massing will be difficult meaning we shall not know for a time who or what has won."

"My fear," Lilith said, "is that we might win most skirmishes and still will not have won the battle. They outnumber us two to one and we cannot lose more hosts than they or we are done."

And a gargantuan battle it was. A thousand, thousand, hosts descended among the seven hills and many ranks were, therefore, invisible and commanders could not coordinate as they would wish since there was no line of sight view of the battlefield.

Lord rode the between the hills and the valleys offering encouragement. Lucifer and Lilith flew above relaying commands from ravine to valley.

There arose a first volley from Lords' hosts upon the central hill as their hosts sought to mount the top of a hill held by Lilt's forces. These were met with an aerial bombardment from Lilt's hosts and a push toward the top, as well, from Lucifer's infantrymen. Backing down, Lord's ranks shrank, pushed back into the valley below with Lucifer's minions in hot pursuit. But Lucifer miscalculated in allowing that pursuit because he could see Lord had planned to have his infantry descend into the valley with hosts he deployed from behind yet another hill. These combined to surround Lucifer's forces. Lucifer's hosts pursuing were now the pursued. There were cries of anguish as the plan hatched and Lucifer saw the loss of an entire battalion, now being decimated rank after rank, outnumbered three to one and they soon fell beneath Lord's forces of purple and green.

Lucifer said to Lilith as they watched; "We see our dream die here at arms and we are helpless. We must choose between hope and clear futility; do we fight on or spare lives and take what fate awaits us before Lord's Throne?"

Lilith spoke quietly, "Not as yet. I'll have my aerials launch another drop to see if mayhem can cause the scatter and help us yet re-coop what our eyes reveal below as sure disaster."

Lilt's forces flew high, their cloud-gasses shooting out, enveloping, but, this was of small consequence since Lord's forces and those of Lucifer were in such close proximity—the cloud-gas had to be sparsely used—least Lucifer's infantrymen be felled along with those Lord had fielded. A drag of time later it became clear that none and nothing would appear to save this battle or to save this day.

Lucifer raised his hand to halt the proceedings, telling all his hosts to cease in resisting and he took Lilith by the hand to begin a slow march through the ranks aimed toward Lord's position on the high hill; each face in the angel hosts looked up to gain sight of what they all understood was the march of surrender, the final battle act, the end of the rebellion.

Slow march and longest time, Lucifer and Lilith then stood before Lord, his mount stomping ground, his eyes piercing down—his judgment ready, his wrath unsheathed, his words coming clear, addressing one and all.

"These two," he began, "were given my greatest fruits, all the gifts I had to give, all the love I possessed and yet, they saw fit to betray me, in my own bed, in my own house and still yet harbor the spawn-seed of that awful union."

"You shall be," he said to Lilith and Lucifer," seated before me and I shall pass judgment upon you befitting the crimes of which you are guilty."

Chapter 5

It was before the assembled hosts that Lord summoned the two to hear sentence passed against them and for them to receive from the parchment read, their fates and transmogrifications.

All hush came upon the group as each stood at Lord's command whereupon he began to read from his rolled up scroll. "I have given each of you the gift of immortality, and mark while this I cannot revoke—this gift is irrevocable--but note, beauty is one gift which is redeemable and I, herewith," he said, raising he sword high so that all could see lowered it over Lucifer's head spoke, "revoke from you the beauty I gave and give you the appearance of the animal of the field with cloven hooves. I place upon you the face of the goat and horns to mark your treachery." Sudden, it was that Lucifer had cloven hooves, and horns on his head, that his whole body was crimson red. A gasp went up from all the hosts.

Lord continued, "You shall have the pitch-fork tail, signal of the forked tongue used to deceive and all shall know you by these presentments and you shall be so named for all eternity, and more, all your hosts and Cheribums shall be as gargoyles—hideous—and they shall cleave with you in this punishment."

165

Lucifer stood now the image of a redden goat; ugly now, with his beauty gone, evaporated.

Lucifer spoke, his mouth was smaller now, but, he still had his eloquence, "You, Lord, have pronounced, and I have received, your judgment and punishments for a crime that has no precedence. I accept your pronouncements but ask Lord that you contemplate that when love given and received is put down viciously, without a shimmer of forgiveness or understanding, when this simple relationship is judged wanting and deemed a threat to kingdoms, what then is the true meaning there? How balanced is this judgment against Lord's own values and sentiments?" How can Love be a crime? Especially since we, Lilith and I, were by your own creation, fated to be attracted one to the other? Should not you Lord forgive and understand that you might have had a hand in the whole scheme?"

Visibly angered, Lord leaned down from his throne-perch and fully-faced Lucifer's new countenance and said "Your sentence is pronounced and you shall be cast down the Pit. You ask if your punishment is just. I answer you that to escape these deeds with your life intact is, in fact, mercy, more mercy that the angels you led received, which now all around us, lay dead. They have not life or limbs whist you walk about full-bodied, uglier true, but full-limbed. Nay, you have mercy."

He turned then to Lilith and spoke close to her face, his tone softening.

"I gave you my all; nothing retained, and allowed all to flow away from my heart to you. I did not anticipate that my reward would be menstrual blood in my own bed and another's embrace round you and conception too, in that very same space. How could you?"

Lord's lament was monstrously sad so great its depth.
"How could you." he said again?"
He paused, "I," he said raising his sword again, "strip from you my beauty gift and make of you a snake to crawl upon your belly henceforth."
And Lilith was, in the instant, a serpent upon the floor.
Lord peered down, gazing upon her lowly form.
"I raise by this kingdom's highest heights this further judgment upon you. So, as the seed you carry is evil sent, I smite it from your belly and thereby prevent its birth in this world and, too, make it such you will forever in your womb be barren."
The hosts gasped as Lilith, even as serpent on the ground had a small bump, which in Lord's pronouncement was gone and dispensed of. Her cry, even with serpent lips was audible in the midst of the hush now over the assembled hosts.

Lord thrust his sword even higher and said "I condemn you and your hosts to the Pit where you will be thrust down its fiery depths. I hereby condemn you, Lucifer and you Lilith, to spend your hideous immortalities on Earth."

Chapter 6

The Earth in that time newly forming was a place of exploding volcanoes, fierce lava flows and it was formless and lifeless. Meteorites and asteroids rained down daily in terrifying numbers, creating huge sulphur and methane gas clouds.

Lord's pronouncement had been carried out instantly and Lucifer and Lilith found themselves on a fiery crag where the heat was unbearable; where their bodies burned with red hot heat, with white fire and a blue blaze but, being immortal there was no relief for their torment. In that instant Lucifer said "we must get away from this Hell and find some place for shelter."

As he spoke, he heard Lord's voice was booming, "And I banish all the hosts who cleaved to them to Hell as well."

All around Lilith and Lucifer could see angels now made into demons descend to be with them exiled by Lord. Thousands arrived, each a gargoyle, no longer the beautiful angels they once were, all cowered and astonished to be in such a place but happy to see Lilith and Lucifer. Many took heart that at least all would be together in the place.

Under fire with brimstone hurtling from the sky Lilith was able to with a great effort take herself from the serpents form temporarily said, "I am able to resume my old form for only brief moments so let me speak while I can." She looked out over the many thousands there--many injured, most frightened--and offered them hope for the future.

"We are in this Hell; true, but some of our strength still remains. Lucifer and I can change our forms, but only for small intervals, so I appear before you in woman form in order to speak with you and to let you know we shall not lose heart despite this circumstance. Place your faith in our resources, even as I know many of you now suffer, sharing a fate which comes from having given us your support. Know you well that we shall survive this and rise again and deny the fate decreed us from Lord. We shall go down this crag and found a new dynasty below. Lord has banned us but he was not able to take from us all our powers. Lucifer and I have many powers left we shall build anew here. Join us."

Lucifer said, "Bear the pain as you will; I see below cooler valleys and we must gather ourselves and clamor down to the valley floor where we can begin to structure a new life."

It was a horrific descent where hot lava and steam burned many horribly step by step. There were cries and pleas of mercy to Lord even as they moved slowly down, passing burning boulders, fiery heaps, steam gardens and pyres. Lucifer could hear cries in his ears-some of the hosts asking for mercy, asking Lord to forgive, but these cries were not heard by Lord. There was only silence from above and in a crevice made of molten sulfur they all sat, to rest before the final descent to the valley below where Lucifer had promised accommodations would be more bearable. Lilith looked at the faces and whispered to Lucifer, "It is clear that, naturally, some among us regret this turn of events and will likely seek redemption from Lord's decree and that will likely be rejected, thus, then, dear one, they will likely turn on us as the progenitors of their now unbearable torment. We, too, shall see," Lilith said, "rebelling rebels and revolutionaries in short order. For that we must have a plan and not be caught by surprise and, thus, suffer more in this horrid place—from a wedding of the specters of Hell and the specters of Politics."

"I agree," Lucifer said, "this is foreseeable."

They arrived at the valley floor to survey the landscape for shelter points and Lucifer pointed across the crevasse to a high cliff which appeared to have caves embedded midway above the valley floor.

"There," he said, "we can find a cooler spot away from this murderous inferno and sit to speak of our plight and our sojourn here."

They all agreed and began the trek up the cliff wall to the cave Lucifer had identified, sore and injured many of them, dispirited were some of them, resentful were others. Lucifer could see the frustration and confusion mix that inhabited them and knew that some of this would spill out and contaminate the new life he and Lilith were planning to build. His thought was to confront the riffs before they became disastrous and thereby cripple the whole enterprise.

That night in counsel, in the cave where they had gathered, he spoke of these issues and more.

"I know some feel our fate here is hell itself and that Lilith and I led, therefore, must take blame for urging you to rebel and now this, 'unbearable eternity.' I see this view. I understand. I understand that some would want to make a plea to Lord to take you back, to forgive and, thereby, relieve this suffering; ask forgiveness for the blasphemy. If that is the wish of some of you I would hear you on this. Stand and let yourselves

---

be seen; how many are of this view? I, myself will help, in this, to see if Lord will recant and punish Lilith and I, but relent among you innocents and take you back. Let me see by standing up, how many are of this view?"

The pause of thought ran threw all of them as they sought to see and feel where their own inclinations lay, and, at some long pause-point, several hundred of the thousands there stood up.

"I see some have declared." Lilith said. "Here, then, is the plan. Choose among you delegates and then prepare to present to Lord your best case. We will then communicate on high and see if Lord will repent. It is a course to try; it is a cause of worth. Let us sleep this night and tomorrow make the attempt to communicate to Lord your desires and see what transpires."

All nodded to Lilt's plan and began to make arrangements for sleep. As they busied themselves
arranging the space Lucifer spoke to them soothingly, "We will on the morrow make a permanent shelter from raining rocks, create a space inside this cave where we can all live normal lives, sheltered. We must plan in our exile to make a new city in this Earth."

The next day the delegation for Lord's review assembled in front of all the hosts and called Lord's name.

"Oh, Lord," the delegation leader said, "we are here, some of us, beseeching you, asking your forgiveness—to take us back, take us away from this dreadful place, to return to your kingdom, give us your salvation."

There was a silent pause and no response came and the group hesitated and started to disperse when that familiar voice, that booming thunder-box of Lord's occurred.

"I hear you; I understand your words and your anguish, and your pleas for redemption at my hand. This makes my mind tend toward salvation for the truly repentant. Here this, I make no promises here, but I will hear from all who want to come to sit with me and make individual personal pleas. Ready yourselves all who would come and I will transport the lot all at once."

The group of several hundred looked at one another understanding Lord would hear them out and in a flash all hundred were gone, taken from where they stood, by Lord for counsel with him.

Astonished, the remaining hosts looked at one another and finally turned their gaze to Lucifer and Lilith who stood stock still mindful that a pardon from Lord for even a few might create an avalanche of those who would, too, ask for forgiveness, thereby abandoning Lucifer and Lilith to a lonelier still, haggard exile.

But Lord's voice instantly returned and was again back in the room; his pronouncement clear.

"I have smited your delegation each and every one."

There was a hush of disbelief spreading among them and a murmuring twanged with fear and loathing.

"How could you Lord?"

"Know this," Lord was saying, "my decree is one of suffering. You have all sinned against me and have, thereby, earned your punishments. There shall be no reprieves. You shall suffer from my command for all eternity. Let this be for you clarity; sin and punishment are not to be severed, but are welded together irretrievably."

There was stunned silence in the room at this.

Lilith spoke, "Lord I can see, especially in the case with me that such a betrayal, from your view, falling in love could warrant the hell you have bequeathed for Lucifer and I, but I am not able to see where such a harsh meting of punishments has been earned by those who merely followed their consciousness. I am of the view that mercy is not a sign of weakness but of strength yet, you by this, show no inclination for forgiveness and, thereby, in my eye reduce your presentation from on high down to lower motivations and pettiness."

All were stunned at Lilt's statement. There was no immediate response from Lord. But soon the cumulative effect of Lord's silence and Lilt's statement ignited among them a cumulative dread awaiting Lord's response to Lilt's speech.

It came.

"By the kingdom which is mine to rule, that the creature I created would affront me so and repay my gift with insolence, blasphemy, and such rejection pains me. Such salt on such wounds do not heal. Such deeds cannot be expunged. These are such dire acts, from which there can be no retraction. As deeds are done, so, too, are they punished, and, you all shall have to suffer yours; and from me know, there will be no, I say again, no reprieve."

"You ask, Lilith, that I make an exception for you and honor your love for Lucifer and stay the hand of punishment. Understand, in this, despite my love for you, I have not allowed in this an exception for myself, even though in my heart, I might sorely wish to…"

"This is done." Lord said with finality.

An awful silence fell. There was no sound or response. Everyone there knew matter had ended.

Lord's disembodied voice was now gone silent.

They all stood mute.

Lilith spoke and said "This is our new home.

―――

170

Title: The Bible as the Oldest Egalitarian Document in History

The bible, usually thought of in religious terms actually has far more dimensions other than the religious one. The bible in "Lilith," as well as in the NOVA special on these topics, makes the point that the document was written over hundreds of years, was and is, the attempt to institute a radically new kind of society, one which had been previously unknown in the world.

Conflict over the bible's religious aspects has obscured, its, perhaps, greatest contribution to Western thought--if not to world history-ideas revolving around egalitarianism, freedom, justice, moral righteousness, social organization and the place of hierarchies in human society.

I have argued above in the Blog "How to Write the Great American Novel" (see the Blog above) precisely these points and illustrated them in the "Lilith" novel.

We see that the ancient Israelites existed in Canaan for centuries as slaves, serfs and vassals of the Canaanite puppet rulers who, in turn, were ruled by Egyptian overlords. The Canaanite puppet rulers fell when Egypt was preoccupied with the Hittite and Assyrian wars, circa 1250 BC and their Canaanite underlings suddenly found themselves free, without overweening power directing their lives.

They set out with nothing less than the objective of creating an entirely new society to replace the oppressive ones they had known under Egyptian rule- a society which had a central premise and requirement-strict equality. The details and the archeological evidence are in the NOVA special (see links to that special above) and is the premise of my novel "The Gospel According to Lilith." Original sin, historically, and in the novel, is violation of the "Rule of Strict Equality"

The bible was written by these former slaves and vassals who undertook to implement this totally new societal concept-- one the opposite of life as they knew it under the Egyptian proxies. This new Canaan was to be free, egalitarian and morally upright; and interestingly, this new egalitarianism included women.

These ideas were by no means common at the time and it took the Canaanite-Israelites hundreds of years to work these ideas out and are part of the Israel's tortured history. However, note too, these themes were

happening simultaneously in other parts of the world driven by the break-down of the divine king system. (See points on this in "How to Write the Great American Novel" in the Blog.)

These critical ideas of these ancient Israelites, therefore, have been obscured but they can yet be seen to be at work all throughout western history to the present day. When the Founding Fathers sought to create a free society, free from English rule, they used the political ideas in the bible as a source of inspiration and guidance.

Let's take these threads from ancient Israel down the centuries to the Enlightenment and see how they have played out over the centuries and are familiar ideas to most of us.

The first idea that these ancient Israelites adopted was the notion of strict equality. The archaeology reveals that their buildings were configured in circular configurations where there were no grand palaces, no elaborate dwellings, or highly decorated pottery. Meals were likely communal and work was shared equally. These were deliberate tacks taken by a people who had seen that hierarchy, kings and Pharaoh-ruled societies brought tyranny. They wanted no part of that way of life, in which they were victims. They, in their society-building, went in the opposite direction.

Strict equality was to be the basis of the new Canaanite societies. The freed Canaanites were to be a new people, and they gradually over hundreds of years saw themselves as a new people-the Israelites. These very same values are seen to be at work in the bible and become the foundation of what the bible views as good and evil.

This strict equality, note, included women, and I think probably had many of the underlying ideas we find in the Essene faith and were likely reflected in the teachings of Jesus. The details of this faith are worth noting and are detailed in "Lilith" for those wanting more information in relation to Jesus specifically. (Note Essence connections are and were made more clear by the discovery of the Dead Sea Scrolls.)

So what is to be the nature of this new egalitarian, anti-authoritarian society? The ideas they developed can be illustrated in the following Essene prayer:

"Bless us, oh Lord, that we might be humble in all we do, each day;
May we not harm any creature, man, woman, child or animal;
May we seek Justice for all; may we seek not, nor participate in, the belittlement of any person or thing;
May we be given the strength to refrain from displaying superior prowess, mental or physical at the expense of no one;
May our very souls stay free of worldly gains and their pursuits.
May we never seek dominion over any man woman or child and we shall not seek or participate in any form of slavery, serfdom or the servitude of others.
May anger never cross our hearts and may we not indulge in unkind emotions.
May we seek moderation in all things and keep our silence among those outside the Brotherhood and speak softly.
We shall only participate in the peaceful trades, carpentry, planting, and merchants;
May we Lord relinquish all our worldly goods and gains to provide for the sick and the poor, the stranger and the downtrodden, for this is our mission in this world."

(This passage is from "Lilith.")

What is striking here is the radical egalitarian nature of their beliefs. Jesus , many believe, was an Essene and adhered to these views. (We are reminded of the Sermon on the Mount.) At the very least many of his preachings and ideas are consistent with Essene beliefs.

There is more to quote from "Lilith."

"None will be wealthy and none will be poor, and all shall work together in the gardens of the Brotherhood. Yet all shall follow his path, and all shall commune with his heart."

"Keep our faith and avoid the blood sacrifice because that is not the way of the Essenes. Do not eat the flesh of animals, thereby keeping your bodies clean. Spread God's new messages that love not curses in the loving God's true way."

Spread God's new message," Joseph continued "one which is one of blessings, not curses and destruction; one where you are called upon to love those that hate you--not war upon them. Blessed are the scribes and meek for they shall inherit the Earth."

"Spread God's message," Joseph said, "that the meek shall be received in heaven by way of the purity of their souls, not by wealth or power. Keep you to the path of the Messiah. Remind all that the soul immortal is salvation from the physical bondage of the sufferings of this Earth."

(The speaker here is Joseph, an Essene leader in the novel.)

Note also the scribes are to be included along with the meek in inheriting the Earth. These scribes wrote down the bible and were revered.

My argument is that these ideas were the ideas of the ancient Israelites and that Jesus, representing those earlier ideas, railed against the Jewish establishment of his time. He claimed the Jewish establishment had abandoned those earlier ideas and ideals. He sacked the temple because of blood sacrifices, the eating of meat, and the hierarchy of the Rabbi's etc. He correctly stated that he came to fulfill prophecy and to bring the Israelites back to Essene views. In the mind of Jesus, they had become like the Egyptian puppet rulers of the past. This was their real sin, and this was The Original Sin in the Essene view

"None will be wealthy and none will be poor, and all shall work together in the gardens of the Brotherhood."

This prayer of the Essenes makes the point around egalitarianism succinctly. The pursuit of wealth, power, was to be eliminated and in its place was a communal society of equals. Hierarchy was to be eliminated among the brotherhood and women were welcome. Seeking dominion over man, woman or child is to be avoided and slavery, serfdom and the servitude of others was expressly forbidden.

Now these are very radical ideas. Moreover, the early Israelites built their small towns and compounds with these ideas in mind. Of course, with the institutionalization of the Jewish religion later these points were lost in the larger society; but note they did not die among smaller groups in the society. The Essenes are the example here. Now the practical ability to maintain this radical equality beyond small groups is highlighted here, but, the fact remains the Essenes did so for hundreds of years and made the communal model of living a reality. Of course this life style has continued to the present day, mostly among monks and nuns.

Note, too, that many of the strictures of these early society-builders are personal. The believer is to speak softly, be humble, never display mental or physical prowess at the expense of others. Anger is not to be displayed and one is to speak quietly. These later become personal sins of pride, anger etc. They, in fact, along with greed become the seven deadly sins which later become part of the church lore.

Conduct in the world is also covered in these restrictions. One is not to participate overtly in civic life; there is to be no war against God's creatures, no animal sacrifices, no participation in human wars and a belief that the meek shall inherit the Earth. All worldly goods have to be surrendered upon joining the brotherhood and are to be distributed to the poor. Travelers are to be welcomed. The washing of feet of strangers maintains the notion of humility among them as well.

These are powerful themes but note that scribes, too, shall inherit the Earth. Scribes write down the holy words and thereby perpetuate the great ideas that these innovators sought to preserve. In fact, it was Jewish scribes, who, in essence, kept the faith alive in the Jewish Diasporas where the homeland and the temple were destroyed by invading hordes. Literacy, writing and scholarship, by implication, have religious overtones in the modern and ancient Jewish traditions.

The special place of scribes is evident here, but a critical follow-on point is the role of writing itself. Writing is wrapped up with a holy mission and that mission has not only has to do with the religious ideas but the social ideas as well. Writing things down is to preserve the very well-springs of society-building, something these early egalitarians sought to preserve and perpetuate via writing. The importance of the ideas of freedom, equality, and justice were inextricably woven into the religion but also the warp and woof of the fledgling Israelite nation. In my Blog "How to Write the Great American Novel" I make a similar point and argue that this sense of the mission of the writer has a place today. It is the duty of the writer, seeking to write for the ages, to keep the best ideas humanity has produced alive.

What happened, we might ask, in the case of the structure of religion in Israel by the time of Jesus? Things by that time had strayed from this early model and that is what motivates Jesus to many of his actions against the then Jewish establishment. His was a call to repent of their sinful ways--sins which went way beyond sins of the flesh to include the corruption of the social structure the early framers of the bible sought to establish.

It also explains the am bivalency Jesus displayed often not seeming to be able to make up his mind as to whether he came to deliver the Jews from Rome by armed rebellion or whether he was, in fact, a pacifist and was urging his follows to render unto Caesar the things which belonged to Caesar. (This is explored in Lilith)

Finally, a last point here is that these early ideas of the writers of the bible are present in both the old and the new testaments. A careful read reveals that the real sin of Lucifer was his advocacy of the life of hierarchy, power, wealth and city temptations which brought slavery, inequalities, serfdom and war. The most powerful messages in the bible, in my view, are its strictures and warnings against social structures which imprison men and women and are, in this biblical view, the true original sin. The simple life of equal brothers in the pastoral context was a consistent message from God in the old testament especially. This message changed in both the old and new testaments as God sought ways to blunt human-kinds apparent attractions to the sins of the city. But the life style argument was one Thomas Jefferson was to repeat centuries later in advocating for the citizen solider and small farmer as the best model for America.

This is also the message of "Lilith" as the novel takes us through biblical events denoting how this seminal struggle actually forms the underpinning of the true meanings being conveyed in both the old and the new testaments and the events they chronicle. They underpin the bibles basic notions of good and evil, their causes and manifestations.

The power of these ideas and the model they represent, while having their ups and downs in history, have nonetheless persevered, albeit changed in many respects, in their march to the present day.
Lets have a look at the list:
a. All men and women are equal as an ideal and goal before God and in society.

b. All people should govern themselves and societies ought to be democratic
c. Peacemakers, writers and scholars are and ought to be at the highest levels of society.
d. Nature is not the enemy; it and its creatures ought to be respected.
e. Slavery, serfdom and vassal relationships are morally wrong.

f. City life, as anonymous living, breeds wrong-doing and is not a sustainable model for living.
g. The soul is prepared for the afterlife by positive actions and personality traits, restraint, and respect for the feelings and inner life of others.
h. The nation-state is to be avoided if possible.
i. Worship is communal, not individual, like the pagans did it.

This is quite a list and we can compare it to the Roman values these ancient Israelite virtues overcame. The Roman model of the million-plus city, values of domination, cruelty, war, disrespect for the individual, slavery and serfdom, were ultimately overcome in the four hundred years after Christ. Of course, the downfall of the Empire was not only due to these Essene ideas but the latter were certainly prominent in Constantine's decision to recognize Christianity as the official religion of the Empire.

The journey of these notions thorough American life and literature is the subject of an upcoming book.

Ah, some of you have said in your emails, "none of this in the bible." Where do these ideas appear? So I cannot leave the topic at this point, nor in staying with it, can I go into great detail. (That will be in an upcoming book) But for now lets explore some of the themes I outline above and demonstrate them as underlying events and the actions of major players in the bible. Let's start with God.

1-God states he is a jealous god-jealous of other gods because indeed the ancient Canaanite world had many gods and the Israelites wanted the pagan Canaanites to give them up. One most prevalent, aside from Baal, was Asherah, a goddess I include in my novel. The creators of the bible had to compromise with their Canaanite prospective converts and allow that their new God was to have a wife, the pagan fertility god- Asherah. The archeological evidence here is irrefutable. Asherah became God's wife for hundreds of years in ancient Canaan. After establishing itself as the major religion, the Jewish fathers banned her worship and you can see many passages in the bible from genesis onward, hostile references to Asherah as pagan and association with her was deemed to be sinful. Asherah, in my novel becomes Lilith.

2-In the bible God is not infallible but makes decisions, changes his mind, cajoles, compromises and laments that he losing in the battle with the devil, whose city-life temptations tempt mankind and they, in God's view, abandon his strictures. God's word is being re-written to match the needs of particular time and compromises were made from the very beginning all the way to Paul who allowed Gentiles into the faith, but the seminal Essene ideas remain through out the document mixed with new revisions, giving the bible its sometimes confusing construction.

Now the bible, written by at least four different writers, and probably many more, stresses obedience to these strictures but we now can say why. Why is it so important to be obedient to God's commandments?

Here are a few instances of God's decision making process and the underlying rationales he used in the bible.
He created man and woman twice- the first time the woman (Lilith) was rebellious and presumably this was corrected with Eve. But free will was the underlying issue and the Tree of the Knowledge of Good and Evil was the critical decision made by Adam and Eve. Why was it so important not to have knowledge of good and evil and why was it represented by a tree? The pagan Goddess Asherahs symbol was a

pole or a tree. Adam and Eve were being forbidden symbolically to "know" or consort with pagan gods and goddesses.

But underlying that stricture was the deeper one of knowing good and evil is tied to the life style of the city, presumed to be evil and indeed the realm of the devil. (This is still held to be the case in modern day American ethos.) But even more importantly here God is saying that knowledge of things like metal, cosmetics, astronomy, magic, etc., was bad for mankind. Why? Because the Egyptian overlords had or practiced all those things, and moreover the acquisition or knowledge of those things led to war, slavery etc., and even more importantly, that life-style was unsustainable and liable to genocide and collapse in the long run. Better to stick to a small, sustainable life style of self-sufficiency. The biblical writers would say of our modern day life-style of progress-"Where has all this progress gotten you- war, grief and the potential destruction of the planet. Better not to have some much of this progress.

This is their view and it is a view which continues to this day among many groups. Finally, many of God's decisions in the old and new testament were made with these values in mind. Cain's gift was not acceptable because it was grain, produced with settled agriculture, a development the framers associated with Egypt and city-states. It was rejected in the bible early on.

The Tree of Knowledge of Good and Evil and the serpent are allusions to Asherah the major female goddess of fertility in the original Canaanite pantheon. Asherahs symbol was a tree and the serpent is a symbol of fertility in ancient times. This allegory is warning the new Israelites to avoid city life and not to listen or worship pagan gods.

All through the old testament from Enoch, Noah to Abraham, God rejects those who hanker after the things of the city, warns the Israelites and brings down upon them mayhem and destruction for not following the strictures. The devil is winning in the old testament. Man appears to choose, wine, women, wealth, city life, and power time and time again.

On a still deeper level the second generation biblical writers then inaugurate the prophets of doom who predict that nothing good will come of Mammon and straying from the values of the Essenes; of course in doing so, they added some pretty extreme new strictures and new threats and punishments to the mix giving the bible a bewildering array of rituals, requirements, observations, laws and commandments such that the document did not retain the consistent

———

message it started with. This involved constant tinkering in the form of the Midrash, commentaries and other "editorializations" on a more or less a continuous basis for hundreds of years.

The writers too, had another goal for the document: they had to put into it sufficient mythical content to attract the Canaanites from the old religion. It is not an easy thing to create an entirely new society whole-cloth. Moreover, as we have seen, the human element can turn even the most pure of beginnings into crass self-aggrandizements and that surely also happened with the evolution of the religious structures in Judah, long after the original framers had left the scene. All of this is the cauldron in which the biblical stew is stirred. We see calls to repent and calls to go back to the original roots and values and then followed by another cycle of falling away from those beginnings. It happens in most societies.

The task of myth-building alluded to above is something every new society, or nation-state has to accomplish. Here myth-building means stories every people tells its self which explains their origins, give explanations of the great issues in life and explains what is special or significant about their people. This involves, as well, hero-building, flags, and special social structures which will elaborate upon and evolve the myth-hero structure.

The founders in ancient Canaan had this exact same problem. So did, to take another example, the founders of the fledgling United States of America. The same processes are and were at work.

Lets look at some of the aspects of myth-building the ancient Israelites wove into their new society. Many of them, if not most, were clearly borrowed from Egyptian sources.

1. Monotheism was introduced into Egypt in 1336 BC by Akhenaton, Pharaoh of Egypt, a mere two or three hundred years before the bible society makers started their task. They were familiar with this idea, at the very least.

2. Yahweh is likely derivative from the Midian God named Yahoo who the early framers became familiar with from Canaanites having traveled through the region and they brought the new Yahweh back imitating what they had seen among the Midianites.

The NOVA special argues that Canaanite slaves returning from Egypt around the time of the fall of the Egyptian vassal states brought this

---

new concept of God to the newly liberated Canaanites and this became Yahweh. The story of Moses and a mass exodus becomes the mythical version of all this. The bible itself, NOVA notes, places Moses in Midian at the same time.

The import, I would argue, of all of these various biblical stories, and I can't go into all of them, is that these myths and hero-creation activities were designed to emphasize not only religious points but political and society precepts we see in the Essene canon above. Moses and the Exodus make him the hero of Freedom, something the Canaanites themselves were in the midst of enshrining.

Seen this way, many of the stories seek to buttress the new values which the framers sought to enshrine, not just religious points.

Now of course, these values become re-interpreted over time and freedom and its pursuits become compromised with the needs of the Jewish religious state and a Jewish nation-state which was at war often, and where defeat was devastating. How can one be a pacifist when the Babylonians, the Assyrians and the Romans burn the temple down, ransack the city, rape your women and children and sell them into slavery? How can Essene values survive in the midst of these realities?

Ah, but that is the story of the holy land, and for that matter many, many other societies.

A follow-on question here is how exactly do themes in American literature interface with those themes I have identified as having originated in the bible?

Let's us take a few themes in American literature and see what might be the nature of the interface.

American Literature themes have included:

1. Who is a hero in society and why

2. The meaning of Freedom, Justice and Equality

3. What is the role, place and rights of the individual in society vs. the government and authority?

4. The role of death, the meaning of life and after-life; religion and faith

5. The nature of human nature and the human condition

6. The nature and aims of community

7. Morality, Guilt Sin and Innocence

8. Friendship, Family and Love

9. Choices, Challenges and the definition of success in life

10. The Nature of the American Dream

We can quickly see that most of these themes are spoken to in the bible and answers are given to those great questions. We see that also that these themes are not strictly American at all, except for number 10. These are themes that most societies and society-builders confront. Who is to be hero in the society: The Romans choose the gladiator, solider, warrior who fought for personal glory a and the Roman state. The Greeks choose the warrior fighting for glory, and the "demos", itself civil society. The American hero has been military in nature and the self-made millionaire, mixed in with the citizen farmer. I have made the point that of all these notions the one most prevalent in early America was the latter, which closely resembles the hero we find in the bible. There the Essene brotherhood mistrusted authority and sought to withdraw from society. Jefferson mistrusted government and at one point recommended revolution every twenty years if necessary to keep authority responsible.

If we compare all of the above points we see that while the answers may vary, and at points even conflict, they reveal that society-builders have taken the questions of the nature of society and its relationships to the individual from the agenda set thousands of years ago in the bible; and society after society seeking to build itself has taken up those questions first written down in the ancient settings we have described.

Now I have also stated that this necessity to build societies from the bottom up and upon different premises was made necessary by simultaneous developments in much of the world at around this same time period, 1250 BC. The ancient Israelites were not the only ones confronted with the task. It was occurring in much of the known world at the time as many of the traditional divine king systems broke

---

down in the face of the development of large massed armies, replacing essentially small chariot based armies and palace guards. Feudal systems with fragmented warlords were no match for massed invading armies. Warfare had become big business, requiring huge investments of time and effort and there was the need for the cooperation of the masses. Classes developed, especially trading classes, which helped to fund these new massive wars. Kings had been shown to be ineffective in protecting the nation and the population lost faith in the Divine King system. The Gods and the King had failed them and now they demanded a role in the state, often as paid, or free men. It was a revolution in political systems and the Israelites are but one example.

The inclusion of classes and the masses has been a hall mark of developing civilizations ever since, despite periods like the middle ages when a serf and vassal systems made a re-appearance. So we see that the bible, as having set this process to writing actually is extremely important in understanding what is and what was involved.

This process and its confluence with religious issues has obscured the formers importance.

The context of American development has, of course, influenced how biblical themes played out on the ground. Each country has exactly this same process at work. Therefore, the history and circumstances of each country has influenced how these ideas were worked out concretely. But note today most countries of the world profess democratic values; even the most tyrannical of these nonetheless profess to being democrats. This is an example of the power of these ideas.

In the American context there were and are four contextual factors which have greatly influenced the themes we have argued came down from the ancient Israelites.

The first of these is that America was founded upon the ideals of freedom, liberty and justice-similar circumstances to those for our ancient example. However, an additional factor was at play. America was an isolated society, surrounded on both sides by an ocean and a huge, largely unexplored, land mass. Americans lived for over 200 years as a frontier society. A frontier society creates unique influences upon, for example, the notion of freedom.

What is and tends to be the notion of freedom in such societies, specifically in the American example? Freedom becomes the right of the individual to own property, to be mobile and not be tied to the land as a vassal; the right to accumulate wealth, and to assert one's own individual personality. Note this is different from the notion of Freedom implicit in the Essene ideas we have examined above. Freedom for the Essenes was the freedom of equals working together, eating, and living in a group. Individualism in expression, and in "standing out" was patently discouraged. American notions of freedom therefore, were and have been clearly influenced by the existence of the frontier. But both notions start with the premise of freedom and not being under the control of the other even as they diverged ultimately.

Justice is a complex of ideas with a long history in western thought. Plato's notion of justice centers on each person or class and city-state fulfilling a specialized role with the outcome being harmony in the just state. Today we have notions of justice intermixed with economic justice, legal justice, moral justice, social justice and many other variations.

Today we look at the notion of Justice in the Essene view and contrast that with the ones we see manifesting in American literature and history.

The Essene view had several components in the notion of Justice. Justice was similar to equality in that all people were equal before God, and that was a just arrangement and had the force of the moral authority of God himself. Justice was bound up with each person having a say or even vote in brotherhood matters. Justice was related to the condition of the soul because the condition of the soul and the conduct of an individual in this life was to be weighted by God himself who would in the afterlife make the final judgment of who had led a just life and who had not. There is a notion of economic justice in that the Essenes were very clear that all wealth was to be shared by the Brotherhood and distributed to the poor. None shall be rich and none shall be poor.

As we can see there are many factors at play in the conception and administration of justice on the material as well as the spiritual plane. Interesting, Justice and its complexities and instruments (judgment by peers and a judge and legal systems; "equal justice under the law" all stem from the rudimentary ideas which have come down to us virtually intact over the centuries.

In the American context Justice as "an eye for an eye" is seen to be at work as well. Where, we may ask does this notion of justice come from. It too, comes from the bible but was not part of its original credo as we can see above. Rebellion against civil authority also was not a part of the Essene credo. These aspects were added later at Jewish stalwarts sought to include in the document justifications for rebellion against various invaders.

Therefore, given these antecedents we see some real confusion around the concept. For example, can one can have justice and inequality at the same time? Apparently. Justice defined as treating everyone equally can occur in a slave system. Justice is equal treatment. Justice and economic equality flies in the face of American notions of getting rich and being as unequal as possible economically. Yet we know that a society dominated by the super rich can and most often is an unjust society. "Equal Justice under the Law" as is stated on the Supreme Court building in Washington DC. has the same dilemma. Here justice is equal treatment and equal Justice meted out by men called judges. Who judges the judges and ensures their solutions are "just?" And finally, even if such justice is equal what does that mean? Are these judges to ensure that "none shall be rich and none shall be poor" or we may ask who is equal to the judges themselves who are making these determinations.

Justice as Re-distribution

Whatever the short-falls of administered Justice by judges, the idea of taking worldly assets and re-distributing them to the needy is an idea of the functioning of the brotherhood which in later centuries becomes the hallmark of the nation state. One critical function of the state is to re-distribute the wealth via taxes and other means, such that "none shall be rich and none shall be poor." Justice here is served in that inequities created by other aspects of society, i.e., capitalist accumulations of wealth, can be righted. Socialism, Communism and even Capitalism take this notion of Justice as central themes and a legitimate function of the state.

185

This in turn has an entire judge-dominated administrative component where rights and wrongs are to be weighed on the scales of justice. All were equal among the Essenes before God and in America, for example, all are equal before God and the law.

An additional function of this notion of Justice is obvious: Allow disproportionate accumulations of wealth, or land or other necessities of life and you invite social disruption if not revolution. In the end a society lacking in justice is an unstable society--another point which is being made not only by the Essenes but one I argue is being made in the bible itself. Sustainability over the long-haul is the reward of the just society. Tyranny fails because tyranny is de-stabilizing.

Given these notions of Freedom and Justice we have seen, and their relation to the frontier character of early American society, we may now ask what other features on the American landscape can be mentioned.

The view that nature is not the enemy did not play well in a frontier society where subduing the land to make it productive seemed necessary. In a land rife with hostile elements, from the settler's point of view, a friendly nature seemed not to fit the facts of their existence. Of course, there was a reaction to this point of view, especially as the frontier receded and new nature-friendly ideas emerged in American thought and literature, as well as new ideas of Freedom and Justice. Interestingly these new strains, were not so new. They hearkened by to some of the original ideas identified in the ancient viewpoints I have identified above.

Cheap Labor

The availability of cheap labor, in the form of immigrant and slave labor in the American scenario had the effect of distorting the ancient prohibitions against slavery and serfdom resident in the bible. Subsequent writers sought to justify the above practices as the developing Jewish state tolerated servant-hood and indeed slavery itself for expedient reasons.

An "Enslave or be enslaved" ethos developed and was countenanced in the name of expediency. These passages in the bible were utilized in the American example to justify slavery in the United States and virtual serfdom in the form of immigrants and children and Africans.

But note this rationalization, driven by economic and later social prejudice factors which had at their core, then and now, purely economic drivers. It paid to have cheap labor with which to tame the frontier and build the industrial empire that America sought to establish. Without this cheap labor the American development vector would have been very different.

Note, however, even in this environment the ideas of freedom and equality have ultimately triumphed, however, weakly, as was true in the Roman example. Much of American history can be seen to be the "cheap labor" components of American society demanding their fair share of the pie and insisting upon reinstalling the original ideas underlying the bible. These movements triumphed because they re-surfaced the moral tenets against slavery and economic domination discoverable in the bible despite these tenets having been obscured by social re-interpretations and obscurations.

<u>Cheap Food</u>

Cheap food also has been a pillar of American strength. Every society must feed itself. Note, however the bible's early framers had notions about food. See above where they were vegetarians and sought to eliminate meat in the diet. But less known is the strictures against animal sacrifices, a practice which the framers had seen replace sacrifices from Pharaohs and Kings which were human in nature. Imagine a world where the King as Divine Messenger of the Gods would sacrifice human beings telling the populace that such sacrifices were necessary to appease those Gods. This human sacrifice component was very common with those king-ship systems.

The request of Abraham to kill his son is not an aberration. It was common practice in societies from Egypt to the Americas. The reaction of the framers and others was to substitute animal sacrifices in place of humans ones. The framers went one step further and sought to ban animal sacrifices altogether and to distinguish their new Yahweh from pagan gods and their demands for sacrifices.

But animal sacrifice continued to the time of Jesus, who also sought its elimination. Note here that this is true even as some have interpreted passages in the bible where Jesus seems be asking his disciples to eat of his body and drink his blood, in the nature of Jesus as the sacrificial lamb. But this is in error, according to at least one scholar who argues that the translation from the original Aramaic was faulty. Blood and body refers to "self-sacrifice" not an analogy to animal sacrifices.

We are seemingly far a field from cheap food, but note that food is an issue and what kinds of animals is it ok to eat or sacrifice. In America grain crops and meat have been the staple. One wonders what the Essenes would think of this American diet. So is the meat and potatoes diet of America "sinful?" The answer is that the framers would likely consider it unsustainable. A vegetarian diet is less costly, and spares the lives of animals would be their conclusion and, they would say, more sparing of the environment. This is not to comment on the Jewish dietary restrictions and later permissions to eat meat. These came later in the bible and were not necessarily present as allowable among the earlier framers.

For those interested in poetry can visit my poetry site which is www.poemhunter.com. Search on Lonnie hicks. The site has over 470 poems, short stories, and essays. There is work there, some of which became books.

Lilith began with a poem call "Asunder" which is on that site.

Note: Here we examine the relationships between religion which we have examined above and science, specifically the scientific ideas of Einstein and modern physic theorists. It was a very instructive journey for me and hopefully it will be for as well for the reader.

Science, Literature, Buddha and Einstein

Title: Einstein, Time, Space, Buddha and Poetry

Update 11/10/2010
Summary: The relation between concepts in modern science, religion and literature. These include sections on Quantum Physics, Einstein's relativity theories, string theory and others. I conclude with my own ideas as regards these elements. I have added the influence of "M" theory to this piece and some thoughts on light and literature
Updated: 5/28/10
Updated 6/4/10: The Nature of Gravity
Updated: 6/5/10: Parallel Universes, The Problem of the Idea, Reincarnation and Multiple Selves Updated: 6/7/10: Belief systems, science and religion
Updated 6/9/10: Is the Universe Alive? Updated: 6/10/10: New mini-chapter: What is Space?
Updated: 6/17/10: The Nature of Reality
Updated: 6/18/10: Toward A New Theory of Gravity
Updated: 6/19/10: A Proposal for a New Theory of Everything: See what you think.
Updated: 6/21/10: Summing Up: All of the Ideas in one Neat Package
Updated: 6/23/10: Merging Universes and Dark Flow Data
Updated: 6/24/10: The Holographic View, God and the Human Brain
Updated: 11/10/10 Looks Like the Plasma Theory of The Universe is Correct.

The most profound thing Einstein said
is that time is taffy, malleable.

And so is space.

If I do it correctly
I can leave earth
and see me coming back again
younger than I am today.

Now practically, this means
that the car ahead of me on the highway
is pushing both time and space ahead of itself
and I am in the rear
observing my own future
since I and my car will soon occupy a future
I can see outside my windshield;
one that will occur as soon as I reach the
spot where that car ahead of me is now,
or was, when I was in the rear observing
that car moving through what was clear to me was my future.
More, I was, (am) in the present behind him
pushing space in front of me
creating time as I proceed
and if my speed is at the speed of light
I can compress both time and space
in doing so.
So a car moving much slower behind me
is actually existing in a different relationship
to time and space than I am;
so different
so as to be almost in another dimension.
So lets assume I am moving at the speed of light;
that much slower car behind me
probably could not even see me
or be aware of me because for all
practical purposes I exist in a separate universe
from my much slower moving compatriot.

But the larger point Einstein says is that you and I
and everything exists in time and space simultaneously
living our past, our future, and our present.

———

That is, all these dimensions exist together.
Look up at the stars and we see what was going on
millions if not billions of years ago because light
takes that long to get here.
But note that other stars also exist in space
in our future, so do we;
so all three dimensions exist simultaneously
in the time-space continuum. Space-time is a fabric and
if we shake one end of the fabric ripples happen all through
the fabric.

Now in the Tibetan Book of the Dead the same point is made
a different way in that when we die and get reincarnated we come back
again probably using Einstein's time space continuum.
Well, look here Christians also believe something very similar
in that after we die we simply enter into another time space continuum and
our atoms, our soul, or what ever, are merely transformed from matter into
another form of energy. Hello Einstein again.

Wonder what want he was reading.

So there is agreement then between religion and science on these things
and therefore what is the big disagreement about? Nothing much it turns
out.

Now the quantum folks come along and they say "wait a minute Einstein,
nice theory but that is not the way things work down at the atomic level.
Time and space are not linear as you imply and you have not recognized
the import of your own idea that time and space, past, future and present
exist simultaneously.
If that is true, and it is at the sub-atomic level, what we get there, and in the
heavens, are small blacks holes in one and big black holes in the other,
and to boot all things existing at the same time is not true. Things at the
sub-atomic level come in and out of existence on a probability basis.

Therefore, things are not stable at all on either level, and at both levels,
things pop in and out of existence; our universe popped into existence from
nothing (the big bang) and we can see parts off our universe popping out
of existence into black and white holes everyday in space.
Therefore, therefore, on the sub atomic level the cat is made up of atoms
which too, pop in and out of existence. It is just that we can't see it very
clearly from our vantage point but we use this fact everyday in computers

---

in the way that every electron popping into and out of existence tracks with its counterpart where ever that counterpart is any where in all of the **universe.** That is how a computer works. Change the charge of electron "a" and electron "b" will instantly change its charge and the gate is open and the computer works. It is called electricity and magnetism.

Now out of all this comes String Theory (look this up) which says that atoms have no intrinsic characteristics by themselves. All properties of everything we know in the universe are generated by tiny strings vibrating at different frequencies and with different numbers of them around the nucleus.(This is the periodic table and note most atoms are spontaneously decaying and losing and gaining electrons.

So red is merely matter vibrating at a frequency we perceive as red. Change the frequency and red becomes blue. Change the vibrations of the atoms in a cat and the cat is dead. Change the vibrations back and the cat is alive; we know this is true because the cat is made up of atoms, true?

Thus simply stated all existence is potentiality, and probabilities and this comes into and out of existence routinely on a potentiality basis. Now add to these factors one more: "M" theory or Membrane theory. This idea is a progression, from quantum theory and initially states that there are many dimensions, more than three or even four.

After much theoretical wresting these folks decided there are 11 dimensions, because the math worked. But the implications of all this grew very quickly because it also became apparent that how can these 11 dimensions exist in the same time and space? Tricky huh? Well the answer is that they exist side by side often just centimeters apart. We may have whole other dimensions and membranes floating in our same time and space, such membranes containing entire universes floating in the Great Nether.

Contemplate that for a moment. A parallel universe may be centimeters from my face and I cannot perceive it. This theory explains the relative weakness of gravity (I can lift my arm and defy the entire pull of planet earth. Why? Because there is a parallel membrane universe centimeters away and in fact our gravity in this membrane universe is the "residual" gravity from that one explaining its weakness in our membrane universe. Further, if two of these universe membranes collide, this would explain the big bang, the volatility of our universe, things popping in and out, etc. My how theory can bake a beautiful cake. And this is all consistent with Einsteinan views.

Let's take a concrete example of membrane theory . Fish swimming below the surface of the ocean live in one universe but fish-world is separated from our world by a thin membrane called the surface of the ocean. The fish are not aware of the air-breathing world yet both exist in the same time and space. Simple. So I will give you a moment to catch your breath to see if you buy into all of this.

All of this can be very confusing, but I promise you that people believe this enough to put billions in the Hadron collider in Switzerland.
My view?
Humm, if all everything does exist simultaneously and we move between these existences, it explains why my Physics professor was so weird. He definitely was not from this planet.

But more profoundly it explains how I can create this very poem from my very own future where it already existed. And more I can access all of my various selves, past, present and future and use the skills I did have, now have, and will have in my future. It may lie in that parallel membrane universe existing right now inches from my face; ideas can hop back and forth between myself and my other poet self in an adjoining universe. So we can have our Einstein cake and eat it too, again.

This, by the way is the way of Buddha who says this exact same thing. Buddha says we can access all of these states of mind through meditation. It is Indian theology as well. There is the world of the unseen and mystical. And in existing we pridefully demand to be able to understand it but that is an impossible dream. We are formed by this universe and are not equipped to sense or really interact with these other worlds. We can only go on faith or test the boundaries which is what the Hadron experiment is doing, literally looking to interact with another parallel universe through particle explosions initiated at the speed of light where these particles disappear, the presumption is that they, like gravity, have gone to that close-by universe.

And in the end no one has an answer to the unknowable question who or what started all this, and more importantly who or what maintains it.

Faith becomes the admission we aim's that smart to know that answer and will never be smart enough to know these answers. Both religious people and scientists now agree on this point.

Well, the more things change, the more it seems like that what we are all saying is the same.
Got to go.
Time for a little meditation.

Apr 5, 2010

Now if, as I am fond of saying, things literally pop in and out of existence, how then does this exactly work? Now keep in mind this is no random problem. Billions have been spent, and billions more, at CERN in the Hadron Collider to answer this question.

Let's take an example of how this works;
We exist in a dimension like the surface of an ocean. The surface of that ocean, as Einstein said is the fabric of space-time. The surface separates the water world from the air world, and both exist in the same time-space but are unaware of each other. Fish don't know we exist and in our example, we don't know the fish world exists. At the intersection of these two dimensions (there can be many--up to eleven dimensions) the surface has little waves which pop up onto the air world and then fall back down into the water world. The surface forms the boundary between the two dimensions and we are seeing that indeed, water is composed of part oxygen and evaporation occurs at that surface and therefore there are exchanges between the two worlds. Now in membrane theory, (see above) the idea is that this is precisely the case between our universe and another "membrane" universe abutting our own. This explains the weak gravitational force, (gravity here is reduced because gravity is actually coming from an abutting universe, and hence by the time it reaches our universe it is weaker. It explains why I can lift my arm and defy the entire gravitational pull of the earth. Gravity is very weak in our universe for the reason stated above.

So far so good.

Now just as our world has more to it than water and air, our universe model has more to it than just two membranes. (Note that collusions between membranes, in this view, caused the big bang.)

But we have bigger fish to fry here. We want to know the nature of dark matter and dark energy. We now know that in our universe only 25% of the universe is accounted for in what we are able to see. There is no question whatsoever that a dark matter exists. We can't see it but we have measured its effects. The same is true for dark energy. It rules the universe of the stars but we want to know its role as well on the sub-atomic level.

Stay with me now. The unseen medium in which dark energy and matter exists we shall call Ether, the unseen. It is all around us yet invisible. The search is on for this ether or particle at CERN where such a particle is called the "graviton" and/or the Higgs Boson. Why all the fuss?

Well to discover such a particle is to discover how mass comes into being and hence the interplay between mass and energy that Einstein describes.

(Notice we have come full circle here)

But even more importantly a discovery of this particle will have implications way beyond physics. Here is my view..

1-A discovery would mean that the world of the unseen and the not directly detectable exists. Humans may simply be unequipped to see or directly experience 75% of the universe. The unseen and the unknowable is therefore most of the world and our universe.

2-No one knows who or what created this huge mechanism.

3-The existence of other universes means the potential for other life forms beyond our comprehension.

4- Popping in and out our universe means that our universe has a basic instability to it. It is mere "potential" as quantum physics discovered. We are constantly interacting with other universes and therefore our universe is constantly changing. It is analogous to the latest gene theory where genes are now seen as merely starting points for the human being but malleable and can be changed by interaction with the environment. They are not immutable, and unchanging. The same must be true, in my view, then, of human nature. This has implications.

5-Finally, such a description of the universe would explain some of the greatest mysteries of all- a. how can all particles in the universe be in touch with every other particle in the universe regardless of time and distance b. how can a particle be in two places at the exact same time. This includes

---

us, individually as well, apparently. c. how can the universe at every level be in touch with itself at every level, the sub-atomic and the galaxy level? This is the "theory of inflation" which is another topic altogether.

This answer takes us back to Mr. E who stated that time-space is a fabric. So if I tug on a piece of fabric on one end, the other end of that piece of fabric moves from my tug on this end of it. Now imagine the fabric in question is our universe floating in space as a thin membrane where a tug at one end of it, no matter how slight, now matter what size, and what is produced is a reaction at the other end of the universe. Time-space is a fabric where all events ripple in the fabric forever. Ether is the medium whereby this is possible.

Once again we can now have our Einstein cake and eat it too.

Now, I take here another theoretical leap. Suppose what we have here is two membrane universes which have not only collided but merged. The larger more dominant universe-membrane is invisible to us yet affects us. This idea would solve a lot of theoretical problems:

1-It is the source of the gravity problem described above.

2-It is the dark matter and dark energy sought by so many

3-A merged universe membrane universe each with its own differing physical laws explains mysteries such as black holes etc.

4-A larger, merged passing-through universe in the some other dimension partially explains the space-time fabric issues. Space-time is a fabric because it is being tugged and pulled by another invisible universe.

5- A last point, how can the universe be constantly expanding and growing, yet remain in touch with itself at all points in space and time at the same time. One answer: This is a characteristic of a living organism. So next time: Is the universe alive" Is it a living organism? One man says so.

That man was Wilhelm Reich. But that is the subject of a separate Blog coming soon. For now I would like to focus on a third aspect of all of this: the transformation of matter into energy and vice versa. This is Einstein's most famous equation: $E=MC2$.

Now the meaning of this equation could take a book but simply put it states matter can be transformed into energy and vice versa. At first this is a common sense observation; burn a log and transformations occur and the log interacts with its environment and we get smoke, charcoal and the matter in the log goes away or is transformed in heat and light energy.

What is new coming from Einstein is that the transformation of tiny bits of matter at the sub-atomic level releases enormous amounts of energy exponentially. The equation above says the energy released will be the amount of mass you have (say a gram of matter) will release energy equal to that mass times the speed of light squared. Stated another way that gram of mass could blow up an entire city, and has.

This is the atom bomb.

Mass here is being transformed at the sub-atomic level into energy.

This is done by shooting protons into the nucleus of say a uranium atom at the speed of light breaking the bonds of force that hold that atom's nucleus together.

But what do you say has this to do with anything? Well, at question at CERN, and now on the table, is where do atoms get their mass from in the first place? We even seem to have particles which have no mass whatsoever and then they seem to acquire it but how? What imparts mass to massless particles? Moreover, how does this search for the graviton and the Higgs Boson relate to the universe of the extremely large, galaxies, black holes, the big bang, dark energy, and dark matter, and of course membrane theory?

Well, no one knows just yet but that is part of the quest at CERN.

I take here another of my famous theoretical leaps and posit the following: we may regard mass and energy as a continuum just as we have seen that space-time is in fact a continuum. What we gain theoretically is all matter and energy are of a piece, are in fact one thing, not two separate things. An analogy would be that body and spirit are one thing not two separate things. Now we see where this is going. If there is the world of the seen and the world of the unseen, physics and religion then must be regarded as part of a single cosmos--a matter-energy continuum.

Given this whole then arguments about the material world and the spiritual world are pointless since both are part of a larger single entity which we have, at this point, not apprehended.

More significantly we have a single whole with differing parts, which interact with one another and each part is aware of and influences all other parts <u>as a single entity.</u>

So if all that we see and cannot see is a single entity, what is that entity?

All is connected to everything else, simultaneously; everything in the universe and beyond and in our physical selves as well, and in our spiritual selves: all one whole.

Sound familiar? It should. It is the basic premise of most of the religions of the world. What is added is an entity which controls this world or at least created it.

So the unity of all things is no idle speculation. It exists. And has been proved to exist over and over again in the world of physics. One astounding implication is that if we are made of these same electrons are we as individuals are also popping in and out of existence as well, or at least between dimensions, if not parallel universes? Some say so.
So now that we have these shiny baubles of wisdom and speculation what do we do with them? What are their practical uses?

That will be the subject of update number four.

Now mentioned above is the famous Einsteinan equation $E=MC2$ and we have explored above the mechanics of how energy is created from mass-- in this example, nuclear energy and the atomic bomb.

Now we want to read the equation backwards. $Mc2=E$ and the allied question of where does mass come from.

For to contemplate that energy can "congeal" into mass puts us into another realm--energy moving at the speed of light becomes mass. Strange to contemplate, I know, but the idea here is that light energy does have mass and can "congeal" into mass. In fact the primal "plasma energy" that existed seconds after the big bang did in fact congeal into the mass we know as stars and planets--so this is no idle speculation. This did occur. But the question is how--especially if we take Einstein's equation seriously--energy moving at the speed of light can congeal or acquire mass.

Well what moves at the speed of light? Answer: Light itself. Light itself here, has mass--which has to come from some where. Enter the graviton and the oft-mentioned Higgs Boson above, dark energy and matter too.

But our focus is more narrow here: what happens at the speed of light to energy moving at 186 thousand miles a second or even faster? Well apparently the laws of physics and objects themselves undergo change or at least encounter change making environments and energy becomes mass: Einstein backwards.

So why do we care? Well this means that indeed electrons, and other objects can pop into and out of existence, that is to say into and out of mass and energy states, and, if light is an example, we often will not perceive these changes since we are creatures who do not move at the speed of light.

Once again proof of an unseen world, if not universes, exist.

Finally, lets take an extreme example: Can energy pulses moving at the speed of light congeal entire planets, solar systems, universes? Yep.

Apparently so.

So now we have energy sources able to materialize, seemingly out of no where in milli–seconds in material form and also disappear as quickly. Scary huh? Yet it is an idea which seems so familiar: Star Trek had a transporter didn't it?

Gravity and its Consorts.

Now we can no longer ignore the elephant in the room, which is the question of what is gravity. Einstein began his inquires which led to his space-time theory and relativity with an inquiry into the nature of gravity.

Surprising to note that no one really knows what gravity is. Many refer to it as "spooky action from a distance." What does this mean? Newton "discovered" gravity but gave up on trying to understand it He settled for describing it's actions and interactions. Simply put gravity is the tendency of masses to attract one another. Large bodies attract smaller bodies and indeed may capture them. Gravity caused Newton's apple to fall. Describing the "laws" which govern these interactions was Newton's great contribution. It gave us Calculus as a means of describing the motions of bodies, to predict orbits and to have a space program.

But we, intrepid reader, like Einstein, want to know what it is.

Einstein, as the story goes was sitting in his patent office looking out the window and imagined that a man jumped from an adjacent building.

Gravity would determine that he would fall and how fast. Now Einstein added to this some of the greatest discoveries of all time. He postulated that as the man fell he was also altering space-time in doing so. In fact he was not only being pulled down by gravity but that space-time was being altered such that the fabric was bending and creating a gap into which the man fell; much like a spinning penny falls into an inverted cone.

Now add to this another factor: gravity as a factor of mass bodies is altering space-time and can do the same thing to light. A third aspect of gravity Einstein noticed is that as objects fall the impact they make as they reach the ground is exponential. That is, if I drop a ball from 10 feet it hits the ground with 20 pounds of force, the anomaly is if I drop the same ball from 20 feet it does not hit the ground with 40 pounds of force as one might expect. It is a higher factor. Why? What is the action of gravity at work here?

Ok, you have been patient here. What is the overall point you may ask?

If gravity is such a powerful force in our universe-for example black holes have the most powerful gravitational pull of any body in the universe and there is a black hole in the center of every galaxy; if gravity can take a massive sun millions of miles in diameter and crush it to an object the size of an asteroid or even a basketball, what is this force?

Well CERN is trying to answer that question. They posit that there must be a particle called the graviton at work, one which gives mass to energy and creates the bodies which then have gravity, except we have not detected it yet. They are in the hunt for it a CERN.

How else to explain the existence of such a powerful force which is otherwise undetectable- and "spooky action at a distance?"

So gravity is all pervasive in our universe, except that it is not the most powerful force in our universe. Given the gravity premise, and that premise is absolutely true, there is a fly in our ointment. Gravity should in fact, at some point, cause all bodies to attract one another and the universe should begin to collapse onto itself or at least remain in a steady state. But no. It is not. The universe is expanding; not only expanding, but expanding at a exponential rate.

This is shocking.

How is that possible if the universe is held together by gravity? Answer: there is another more powerful force than gravity: Dark energy. Dark energy is pushing the universe apart, and is stronger than gravity and, astoundingly, space itself is expanding as well, *dragging the stars, planets and galaxies along with it. Empty* space has properties we don't understand. How can space itself expand?

Our universe is a strange place.

So now we are confronted with the issue of dark energy and it's travel-mate dark matter as possible factors in all of this.

And we know very little about either, and starting to feel very small in the very large place we call the universe.

Maybe CERN will give us some answers or CERN itself may disappear into another universe and we'll not know why. LOL

Well we have come a long way with this topic and now we take a leap off the conceptual cliff. Among the string theory people, the membrane people, the quantum people, and Einsteinan is a startling consensus.

Einstein started it with the suggestion that the past, present and the future all exist simultaneously in the same time and space. The quantum people added to the mix the idea that electrons can be in two places at the same time and are in contact at every point in the universe, and membrane people suggest that parallel universes exist centimeters away from my face and there might be millions of them, all occupying the same time and space connected by 11 dimensions-some of these universes may be tiny pin-pricks, likes ours was at the beginning and others large.

We now add the cosmologist group which suggested that laser shots into the universe show that the universe is flat or at least wavy. Repeat flat.

Others claim no, there are bubble universi, and they break off from one another. But, I like the flat and wayy gravy theory.

Laser shots into the deep cosmos by these folks show that a perfect triangulation was achieved.

Astounding.

That meant the universe is *flat.*

An isosceles triangle does not lie.

Universes folded upon universes, all occupying the same space and time. Or millions of parallel universes-take your choice, but all somehow connected and ours is flat or mostly flat.

Now we, our heads spinning, ask the question what oes this have to do with me, literature, religion, and the price of sanity?

Well, undaunted by those questions, the physicists leap right over that cliff and argue:

We are made up of these electrons, popping in and out of existence. Does this mean we as individuals are popping in and out of existence and god forbid popping between and among parallel universes? Can there be duplicates of me in these parallel universes, slightly different but all existing

at the same time, in the same space? Answer: Yes indeedy.

Then, if ideas in the brain, therefore, participate in this process coming from my past, present and future might I be communicating with these other selves both from the parallel membrane and my own past and future self? How does one have aptitude and skills at three to be a great piano player?

Answer: the skill was acquired in a past or future life. Enter as well notions of reincarnation.

Creativity then has a past and a future origin.

Once all of this is contemplated anything can happen.

Let us pause here to catch our breath.

This is a lot to take in and some of us are edging toward the door labeled "crackpot ideas." Could all of this stuff be true, or proven?

Well let me assure you that among these folks, many do believe it and are busy offering proof if you look in the right places and read the right journals.

The facts are that in a logic-dominated culture no one knows what an idea is or where they come from. All we know is which areas of the brain light up when people are doing specific tasks.

That is not much.

Where do these ideas come from? What is an idea in the brain. How does the brain and its ideas relate at the quantum level to this universe? Where do talents come from?

Some talents and aptitudes to be sure come from hard work, but a three year old progeny has not had much time for hard work.

Finally, multiple universes or parallel universes might mean multiple selves for each of us individually, each living *in their own universe*, living similar or slightly or wholly different lives.

This is a lot to absorb.

Time for ice cream.

But I assure you these ideas are now common in physics circles.

And, there is more.

While these ideas sound strange, they also sound familiar. The idea that there are other worlds of the not-detectable, whole undetected realms, are familiar to many as heaven and hell; as Nirvana, as visions of underworlds, of Hindu notions of reincarnation, cosmic cycles in the Veda are pegged at 8.6 billion years each. Most religions believe in other worlds where other beings, Gods for example live. Multiple selves for example is expressed in the concept of the soul which we find everywhere from the ancient Egyptian concept of actually having one's soul weighed after death, to the Christian notion of the soul which lives after death and resides in heaven or hell or limbo.

Other realms, unseen, where versions of our earthly presence are duplicated or live in transformed state, indeed, are common. What is uncommon is that modern science is now saying virtually the same thing.

Here again we see the worlds of the religious and the not-religious sounding similar. But are these ideas really all that different? Einstein was religious, Darwin was religious, and Newton was religious.

So where are we?

Differing belief systems when examined closely it seems, end up sounding similar. We discover we are all really brothers and sisters sharing the same family of ideas and that feels sorta nice.

But where do we go to from here? Hold your breath here because the CERN experiment is about trying to throw light on some of the above issues.

The collider has been fired up at 50% level already. (No results for months.)

But when it does fire up 100% in approximately a year we might get answers or we might get more questions, but for sure things will never be the same on planet Earth.

Think about this; the greatest experiment in the history of Earth might bring back a result which states that we are not alone, there might be other parallel universes and no, we cannot ever really know all of the whole story because we are from this universe.

Let's go for the double-scoop.

June 9, 2010
Lurking in the above analysis is one which is so fantastic I hesitate to bring it up. But Einstein was not afraid to bring up his fantastic idea; should I be?

No.

Here goes.

What is striking above with an expanding universe analysis and, the all connectedness of all things view, and the single unity idea is that this is reminiscent of the characteristics of a *living* organism. Berkley said "we only exist in the mind of God" is now scary. Riech died believing in an unfound particle which he called a "bion" --tiny units of life which we have not discovered; a form of life-cell all around us. With an expanding universe can we call that growth in a living entity? Maybe dark matter is not matter at all but a form of life-along the matter-energy continuum. Fish again, failing to recognize water. So if we were to entertain such a notion. (I am reminded of the Indian Theological view that all things have a spirit, and may be alive etc. Animists, pagan theologies also come to mind. Is all the world alive?

Let's pretend that this is possible. Is this perhaps the true secret of dark energy and dark matter. If so how can it be proven? How can "bions" be discovered or examined? Is it matter, is it energy, and is it the form of life that is this universe? Pretty scary stuff for a people living on a shiny blue ball floating in space, in space-time that is.

Well, my brain has had enough. What about yours? We have had our ice cream, now let's go for the chocolate.

June 17, 2010
We have above looked at various ideas about the nature of the universe, ranging from Einstein to laser theories of a flat universe. Now we are at the point where we want to know what it all means and ultimately what do all of these theories have to say about the nature of reality. Can all of these ideas be combined into the elusive "Theory of Everything:" the holy grail of Physics. Well maybe.

I will begin here with my modest offering. (Did you think I would miss this party?)
Let's go over the facts first: such a theory would have to take into consideration of the ideas of Einstein, String Theory, Quantum Mechanics, Inflation Theory and even the living universe theory. It also must produce an idea which explains an idea; how the world of the very large (galaxies and stars) relate to the world of the very small (sub-atomic particles) and last, but equally important, this theory must explain "reality" not only for us humans but for all of nature and its creatures. Not much huh?
Well here goes. Obviously I cannot do it in one blog but I'll start the conversation and you can start the hole-poking at your leisure.
Let's start the process of explaining the nature of the reality of everything with the re-introduction of the ideas of String Theory, because that is, in fact, the way this story started. Hawking, the world renown physicist ("A Short History of Time" did important work on the nature of black holes. He posited that nothing escapes a black hole and argued that things go into a black hole but nothing comes out, except for radiation which occurs when paired electrons/ photons get separated at the event horizon. Humm, event horizon what is that? Well it is at the point where an object is no longer visible as it goes into a black hole because the gravity of the black hole is so strong light itself can no longer escape, and at that point, Hawking argues, the laws of physics becomes very peculiar and are in fact altered. The implication was that whole stars could simply disappear without a trace in the maw of a black hole.
Now this sparked a huge controversy where other physicists declared this was not possible because it violates the law of physics called "the conservation of information" which is just another version of an old precept that was called the "conservation of matter and energy." In all transactions

---

in nature things are transformed, matter to energy and vice versa, but nothing is ever lost. It is a law.

Now the fight was on.

Hawking seemed to be saying that this was not true in the special case of black holes.

Holy Smokes Batman, all Hades broke out and the controversy between Hawking and other physicists proceeded.

If Hawking was accurate, the nature of reality itself was at stake and physics itself. The leader of the loyal opposition was Leonard Susskind, string theorist who sought to disapprove the Hawking thesis. Nothing in physics should ever be lost he said

He came up with a solution that proved perhaps to prove too much. See what you think.

He argued that information is not lost as stars disappear into a black hole because elementary particles which are, in string theory, vibrating strings operate in the black hole example to produce a three dimensional event and the star is swallowed but also there is a simultaneous two dimensional event or "hologram" produced which is two-dimensional in nature which is then projected out into space and exists at the edge of our universe in the two dimensional universe. In another version Susskind also posited that at the event horizon time essentially ceases and information exists on the rim of that event horizon and never actually enters the black hole, hence no infomation of lost. This is consistent with relativity theory.

However, in promoting this idea a whole new concept of reality is created. That is to say that as I sit here in my living room there is the three dimensional version (four including space-time) of me but all around me are two dimensional holographic versions of me (we don't know how many, sort of ghost images of me but just as real as the three dimensional version of me we are used to and, get this, these events in the case of the black hole exit the black hole at speeds exceeding that of light.

Now, this is explained in the black hole example by the notion that black holes distort not only matter and gravity but the nature of reality and space-time itself and; elementary particles vibrating are seen to have multiple two dimensional ghosts stretching to infinity. Since we are three dimensional people, living in three dimensional space and in a three dimensional universe we do not see these ghosts of holograms, but they exist.

Now this does go a ways toward unifying all of the other ideas above from

———

Einstein to Quantum Mechanics to String theory etc., but it does leave more questions in its wake than answers..
Tomorrow I will explain why.

June 18, 2010
Hopefully I have accurately reflected Susskind''s views above but, I am taking the tack that what is being said here, aside from the spat between he and Hawking over the black hole, is that we have multiples of our selves in other dimensions, whether they be two dimensions or many dimensions. Well we have heard that before and it is not new.

What is interesting to me is an idea that Susskind did surface in another context: that is his idea about the origin of gravity.
His theory goes that strings sometimes close in upon themselves, or close, and these strings vibrate, can and do pop into and out of existence and are paired. But these strings can and often close and essentially bifurcate themselves, (divide) and that "string division" and as pairs seek to re-entangle and match up often miss and create a graviton, hence gravity is born. Gravity is string DNA missing or miss-coding once in a while and the product is gravity from the graviton created.
Well this is interesting, but no cigar.
Here is an alternative view (mine.)
How about the following explanation for gravity:
1- Gravity may be in fact the result of several forces: the first is that seconds after the big bang anti-matter and matter existed. But there was a little bit more matter than anti matter so matter became dominant in our universe. This is current theory.
Now suppose, if you will, this was not really the case. Suppose that anti-gravity did not go away but became transformed into (hold your hat here) dark matter. This is a special form of anti-matter and it becomes dark matter and it is moving speeds exceeding that of light--notice that the theory of inflation is relevant here, and this special form of anti-matter as dark matter still exists. Now add to this dark energy. Dark energy here in this idea is the result of anti-matter being created by contact with matter (the graviton) and there is a resultant explosion of energy (dark energy) also moving at speeds exceeding that of light. Dark energy also is created by the big bang itself and enters our membrane via black holes. (More on this later.)
Now we have to account for the creation of gravity in this scenario. I like the idea that strings in fact play a role in the creation of gravity that would fit at both the macro level and at the micro level. But we need to add another element--that of electro-magnetism. We need to know its role in all of this.

I have a modest suggestion:

Electro-magnetism is the force which in its fluctuations press down upon matter (gravity-the graviton) causing the creation of a special form of anti-matter and then an explosion of this special kind of anti-matter also creates dark energy which is why the universe of flying apart and expanding. It is a thought.

Therefore, to repeat Einstein's thought experiment of the man jumping of the building. The man is actually being pushed downward by anti-gravity (dark energy) because the motion, space and time of his falling creates an imbalance in electromagnetic fields and in space-time which subsists among all three.

Another example, when a star collapses, or even a black whole we see enormous explosions of electromagnetic waves. What is collapsing here and why are electromagnetic waves a product of this process?

Well, no one really knows, that being the case I will jump in and offer my view.

The special anti-matter and anti-gravitons are all around us and it is this anti-matter and dark energy at work pressing gravitons down into that collapsing star and its matter molecules. The result is an explosion linked to electro-magnetism and an explosion which produces dark energy which expands the universe and in doing so creates space.(Note here there are two kinds of dark energy at play.)

Running the movie backward in the case of the black hole is the next interesting idea. But let's save that for later.

Now what is new with these ideas is the one which postulates that what if dark energy and dark matter do in fact move faster than the speed of light, breaking Einstein's speed limit in the universe. (He said nothing can move faster than the speed of light. But what if that is not true?

We would have a very different assessment of the universe. My candidates for the cosmic speed limit breakers? Dark energy and Dark Matter and Dark Space.

It would illuminate the whole idea of parallel universes, gravity, and anti-matter would here play a somewhat paradoxal role; and the elephant in the Physics study is the following: how can the conservation of information reconcile with the idea of multiple universes and exchanges between same? That is a tough one, even for Susskind. This is a true Goldilocks paradox.

I like this game. Everyone can play. Of course my view lacks certain details but that is for tomorrow.

But we may ask do these ideas in fact unite all of the theories above. Well let's have a look tomorrow.

June 19, 2010

Time now to get down to cases.

First, let's imagine that in the big bang, anti-matter, dark energy and dark matter did not in fact disappear but are still with us and cycle through our universe involving black holes.

In addition we have the graviton and the anti-graviton- all swiming in the Great Nether, in the ocean soup just below our visible universe of matter and energy. But where do all these particles live?

Our flat universe is a thin layer floating above this ocean-soup and there are exchanges between the two at the boundaries. Our matter pops out of our universe and anti-matter, dark energy and dark matter, anti-graviton and gravitons from our universe interact under specific conditions and can move between universes.

So we swim just above the dark energy, dark matter ocean which we don't see because these items along with the anti-graviton move in excess of the speed of light and may be massless or at least a different kind of mass from that which exists in our universe.

Now we want to know the nature of the interactions in this arrangement. Let's use the black hole as an example. Why should there be massive black holes at the center of many if not most galaxies? They surely must play a role in the above paradigm. Let's imagine that objects passing through the event horizon not only experience space and time distortions but gravity and its gravitons in this case are being pressed down toward the singularity by anti-gravitons and anti-matter from the soup. Space itself in crashing down the black hole moves faster that the speed of light and can come back out of the black hole moving faster than the speed of light. The distortion over-all is actually a boundary exchange point. Add to this mix the action of dark energy and dark matter as well.

We know that huge anti-matter (and perhaps anti-graviton) clouds exist and they have been identified in our space, now visible to us. (How did this occur you wonder.)

So what is happening in the special case of a black hole is that boundary exchanges are occurring where anti-gravitons and anti-matter, due to distortions at the event horizon are pressing gravitons and matter down to incredibly small dimensions. What happens next is the fun part.

Suppose what we are witnessing in all of this is a form of black hole fusion where the product is not only gamma rays but dark energy and dark matter. Gravity is being overcome and dark energy is being produced along with dark matter and anti-matter. (We saw the cloud didn't we?) I suspect that also at play here are the laws of electro-magnetism which are also altered in this process. But I don't have a notion about that yet. But now we want to formularize what the process might look like.

209

The formula would be a version of Einstein's E=Mc2.

It would be: DE= Dark energy; DM= Dark matter

DE=DM times the exponential of such speed in excess of light speed equal to a velocity of 3.2 million light years per hour (the rate of expansion of the universe exponentially expressed.) (There is another unstated implication here: Space itself must be expanding and is a factor in this formulation. But I have no notation of that aspect.)

What we are doing here is trying to answer the question of how dark energy is produced and tying it to black holes processes.

The alternative would be to say that dark energy and dark matter existed from seconds after the big bang and essentially have not changed since.

I prefer the former notion.

So does the above notion tie together all of the ideas above?

Mostly.

Here is how:

1-It incorporates string theory in the terms of explaining how gravity comes into being

2-It accepts parallel world notions and 11 dimensions

3-It incorporates Einstein's equation and extends it to dark matter and dark energy

4-It accepts the theory of inflation and extends it beyond a steady state notion of the universe and explains how dark energy and matter production can be seen as analogous to nuclear fusion. (The black hole can be seen as the nucleus of an atom being acted upon in a nuclear fusion process with anti-gravity- anti-gravitons as protagonists and dark energy the product-hence explaining the expansion of the universe.

5- It gives black holes a rationale for being and suggests how transactions at the boundaries between the seen and unseen might work.

It is testable in that we look not only for the graviton but the anti-graviton as well, the anti-gravity wave as well as the gravity wave. And it tells us there is much more going on with black hole distortions of space, time and universe boundaries than we thought.

The best point of this theory is its premise is testable: if we do exist as thin layer above a dark energy, dark matter universe then CERN might detect it. What we have done is try to explain the nature of the interactions at the boundary points.

So we have come full circle, all the world is connected, sub-atomically and glaxctically and this too would explain how ants as a mass can communicate and make intelligent decisions without have a really big brain.

There is obviously communication possible in the Ether. (I couldn't resist)

So finally what about our "The Universe is Alive" thesis. Not entirely sure about it, but, I would not rule it out. Would you?

I close the blog today with a tribute to the great Albert Einstein:

Where ever I go in the cosmos I encounter Albert Einstein coming back, with a big fat smile on his face.

Jun 21, 2010
Now we step back and take a longer view and see what kind of cake we have baked. We have focused upon process above and now we want to have a look at context.

The context is:

1- The big bang did not end. It is still going on between two membranes which collided and then have proceeded to merge or pass through one another and exchanges between the two still occur at boundary points involving black holes.

The nature of space itself in this is still largely a mystery and must be seen as an entity which itself perhaps can expand at speeds faster than the speed of light.

211

2-The big bang involved our universe and a larger one-both passing through and sharing the same time and space. Both "branes" may make up and be part of a larger complex of brains or even "bubble universes."

3- Dark matter and Dark energy may in fact be (along with gravity) function as part of the larger more dominant membrane universe. Matter in the larger membrane is not just "anti-matter" it is the form of matter in that dominant universe and can move and exceed the speed light, and has a very different kind of mass aspect. So different that we must allow that we may never be able to comprehend it's outlines in detail. I have suggested above what the nature of interactions at the boundaries might be between the two universes. But it is a merged universe idea but with seperation between the two. The larger universe is composed of DM and DE and is the source of the expansion in our universe.

4-Therefore CERN may discover particles but indeed we may not be able to comprehend such particles moving at speeds in excess of light. Einstein, by the way did not say nothing can exceed the speed of light in general relativity, that maxim only applied in the case of special relativity.

5- Such assumptions explain further the theory of inflation, the behavior of black holes, the notions of extra dimensions, dark energy, dark matter, universe expansion, particle pairing to some degree, and identifies the sub-atomic process and the galactic processes as similar if black holes are seen as interaction boundaries between two membrane universes of different physics; it explains space-time distortions and evidence of such interactions and the weakness of gravity and it extends the notion of the big bang to include continuing manifestations.

Finally it raises questions around the issue of information loss and places it in the context where loss does not occur but must be seen as information flow between conjoint and mingled membranes. Susskind"s solution was similar as the one I have proposed here except he exiled that information to the edge of the cosmos. I have kept it at home and tried to explain its interactions and transformation processes.

At the end of all this we are left with two conclusions, one good and the other discouraging. We may get hints of the whole universe complex, and those is exciting but are not smart enough to really understand all of it because we are from this universe.

So, as we eat our Einstein-cake, we must overcome our deep suspicion that a much better and more delicious cake is somewhere in the room, out of reach and unreachable and unknowable.

———

Such is life.

Jun 22,2010
Every time I think I am through with this blog I get an email from one of you which makes me realize there is more to deal with.

Here is the next candidate. If the above ideas are valid, we have to alter the Standard Model's idea of the big bang and Inflation Theory to account for the presence of Dark Matter and Dark Energy. We can not take a simple anti-matter notion and forget about it thereafter.

We have to take into account how merged and merging membranes account for them and now for black holes and their roles in all of this.

And of course we want to know what are the dynamics of this merging process everyday that is observable to us.

These are weighty matters.

Time for more ice cream.

See you tomorrow.

June 23, 2010
With the merging concept there is yet another potential fly in our ointment; that of Dark Flow.

Dark Flow is an observation made in 2008 of an astounding movement of whole clusters of galaxies at about 2 o'clock in the visible universe where whole clusters of galaxies are *in a line* moving at speeds of three million hours per hour toward a single point! Millions of light years in diameter this "Dark Flow" was totally unexpected and not supposed to be happening according to the big bang theory. (They are revising I understand)

The universe is supposed to be uniform in that mass is evenly distributed and temperature as well since the big bang. This huge movement of whole galaxy clusters is heading toward a spot between the star systems of Centarus and Vela is a shock if the observations hold up.

What can be causing this?

Well there are basically three possible explanations:

1- A huge mass outside our visible universe is drawing these clusters. This would mean that such a huge mass might be another universe or some super galaxy inside our universe but beyond the visible horizon is drawing upon matter.

String theory and bubble universe, inflation people and multiverse people claim the "other universe" is a logical explanation.

2- This phenomena might simply be dark energy at work and *space itself* is expanding and our universe is simply larger than we think.

3- I have suggested a merged universe theory (see above) where dark energy and merged expanding space itself is creating a **singularity.**

I have suggested that black holes might be manifestations of merged universes interacting and now I am suggesting that this dark flow might simply be the two membranes creating the Mother of All Black Holes.

After all, all of these galaxies are moving in a line toward a single center. Would another universe outside our own create such a straight line? A pull would create a more diffuse pattern not a straight line unless there was something like a peep-hole phenomena going on, in which case the singularity thesis is reinforced not disproven.

Ah, but again all three speculations demand some kind of proof; and that is the hard part.

Jun 23, 2010
In our never-ending blog we come back to an aspect we passed over lightly above. But careful readers will note that we discussed the idea of a holographic theory of the universe which some string theory people embrace. But note there are implications of this for what we have described as the problem of the idea.

And that believe it or not gets us back to literature, religion and the life because one implication is that our brains, just like it does with memory has created individual universes (multitudes of them) as a function of our brains interaction with what we conceive of as the material universe. In other words, we are creatures with brains which have the capacity to interact with our universe to create individual versions of ourselves in multiple universes-holographic versions if you will.

More on this tomorrow in a separate entry-see the companion item on this site call "Everything You Heard About the Universe is Wrong."

Nov 11, 2010

A new discovery denoted in the New York Times announces that two huge bubbles of energy exist at the center of our galaxy. The import of this discovery cannot be understated. These bubbles are 50 light years across, covering half of the entire milky way, and, note this fit exactly with the Plasma Theory of the Universe. (See my blog "Everything you Heard About the Universe is Wrong"

Their mere existence radically changes our notions of the universe. See the "Wrong" blog for details.

Title: Everything You Heard About the Universe is Wrong

Summary: This is part of the Einstein essay series. See the ongoing series on this site.
Updated: 6/25/10: White Holes and Dark Energy
Updated: 6/27/10 The Idea of Dark Space and God as embodying the Universe. (Free Popcorn for the show.)
Updated 6/28/10: A New Theory of Black Holes and Their Role in the Universe
Updated: 6/28/10: Living in Two Universes At The Same Time?
Updated: 7/1/10 The Dynamics of the Mergered Universes Idea and Supersymmetry
Updated: 7/2/10 The Merger Process -Retro-Engineering the Merger Process
Updated: 7/4/10 Views and Critiques of the Standard Model of Physics
Updated: 7/5/10 Critiques of Einstein-Is the Relativity Theory Wrong?
Updated: 7/6/10 Superfluids and Ether
Updated: 7/7/10 A Entirely New Model of Physics--What is that?
Updated: 7/8-9/10
Updated 7/10/10 Who is Hannes Alfven and Why Is He Saying Those Terrible Things About Physics?
Updated: 7/12/10 Was Hannes Alfven Persecuted in Physics?
Updated: 7/13/10 Let's Have A Cler Look At Plasma Theory in the Last Ten Years
Updated: 7/15/10 The Electric Universe Ideas About the Nature of Matter, Gravity and Light
Updated: 7/17/10 Photos of the Electric Sun
Updated: 7/18/10 Just When You Thought You Understand Things Someone Comes Along And Applies Another Big Bang To Your Hard Won Wisdom.
Updated: 9/12/10 Superwave Theory
Updated: 9/13/10 Elementary Wave Theory- And What, We Ask Is That?
Updated: 11/10/10 Looks Like the Plasma Theory of the Universe Might Be the Correct One
Updated: 11/11/10 One Would Hate For Plasma Theory to Be Correct.

Jun 24, 2010 (Continued from the blog "Einstein: Time, Space, Buddha and Poetry)

The Holographic view of the universe takes the view that the brain is the creator of our notions of the universe or, at the very least, the brain is fine-tuned to be in touch with the seen and unseen universe we have been describing in this blog. (Notice how strange ideas are not so strange when examined closely.) Here is yet another example.

Religious people have claimed for centuries of contact with the unseen, with God, and other visions from that unseen world. Now some scientists are saying that may very well, not only be possible, but verifiable at some time in the future. The experiment at CERN (remember that?) may provide some part of that proof.

Wow you say-and rightly so.

Think about that idea for a moment; and aren't you glad you have endured all of my prognostications to get to this point?

Think of the brain on a quantum level as having electrons which indeed pop in and out of existence, have the capacity to bridge across dimensions, participate in all of the processes we have described above and understandings from both science and religion seem to be saying the same things in the end:

1-There is an unseen and mostly unknowable realm out there.

2- We humans may never be able to comprehend all of it.

3- There may be some force, God or some entity or invisible force involved.

4- We are personally affected by all of this everyday in ways we are just beginning to understand.

5-That my actions in this world may reverberate across time-lines and indeed across other dimensions or realms.(That is a mouthful.)

6- All of the universe is a single unity, in contact with itself at all times and at all points.;

We are our brother's keeper and every thought manifests itself on both the physical as well as the spiritual plane across the fabric of space-time.(Another mouthful and I am getting very full.)

So who is God? So what is the supreme force in the universe?

No one really knows, except maybe it is in the human brain or accessible there. (Experiments are underway to tap the "God" experience in the laboratory and some progress has been made. But no one know how or why it occurs or even how to interpret the results. In any event you heard it here first.

The point though is that the brain and its connections to what we loosely called the universe remains mysterious. Some of the Holo people think the brain has created the illusion of all we see.

Quantum folks, and their view is as described above, root their view in Quantum physics and string theory, and we saw them above argue that a two dimensional holographic version of each and everyone of us exists in two dimensional space inches away but not detected by us (See Einstein series above)

Others still relate it all to religious experiences which refer to deep religious experiences, contact with God, angels, spirits and the like.

And still others make the point that the brain stores data and memory and reassembles it in what can be described as the holograph of the mind. One implication is that we are all in a Sims or Matrix stimulation, or only exist in the mind of our creator, divine or computer. Or even that we are all simulations created by our own future ancestors. Remember Einstein said past, present and future all exist simultaneously and, perhaps, accessible to us

So there you have it.

So, at this point, there is no overall unified Holographic View, except that all focus on "in here" rather than the "out there." One commentator remarked that Jesus, Buddha, and other religious folks have always counseled us to look within for answers. Maybe "within" is related to the workings of the human brain and its connections to the universe. Therefore, the brain is the focus of research.

This is the view of the some of holographic folks and scientists who are looking to the structure of the brain for answers.

But is it true? Not sure, but here is another thought which I have waited to discuss until after you have had your ice cream:

We are, from the point of view of science, at an earth-shaking point: Einstein's field equations fail, repeat fail, beyond the event horizon of a black hole to explain reality and they end up with impossible answers, and just as importantly, so do the equations of quantum mechanics. Neither one can claim at this point to have real answers.

If all this holds, it is of incredible importance because the Physics of our universe also fails as well. Everyone realizes how little is really known but the implications on this "not knowing" are enormous.

The Quantum folks are seeking to extend their ideas to fix this problem with a quest for a Theory of Quantum Gravity but nothing so far. Meantime, we are in this theoretical backwater -no verifiable answers from any quarter. And, even if there were, we might not be equipped to understand those answers. Tough spot.

But note science has moved more toward religious pre-suppositions rather than the other way around. (The Poet smiles)   But, stay tuned. Things change daily as we continue our explorations.

Next time.

June 26,2010
Now we want to take up the evaluation of the Holographic view as regards string theory in more detail and compare it to my own view.

I postulate that with the breakdown of Einsteinian equations and Quantum mechanics in the context of black hole events, space itself, not gravity, not neutrinos, not gravity vs. anti-gravity, is the critical issue.

The latter become side issues because we see now see how important it is to understand the nature of space itself..

We want to know the nature of space especially in the black hole context. Space is the grand mystery here, in terms of its behavior inside a black hole below the event horizon.

We have Space itself moving at the speed of light in the black hole, expanding beyond the event horizon and space itself expanding in the universe as a whole possibly in both examples moving beyond the speed of light. Space is therefore, poorly understood.

219

I assure you, as you can see, that whatever is happening with space, it is very, very strange.

Now lets go slowly because my brain is on unfamiliar ground and I am working this out as I type. You can see this, therefore, getting born in the black hole of my own mind.

Here is my logic: (see above for details) if we now understand empty space is not empty at all, and can exceed the speed of light and is filled up with energetic particles in what I have called the ocean-soup, then we want to know how the interaction of that energetic soup-space works in the context of a black hole.

But first we want to know what are the details of the characteristics of this empty space.

Here are a few guesses:

1- It can exceed the speed of light.

2- It is malleable.

3- It is allied with dark matter and dark energy

4- It might in fact be part of a larger universe structure, not our own, and that universe may obey different laws of physics, or can void ours upon contact.

5- It may be the real source of gravity

6. It can be seen, theoretically, to crush down upon gravitons or even electromagnetic fields to produce huge magnetic storms in some sort of fusion process.

7- It may be the answer to what white holes are; that is, if gravity collapses large stars and they become black holes and swallow other stars, where does all that star material go to? Einstein's field equations claimed that they go to infinity in mass structure, but that is impossible. But contemplate this idea: black holes sink and are the mirror image of white holes which may involve material leaving our membrane universe and entering that other one I have postulated. Therefore, this becomes the function of black holes and explains why there are millions of them in our membrane universe. (It may be that our universe is the result of a singularity we now

---

call the big bang and we are the white hole of that other universe. (Amazing stuff huh?)

Back to the black hole: Some of the material from black hole fusion goes back into the ocean-soup via space itself; going back into our ocean soup- at the speed of light in the process- creating new dark energy as a result of fusion occurring in the heart of the black hole-that dark energy fueling the expansion of our universe. Our black hole mirrors more or less the nucleus of the atom, where similar processes may be at work. (I am just bloated on mouthfuls now, aren't you?)

At last the small and the large are seen to behave similarly. Atoms and their sub-particles pop into and out of existence. Maybe black holes and their constituents parts do also. Just a thought.

This means that black holes may function as exchange points between the two universes I have postulated (ours and another) which are currently occupying the same space and time; again, a lot in these ideas.

Are they true and can they be tested?

Let's sleep on it. (This is the never-ending blog; let's age together.)

June 27, 2010
Above, we alluded to the importance of space in attempting to understand how black hole processes beyond the event horizon correlate with events at the quantum level. The idea here is that the space factor at the sub-atomic level can also be seen as filled with an energetic soup of energetic particles popping in and out of existence. The question is popping from where to where and what is driving the process.?

Aside from the electromagnetism theory there is no explanation of the Space itself which exists in that micro-sub-atomic realm. After all most of the volume of an atom is "empty space."
The proposal here is that dark energy and dark matter may be involved at the sub-atomic level as well as the galaxy level. Since both Einstein and Quantum have no explanation otherwise, let us explore this idea for a moment.
Just as virtual particles come into and out of existence at the quantum level let us postulate that the model we see at work at both the micro and the macro level is identical and that the two-universe model I have proposed

exists and that particles-waves in both meet and interact at both levels. Bear with me, now.

I do not find that electromagnetism alone can account for what is transpiring at the quantum level nor at the below event horizon level with black holes. So-called empty space exists at both levels.

Let assume that at the mico-level:
1-energetic processes involving dark energy and dark matter are at play.
2- The interplay involves exchanges at the boundaries between the two membranes I postulate.
3- The interplay involves the annihilation of particles, as currently believed, but more, some of these particles actually move over and into the other universe and back and this is a process whereby a dynamic tension is at play and is maintained between the two membrane universes.
This becomes the real reason electrons stay in place, not just from electromagnetism alone. Let's further assume that quantum gravity also exists but it a predominately one-way residual gravity coming at us from that other universe.
It is weak as a result but the process at the macro level also involves space itself creating dark energy from that interaction as well and hence universe expansion on the macro level. Since this dark energy is negligible at the micro level and doesn't have to be particularly strong to hold particles in place there but is much stronger at the macro level.
At the macro level the exchanges occur below the event horizon level and what is being ejected is not just Hawking radiation or gamma rays but also dark energy and dark matter as the result of a fusion process occurring below the event horizon and the latter two energies are ejected at speeds faster than light and the universe expands as a result of not just dark energy but of Space itself expanding as well as a function of the interchanges between the two membranes in the context of the millions of black holes we know are in the Milky Way alone. This is a two way exchange. This process keeps the tension between the two universes at manageable levels and things are more stable as a result, except for the dark energy part because our gravity in this universe does not balance off the dark energy processes coming through from the other.
I propose this because it would give us the same model of interaction at both the micro and the macro level—why would nature waste a perfectly good model if it can be used in both places, the very small and the very large?
Now interestingly the CERN experiment might provide some proofs or hints.
But the larger point, is that we are postulating that dark energy and matter are just facets of Dark Space which has its origins in the merged membrane we keep alluding to.
Now that would be interesting, if it turns out to be a valid way of looking at things.

But, by the time this never ending blog is finished I will be old and tottering and perhaps you as well. But we solider on, don't we?

Next time let's look at the notion that if our universe is part of a larger structure and has exponential growth as its characteristic, are we foolish to rule out that this whole structure might be alive--especially if we take Susskind"s "string division" ideas seriously and push them just a little bit to ask: who are we to say that we do not exist inside a universe, (the mind of God) that is alive?

Now that would be truly interesting. Next time, let's examine that idea. Don't touch anything; we are on delicate premises here.

June 28, 2010:
But first, a detour which is not really a detour. That detour is to have another look at black holes (they keep coming up) and relate them to the idea of the "living universe" (this is just for fun, ok? We just want to push this idea and see where it leads. After all who knows anything for sure these days)

Now we know that black holes exist in their millions in our very own galaxy and it is safe to say they exist in other galaxies as well. Every galaxy, it seems, also, has a massive black hole at its center and black holes may in fact create those galaxies and such creation may go all the way back to the big bang. So black holes were present very early.

So what, we may ask, accounts for this phenomena? Why all these black holes? We see that they are not anomalies but seem to be central features of the universe and galaxy-making. Most of the stuff and matter our universe exist in black-hole dominated galaxies.

So here we go:
Let's assume that our merged universe idea is true and that these two merged universes collided and produced the big bang. Since both membrane universes were wavy or had ripples, contact created the equivalent of tides and rip-tides as they began the process of merging. Like fluids the two universes had several forms of interaction at this point:

1-A rip tide motion is created as matter from both universes intermingled
2-Tectonic plate like motions occurred continuously where one ripple in a membrane perhaps dived below a ripple in the other membrane causing an earth-quake like responses and constructive and destructive wave patterns.
3-These crashes created disequilibrium between matter and energy in both membranes and the two systems sought almost immediately to both "wall off their matter and energy structures, one from the other, and establish some sort of equilibrium between the two. (Membranes in this theory seek equilibrium and resist total emulsion and this is accomplished by a "safety

---

223

value" function which explains the creation of black holes as boundary keepers between the two and where some exchanges, for equilibrium purposes, are in fact happening.

Moreover, after the collision, tensions between the two universes remain, and over time black holes emerged as both boundary maintainers but also to facilitate energy and matter exchanges between the two universes which would not de-stabilize either.

We have mentioned another kinds of interactions such as rip tides and plate interactions between the two membranes. Could black holes be the rip-tides produced as a part of the merging process and interaction points? Maybe.

4- This would explain quantum mechanics and Einstein's field theories in that the energy soup I have postulated includes boundary particles moving between the two membranes. An imbalance of forces between the two membranes, such as the strength of gravity, has effects in both. Now what would be interesting is to deduce the nature of the dominant membrane by its effects on our own.

5-Black holes perform these boundary and matter and energy exchange functions between the two membranes, and may be typical of such functions between dimensions as well.

After all, how is boundary integrity maintained between dimensions anyway?

So now you ask what in Hades does this have to do with the "living organism" idea anyway?

Well, here goes; and hold the derision for a sec; can black holes be the equivalent of "cell structures" inside a living organism of gigantic proportions? Is this on the quantum level analogous to "string division?" Probably not; but an interesting idea. But more importantly it gives us some new ideas to work with. Here they are:

1. String theory, cosmic theory, and even Einstein ignore the issue of boundary making in discussing how the universe and dimensions work. The CERN experiment is essentially an experiment at testing those boundaries; so what I am saying is not entirely true. Boundary testing is coming to the fore.

But once you focus on boundaries at the micro and macro levels you have to play the cards you have: to wit what roles do black holes play in boundary and equilibrium maintenance between the dimensions we postulate and in our own universe? Put simply, at the quantum level, the simplest question is how are the boundaries of the atom (electrons in their orbits) maintained if we discount the assertion that it is all electromagnetism?

So with this view, we get our Physics back and everyone goes away happy.
But no. (Did you think it would be this easy?)
There is more to this tale.
Tomorrow.

June 29, 2010
Now we look at another of our examinations of black hole interactions in the context of galaxy formation. We want to know because there might be analogs at the quantum level.

Let's say my merged theory is correct and black holes in fact pre-date galaxies and that galaxies were in fact created by these very same black holes. Black holes are also exchange points and now I am guessing are the real engine of the inflation process and perhaps even dark energy expansion.

If contact is made, let say there was not one big bang, but perhaps millions as the contact process proceeded between the two membranes. The product was millions of black holes as forces from the two membranes intermingled, repelled in some cases and attracted one another but tremendous amounts of energy spewed instantly into our universe as part of an equilibrium-seeking process. Black holes are these entry and interaction points in the early two-membrane contact process.

Inflation instantly occurs as a function of dark energy pouring into our universe moving at speeds which exceed the speed of light. Thus inflation happens simultaneously at millions of points.

This model explains why stars at the outer rim of a massive black hole galaxy are moving at the same velocity as stars closer in. That is to say that massive black holes at the center of galaxies seem to be affecting stars way beyond their gravitational pull. This tight relationship apparently exists in most galaxies and are not explained in Newton models, Einstein or quantum models.

I have proposed it makes sense if we see space itself as an actor in this phenomena as well as black hole processes involving dark energy transfers between two branes. I have added a third aspect at this point: that of early inflation process from membrane contact and suggest that such contact is still going on.

Finally I end the blog today with two additional thoughts: suppose our universe is not expanding but being "blown up" (like a balloon) or

———

expanded by dark energy interacting with in-coming dark energy from another universe? Now this would make sense and I officially abandon the "mind of God" notion for now. We, should, I think, explore this idea's utility as regards other mysteries in Einstein and quantum mechanics. As always, we want to know what theories explain best what we see happening at the micro and maco level. And of course, how such ideas can be tested.

Well I have had enough for one day, how about you?

July 1, 2010
Continuing with our investigation of "empty space" I have been vague but vague is all we really have now. My argument is that I am vague in a better way than others I have read.

One candidate of super vague is Supersymmetry. I don't pretend to understand it (few do) but I propose not to look it from a physics point of view but from the point of view of a central organizing principle. Much of physics in my view has gone to a way of working where physicists discover or create new particles every day but do it from a bottom up point of view rather than from some central concept which is then tested.

Einstein did this. He conceived a new theory of gravity and then conceived how it could be tested. In his later years in search of a theory of everything he sought merely mathematical solutions instead of asking what kind of idea or organizing principle can explain what we can currently observe. That tack proved fruitless and he hit a dead end for the remainder of his career. His earlier work was around organizing principles (gravity, light, relativity etc, not particle finding and mathematical conception-making.

To complicate matters even more the Nobel Prize people started handing out the prize to anyone who could claim they had discovered a new particle and viola, physicists started chasing or hypothesizing new particles in unprecedented numbers. But where has all this particle inflation (couldn't resist the pun) gotten us? Deep into the black hole. (smile)

Inventing new particles creates a process of punting when these particles cannot be detected except by increasingly more expensive equipment until finally at the CERN the biggest machine in history has been built to tackle the problem.

This had better work.

Super symmetry is perhaps a whole new example. It produces great equations and mathematical models, but has, as well, invented whole new

---

super symmetrical particles and models of the universe in seeking a unified model of the universe. The number of particles doubled. It invented an entire universe of particles to match the observable one, much like anti-gravity was postulated to explain quantum dynamics.

This is tantamount to saying "the check is in the mail" in that solutions to theoretical problems get buried by inventing another particle or class of particles or indeed whole unseen worlds and dare I say dimensions-particles which may not be verifiable. Supersymmetry does this with particles with names too exotic to name here. But the point of creating these particles is to create equilibrium in the micro and macro systems. If that is the case better to go to the root of the problem--equilibrium rather that constantly seek to examine its parts without identifying the nature of the whole.

Such systems keep chasing the carrot without verifying if the carrot exists at all.

My suggestion is a simple one, which is of all of our ways of looking at the universe a merging of membranes presents the best idea in terms of creating an organizing principle for observable effects and for proposing components which are testable. (There are other candidates which I will examine later)

My suggestion was the merged universe idea with a motivating or driving tendency toward equilibrium. This fits with:

1- The principle conservation of energy--all systems seek some sort of equilibrium

3- It assumes a dynamical relationship with all matter and energy and this matches with both quantum and Einsteinian physics. (The aforementioned energetic soup idea)

4- It can potentially be verified at CERN.

5- It uses the precepts of both gravity and electro-magnetism which argue there are balancing forces in nature which can overcome inertia

What I have added is the two universe notions, which look like they might be described with simple electromagnetic and theory of fluid laws. Research would then focus on the functions of dark energy and space in our universe as a corollary and just might explain the Higgs field (or mass creating Ether) as having originated from the merging process which is described here as an on-going process

---

227

Now, of course, there are as yet undiscovered particles and forces involved but the ones I postulate actually do exist, i.e., dark matter and dark energy and the only new assumption is that the Higgs field is an entangled membrane. Note field, not particle)

My argument is that we have to identify how this functions at the micro and macro level. Process, not particles and waves, might be a better approach, especially in a dynamical system--and that is, after all, is what quantum and Einstein physics have in common and both contrast with Newton.

So my last arguments in these regards are that while I don't have all the answers I know where they live. (smile)

Maybe.

We will not know for Cern-tain until next year.

Now as an example of the above approach I offer the following:

Let's try to understand our universe in terms of process as it relates to the merger process.

I propose we examine the Pre-Universe characteristics of both membranes as a way to understand what processes we currently see at play in our own four dimensional universe and then back up the tape and see what we have.

(By the way what is slightly embarrassing to me, a lay person, is that modern physics seems to be in the business of postulating more and more particles, and indeed discovering some of them, but having to theorize to explain how the remaining undiscovered particles all fit into an over-arching theory, hence robbing us of the understanding such activities are supposed to produce. And to boot we are asked to swallow the idea that light itself is both a particle and a wave or can function either way, depending upon circumstances and probabilities. Really.

Also take the Hierarchy Problem where the strong force, weak force, electro-magnetic force and gravity are hypothesized as once being unified but that re-unification only can take place at temperatures never theoretically possible. Really. (Forgive this diversion.)

Back to the issue at hand:

Here are the parameters of any merger theory.

1- The merger process must result in a Goldilocks world, that is, once the two membranes start the merger process it must result in a universe where the forces involved result in a universe capable of supporting life.

Us.

2- Second it must explain why at short distances the weak force is so much stronger than gravity.

3. It must hypothesize the temperature at which all of the four forces were unified and then have become separated in our universe.

4- It must explain the nature and role of black holes.

5. It must not result in more particles which are never detectable.

So off we go. (We will have to do this in stages and not all in one day.

Let's take gravity first:

Gravity is very weak at the quantum level and apparently also at the macro level as well.

Let's assume the Lisa Randall theory that the incoming membrane is a strong gravity universe where gravity is indeed very strong, so strong such that, as a result of the merger, (she did not assume merger as far as I know, I am the one guilty of that assumption) there are enough gravitons left over so as to provide gravity, in the right amounts, for our universe.

Now this is interesting

First it means that the In-Coming is a heavy gravity membrane. What would that look like?

Let's speculate for moment:

1- It could mean that Incoming could be a membrane of black holes the most extreme gravity environment we know of .Or that the incoming is a gigantic black hole itself; or last simply a heavy gravity environment.

This heavy gravity membrane might, if similar to our black holes, be composed of heavy, compacted neutrinos, massless or of the low mass variety or of photons and electrons and that is all.

Upon collision (remember that) a soup ocean of these initial particles spew into our universe. (I can just see the photons flying.)

Further, let's hypothesize that our own pre-universe had the following traits.

1-It is a weak force universe with little or no gravity.

2- The collision with In-Coming generates faster than the speed of light movements in the soup which is now defined as space itself. So space itself and it's sea of energetic particles also pour into our universe in an initial collusion which generates temperatures approaching a trillion degrees.

3-So our pre-Universe did exist with just the strong nuclear force, the weak and the electro. But how and in what configurations, and with what strengths? It is a possible that this universe is likely composed, however, of only thin particles including atoms, flying around in a great magnetic cloud with lines of force providing to it all some structure. Gravity enters the changes all that.

Under specified high temperatures at the collision, all four of the forces combine and become one source. Under cooling conditions gravity separates out because its source is not in our pre-Universe. It is coming from the other.

But this process has made life possible in our universe where it had not been possible before.

More tomorrow- establishing equilibrium in the joined and merging universes.

Note:

According to our present understanding, the electromagnetic field itself is produced by photons, which in turn result from a local gauge symmetry. But is this pre-or post collusion? And which universe had the photons, in-coming or native?

July 4.2010
But first another diversion. In response to some of your emails it is proper to look at the counter-views to all of this. You will recall I have stated there was a crisis in physics. It became clear that when Einsteinian and Quantum field equations failed in the black hole example; other discrepancies in these two models (collectively known as "The Standard Model" also have become apparent.

This has spawned other alternative views and rebels in the ranks. Of course, the Physics establishment has ignored both the newly proposed models and also the critiques of its own model. The massive response was to create more particles without dealing with the central critiques being made.

In fact, the theory of inflation was created as a response to the many questions created by particle physics.

The nature of these counter models are detailed and I won't bore you will them, instead I will focus on the discrepancies in the Standard Model these models sought to address. The three areas I will address include:

1- The nature of space, the vacuum, and the battered notion of Ether

2- The nature of gravity and its relation to the other forces of nature.

3- The nature of the electromagnetic force, Superfluids, and crystallization theories and the idea that even our three dimensional world is actually a five dimensional universe shaped like a box. (Yes, box.)

4. Arguments over the nature of light and its so-called speed limit.

Well as you can see there are a lot of rebels in the woods. We will, in the coming days, have a look at some of them. My take off on the Lisa Randall's idea isn't exactly rebel in the woods but it does live on the edge of the woods.

Watch your dimensions--three, four, or five and don't forget number two.

July 5.2010
A lot of the problems and critique of modern physics ultimately centers on the question of is space empty? If it is not (and it certainly is not) what is its nature? The idea of a vacuum in space now turns out to be inaccurate. Space is not empty and as we have seen can move at the speed of light

---

231

and has huge influences on galaxies as well as atoms. So again what are the properties of space. What is in there?

Interestingly, this is precisely where we can demarcate the boundary line between so-called modern physics and so-called classical physics. And wouldn't you know it Einstein was in the center of it all.

This is a juicy story and I know how you all out there love a good juicy, true story.

Get the popcorn out and give a listen.

Einstein in his earth-shaking new theory did not create it in a vacuum (smile) He was aiming to disagree with an existing theory of space that said space was filled with an Ether that acted like a fluid. Einstein, who was working at the time on how light propagates argued that light could not propagate in a fluid. (Yes, we saying these folks were making the argument that empty space is actually a fluid and behaves like a fluid and we are affected by the motion of this Ether fluid which is all around us.)

Einstein comes along and basically joined the gang who argue: "There is no Ether at all because as everyone knows liquids can diffuse and refract light and light does not behave that way, hence there is no fluid or Ether.

This was big news back in the day. Physics quickly choose sides in the controversy. Who to support, the new upstart or the old professionals who needed to have explained what do you put in the place of Ether, if you drop the concept altogether?

Einstein and the quantum folks had an answer. They put quantum mechanics in the place of the Ether on the atomic level, and Einstein solved the problem by simply ignoring it and stated axiomatically that light moves at the speed of light and at a constant rate since there is no Ether to hinder its propagation.

Gravity, Einstein said is related to space-time which is moving around, not any fluid. Wow, talk about turning things on its head.

Einstein's antagonist in all of this was Dayton Miller, a well-known and respected scientist in his day who set out to prove the existence of ether by measuring its effects on the absolute velocity of the earth and as affected by this ether. This would disprove Einstein's whole edifice that everything is relative and dependent upon the vantage point of the observer. He was trying to prove there aim's no relativity at all and that light has no constant speed because space is really filled with fluid or ether.

The line of conflict was drawn. Miller published the results of his experiments in 1928 which showed there was an ether which the earth and all matter in the universe floats in and it moves. The absolute velocity of the earth and the speed of this moving ether itself could be computed and its velocity he said was moving toward a specific constellation. Wow again. This story is riveting.

You can see the threat to Einstein here who claimed; no everything is relative and the quantum folks added to all this, "therefore we can never know the position of particles at the quantum level with any certainty." Einstein's relativism on the macro level now had an analog on the micro level although later there was to be real problems with simply assuming that relativity worked the same on both levels.

Einstein's view prevailed and he actively sought to bury the Miller data and that point of view. He knew upon which slice of bread his Nobel prize lay.

In July of 1925 Einstein, writing to a friend stated:

"My opinion about Miller's experiments is the following. ... Should the positive result be confirmed, then the special theory of relativity and with it the general theory of relativity, in its current form, would be invalid. Experimentum summus judex. Only the equivalence of inertia and gravitation would remain, however, they would have to lead to a significantly different theory."
— Albert Einstein, in a letter to Edwin E. Slosson, 8 July 1925 (from copy in Hebrew University Archive, Jerusalem.) See citations below for Silberstein 1925 and Einstein 1926.

"I believe that I have really found the relationship between gravitation and electricity, assuming that the Miller experiments are based on a fundamental error. Otherwise, the whole relativity theory collapses like a house of cards."
— Albert Einstein, in a letter to Robert Millikan, June 1921 (in Clark 1971, p.328)

Cited from Dayton Miller's Ether-Drift Experiments: A Fresh Look* by James DeMeo, Ph.D.

But as quantum mechanics took hold in the world of physics it, apparently had to re-invent the notion of ether fluid, calling it

"Quantum Foam" and many other labels which essentially re-introduced the notion proclaiming that because of the foam (I have called it an ocean-soup of particles) only probabilities can exist at the mico level. Think about it: if elemental particles dissipate upon observation that could be someone interrupting the flow of a wave through a fluid, couldn't it?

Einstein had his doubts about quantum mechanics and even though he helped to create it he never really accepted it wholeheartedly.

But note, in later life, he seemed to doubt most of his relativity work as well. In a letter to a friend he wrote:

— Albert Einstein, on his 70th birthday, in a letter to Maurice Solovine, 28 March 1949 (in B. Hoffman *Albert Einstein: Creator and Rebel* 1972, p.328)

"You imagine that I look back on my life's work with calm satisfaction. But from nearby it looks quite different. There is not a single concept of which I am convinced that it will stand firm, and I feel uncertain whether I am in general on the right track."

So quantum mechanics gives us ether without calling it ether. Interesting, even the string theory people are backing into a fluid like notion of space filled with strings, of course which vibrate and above all else, properties and characteristics of matter flow from these strings. For example Andrew Strominger says that space itself is composed of strings and behaves like a wave. or something close to it. Here comes those pesky fluid notions back again, one more time. Pardon me, critics say, but don't waves move in a fluid, elastic or otherwise?

So what is the difference we may ask between this quantum ether and classical notions of ether and a modern notion of ether which is often referred to as Superfluids.

So you thought this story would be simple huh?

July 6.2010
Well like many theories in Physics we will see an initial attempt to distinguish a new theory from old ones, but then we see movements where the new tries to incorporate the old ideas after having declared them defunct or full of fundamental errors; but then later still make the claim that should new facts arise, claim," yes I was saying that too; my theory is

consistent with what the facts that I now see emerging. It is just that you and I were saying it differently; and by the way; a minor difference I will stress as a way of trying to maintain my ideas are also different than yours still, especially if I blow up this minor difference and pretend it is of greater import than it really is. And besides, just as you can't produce your particle, neither can I and last, but not least, I will hide my ideas in a blackboard filled with equations with terms I have not defined, and, in which I have hidden dubious terms which I am having my graduate students try to figure it out for me, and since that takes time--lets say thirty years to clarify what I was talking about in the first place. I proclaim now new knowledge is difficult to obtain and takes time, urging my students and colleges to be patient while I try to figure out what the hell went wrong with my ideas and while I secretly nurse a dry bitterness about those who don't appreciate the mathematical beauty of what I have been trying to do all these years.

But the above is a typical process not only in academia but also in many professions. I do not undervalue the work being done in advancing our knowledge in Physics and many other fields. It is just I see the humor in it emanating from the capacity of human beings to move peas and shells around when pressed for concrete answers to complex questions.

This is life and life only.

Tomorrow: Let's look at crystallization theories, more on fluid theory and the "We all live in a big box theory" and sundries. Oh, I am tired already.

Will fluid save us? Let's just say that for now we can only describe the situation in Physics as very fluid. The Ghost of Ether is everywhere.

July,8-9 2010
So here we are at ether, like Einstein, we have to deal with it. We know what he did, he dismissed it and invented an arbitrary speed limit for light and there by eliminated the problem of ether. Now this is an indication of how difficult the problem is for Einstein to have made this maneuver.

I am no Einstein and don't have the brains even to dismiss ether so, I too, want to through up my metaphorical hands and invent something entirely new.

Well I don't and can do it but others have re-tacked the problem.

Now what would that be, you ask?

Well there are many alternatives out there and I can't go over all of them. But let's take a few conceptual ideas and see what categories they fall into.

First let's just take a huge idea totally different from the standard model then we'll let the idea sit for 24 hours.;

Here is the idea:

Einstein said let's see what happens to our thinking if we see space-time as one concept. Here is one he missed: What would happen to our thinking if we see matter-space as a single entity and related in such a way so as to explain everything we see in the universe. That is a very interesting idea.

But first a hint: Why is the speed of light constant? Einstein said so and its speed is a constant but he never had an answer as to why.

Answer to ponder: Space is the inverse of matter and matter is the reciprocal of space--each aspect of this single reality interact with one another via disturbances in the two different electrical fields they propagate and all of that interaction can be described by wave functions in this (dare we say ether) along with vortex and super fluid like characteristics.

One variety of this view says that particles are merely aspects of wave functions and vortex interactions and condensates. A similar pattern exists they say in Helium 3 experiments where normal liquid helium interacts with superconductive Heliium3.

To summarize matter is enfolded space and space is expanding matter. These are the two major forces at work in the universe. Gravity becomes a disturbance created in the Space-Matter continuum (we don't need Einstein's time component) Light is a wave propagating in space defined as having super fluidity components. Light does not move but excites waves like a ripple in a pond propagating outward. These waves quantum folks call "quanta" all of this existing in a quantum soup or in the "quantum vacuum."

Finally these super fluid aspects of matter found at the quantum level are also found in the core of neutron stars. Finally one theory (Scoce) identifies light as the manifestation of photons embedded in this elemental space and propagation is via wave functions across the medium of space which is defined as the ultimate super fluid.

Matter becomes congealed space. Note here E=mc2 is to be understood that matter as congealed space can be transformed back into it's space

---

236

component and it is the dark energy of space itself expanding from the dynamics of the Einstein equation. Matter equals condensed space and can be transformed into energy or exploding space moving at speeds up to and exceeding the speed of light squared. And, then you can also read the equation backwards. Add to this the concept of space as a plasma-like super fluid and you have the basic idea.

Now that is a clever turn on Einstein, don't you think?

We end up in this category of theories with basically only two elemental particles in the universe: photons and electrons and ions out of which everything else is built via a process acting in this vortex- interacting model and all other elements are created via "condensation" processes operating between the two processes, one positive and the other negative involved as wave functions. Goodbye particles--which in the end are wave condensations.

The argument, this group says, is that Physics got off on the wrong track with quantum mechanics and Einstein where causality was severed from effect and we have ended up with non-inquisitive notions tied to math models which custom fit the results and produce the Uncertainty Models. If everything is uncertain then nothing can be known. They argue that we were better of with minor corrections to a previous model of ether, even as we notice that quantum folks in fact inch back toward that model while denying that they are doing so.

So the past is re-introduced via Superfluids theories which are ether by another name.

Finally, they point out that the original equations around ether pointed out that the expansion of space as ether was infinite and Einstein's generation revolted against that outcome. Einstein's equation also ended up with infinity as a result in the context of a black hole. Now, point out the critics,, the expansion of space infinitely is not so fantastic as it once seemed. After all Superfluids under laboratory conditions are frictionless and once set in motion can continue to move forever. Humm, this is getting more and more confusing. But we like that don't we? It must mean we are on to something.

I know.

This is a lot to absorb at a single sitting.

Let's sleep on it.

July 10 2010
Now many of the alternate theories of how the universe works center on two of the most glaring problems that the standard model face:

1- The first is why is it that galaxies do not seem to obey Newton or Einstein and those black holes as well present problems.

2- The second is the astounding fact that the entire universe is expanding exponentially. The further out the galaxy the faster it is receding from us.

These two problems were answered by the Standard Model with the postulation of dark matter, dark energy, and a myriad of particles with strange names like Machos Wimp's, neutrinos with mass etc.

After all it is embarrassing to note that 95% of the universe is made of up stuff nobody knows and can't detect.

Into this intellectual breach ride still other alternative views which offer the following answers:

1-The galaxy problem can be solved if we conceive of space as a super fluid. This kind of behavior has been observed in the lab with He3 and this might be the case on the macro level as well.

2-The galaxy problem might be "electric plasma.". Space is gigantic electrical fields and can be understood so as such to explain the galaxy problem. Gravity becomes a function of electrical field interactions. Particles and their interactions become photons and electrons interacting within these electrical fields and within this plasma, which by the way ,has some of the same characteristics as a super fluid.

The expansion of the universe in the one example is due to the capacity of space to expand infinitely propelled by the mass within space to transform itself into space which can travel at or above light speeds.

In other alternative theories the interaction of these plasma fields account for expansion in ordinary electrical and charge terms--although this is little vague in terms of what I have read. The idea though is that just as lightening strikes powerfully, it is the power of electricity which drives the

great movements we see in the universe. The same would be true on the quantum level as well. The electric plasma group has a pedigree. See the work of Hannes Alfven who virtually created the field won a noble prize and basically challenge all of the major premises of the Standard Model:

To wit:

1-There was no big bang.

2-There is no expansion of the universe

3- There are no black holes

4-The universe is infinite, always was and always will be

5- The Sun does not produce energy by nuclear fusion

6- Stars are not created or destroyed by "collapsing gravity"

5- Most of the process we see in the universe can be explained and, indeed predicted, by electro-magnetism and positive and negative gas plasma clouds clearly visible in the universe. I will give some citations next time for those wanting to track down this gentleman most of us have never heard of.

Now of the groups of theories above only the super fluid example addresses the quantum issues. And Superfluids are being accepted by mainstream physics at this point, and quantum theory itself is slowly backing into adopting the experimental results. I have argued that I am not seeing much difference between Superfluids behaviors on the macro and the micro levels but that has to be verified experimentally.

How? Well we will always have CERN. Isn't that in Paris?

Next time--what about my merging universe theory; and who are those electric plasma people and why are they saying those terrible things about the Standard Model?

July 12, 2010
The challenger with all of the above assertions is Hannes Alfven. His student writes on a website devoted to Alfven:

"Alfven"s approach to physics was based on insight and intuition. He was quick to understand how nature works and he was able to place new observations into a framework larger than that required to explain the observations themselves. For example, in the early 1930"s, cosmic rays were commonly thought to be gamma rays filling the entire universe. However, when they were discovered to be charged particles, Alfven offered in 1937 the novel suggestion that the galaxy contained a large-scale magnetic field and that the cosmic rays moved in spiral orbits within the galaxy, owing to the forces exerted by the magnetic field. He argued that there could be a magnetic field pervading the entire galaxy if plasma was spread throughout the galaxy. This plasma could carry the electrical currents that would then create the galactic magnetic field.

Alfven was a Nobel prize winner (1970) and the lists of his credentials are quite impressive for someone few have heard of.

He is credited generally which discovering: electrons and ions moving in orbits through gigantic galaxy-sized magnetic fields in space create electric current flows and argues that this is the real explanation for galaxy behavior and missing matter better than gravity or dark matter.

He apparently, according to his supporters discovered:

1- The explanation of the Van Allen radiation belt

2- The cause of fluctuations in the earth's magnetic field during magnetic storms

3- alternative explanations of the birth of our galaxies, stars, our solar system and the universe itself in terms of these gigantic magnetic fields where electrons and ions fly sometimes exceeding the speed of light in what has been dubbed the "electric plasma" which dominate space. Ether is apparently magnetic and has current flows.

4- He predicted the filamentary structure of the universe in 1963 saying that space is filled with current flows and essentially operates like the familiar dynamo we know on earth.

5- He presented explanations of a large magnetic field which dominates our own galaxy and connected that to the behavior and creation of our Sun; identifying nonthermal astronomical radiation sources. He argued that nearly all radiation recorded by radio telescopes derive from these gigantic magnetic clouds and their radiation. (I am reminded of "black body radiation" experiments Einstein sought to explain in his photoelectric experiments, for which he received a Nobel prize. This is important because his answers in that regard were designed to explain away black body radiation which Alfren explains. The attempt to explain away black body radiation and its experimental findings gave us quantum mechanics, such experiments show that heat is generated to infinity up and down the spectrum. Unacceptable this was, so the concept of "quanta" in light and

Planck's theorems were get around the problem. Alfren counters that was a wrong turn. The black body radiation is particles moving in galactic magnetic fields and understood today; all of this is moving in a gigantic magnetic field, nothing more; -- all of Einstein's and quantum theories are overkill and incorrect.)

The principle is the same as in a linear accelerator--magnets can move particles to speeds approaching light. This is happening in our universe as well according to Alfven.

Alfven "s supporters claim every day measurements of his claims are available but are discounted by the Physics establishment even as it uses his tools and concepts everyday. Giant magnetic clouds are discovered every day in astronomy but their meaning is never discussed.

Well, this is quite a bit. Reality all around me is changing. Alfven sounds like another Einstein critic and, by the way, what does Alfven have to say about relativity and quantum mechanics? That on tomorrow.

Me? I am going to have another look at that suspicious magnet on my refrigerator. Apparently a lot more than I thought is going on there.

Note for tomorrow:

Alfven is generally given credit as the father of Magnetohydrodynamics, for which he won an Nobel prize.

Magnetohydrodynamics (**MHD**) (*magnetofluiddynamics or hydromagnetics*) is the **academic discipline** which studies the **dynamics** of **electrically conducting fluids**. Examples of such fluids include **plasmas**, liquid metals, and **salt water**. The word *magnetohydrodynamics (MHD)* is derived from *magneto-* meaning **magnetic field**, and *hydro-* meaning **liquid**, and -dynamics meaning movement. The field of MHD was initiated by **Hannes Alfvén**[1], for which he received the **Nobel Prize** in Physics in 1970.

From Wikipedia

More Notes for Tomorrow:

In 1937, Alfvén argued that if plasma pervaded the universe, it could then carry electric currents capable of generating a galactic magnetic field.

[1]

After winning the Nobel Prize for his works in **magnetohydrodynamics**

he emphasized that:

In order to understand the phenomena in a certain plasma region, it is necessary to map not only the magnetic but also the electric field and the electric currents. Space is filled with a network of currents which transfer energy and momentum over large or very large distances. The currents often pinch to filamentary or surface currents. The latter are likely to give space, as also interstellar and intergalactic space, a cellular structure.[2]

His theoretical work on field-aligned electric currents in the aurora (based on earlier work by **Kristian Birkeland**) was confirmed by satellite observations, in 1974, resulting in the discovery of **Birkeland currents**.

7/13/10
So here we are dear reader ready to explore more of the electric plasma idea and to evaluate it.

There can be no question that many if not most of Alfven''s ideas about magnetic and electrical stellar fields have been actively accepted and a whole new field of magnetohydrodynamics has evolved to examine the nature of the universe and the stars from that vantage point

A cursory look at Science Daily and other sources show discoveries which seem to verify his ideas of how the magnetic-electrical universe works.

What would be the summary of it in terms of what has been verified independently?

1- The Universe indeed is populated by plasmas of huge size which include particles (hydrogen ions and charged electrons mostly) which interact with star and planetary magneto-electrical fields of immense size and these are likely the cause of star formation and even destruction. Gravitational effects are much less. (Those wanting citations for this can email me.) But you can search on "electric plasma" in Science Daily and there are over three thousand results. His results are now given names like "magnetic reconnection" "pinching in magnetic fields" but they are predicted by his writings. Huge magnetic dust clouds funnel particles along magnetic lines of force and pinch or reconcile at some points of interaction with other galaxy sized fields and help create stars and planets, not gravity alone. In fact these fields have cosmic rays and ions orbiting entire regions hundreds and thousands of light years in diameter. In dense ion areas these concentrations light up in the visible light range in others they are dark until these ions become energized by entering magnetic fields.

The four-satellite European Cluster group more or less verified these processes at work in connection with the earth's magneto-sphere and plasma, beginning in 2001 and again in 2004.

2- His ideas are accepted in electro-magnetic fluid dynamics and particular wave behaviors in these type fluids are called Alfven waves.

Therefore, much of Alfven''s work has been verified.

What is still controversial is his conclusions from the above observations and theories. Let's see what his conclusions were and why he came to them, and how they constitute a serious challenge to the Standard Model, Einstein's views and those of quantum mechanics.

We will take them one blog at a time.

The first is that Alfven challenged the notion that the universe is expanding; (and just when I was getting used to that notion.) His reasoning was that the famous Hubble experiment was erroneous and Hubble himself later in life said so and so did his assistant. (More detail on this later.)

The universe is not expanding Alfven says (the red shift analysis of the light of stars was made without understanding the role of the electro-magnetic plasma at work. Alfven makes the assertion that this is an error. The red shift in fact is a gas plasma indication a young star being born not a receding star or cluster. He indicates that the idea that the further away a star or galaxy is the faster it is receding does not makes sense and is not backed up by any real data other than this so-called red-shift data. Others of his followers also indicate that "gravitational lensing" techniques which are used to buttress this proposition makes no sense either.

For those who may not know, "gravitational lensing" is the purported process where by light from distant galaxies, say ones from the youth of the universe, "bends" around intervening and younger galaxies allowing us to observe them. The rationale is that light is affected by the gravity of these intervening galaxies and this "bending" allows that light to continue

---

on to us as opposed to being blocked. Einstein is cited to account for this effect.

Alfven and his later supporters point out that this lensing would require such precise lining up of the near and far galaxies so as to be exceeding rare and probably not exist at all. After all how many galaxies must be between the earliest ones and our own? Lots. So lensing would be broken up at some point along the way and all we would get is a distorted view at best.

This second technique of measuring the receding is also flawed.

Here we go. Does this mean that Einstein's "cosmological constant" is being dusted off and brought back in to the conversation? Yes, indeedy.

The implication of an non-expanding universe? Hold your hat. They are;

1-No expansion, no dark energy

2-No expansion ,no big bang, no inflation theory, and a whole new theory of cosmic radiation is needed because that is supposed to be what was discovered in the 60"s and the smooth texture and temperature of the cosmos therefore, doesn't make sense. Something, the Alfven people say, is wrong with that map.

Let's have a look tomorrow at the Hubble data and also at Alfven''s own description of how the now-expanding universe works.

Tomorrow: Oh boy. What do we do now?

July 15, 2010
Well lets evaluate Plasma and Electric Notions of matter and ether (yes we are back to that never-ending discussion of ether or aether.

What do the electric universe people have to say about the major issues we have discussed? Lets take gravity first and it's nature.

Newton gave up on understanding it. Einstein ridiculed it as "spooky action at a distance" in classical terms and offered an explanation of gravity as space-time interacting with mass and the former bending- creating gravity. I and others have placed gravity as an external force from another membrane universe, still others postulate gravity as part of a unified field of particles but don't offer much more insight as to what it is. Quantum mechanics has nothing real to add to this.

Desperate for answers we turn to electric plasma theory people and see what they have to say.

Here goes: Wal Thornhill and Donald Scott "the latter a leading string theorist and Nobel prize winner) appear to agree on some main electric universe ideas on gravity.

I will quote Thornhill at length since any attempt on my part to paraphrase will likely fail.

"The equivalence of inertial and gravitational mass implies that gravity is also an electrical force. Before Einstein, some noted scientists were suggesting that the gravitational force between neutral particles might ultimately be due to electrical polarization within the particles. In 1882, Friedrich Zöllner wrote in the introduction to his book, Explanation of Universal Gravitation through the Static Action of Electricity and The General Importance of Weber's Laws, "we are to conclude that pair of electrical particles of opposite signs, i.e. two Weberian molecular pairs attract each other. This attraction is Gravity, it is proportional to the number of molecular pairs." Indeed, gravity can be represented as the sum of the radically aligned electric dipoles formed by all subatomic particles within a charged planet or star."

Gravity here is the electrical components of particles realigning (like iron filings to a magnet?) and this true as well as in planets and stars. Wow, again. Gravity in this is a measure of the charge of sub-atomic particles in what we call matter. The distributions and intensity of the charge sub-atomically and at the star and indeed galaxy level determines the currents in space and its effects are seen as what we describe as gravity.

Humm, this is getting interesting. Go on Mr. Thornhill.

"This new electrical concept suggests that Newton's "universal constant of gravitation," or "G," is a dependent variable. G depends upon the charge distribution within a celestial body. Highly charged objects like comets look like solid rock, yet they have a gravitational field that suggests they are fluff-balls. And as they discharge they suffer what is euphemistically called "non-gravitational" accelerations. The extreme weakness of the force of gravity, compared to the electric force, is a measure of the minuscule electric dipolar distortion of nucleons."

Thornhill goes on to say that magnetism is also a manifestation the charge distribution in matter. He comes to a startling conclusion from all of this:

———

245

"This simple electrical model of matter has the great virtue of reducing all known forces to a single one – the electric force."

So all four of the fundamental forces end up being one-the electric force. But, we are warned, this comes at a price:

"However, it has a price. We must abandon our peculiar phobia against a force acting at a distance. And we must give up the notion that the speed of light is a real speed barrier. It may seem fast to us, but on a cosmic scale it is glacial. Imposing such a speed limit and requiring force to be transmitted by particles would render the universe completely incoherent. If an electron is composed of smaller subunits of charge orbiting within the classical radius of an electron, then the electric force must operate at a speed far in excess of the speed of light for the electron to remain a coherent object. In fact, it has been calculated that if released, the subunits of charge in the electron could travel from here to the far side of the Andromeda galaxy in one second!

We have direct evidence of the superluminal action of the electric force, given that gravity is a longitudinal electric force. Indeed, Newton's celebrated equation requires that gravity act instantly on the scale of the solar system. It has been calculated that gravity must operate at a speed of at least 2×10^{10} times the speed of light, otherwise closely orbiting stars would experience a torque that would sling them apart in mere hundreds of years. Similarly, the Earth responds to the gravitational pull of the Sun where it is at the moment, not where the Sun was 8 minutes ago. If this were not so, the Earth and all other planets in the solar system would be slung into deep space within a few thousand years. Gravity is therefore an electrical property of matter, not a geometrical property of space.

What is the nature of light? Einstein's special theory of relativity was disconfirmed right at the start by the Michelson-Morley experiment, which showed a residual due to the æther. This was later confirmed by far more rigorous repeats of the experiment by Dayton Miller. But by then popular delusion and the madness of crowds had taken hold and contrary evidence would not be tolerated. The Dayton Miller story makes interesting reading. If it weren't for the extraordinary power of self-delusion, commonsense would tell us that a wave cannot exist in nothing. So Maxwell was right, light is a transverse electromagnetic wave moving through a medium, the æther."

———

Sorry for the long quote here but I thought you should get the argument direct from the horse's mouth so to speak. But here comes another long quote. After that I promise no more.

"But what is the æther?" Thornhill says:

"In the vacuum of space, each cubic centimeter is teeming with neutrinos. And since neutrinos are resonant orbiting systems of charge, like all matter, they will respond to the electric force by distorting to form a weak electric dipole aligned with the electric field. The speed of light in a vacuum is therefore a measure of the delay in response of the neutrino to the electric force.

What about the bending of starlight by the Sun, which discovery raised Einstein to megastar status? The residual found in the Michelson-Morley experiments shows that the Earth and all ponder able bodies "drag" the Æther along with them. The bending of starlight near the Sun is simply the effect expected of an extensive neutrino atmosphere held to the Sun by gravity. Light will be slowed in the denser medium – causing normal refraction or bending of light.

What about time? With all bodies in the Milky Way galaxy communicating their positions effectively in real time through the electric force of gravity, it means there is a universal time. There can be no time distortion or time travel – something that common sense always told us.

What about black holes? They are a mathematical fiction, a near-infinite concentration of mass, required to explain concentrated sources of energy seen at galactic centers, by employing the weakest force in Nature – gravity. It is the high-school howler of dividing by zero. Plasma cosmology shows that where electrical energy is concentrated at the center of a galaxy, gravity can be ignored in favor of far more powerful electromagnetic forces. The collimated jets of matter coming from that focus are also replicated to scale in plasma labs. The jets are inexplicable if a black hole is supposed to be a cosmic sink for matter."

All quotes from http://www.holoscience.com/news.php?article=gdaqg8df

Well these ideas are far-reaching indeed. I am far-reaching for the Maalox because the story is getting scarier and scarier. Let's try to recover by tomorrow. See you then. But before that here is a definition of plasma:

Definition of Electric Plasma:

"Plasma has been called the "fourth state" of matter, after solids, liquids and gases. Most of the matter in the universe is in the form of plasma. A plasma is formed if some of the negatively charged electrons are separated from their host atoms in a gas, leaving the atoms with a positive charge. The negatively charged electrons, and the positively charged atoms (known as positive ions) are then free to move separately under the influence of an applied voltage or magnetic field. Their net movement constitutes an electrical current. So, one of the more important properties of a plasma is that it can conduct electrical current. It does so by forming current filaments that follow magnetic field lines. Filamentary patterns are ubiquitous in the cosmos."

July 17,2010

A diagram from **The Sun e-book** is interesting. The simplistic estimate of the size of the body of the Sun is intended to show that the atmosphere of a star can contribute a substantial amount to its apparent size, given by the thin yellow photosphere.

From http://www.holoscience.com/news.php?article=ah63dzac

This diagram purports to make a radical statement about the stars, our sun, our solar system and the universe. To wit:

1-The existence of large scale, galaxy-sized electro-magnetic fields in space drive the star formation process, not hydrogen and helium. Stars are not nuclear reactors. Rather they are formed by galaxy-sized magnetic fields in what is described as z-pinch and double-layer formations. More, this energy from stars comes from these external galaxy-sized magnetic fields which stream particles at light speed speeds, resulting in a discharge of particles (neutrinos and the solar wind for example) outward. These neutrinos, winds and cosmic rays interact with the Earth's magnetosphere and, indeed, with the magneto-spheres of all of the planets in our solar system. But note this is all part of a galaxy wide electro-magnetic field which has particles in orbit--all within this galaxy-wide plasma.

Numerous citations are given for this view. It goes on to assert:

1-Stars do not follow nuclear fuel exhaustion cycles which can take millions of years but, instead, say the Plasma Model, stars can form and die in a single life-time and they offer examples from current astrological observations of stars doing just that. Stars are not nuclear reactors.

248

2-Stars emit huge magnetic x-ray and gamma rays filaments because these discharges are electrical in nature and origin, not solely coming from black holes. Recent observations show huge comic dust trails from recently exploding stars. This is the normal expulsion via z-pinching and electrical discharge which is part of the evolution of starts. To be clear, depending upon the strength and density of the ion field and the magnetic field, a given star can explode at any time and evolve very quickly to its demise, even in as little as forty or fifty years.

3- They argue that the famous red shift is way overstated. The red shift is a measure of the youth of a star (young stars will emit a red-shift and even stars rotating away from us will emit a red-shift. The idea that the red-shift means only a receding star ends up with a prediction that the stars

furtherest away from us are moving away from us at speeds exceeding that of light, an absurd claim.

4- The issues around Dark Flow are best explained by a huge magnetic cloud field. Current theory has no explanation of dark flow.

5- There is no need for dark energy, dark matter theories, all are explained by the plasma theory.

6- No need for elaborate big bang and inflation theories.

In short the universe is relatively static and is probably infinite.

The best fit, in my view, with the Plasma theory is the membrane theory which does postulate a huge influx of plasma from one membrane to another, upon contact. But we shall in a later blog compare the Plasma theory with all others and try to judge which explains current observations and experimental results.

But first you may ask does Plasma Theory have to say about Quantum mechanics. What role does Plasma play at the quantum level?

I thought you would never ask.

But hold your Plasma until tomorrow.

July 18, 2010

Well at the quantum level the answer is all electric. Gravity is the attraction between the elemental particles, the electric force is prevalent, electrons can be easily placed within the "black body radiation" matrix but what has to be added is that the elemental particles exist inside galaxy-wide field currents driven by huge magnetic fields these currents themselves help generate.

Gravity then at the quantum and the galaxy level is the instantaneous realignment of the charges of ions and electrons which indeed exceed the speed of light. All of the universe is connected, as quantum holds, and entangled and these charged particles operate in pairs as quantum theory holds.

Einstein here is considered incorrect. String Theory is considered incorrect. Current astrological theories of what is happening with galaxies and stars are considered incorrect. Big bang and inflation theory is considered incorrect .Quantum theory is misapplying the role of electric forces at the

quantum level. Super fluid theory does seem to have utility because superfluids are a kind of plasma.

So with this kind of house cleaning what is left for Plasma to explain? They argue that the so-called search for the theory of everything, black holes, unified field theories, eleven dimensions is also flawed.

So what is left we ask again?

For that we have to wait until tomorrow, where we will examine the questions of how does a Plasma theory answer question which physicists today don't seem to have answers to.

Sept 12, 2010

Plasma theory has new adherents and some of it tenets seem to have ice core empirical confirmation.

Research findings seem to be consistent with its theories. The researcher I am familiar is Dr. Paul La Violette (his book is "Earth Under Fire") who was conducting ice core analyses in Antarctica and in Greenland. Dr. Paul, as he is known, while working on his PhD. discovered evidence of regular huge cosmic ray bombardments in the ice cores occurring at regular intervals. These cosmic ray bombardments are routine and of course and are generally related to solar flares.

But Dr. Paul is saying some thing very different:

He argues:

1-These bombardments originate from explosions from super novas and pulsars and quasars in our galaxy and even other galaxies.

2-This occurs regularly in "Superwaves"

3-They are related to earth extinctions, our ice ages and climate changes.

4-He produces ice core evidence of their frequency and categorizes them as falling into four categories of strength from one to four.

5-The evidence he offers are high levels of iridium, nickel and gold in these ice samples and connect these concentrations to mass extinctions, star explosions and ice ages here on earth alternating with periods of climate warming.

Now I am not sure if Dr. Paul (a John's Hopkins graduate in physics and a PhD from Portland) subscribes to Plasma theory but his ice core findings are consistent with Plasma theory data and theories.

Cosmic rays bombardments originating in our galaxies and others fit with the idea that these star explosions are electro-magnetic in origin and the cosmic storms reach our solar system and the earth itself.

The consequences Dr. Paul warns, of even a category one bombardment would be devastating now because since the last large one 700 years ago we now have satellites and other technology which now which would be effected. The whole planet, he argues, could be brought to its knees. Repairs might take months or years. Moreover, he argues we have solar flares and bombardments of a less intense nature often-every 11 years in the case of solar flares; and other bombardments from outside our galaxy virtually every day.

This is gloomy stuff.

This is all the more gloomy since we are generally being told that such cosmic rays come from our sun. But Dr. Paul argues that is not the case entirely. They come from exploding stars as well and can activate the sun to produce more rays than it normally does. So the bombardments come directly from our galaxy and other galaxies and the stronger waves can and have induced our sun to emit more rays than it normally does. Note these outbursts are electrical in nature.

Plasma theories of huge magnetic fields, galaxy-sized, sending huge moving currents of charged particles in orbits which regularly impact the earth is the up-shot of all this.

Now there is physical evidence of such occurrences being offered in the ice core samples.

Large super waves can last 100 to a thousand years. There have been over 14 events, he states, in the last 5 thousand years. The large ones appear to occurs every 13 to 26 thousand years. The last occurring about 14,000 bc according to the ice samples. You do the math.

Several groups are apparently monitoring the lesser events which last from 300 to 700 seconds and can occur without warning.

So what we may ask can be done?

More in the coming days.

Sept 13th 2010
Elementary Wave Theory Dr. Boyd Theories

Now there is yet another theory which we might consider. Yes I know this is all getting complicated. But not that all of it is now seeming borrow from one another. See the website: http://elwave.org/nonphysicists/

In brief this theory states that quantum mechanics theory is flawed in that it resorts to math models and probabilities. He called the findings of quantum physics "weird." and counter intuitive. While some of the findings make sense but some of the basic ideas do not make sense.

He argues the following "peculiar" ideas:

1- Ether exists and heretofore undetected waves exist at all wave lengths and frequencies. And more, these waves travel in both directions with electrons responding to these waves. For example he argues that waves propagate from for example the human body and photons from the sun become excited and travel back to the body. Electrons excited by waves

---

252

create photon reactions. These elementary wave (none dare call it ether, permeate the entire cosmos and are neither matter nor energy but form the backdrop medium in which matter and energy interact.

2-Using the famous split experiment he seeks to demonstrate the differences between his theory and the explanations offered by quantum theorists who argue that an electron gun firing electrons at two slits in a board mounted between it and a plate will initiate with a particle but end up after passing through the slits looking like a wave function.

3- This outcome is explained in quantum mechanics as the observational effect. An electron exists in a quantum cloud until observed and then it becomes a particle when measurement is sought. Boyd states this arguments makes no sense.

4- He argues that it makes more sense to see the behavior of the electron as propagating within a two way wave field in which the electron excites a wave reaction from objects and are pre-existing.

Yes I know. This is mind-tingling.

More on this tomorrow since it feels like my brain has just been administered a super strong Altoid.
 Meantime see: http://physics.prodos.org/stephenspeicherexplains/

Nov 10, 2010
The Plasma-Electric Theory of the Universe received a tremendous boost as can be read in the Nov 9 issue of the New York Times. There scientists report they have discovered two huge bubbles of energy at the center of our galaxy, the Milky Way.

Tremendous in size, they cover *half* of the galaxy and contain tremendous amounts of energy. This is consistent with the Plasma theory and has tremendous import for our understanding of how the universe works.

It means that these highly energetic, galaxy sized bubbles fit perfectly with Plasma theories. (See above) To wit:

1-There are huge magnetic clouds moving electrical currents in huge orbits around the entire milky way galaxy as predicted by Plasma Theory. To find one in the very center of the galaxy is astonishing.

2-The corollary proposition to this empirical data, in Plasma Theory is that these huge currents dominate the universe, are the real incubators of stars and impact our very sun, where these electrical currents in orbit, can and has caused the sun to emit huge bursts of cosmic rays. These cosmic rays bombardments are documented in ice core samples going back thousands of years in 700 year cycles, the last being about 700 years ago.

While in the past these bombardments did little damage, in today's highly electronic and computer environments such a bombardment now could effectively end our way of life.

3- The argument is that modern physics and astronomers have ignored the evidence of this threat and now need to urge upon us the necessary steps to protect the earth.

As you can see this is not of small import.

But what would be those steps you say?Tomorrow.

Title: New Evidence For The Plasma Theory of The Universe

Summary: New Evidence That Plasma Theory of the Universe Might Be Correct
Updated: 11/12/10 More Evidence for The Plasma Theory

The Plasma Theory of the Universe stands as a major alternate theory of how the universe works and centers on the most glaring problems that the standard model of Physics does not explain:

1- The first problem is that the Standard Model of physics does not explain why it is that galaxies do not seem to obey Newtonian or Einsteinian theories; and the latter do not explain black holes either.

2- The second is the astounding fact that the entire universe is considered to be expanding exponentially. The further out the galaxy the faster it is receding from us. This is challenged by Plasma Theory.

These two problems were answered by the Standard Model with the postulation of dark matter, dark energy, and a myriad of particles with strange names like MACHOs Wimp's, neutrinos with mass etc.

After all, it is embarrassing to note, Plasma theorists say, that 95% of the universe is made of up stuff nobody in the standard model can detect.

Into this intellectual breach ride Plasma Theory ideas which offer the following answers:

1-The galaxy problem can be solved if we conceive of space as a super fluid. This kind of behavior has been observed in the lab with He3 and this might be the case on the macro level as well.

2-The galaxy problem is solved if space is filled with an "electric plasma.". Space is gigantic electrical fields and can be understood as such to explain the galaxy problem. Gravity becomes a function of electrical field interactions. Particles and their interactions become photons and electrons interacting within these electrical fields and within this plasma, which by the way, has some of the same characteristics as a super fluid.

The expansion of the universe, in the one example, is due to the capacity of space to expand infinitely propelled by the mass within space to transform itself into space which can travel at or above light speeds with galaxy sized orbits containing x and gamma rays.

These plasma fields account for expansion in ordinary electrical and charge terms--although this is little vague in terms of what I have read. The idea though is that just as lightening strikes powerfully, it is the power of electricity which drives the great movements we see in the universe. The same would be true on the quantum level as well.

The electric plasma group has a pedigree. See the work of Hannes Alfven who virtually created the field won a Noble prize and basically challenges all of the major premises of the Standard Model:

To wit:

1-There was no big bang.

2-There is no expansion of the universe

3- There are no black holes

4-The universe is infinite, always was and always will be

5- The Sun does not produce energy by nuclear fusion

6- Stars are not created or destroyed by "collapsing gravity"

5- Most of the process we see in the universe, he says, can be explained and, indeed predicted, by electro-magnetism and positive and negative gas plasma clouds clearly visible in the universe. I will give some citations next time for those wanting to track down this gentleman most of us have never heard of.

Now of the groups of theories above only the super fluid example addresses the quantum issues. And super fluids are being accepted by mainstream physics at this point, and quantum theory itself is slowly backing into adopting the experimental results. I have argued that I am not seeing much difference between super fluids behaviors on the macro and the micro levels but that has to be verified experimentally.

How? Well we will always have CERN. Isn't that in Paris?

Next time--what about my merging universe theory; and who are those electric plasma people and why are they saying those terrible things about the Standard Model?

Jul 12, 2010

The challenger with all of the above assertions is Hannes Alfven. His student writes on a website devoted to Aflven:

"Alfven"s approach to physics was based on insight and intuition. He was quick to understand how nature works and he was able to place new observations into a framework larger than that required to explain the observations themselves. For example, in the early 1930"s, cosmic rays were commonly thought to be gamma rays filling the entire universe. However, when they were discovered to be charged particles, Alfven offered in 1937 the novel suggestion that the galaxy contained a large-scale magnetic field and that the cosmic rays moved in spiral orbits within the galaxy, owing to the forces exerted by the magnetic field. He argued that there could be a magnetic field pervading the entire galaxy if plasma was spread throughout the galaxy. This plasma could carry the electrical currents that would then create the galactic magnetic field.

See the following website:

http://www.tmgnow.com/repository/cosmology/alfven.html

Alfven was a Nobel prize winner (1970) and the list of his credentials is quite impressive for someone few have heard of.

He is credited generally with discovering: electrons and ions move in orbits through gigantic galaxy-sized magnetic fields in space creating electric current flows and argues that this is the real explanation for galaxy behavior and missing matter better than gravity or dark matter.

He apparently, according to his supporters, discovered:

1- The explanation of the Van Allen radiation belt

2- The cause of fluctuations in the earth's magnetic field during magnetic storms

3- alternative explanations of the birth of our galaxies, stars, our solar system and the universe itself in terms of these gigantic magnetic fields where electrons and ions fly sometimes exceeding the speed of light in what has been dubbed the "electric plasma" which dominates space. "Ether" is apparently magnetic and has current flows.

4- He predicted the filamentary structure of the universe in 1963 saying that space is filled with current flows and essentially operates like the

familiar dynamo we know on earth.

5- He presented explanations of a large magnetic field which dominates our own galaxy and connected that to the behavior and creation of our Sun; identifying nonthermal astronomical radiation sources. He argued that nearly all radiation recorded by radio telescopes derive from these gigantic magnetic clouds and their radiation.

I am reminded of "black body radiation" experiments Einstein sought to explain in his photoelectric experiments, for which he received a Nobel prize. This is important because his answers in that regard were designed to explain away black body radiation which Alfren explains.

The attempt to explain away black body radiation and its experimental findings gave us quantum mechanics; such experiments show that heat is generated to infinity up and down the spectrum. Unacceptable this was, so the concept of "quanta" in light and Planck's theorems were get around the problem.

Alfren counters that was a wrong turn. The black body radiation is particles moving in galactic magnetic fields and understood today; all of this is moving in a gigantic magnetic field, nothing more; -- all of Einstein's and quantum theories are overkill and incorrect.)

The principle is the same as in a linear accelerator--magnets can move particles to speeds approaching light. This is happening in our universe as well according to Alfven.

Alfven's supporters claim every day measurements of his claims are available but are discounted by the Physics establishment even as it uses his tools and concepts everyday. Giant magnetic clouds are discovered every day in astronomy but their meaning is never discussed.

Well, this is quite a bit. Reality all around me is changing. Alfven sounds like another Einstein critic and, by the way, what does Alfven have to say about relativity and quantum mechanics? That on tomorrow.

Me? I am going to have another look at that suspicious magnet on my refrigerator. Apparently a lot more than I thought is going on there.

Note for tomorrow:

Alfven is generally given credit as the father of Magneto hydrodynamics, for which he won a Nobel prize.

Magneto hydrodynamics (**MHD**) (*magnetofluiddynamics* or *hydromagnetics*) is the **academic discipline** which studies the **dynamics** of **electrically conducting fluids**. Examples of such fluids include **plasmas**, liquid metals, and **salt water**. The word *magnetohydrodynamics (MHD)* is derived from *magneto-* meaning **magnetic field**, and *hydro-* meaning **liquid**, and -dynamics meaning movement. The field of MHD was initiated by **Hannes Alfvén** [1], for which he received the **Nobel Prize** in Physics in 1970.

From Wikipedia

More Notes for Tomorrow:

In 1937, Alfvén argued that if plasma pervaded the universe, it could then carry electric currents capable of generating a galactic magnetic field.

[1]

After winning the Nobel Prize for his works in **magnetohydrodynamics**

he emphasized that:
In order to understand the phenomena in a certain plasma region, it is necessary to map not only the magnetic but also the electric field and the electric currents. Space is filled with a network of currents which transfer energy and momentum over large or very large distances. The currents often pinch to filamentary or surface currents. The latter are likely to give space, as also interstellar and intergalactic space, a cellular structure.[2]

His theoretical work on field-aligned electric currents in the aurora (based on earlier work by **Kristian Birkeland**) was confirmed by satellite observations, in 1974, resulting in the discovery of **Birkeland currents**.

Jul 13, 2010
So here we are dear reader ready to explore more of the electric plasma idea and to evaluate it.

There can be no question that many if not most of Alfven''s ideas about magnetic and electrical stellar fields have been actively accepted and a

whole new field of magnetohydrodynamics has evolved to examine the nature of the universe and the stars from that vantage point

----

A cursory look at Science Daily and other sources show discoveries which seem to verify his ideas of how the magnetic-electrical universe works.

What would be the summary of it in terms of what can be empirically verified?

1- The Universe indeed seem to be populated by plasmas of huge size which include particles (hydrogen ions and charged electrons mostly) which interact with star and planetary magneto-electrical fields of immense size and these and may be involved in star formation and even destruction. Gravitational effects are much less. (Those wanting citations for this can email me.) But you can search on "electric plasma" in Science Daily and there are over three thousand results.

His results are now given names like "magnetic reconnection" "pinching in magnetic fields" but they are predicted by his writings. Huge magnetic dust clouds funnel particles along magnetic lines of force and pinch or reconcile at some points of interaction with other galaxy sized fields and help create stars and planets, not gravity alone. In fact, these fields have cosmic rays and ions orbiting entire regions hundreds and thousands of light years in diameter. In dense ion areas these concentrations light up in the visible light range in others they are dark until these ions become energized by entering magnetic fields.

The four-satellite European Cluster group more or less verified these processes at work in connection with the earth's magneto-sphere and plasma, beginning in 2001 and again in 2004.

2- His ideas are accepted in electro-magnetic fluid dynamics and a particular wave behavior in these type fluids is called Alfven waves.

Therefore, much of Alfven''s work has been verified.

What are still controversial are his conclusions from the above observations and theories. Let's see what his conclusions were and why he came to them, and how they constitute a serious challenge to the Standard Model, Einstein's views and those of quantum mechanics.

We will take them one blog at a time.

The first is that Alfven challenged the notion that the universe is expanding; (and just when I was getting used to that notion.) His reasoning was that

---

the famous Hubble experiment was erroneous and Hubble himself later in life said so and so did his assistant. (More detail on this later.)

The universe is not expanding Alfven says (the red shift analysis of the light of stars was made without understanding the role of the electro-magnetic plasma at work. Alfven makes the assertion that this is an error. The red shift, in fact, is a gas plasma indication a young star being born not a receding star or cluster. He indicates that the idea that the further away a star or galaxy is the faster it is receding does not makes sense and is not backed up by any real data other than this so-called red-shift data. Others of his followers also indicate that "gravitational lensing" techniques which are used to buttress this proposition makes no sense either.

For those who may not know, "gravitational lensing" is the purported process where by light from distant galaxies, say ones from the youth of the universe, "bends" around intervening and younger galaxies allowing us to observe them. The rationale is that light is affected by the gravity of these intervening galaxies and this "bending" allows that light to continue on to us as opposed to being blocked. Einstein is cited to account for this effect.

Alfven and his later supporters point out that this lensing would require such precise lining up of the near and far galaxies so as to be exceeding rare and probably not exist at all. After all how many galaxies must be between the earliest ones and our own? Lots. So lensing would be broken up at some point along the way and all we would get is a distorted view at best.

This second technique of measuring the so-called receding universe is also flawed.

Here we go. Does this mean that Einstein's "cosmological constant" is being dusted off and brought back in to the conversation? Yes, indeedy.

The implication of a non-expanding universe? Hold your hat. They are:

1-No expanding universe and no dark energy

2-No expansion, no big bang, no inflation theory, and a whole new theory of background cosmic radiation is needed because while this radiation was supposed to be what was discovered in the 60"s and has a smooth texture and temperature of the entire cosmos, therefore, doesn't make sense.

Something, the Alfven people say, is wrong with that map because there was no big bang to produce such a phenomena.

Let's have a look tomorrow at the Hubble data and also at Alfven''s own description of how this now-expanding universe works.

Tomorrow: Oh boy. What do we do now?

Jul 15, 2010
Well lets evaluate Plasma and Electric Notions of matter and ether (yes we are back to that never-ending discussion of ether or aether.

What do the electric universe people have to say about the major issues we have discussed?

Lets take gravity first and it's nature.

Newton gave up on understanding it. Einstein ridiculed it as "spooky action at a distance" in classical terms and offered an explanation of gravity as space-time interacting with mass and the former bending- and creating gravity. I and others have placed gravity as an external force from another membrane universe; still others postulate gravity as part of a unified field of particles but don't offer much more insight as to what it is. Quantum mechanics has nothing real to add to this.

Desperate for answers we turn to electric plasma theory people and see what they have to say.

Here goes: Wal Thornhill and Donald Scott "the latter a leading string theorist and Nobel prize winner) appear to agree on some main electric universe ideas on gravity.

I will quote Thornhill at length since any attempt on my part to paraphrase will likely fail.

"The equivalence of inertial and gravitational mass implies that gravity is also an electrical force. Before Einstein, some noted scientists were suggesting that the gravitational force between neutral particles might ultimately be due to electrical polarization within the particles. In 1882, Friedrich Zöllner wrote in the introduction to his book, Explanation of Universal Gravitation through the Static Action of Electricity and The General Importance of Weber's Laws, "we are to conclude that a pair of electrical particles of opposite signs, i.e. two Weberian molecular pairs

attracts each other. This attraction is Gravity; it is proportional to the number of molecular pairs." Indeed, gravity can be represented as the sum of the radically aligned electric dipoles formed by all subatomic particles within a charged planet or star."

Gravity here is the electrical components of particles realigning (like iron filings to a magnet?) and this true as well as in planets and stars.

Wow, again.

Gravity in this is a measure of the charge of sub-atomic particles in what we call matter. The distributions and intensity of the charge sub-atomically and at the star and indeed galaxy level determines the currents in space and its effects are seen as what we describe as gravity.

Humm, this is getting interesting. Go on Mr. Thornhill:

"This new electrical concept suggests that Newton's "universal constant of gravitation," or "G," is a dependent variable. G depends upon the charge distribution within a celestial body. Highly charged objects like comets look like solid rock, yet they have a gravitational field that suggests they are fluff-balls. And as they discharge they suffer what is euphemistically called "non-gravitational" accelerations. The extreme weakness of the force of gravity, compared to the electric force, is a measure of the minuscule electric dipolar distortion of nucleons."

Thornhill goes on to say that magnetism is also a manifestation of the charge distribution in matter. He comes to a startling conclusion from all of this:

"This simple electrical model of matter has the great virtue of reducing all known forces to a single one – the electric force."

So all four of the fundamental forces end up being one-the electric force. But, we are warned, this comes at a price:

"However, it has a price. We must abandon our peculiar phobia against force acting at a distance. And we must give up the notion that the speed of light is a real speed barrier.

It may seem fast to us, but on a cosmic scale it is glacial. Imposing such a speed limit and requiring force to be transmitted by particles would render the universe completely incoherent. If an electron is composed of smaller subunits of charge orbiting within the classical radius of an electron, then

the electric force must operate at a speed far in excess of the speed of light for the electron to remain a coherent object.

In fact, it has been calculated that if released, the subunits of charge in the electron could travel from here to the far side of the Andromeda galaxy in one second!

We have direct evidence of the superluminal action of the electric force, given that gravity is a longitudinal electric force. Indeed, Newton's celebrated equation requires that gravity act instantly on the scale of the solar system. It has been calculated that gravity must operate at a speed of at least $2x10^{10}$ times the speed of light; otherwise closely orbiting stars would experience a torque that would sling them apart in mere hundreds of years. Similarly, the Earth responds to the gravitational pull of the Sun where it is at the moment, not where the Sun was 8 minutes ago. If this were not so, the Earth and all other planets in the solar system would be slung into deep space within a few thousand years. Gravity is therefore an electrical property of matter, not a geometrical property of space.

What is the nature of light? Einstein's special theory of relativity was disconfirmed right at the start by the Michelson-Morley experiment, which showed a residual due to the æther. This was later confirmed by far more rigorous repeats of the experiment by Dayton Miller. But by then popular delusion and the madness of crowds had taken hold and contrary evidence would not be tolerated. The Dayton Miller story makes interesting reading. If it weren't for the extraordinary power of self-delusion, commonsense would tell us that a wave cannot exist in nothing. So Maxwell was right, light is a transverse electromagnetic wave moving through a medium, the æther."

Sorry for the long quote here but I thought you should get the argument direct from the horse's mouth so to speak. But here comes another long quote. After that I promise no more.

"But what is the æther?" Thornhill says:

"In the vacuum of space, each cubic centimeter is teeming with neutrinos. And since neutrinos are resonant orbiting systems of charge, like all matter, they will respond to the electric force by distorting to form a weak electric dipole aligned with the electric field. The speed of light in a vacuum is therefore a measure of the delay in response of the neutrino to the electric force.
What about the bending of starlight by the Sun, which discovery raised Einstein to megastar status?

264

The residual found in the Michelson-Morley experiments shows that the Earth and all ponder able bodies "drag" the Æther along with them. The bending of starlight near the Sun is simply the effect expected of an extensive neutrino atmosphere held to the Sun by gravity. Light will be slowed in the denser medium – causing normal refraction or bending of light.

What about time?

With all bodies in the Milky Way galaxy communicating their positions effectively in real time through the electric force of gravity, it means there is a universal time. There can be no time distortion or time travel – something that common sense always told us.

What about black holes?

They are a mathematical fiction, a near-infinite concentration of mass, is required to explain concentrated sources of energy seen at galactic centers, by employing the weakest force in Nature – gravity.

It is the high-school howler of dividing by zero. Plasma cosmology shows that where electrical energy is concentrated at the center of a galaxy, gravity can be ignored in favor of far more powerful electromagnetic forces. The collimated jets of matter coming from that focus are also replicated to scale in plasma labs. The jets are inexplicable if a black hole is supposed to be a cosmic sink for matter."

All quotes from
http://www.holoscience.com/news.php?article=gdaqg8df

Well these ideas are far-reaching indeed. I am far-reaching for the Maalox because the story is getting scarier and scarier. Let's try to recover by tomorrow. See you then. But before that here is a definition of plasma:

Definition of Electric Plasma:

"Plasma has been called the "fourth state" of matter, after solids, liquids and gases. Most of the matter in the universe is in the form of plasma. A plasma is formed if some of the negatively charged electrons are

separated from their host atoms in a gas, leaving the atoms with a positive charge. The negatively charged electrons and the positively charged atoms (known as positive ions) are then free to move separately under the influence of an applied voltage or magnetic field. Their net movement constitutes an electrical current. So, one of the more important properties of a plasma is that it can conduct electrical current. It does so by forming current filaments that follow magnetic field lines. Filamentary patterns are ubiquitous in the cosmos."

Jul 17, 2010
A diagram from The Sun e-book will show a simplistic estimate of the size of the body of the Sun is intended to show that the atmosphere of a star can contribute a substantial amount to its apparent size, given by the thin yellow photosphere.

From **http://www.holoscience.com/news.php?article=ah63dzac**

This diagram purports to make a radical statement about the stars, our sun, our solar system and the universe. To wit:

1-The existence of large scale, galaxy-sized electro-magnetic fields in space drive the star formation process, not hydrogen and helium.

Stars are not nuclear reactors.

Rather they are formed by galaxy-sized magnetic fields in what is described as z-pinch and double-layer formations. More, this energy from stars comes from these external galaxy-sized magnetic fields which stream particles at light speed speeds, resulting in a discharge of particles (neutrinos and the solar wind for example) outward. These neutrinos, winds and cosmic rays interact with the Earth's magnetosphere and, indeed, with the magneto-spheres of all of the planets in our solar system.

But note this is all part of a galaxy wide electro-magnetic field which has particles in orbit--all within this galaxy-wide plasma.

Numerous citations are given for this view. It goes on to assert:

1-Stars do not follow nuclear fuel exhaustion cycles which can take millions of years but, instead, say the Plasma Model, stars can form and die in a single life-time and they offer examples from current astrological observations of stars doing just that. Stars are not nuclear reactors.

2-Stars emit huge magnetic x-ray and gamma rays filaments because these discharges are electrical in nature and origin, not solely coming from black holes.

Recent observations show huge comic dust trails from recently exploding stars. This is the normal expulsion via z-pinching and electrical discharge which is part of the evolution of starts.

To be clear, depending upon the strength and density of the ion field and the magnetic field, a given star can explode at any time and evolve very quickly to its demise, even in as little as *forty or fifty* years.

3- They argue that the famous red shift is way overstated. The red shift is a measure of the youth of a star (young stars will emit a red-shift and even stars rotating away from us will emit a red-shift. The idea that the red-shift means only a receding star ends up with a prediction that the stars furthers away from us are moving away from us at speeds exceeding that of light, an absurd claim.

4- The issues around Dark Flow are best explained by a huge magnetic cloud field. Current theory has no explanation of dark flow.

5- There is no need for dark energy, dark matter theories, all are explained by the plasma theory.

6- No need for elaborate big bang and inflation theories.

In short the universe is relatively static and is probably infinite.

The best fit, in my view, with the Plasma theory is the membrane theory which does postulate a huge influx of plasma from one membrane to another, upon contact. But we shall, in a later blog, compare the Plasma theory with all others and try to judge which explains current observations and experimental results.

But first you may ask what does Plasma Theory have to say about Quantum mechanics? What role does Plasma play at the quantum level?

I thought you would never ask.

But hold your Plasma until tomorrow.

Jul 18, 2010
Well at the quantum level the answer is all electric. Gravity is the attraction between the elemental particles, the electric force is prevalent, electrons can be easily placed within the "black body radiation" matrix but what has to be added is that the elemental particles exist inside galaxy-wide field currents driven by huge magnetic fields these currents themselves help generate.

Gravity then, at the quantum and the galaxy level, is the instantaneous realignment of the charges of ions and electrons which indeed exceed the speed of light. All of the universe is connected, as quantum holds, and entangled and these charged particles operate in pairs as quantum theory holds.

Einstein here is considered incorrect. String Theory is considered incorrect. Current astrological theories of what is happening with galaxies and stars are considered incorrect. Big bang and inflation theory is considered incorrect .

Quantum theory is misapplying the role of electric forces at the quantum level. Super fluid theory does seem to have utility because super fluids are a kind of plasma.

So with this kind of house cleaning what is left for Plasma to explain?

They argue that the so-called search for the theory of everything, black holes, unified field theories, eleven dimensions is also flawed.

So what is left we ask again?

For that we have to wait until tomorrow, where we will examine the questions of how do Plasma theory answer questions which physicists today don't seem to have answers to.

Sept 12, 2010
Plasma theory has new adherents and some of it tenets seem to have ice core empirical confirmation.

Research findings seem to be consistent with its theories.

The researcher I am familiar is Dr. Paul La Violette (his book is "Earth Under Fire") who was conducting ice core analyses in Antarctica and in Greenland. Dr. Paul, as he is known, while working on his PhD. discovered evidence of regular huge cosmic ray bombardments in the ice cores occurring at regular intervals. These cosmic ray bombardments are routine and of course and are generally related to solar flares.

But Dr. Paul is saying some thing very different:

268

He argues:

1-These bombardments originate from explosions from super novas and pulsars and quasars in our galaxy and even other galaxies.

2-This occurs regularly in "Super waves"

3-They are related to earth extinctions, our ice ages and climate changes.

4-He produces ice core evidence of their frequency and categorizes them as falling into four categories of strength from one to four.

5-The evidence he offers are high levels of iridium, nickel and gold in these ice samples and connect these concentrations to mass extinctions, star explosions and ice ages here on earth alternating with periods of climate warming.

Now I am not sure if Dr. Paul (a John's Hopkins graduate in physics and a PhD from Portland) subscribes to Plasma theory but his ice core findings are consistent with Plasma theory data and theories.

Cosmic rays bombardments originating in our galaxy, and others, fit with the idea that these star explosions are electro-magnetic in origin and the cosmic storms reach our solar system and the earth itself.

The consequences Dr. Paul warns, of even a category one bombardment would be devastating now because since the last large one 700 years ago we now have satellites and other technology which now which would be effected. The whole planet, he argues, could be brought to its knees. Repairs might take months or years. Moreover, he argues we have solar flares and bombardments of a less intense nature often-every 11 years in the case of solar flares; and other bombardments from outside our galaxy virtually every day.

This is gloomy stuff.

This is all the more gloomy since we are generally being told that such cosmic rays come from our sun. But Dr. Paul argues that is not the case entirely. They come from exploding stars as well and can activate the sun

to produce more rays than it normally does. So the bombardments come directly from our galaxy and other galaxies and the stronger waves can and have induced our sun to emit more rays than it normally does. Note these outbursts are electrical in nature. They have regularity because the particles have super galaxy, regular orbits.

Plasma theories of huge magnetic fields, galaxy-sized, sending huge moving currents of charged particles in orbits which regularly impact the earth is the up-shot of all this.

Now there is physical evidence of such occurrences being offered in the ice core samples.

Large super waves can last 100 to a thousand years. There have been over 14 events, he states, in the last 5 thousand years. The large ones appear to occur every 13 to 26 thousand years. The last occurring about 14,000 BC according to the ice samples. You do the math.

Several groups are apparently monitoring the lesser events which last from 300 to 700 seconds and can occur without warning.

So what we may ask can be done?

More in the coming days.

Sept 13. 2010 Elementary Wave Theory: Dr. Boyd.
Now there is yet another theory which we might consider. Yes I know this is all getting complicated. Several seem to borrow from another. See the website: http://elwave.org/nonphysicists/

In brief, this theory states that quantum mechanics theory is flawed in that it resorts to math models and probabilities. He called the findings of quantum physics "weird." and counter intuitive. While some of the findings make sense but some of the basic ideas do not make sense.

He argues the following "peculiar" ideas:

1- Ether exists and heretofore undetected waves exist at all wave lengths and frequencies. And more, these waves travel in both directions with electrons responding to these waves. For example, he argues, that waves propagate from, for example the human body, and photons from the sun become excited and travel back to the body. Electrons excited by waves create photon reactions. These elementary waves (none dare call it ether,) permeate the entire cosmos and are neither matter nor energy but form the backdrop medium in which matter and energy interact.

2-Using the famous split experiment he seeks to demonstrate the differences between his theory and the explanations offered by quantum theorists who argue that an electron gun firing electrons at two slits in a board mounted between it and a plate will initiate with a particle but end up after passing through the slits looking like a wave function.

3- This outcome is explained in quantum mechanics as the observational effect. An electron exists in a quantum cloud until observed and then it becomes a particle when measurement is sought. Boyd states this argument makes no sense.

4- He argues that it does make more sense to see the behavior of the electron as propagating within a two way wave field in which the electron excites a wave reaction from objects and are pre-existing.

Yes I know. This is mind-tingling.

More on this tomorrow since it feels like my brain has just been administered a super strong Altoid.
Meantime see: http://physics.prodos.org/stephenspeicherexplains/

The relevance to Plasma theory is that one could add the proposition that electrical fields can suddenly shift direction and z-pinch backwards.

Nov 10, 2010
The Plasma-Electric Theory of the Universe received today a tremendous boost as can be read in the Nov 9, 2010 issue of the New York Times. There, scientists report they have discovered two huge bubbles of energy at the center of our galaxy, the Milky Way.

Tremendous in size, they cover *half* of the galaxy and contain tremendous amounts of energy radiating out 50,000 light years across the Milky Way which itself is only 100,000 light years across.

This is consistent with the Plasma theory and has tremendous import for our understanding of how the universe works.

It means that these highly energetic, galaxy sized bubbles fit perfectly with Plasma theories. To wit:

1-There are huge magnetic clouds moving electrical currents in huge orbits around the entire milky way galaxy as predicted by Plasma Theory. To find one in the very center of the galaxy is astonishing.

2-The corollary proposition to this empirical data, in Plasma Theory, is that these huge currents dominate the universe, are the real incubators of stars

———
271

and impact our very sun, where these electrical currents in orbit, can and has caused the sun to emit huge bursts of cosmic rays. These cosmic ray bombardments are documented in ice core samples going back thousands of years in 700 year cycles, the last being about 700 years ago.

While in the past these bombardments did little damage, in today's highly electronic and computer environments, such a bombardment now could effectively end our way of life or damage it severely.

3- The argument is that modern physics and astronomers have ignored the evidence of this threat and now need to urged to take the necessary steps to protect the earth.

As you can see this is not of small import.

But what would be those steps you say?

Tomorrow.

Nov 12, 2010
The two bubbles discovered above also fit with other aspects of Plasma theory and predictions. To wit:

1-PT states that the z-pinch aspect of electro-magnetic galaxy sized fields creates a cell or filamentary topography for the universe. This has turned out to be true.

2-PT argues this same z-pinch effect will in fact create a binary star pattern for stars. That is most stars are not stand alone. They have companion stars which may not be in the visible light spectrum. These binary patterns is now becoming more and more observed and note that the bubbles above are binary, there are two bubbles.

3-This binary pattern and its interactions with z-pinch phenomenon is the cause of star formation and of supernovas in Plasma Theory which the details of which are in the citations above.

4-Plasma Theory argues this is driver in our galaxy not a massive black hole.

There are more predictions which essentially argue that the magnetic orbits of these huge fields will give us some ability not only to understand the sky but perhaps predict events.

272

Finally, we can speculate, if the entire universe is electric and z-pinch involved, how this idea relates to Dark Flow, the phenomenon observed in which a large section of the night sky is moving in one direction pulled by some enormous unseen force. (See my blogs on Einstein.)
What would the Plasma people say about that?

Lets see tomorrow.

Title: The LHC Collider at CERN: A Threat to the Entire Planet?

Updated Nov 23, 2010
Summary: The Experiments At CERN--A Threat To The Planet? For a video from professor on all of this go to the link below:
http://www.notepad.ch/blogs/index.php/2010/03/26/breaking-news-video-of-interview-mit-pro
Updated: Jul 30, 2010 Responses to the Critics
Updated: October 16, 2010 -So Where Are We Now?
Updated:
Updated: October 30, 2010--Are the Tsunami, the Volcano Eruption and the LHC collider tests connected?
Updated: Nov 30, 2010 How Long Will It Take To See If CERN Is Affecting the Planet?

See:
www.notepad.ch/blogs/index.php/2010/03/26/breaking-news-video-of-interview-mit-pro

Those of you who have followed my blogs on Einstein and Physics theory will recall that I frequently referenced CERN which is an international project near Geneva Switzerland which has as it's goal the re-creation of the conditions of the Big Bang.

The project, planned for years, first fired up in 2009 with mixed results and limited power and problems with the gigantic magnets which accelerate the particles. But, the multi-billion dollar project has drawn fire as the most dangerous tinkering in the history of the world and has been described as a threat to the entire planet. Lawsuits seeking to in joint its operations have been filed.

Below find a citation on the CERN project from the NY Times of October, 2009.

October 31, 2009, "The Cosmic Countdown in Geneva Goes On"
By **DENNIS OVERBYE**

(For a video on this from a prominent critic of the project go to the link below: Copy and paste into your browser window.)

http://www.notepad.ch/blogs/index.php/2010/03/26/breaking-news-video-of-interview-mit-pro

The issue is that, if successful, no one knows what will really happen. The horrendous prediction of Luis Sancho, in a law suit to shut CERN down, claims that there is a 78% chance that the *entire* earth can be swallowed up by a black hole created by the collider. No one, he says, can predict that it will *not* happen.

Others predict that the accelerator has the goal creating some of the most explosive atomic reactions in the known universe and, if successful, puts the entire planet at risk and no one is looking closely at these Dr. Frankenstein Physicists, tinkering with what they, in fact, can not control. What is the truth here?

Other critics say that the HLC can disrupt the entire magnetic field of the earth with disastrous results--including deadly exposure of earth from cosmic rays, earthquakes, electrical disruptions of unimaginable destruction if our satellite systems are destroyed. After all, they point out, a collider is a gigantic magnet running electrons and protons through the largest machine in the history of the world.

So what is the truth of all this, and when, for my calendar, are the next tests to be held?

Let's take up these arguments pro and con in the next coming days.

Also see the scenario critics create at the following link.

http://www.cerntruth.com/?p=

For those that want to read the entire article, I have reproduced it below.

How it Will Happen: Earthquakes, Strangelets and Black Holes.

Published: March 10, 2010

FIRST SIGNS: EARLIER 2010. THE PROTON C-SPEED RING:
EARTHQUAKES AND VOLCANIC ACTIVITY.

The first hints that the LHC is seriously damaging life on Earth will come
from an increase on earthquake and volcano activity. This is due to the
fact that the LHC is creating a powerful gravito-magnetic field, a 'ring' of
charged, massive particles that can interact with the magnetic fields of the
magma and Earth's center.

Disturbances on the Earth's magnetic field by the magnets of the LHC and
specially THE CHARGED POSITIVE C-SPEED FLOW OF PROTONS can
come through 3 different processes:

- The possibility that the 27 kilometers continuous ring of charged protons
can interact with self-similar charged flows in the magma or earth's center,
creating a powerful electro-magnetic effect, displacing magma and causing
earthquakes and volcano activity. It is a fact that THE FIRST DAY THAT
THE CHARGED, PROTON RING WAS CREATED IN 2008 IT CAUSED **4
significant Earthquakes, the first one in Iran**, SECONDS AFTER IT
WAS POWERED UP.
The proton, charged ring could act as a new pole of a magnetic field with
Earth's inner fields.

- The creation of strange liquid, already produced in the first experiments,
(Kaons at the LHC, hyperons at RHIC) could also provoke explosions in
the magma. If stable, it will leak in increasing quantities to the center of the
Earth. Some of it will remain in the center, forming the seed of a strangelet.

Some will accrete and/or explode in the mantle, in highly energetic, tiny
bombs.

- The creation of **gravitational waves**. The LHC is a 27 Kilometer ring of
positive charged massive particles, turning at c -speed. This is essentially
equivalent to the 'singularity' of a **Kerr black hole** - a rotating c-speed
charged ring of mass. Since a Kerr singularity can produce
transversal gravitational waves; the LHC might produce perpendicular
gravitational waves that will sink straight towards the center of the Earth
(in a similar process a rotating , charged coil is used to produce
electromagnetic waves). If so those Gravitational waves, which are
undetectable will affect magnetic fields, provoking earthquake waves and
increase volcano activity.

Each time the machine increases its speed and 'luminosity' (mass), as
CERN powers up the LHC, **we should observe an increase of**

earthquakes and collateral deaths, till the 2 possible 'doomsday events' happen:

Strangelet Scenario: FALL 2010; 2012

In the fall of 2010 CERN will begin colliding groups of **70 million lead hadrons** at 287 tev, unpacking millions of quarks in each collision. Those quarks will be first accelerated at light speed, acquiring **relativistic mass**, becoming heavier **strange quarks**, the substance of a strange quark-gluon soup called a '**strangelet'**. The strange liquid has the potential to become stable and start an **'ice-9' big-bang reaction**. If that happens that effectively transforms the Earth into a **pulsar.**

During 2010 and 2011 as the LHC increases the potency and number of quarks it collides in its experiments, it will create greater quantities of atoms of strangelet liquid, called hyperons, made of up, down and strange quarks, which **it has already produced in unexpected numbers** at low energies, despite all their safety reports that **said it would never produce them**.

As quarks accelerate at c-speed, they acquire mass, because energy cannot go beyond light speed. Energy curls tiny vortices of space-time (Einstein's definition of mass), making those quarks heavier. At light speed our protons made of up and down quarks (and) will become strange quarks, converting the colliding protons into **hyperons** (usd particles, atoms of usd=**strange liquid**). Within the point of collision hyperons merge in pairs becoming **dibaryons**, which are stable and neutral and so they cannot be detected.

Thus dibaryons once formed, will fall to the center of the Earth, accreting matter as they form a growing ball of strange liquid. Most of them will explode in their path to the center of the Earth provoking mini-big bangs in the mantle, which will cause **an increase in earthquake activity during the years 2010** and 2011. But some will arrive to the center of the Earth, where they will form a growing ball of ultradense strange liquid, which finally will crunch the Earth into a **strange star**. We will know this scenario's end is closer, when we experience magnitude 9 earthquakes that kill hundreds of thousands of human beings.

Black Hole Scenario: 2013

In 2013 the LHC will accelerate protons and hadrons at maximal energy, colliding them at over 1 Pev, producing heavy, bottom, charm and top quark-gluon liquid condensates, aka Higgs, possible substances of black holes. The quark-gluon soup it will produce will be far denser and attractive than strangelet liquid, hence the process of accretion of the Earth will be self-similar to the strangelet event but much faster.

Those collisions have the potential to create micro-black holes and top quark condensates (the real Higgs). The top quark condensates have properties similar to black holes, which according to Albert Einstein will not evaporate, rather convert matter (the Earth) into a 3 cm Black Hole or Frozen star.

A black hole is made of strings (the minimal components of quarks) which are the components of gluons and quarks. Their mathematical description is equivalent (a 5th dimensional world of strings is equivalent to a 4 dimensional world of quarks); which reinforces the idea that a black hole is a top quark star.

The LHC was created to produce massive quantities of top quarks since the Higgs and a top quark condensate are the same substance, (the Higgs was promoted as the new 'God particle' just to get more research resources, not allocated to study known-particles). It will not form black holes that evaporate. Since quarks don't evaporate.

The black hole will not fall to the Earth but it will become the new, densest center of the Earth and the Earth will fall into LHC's creation. The process will last a very short time. Some images might be captured on TV but most likely wherever we are, we will just feel a strong wind, and then a blast of attractive forces will crunch and kill us, as the Earth explodes into a Nova."

Well this is a very cheery scenario! But is it true? Who is Luis Sancho and why is he saying these awful scary things about the CERN project?

Next time let's find out.

Below another critic speaks.

The LHC (Large Hadron Collider) experiments: Where might equals right.

By Marguerite Thoresen (B. Journ)

Abstract: This paper discusses why the LHC experiments at CERN are unsafe and a danger to life on Earth. Discussions using the precautionary principle, safety aspects, ecofeminism and risk analysis enable an understanding of the issue. The Large Hadron Collider took 20 years to design and build. New and revised scientific theories indicate the LHC experiments recently commenced at CERN may lead to destruction of planet Earth. Obtaining a legal injunction to stop the LHC experiments while safety issues are discussed is difficult and several attempts have failed. Meanwhile, the LHC machine continues to operate at ever increasing rates of power while CERN avoids open and honest discussion of safety issues. This authoritarian approach by CERN and its scientists marginalizes, disempowers and devoices world citizens and concerned scientists. In the past, authoritarian approaches of those in power pursuing deemed justifiable but abhorrent courses of action, resulted in the development and use of the atomic bomb used to kill at least 70,000 people in Hiroshima alone. Authoritarian approaches in Nazi Germany resulted in the holocaust, killing over 6 million people. In both these cases the average person could do little to stop these atrocities.

The issues: The Large Hadron Collider experiments at CERN have outcomes which CERN scientists themselves cannot fully predict. In a 2007 interview with the "New Yorker" magazine", Jos Engelen , CERN's Chief Scientific Officer, was quoted as saying that "CERN officials are now instructed with respect to the LHC world-destroying potential 'not to say the probability is very small but that the probability is zero.'"[1]

Professor Otto E. Roessler is one of many scientists who say the LHC experiments are a danger to our planet. Professor Roessler is a Professor of Theoretical BioChemistry and a Chaos theorist at the University of Tubingen, Germany. He has a medical degree, has published Physics papers, taught theoretical physics and has over 300 scientific papers published. Professor Roessler says that LHC experiments could lead to the destruction of Earth and other planets. One of the main problems discussed by Professor Roessler is that the LHC experiments could create micro black holes, some of which would be drawn to the centre of the Earth by the Earth's gravitational pull to eventually grow and cause the destruction of our planet. CERN admits to the fact that the LHC may create unknown numbers of micro black holes but CERN scientists rely on a theory by theoretical physicist Stephen Hawking who says micro black holes will evaporate. The rate of production of micro black holes produced by the LHC is estimated by German Astrophysicist Dr Rainer Plaga in his paper "On the potential catastrophic risk from metastable quantum-black holes produced at particle colliders". Dr Plaga says "A production rate of up to about one BH per second could then occur at the nominal LHC luminosity i.e, the LHC would be a "black hole factory". He says "The possibility that a collider-produced black hole (BH) - or another exotic object -might catastrophically grow by accretion and thus injure or kill humans deserves careful attention". [2]

In explaining the outcome of LHC experiments at CERN, Professor Otto Roessler says one outcome might be that a positive or negative outcome from the experiment "is indistinguishable as the mini black hole leaves no decipherable sign of their existence – at first". Professor Roessler says "This difference to its predecessors makes the current experiment a guaranteed success: at causing an unprecedented amount of human suffering. For there will be no way to explain to anyone that he or she is safe or to apologize for the suffering to expect. The rational fear unavoidably caused can only be made go away by convening a post-facto scientific world conference that proclaims absolute safety. Unfortunately, every scientist who would not agree with this preassigned verdict would act irresponsibly. Since this will be obvious, no one would ever again believe a single world from a scientist. Anti-scientific fundamentalism would have won –even if the experiment proves innocuous in hindsight" [3].

Risk Assessment

In a paper *"The Black Hole Case: The injunction against the end of the world"*, Eric. E Johnson, Assistant Professor of Law at the University of North Dakota in Grand Forks, gives a detailed summation of most of the issues that different scientists are raising as potential threats from the LHC experiments. Johnson says "critics, of course, fear that particle-physics experiments will annihilate humanity. At the same time, particle physicists fear that humanity will annihilate their experiments. The angst felt by the physics community is not trivial. One top CERN physicist said that most of CERN's member-nation governments are "desperately waiting for the right opportunity to shut down the place. There is nobody fighting for this to survive, to continue" he said. "We have to fight ourselves – the physicists"" [4]. Johnson outlines at least five threats from the LHC experiments including black holes, strangelets, magnetic monopoles, a bosenova, and a vacuum transition which could destroy not only Earth, but the universe. These threats are credible scientific theories and all have merit.

In allowing a dangerous project to proceed in a community or on this planet, risk assessment (in this case the threat to our planet from these experiments) should be explained in an environmental impact statement or a safety report. In 2008 a court case against CERN stated "CERN has failed to provide an environmental-impact statement as required under the National Environmental Policy Act" [5]. Safety reports issued from CERN will of course be biased since they have a vested interest in keeping the experiments going.

In her article *"Green Justice: A holistic approach to environmental injustice"*, American lawyer Nicole C Kibert writes "When a potentially hazardous project is being proposed, if it is a well-organized and economically well-off community, the community members will be able to come up with their own risk analysis numbers showing an unacceptable risk resulting in permit denial. However, if the negative impact is going to

fall mainly on people who are not able to fight back, then the project will most likely go ahead with a risk analysis showing an acceptable risk by the permitting agency" [7].

Industrial Risk Assessment when applied to projects such as the LHC is extremely difficult to quantify and even if you can prove that enough risk of danger exists to warrant stopping the project, jurisdiction and lack of rules and regulations that normally deal with keeping such things in check in any one country are lacking in this case. Therefore without a huge global outcry and the majority of physicists speaking against the project, it is unlikely those in charge of the LHC will consider stopping the experiments when so much time and money has been invested.

In the case of the LHC which cost over $6 billion dollars to build, it is unlikely that proponents of the project will accept requests to stop the experiments, even if it would alleviate concerns and enable some open and honest discussion of the risks of the LHC. If such a Risk Assessment was undertaken, there could be a consideration of cost benefit analysis. In the paper by Eric E. Johnson, *The Black Hole Case: The injunction against the end of the world*, human life was given a value by Judge Richard A. Posner in calculating the value of all human life. He valued the extinction of all human life at 600 trillion dollars. Posner says "valuing human lives is not... quite so arbitrary a procedure as it may seen. It sounds like an ethical or metaphysical undertaking, but what actually is involved is determining the value that people place on avoiding small risks of death" [4]. In this paper, Posner arrived at this figure by valuing each human life at $50,000 and multiplying that number by the world population of 6 billion to arrive at 300 trillion dollars and he then doubles this to adjust for future lives that haven't been accounted for.

Which ever way you consider these equations, the sum of money put on a human life is arbitrary and if the world ended there would be no-one left to pay the claim and no recipients either. What value should we give the life of the 16 year old girl who committed suicide because she could not bear to see the destruction of all that was dear to her (by the LHC experiments) and therefore thought it was better to end her life. Isn't her life worth more than all of the LHC? Isn't one life worth more than the LHC?

The LHC has no real focus except to look for answers to questions about matter and antimatter and how the universe was formed. If there was no LHC, life would go on as normal tomorrow. In examining how people might feel who have spent so much time and effort on a project that might explain unexplained matters of physics but which also may result in the end of the world, a quote by author C. S. Lewis who wrote about the Lord of the Rings by J R Tolkien seems relevant. He implied that the weapon mentioned in Lord of the Rings was based on the atomic bomb (also a threat to humanity). "Here is a book published when everyone was preoccupied by that sinister invention [the atomic bomb]; here in the centre of the book is **a weapon which it seems madness to throw away yet fatal to use"** [8].

Cost benefit analysis is difficult to apply to the LHC since you cannot really quantify human life and the benefits are largely unknown. Death is simply not a redressable injury under law.

The Precautionary Principle
"When an activity raises threats of harm to human health or the environment, precautionary measures should be taken even if some cause – and – effect relationships are not fully established scientifically"(From the January 1998 Wingspread statement on the Precautionary Principle) [15].
 The precautionary principle states that "if an action or policy has a suspected risk of causing harm to the public or to the environment, in the absence of scientific consensus, that the action or policy is harmful, the burden of proof that it is not harmful falls on those who advocate taking the action" [16].

In the court case to obtain an injunction against the LHC where the applicants were Luis Sancho and Walter L. Wagner (nuclear safety expert), it was stated that " Neither CERN nor the government defendants have engaged in any form of hearings or other meetings in which the plaintiffs or members of the public would have been allowed to attend so as to comply with requirements for Environmental Assessment [EA] findings, Findings of No Significant Impact [FNSI], or Environmental Impact Statements [EIS], or any other NEPA requirements or European Commission requirements pertaining to the Precautionary Principle" [6]. Therefore it can be seen that there was little consultation with experts and the public to have any say in whether the LHC machine should be used. This application to the court in Hawaii also stated that the LSAG (safety report) is biased towards defendant CERN in that it was prepared by a committee consisting entirely of CERN employees or former employees.

In the document titled "*Communication under the optional protocol to the international covenant on civil and political rights*" addressed to the Human Rights Committee at the UN, it is stated "The European Union has formally accepted the precautionary principle. However, in the case of CERN, we could not find an official willing to take responsibility for enforcement of that principle". This document also quotes the Future of Humanity Institute of Oxford University, U.K, as saying "While the arguments for the safety of the LHC are commendable for their thoroughness, they are not infallible. Although the report considered several possible physical theories, it is eminently possible that these are all inadequate representations of the underlying physical reality. It is also possible that the models of processors in the LHC or the astronomical processes appealed to in the cosmic ray argument are flawed in an important way. Finally, it is possible that there is a calculation error in the report...However, our analysis implies that the current safety report should not be the final word in the safety assessment of the LHC. Such work would require expertise beyond theoretical physics, and an interdisciplinary group would be essential" [1].

CERN's answer to any criticisms is to say that the LHC is safe to use. CERN documents say "If the LHC can produce microscopic black holes, cosmic rays of much higher energies would already have produced many more. Since the Earth is still here, there is no reason to believe that collisions inside the LHC are harmful" [18]. Many scientists have commented on this statement with rebuttals which include the fact that the experiment being undertaken at CERN is extremely different to what happens in space because, firstly, particles in space are moving freely and are not set up to clash in such a focused way and in the conditions that exist in the CERN LHC experiments.

In 2007, CERN's chief scientific officer Jos Engelen was quoted as saying that "CERN officials are now instructed with respect to the LHC's world-destroying potential 'not to say that the probability is very small but that the probability is zero'". The zero-risk policy was questioned by collider supporter Kapusta who said "The odds [1 in 5 million] are tiny but not zero. A physicist never says never. Is this tiny probability acceptable... given the potentially devastating consequences?" [1].

It is obvious that the precautionary principle has not been observed by CERN and that no committees have been allowed to form made of experts from different fields and members of the public and that CERN has disregarded and ignored the voices of those who have spoken out and asked for a safety conference. Experts have said that there are risks including risks we can theorise about and risks that we may not even comprehend.

Clues to the unknowns of the CERN experiments can be found in much of their documentation. For instance, in corrected update 3 [CERN, 30th March 2010], CERN research director Sergio Bertolucci says "This is a step into the unknown. We are doing something that no-one has done before. We hope we find things that are really new. There are known unknowns out there, like dark matter and new dimensions about which we hope to learn. But it is possible that we will find some unknown unknowns which could be hugely important for mankind. With the LHC, we have the tool that we need" [19].

Probable risks are being taken that rival and eclipse those known risks of terrible events such as exploding huge atomic bombs. The people who publicly discuss these issues have no other recourse to date other than interviews and open publications and discourse since CERN is unlikely to agree to stopping the experiments while debate is allowed. People are asked to accept CERN's word that everything will be all right based on unproven theories and PR releases that make dubious comparisons between the LHC experiments and what happens in space. The fear caused by CERN has contributed to the death of one young girl and it has contributed to the sadness felt by many other people who feel that CERN has disregarded their civil and human rights by conducting these experiments knowing full well safety concerns are not addressed and all life risks being destroyed.

The Precautionary Principle includes a consideration of social justice issues compatible with Ecofeminist principles because feminist environmentalists and health activists contributed to the original conception of the Principle and the ensuing Wingspread statement on the precautionary principle (1998) The precautionary principle embraces the idea of "forecare" and "caring for" which are distinctly feminine concepts that women have articulated for years [17]. These principles have not been addressed or discussed by CERN, nor has CERN shown any formal attempt to satisfy the Precautionary Principal.

Safety issues

In a document submitted to the Human Rights Committee at the UN by people from "conCERNed international" (www.concerned-international.com), it was stated that "composition of the panels that conducted the LHC safety reviews in 2003 and 2008 failed to address issues of conflict of interest, diversity of specialization, and consultation of the public" [1]. "The first panel was composed only of collider physicists. This led to complaints about conflict of interest. This lack of a fully disinterested arms-length safety assessment was also the model for the safety assessment of a previous U.S collider, the RHIC at Brookhaven which was started up in 2000" [1].

In a book "*Catastrophe: Risk and response*", Professor Richard Posner observed the lack of arms-length assessment and called for strict regulation of colliders. Posner wrote many scientists have an "attitude gap created by the different goals, and resulting different mindsets of science on the one hand and public policy on the other. The scientist qua scientist wants to increase scientific knowledge, not make the world safer – especially from science" [20].

Other safety concerns raised in the document to the Human Rights Committee at the UN quote an expert's report on the LHC Risk management practices: review of the risk assessment process used for the 2008 LHC safety study" (Leggett 2009). Leggett's paper reported that the 2008 LHC study "shows that the LSAG report has less than a quarter (in fact, only 18%) of the elements that would be present if current recommendations for best-practice safety assessments were followed as shown in the survey" [1].

The report to the Human Rights Committee states all direct and non-direct contributors to the 2008 safety review were particle physicists. All the contributors to the 2008 safety review (including the SPC report) are presently listed in the CERN directory (at the time of the publication of the report). Therefore none were "experts beyond the scientific community... for example, lawyers, ethicists" et cetera despite that being recommended by the European Commission. The document quoted one of the rules of natural justice or procedural fairness: the rule against bias – no one to be a judge in their own cause [1]. This paper also said the question (about safety to be considered) should have been "Can there in fact be a way that

a catastrophe could occur from collision from the available physics? Not 'how can it be argued that there is safety?'" [1].

Calls for a safety conference where all the perceived threats from the LHC experiments could be discussed have so far been ignored by CERN. In a recent interview with Professor Otto E. Roessler, he said that "I want to be disproved. It would be wonderful if one could disprove this main danger that black holes would not evaporate, would be therefore eternal essentially, so they would eventually eat the Earth. Whether I'm right that it's only 5 years or it takes longer is less important in comparison. But this is the basic question on the table and the public should be allowed to participate in a discussion about this question. I call it a security or safety conference and this conference doesn't cost much. It doesn't take more than a week to arrange. It can be done. And CERN can wait for this week. And if enough people on the planet say, why not go the safe way, then everything is fine" (Professor Dr Otto E. Roessler) [14].

In discussions of the safety of our planet and LHC experiments, Russian academic Evgeni Dovgel says "The energy of particle collisions which can be achieved in this collider is millions of times higher than the energy of the synthesis of helium atoms out of hydrogen atoms in a hydrogen bomb explosion, the frequency of collisions to be achieved is a million times per second, while the temperature at the point of particle collisions is to be 100 thousand times as high as the one at the center of the sun. They say, this will help scientists reproduce in the collider (on the inhabited planet!) those conditions which existed in the universe for the first fractions of a second after the big bang, which supposedly created the universe (but the cause of which is unknown to them), as well as helped them clarify their assumptions concerning physical laws" [21]. Dovgel points out that the safety report produced by CERN scientists is flawed and he also says that the report conclusions are erroneous. He also says that many scientists seriously criticize this report but it is being ignored by CERN. Dovgel is another example of another voice speaking out against the dangers of the

LHC being ignored by CERN.

Attempts to stop the experiments have been tried using legal means including a law suit pursued in a Federal court in Hawaii by Walter L. Wagner (nuclear safety expert) and Luis Sancho. This case failed. They sought to require an environmental impact statement from the U.S government in its role of funding and participating in the LHC project. The case was dismissed on jurisdictional grounds, but Judge Helen Gillmor wrote "It is clear that Plaintiffs' action reflects disagreement among scientists about the possible ramifications of the operation of the Large Hadron Collider. This extremely complex debate is of concern to more than just the physicists". Other court cases including a case in the Swiss courts in 2008 and a law suit in Germany in 2009 to prevent full-power operation of the LHC at CERN also failed. And Eric Johnson says "Suing to stop the LHC is a unique litigation endeavor. Problems abound. The only thing that seems straightforward is the prayer for relief (a remedy in civil law) but what is the claim? In what court do you file it? And how do you get personal jurisdiction over CERN?" [4].

Conclusion

Situations such as CERN would not arise if we had a world that respected an Ethic of Care which is discussed by people involved in the environmental movement as well as being implied by scientists such as Roessler who advocated that all scientists take a Hippocratic Oath. In "*Green Justice: A holistic approach to environmental injustice*" by Nicole C Kibert, Kibert says "Ecofeminists have stated that to begin working towards breaking down the oppression systems that perpetuate the degradation of both the earth and disenfranchised people, we must shift to an ethic "that makes a central place for values of care, love, friendship, trust, and appropriate reciprocity-values that presuppose that our relationships to others are central to our understanding of who we are [22]." Kibert says "This ideal is something that can also be included in environmental education programs, but to really work it has to be implemented on a much larger scale, on the level of a paradigm shift [7]."

Unfortunately the universal adoption of an Ethic of Care is yet to happen and it may be an ideological dream opposed by groups who want to dominate and control others. In the case of the LHC experiments, the human race now looks on at discussions, theoretical postulating and arguments more suited to an unreal world of science fiction stories than

real life. The reality of the sunrise on any given day being the last sunrise for everyone on the planet is no longer a nightmare but reality.

In past scenarios of huge loss of life, such as the atomic bomb or tsunamis or the Nazi Germany holocaust, there was some knowledge that the human race as a whole would still survive. People had some certainty, other that a meteor hitting the Earth or death by accident, murder, war or sickness of at least having the chance to plan for old age. There was a knowledge that when an individual died, the rest of humanity would keep going; that the birds would still sing and the forests would still grow and those remaining on this beautiful planet would keep looking for solutions to the problems of the world.

Has science in the pursuit of science chosen to ignore safety and risk assessment thus gambling with all human and animal and plant life and our planet? Who gave science that authority? Did we? In our everyday lives there are rules and regulations and laws that reflect society's norms and safeguard all of us. Cars that go too fast are stopped by police and police will apprehend a man with a gun threatening the innocent (hopefully but not always before he has killed people). Wars are still fought disempowering some and empowering others but these are usually localized. In the global scheme of things, where are the laws and regulations that hold CERN to account and what is to stop other scientific establishments also taking great risks with people's collective lives? Until international laws are changed and/or until a predominantly Ecofeminist nurturing, non-violent, sustainable, precautionary and environmentally friendly approach becomes reality in our world, we will be faced with situations such as CERN and the LHC experiments where "might equals right" and where those who dispute such an organization are told to shut up or are personally attacked, marginalized or rebutted with answers that are neither sound or satisfactory.

Dedications and thanks
Much thanks and kudos to all the scientists who have voiced their concerns openly about the dangers to our planet Earth from the LHC experiments. These scientists have shown courage, integrity and bravery in speaking out against those who would impose potentially deadly experiments on a planet inhabited by over 6 billion people. Our planet also contains an incredible array of flora and fauna over which we humans have stewardship. Scientists such as Dr Otto Roessler, Dr Walter Wagner and others such as law Professor Eric E. Johnson and Russian academic Evgeni Dovgel all deserve Nobel peace prizes in my opinion much more

than the perpetrators of potentially life threatening experiments at LHC that could exterminate our planet and all who live on it.

Notable quote

Evgeni Dovgel quoted Oppenheimer (father of the atomic bomb) as saying it wouldn't matter if the atomic bomb had blown the world up because there would be no-one left to judge him (Oppenheimer) or the other scientists involved. In his paper (see link below) Evgeni Dovgel wonders will we be so lucky with the LHC experiments that we survive the dangers they may bring? In our world, recent risk versus benefit failures include the space shuttle Challenger that blew up, killing the crew on board, and the recent disaster from the BP oil rig leaking an unstoppable flow of oil into the ocean. These are examples of humans miscalculating risk.

Dovgel says "The connection between madness and genius has been proved many times. After the explosion of the first atomic bomb, its "father" R. Oppenheimer was "joking" that, of course, they hesitated, too, but decided, if everything ended well, no one would condemn them. And if not, then there would be no one to judge them... They took the risk and became famous: they were the first who exploded the atomic bomb. Today's nuclear physicists are also ready to take the risk to become famous for 'such discoveries, which are not yet even conceived,' in the course of 'experiments, whose results may not be predictable in principle'."
-Evgeni Dovgel

The fate of the planet is in the hands of nuclear physicists: shall we be lucky this time?
http://dovgel.com/engl/kve.htm
Specific concerns and responses

Otto Rössler, a German chemistry professor at the University of Tübingen, argues that micro black holes created in the LHC could grow exponentially.[67][68][69][70][71] On 4 July 2008, Rössler met with a CERN physicist, Rolf Landua, with whom he discussed his safety concerns.[72] Following the meeting, Landua asked another expert, Hermann Nicolai, Director of the Albert Einstein Institute, in Germany, to examine Rössler"s arguments.[72] Nicolai reviewed Otto Rössler"s research paper on the safety of the LHC[68] and issued a statement highlighting logical inconsistencies and physical misunderstandings in Rössler"s arguments.[73] Nicolai concluded that "this text would not pass the referee process in a serious journal."[71][73] Domenico Giulini also commented with Hermann Nicolai on Otto Rössler"s thesis, concluding that "his argument concerns only the General Theory of Relativity (GRT), and makes no logical connection to LHC physics; the argument is not valid; the argument is not self-consistent."[74] On 1 August 2008, a group of German physicists, the Committee for Elementary Particle Physics (KET),[54] published an open letter further dismissing Rössler''s concerns and carrying assurances that the LHC is safe.[2][55] Otto Rössler was due to meet Swiss president Pascal Couchepin in August 2008 to discuss this concern,[75] but it was later reported that the meeting had been canceled as it was believed Rössler and his fellow opponents would have used the meeting for their own publicity.[76]

On 10 August 2008, Rainer Plaga, a German astrophysicist, posted a research paper on the arXiv Web archive concluding that LHC safety studies have not definitely ruled out the potential catastrophic threat from microscopic black holes, including the possible danger from Hawking radiation emitted by black holes.[3][77][78][79] In a follow-up paper posted on the arXiv on 29 August 2008, Steven Giddings and Michelangelo Mangano, the authors of the research paper "Astrophysical implications of hypothetical stable TeV-scale black holes",[56] responded to Plaga''s concerns.[80] They pointed out what they see as a basic inconsistency in Plaga''s calculation, and argued that their own conclusions on the safety of the collider, as referred to in the LHC safety assessment (LSAG) report,[5] remain robust.[80] Giddings and Mangano also referred to the research paper "Exclusion of black hole disaster scenarios at the LHC", which relies on a number of new arguments to conclude that there is no risk due to mini black holes at the LHC.[3][59]. On 19 January 2009 Roberto Casadio, Sergio Fabi and Benjamin Harms posted on the arXiv a paper, later published on Physical Review D, ruling out the catastrophic growth of black holes in the scenario considered by Plaga.[81] In reaction to the criticisms, Plaga updated his paper on the arXiv on 26 September 2008 and again on 9 August 2009.[77] So far, Plaga''s paper has not been published in a peer-reviewed journal.
[edit] Legal challenges

On 21 March 2008, a complaint requesting an injunction to halt the LHC's startup was filed by Walter L. Wagner and Luis Sancho against CERN and its American collaborators, the US Department of Energy, the National Science Foundation and the Fermi National Accelerator Laboratory, before the United States District Court for the District of Hawaii.[19][82][83] The plaintiffs demanded an injunction against the LHC's activation for 4 months after issuance of the LHC Safety Assessment Group's (LSAG) most recent safety documentation, and a permanent injunction until the LHC can be demonstrated to be reasonably safe within industry standards.[84] The US Federal Court scheduled trial to begin 16 June 2009.[85]

The LSAG review, issued on 20 June 2008 after outside review, found "no basis for any concerns about the consequences of new particles or forms of matter that could possibly be produced by the LHC".[5] The US Government, in response, called for summary dismissal of the suit against the government defendants as untimely due to the expiration of a six-year statute of limitations (since funding began by 1999 and has essentially been completed already), and also called the hazards claimed by the plaintiffs "overly speculative and not credible".[86] The Hawaii District Court heard the government's motion to dismiss on 2 September 2008,[1] and on, 26 September, the Court issued an order granting the motion to dismiss on the grounds that it had no jurisdiction over the LHC project.[87]

On 26 August 2008, a group of European citizens, led by a German biochemist Otto Rössler, filed a suit against CERN in the European Court of Human Rights in Strasbourg.[69] The suit, which was summarily rejected on the same day, alleged that the Large Hadron Collider posed grave risks for the safety of the 27 member states of the European Union and their citizens.[31][35][69].

Late in 2009 a review of the legal situation by Eric Johnson, a lawyer, was published in the *Tennessee Law Review*.[88][89][90] In February 2010 a summary of Johnson's article appeared as an opinion piece in New Scientist.[91]

In February 2010, the German Constitutional Court (Bundesverfassungsgericht) rejected an injunction petition to halt the LHC's operation as unfounded, without hearing the case, stating that the opponents had failed to produce plausible evidence for their theories.[92]

So what do we have here? What are the facts. In the coming days I will publish other comments and views pro and con and see where we stand at that point.

For a look at an official report on the safety of the CERN project click on the link below.

http://lsag.web.cern.ch/lsag/LSAG-Report.pdf

292

Oct 16, 2010

So where are we now in the CERN project? Information is very difficult to come by; but here is what my look at it reveals:

They are going ahead but seemingly much more cautionously since the "accident" of last year and the year before, essentially at one-third to half power. Full power would be 14 mil. TEV (total electron volts.)

Several of the purely physics theory issues remain resolved, even as the law suits to stop the project have failed.

A central issue among the physicists was the examination of the central equations involved--that is whose equations are correct in the context of the possible threat CERN might contain-Hawking or Einstein.

This is interesting because CERN advocates state that Hawkins's idea on black hole formation is correct because he argued, on paper, that such black holes would be tiny and dissipate, immediately, presumably by other particles ranging from anti-matter, to even strangelets themselves.

(See my blog Einstein, on this site for some background on Stephen Hawking.)

The problem with relying on Hawking's equations is that I have not read where he endorses those equations himself, anymore especially since his views on black holes were rejected by Hawking's himself in a titanic battle with Susskind, another physicists. (Again, see my blog on this site for more background.

Therefore, if the Hawking equations cannot be relied upon to prove the experiment is safe where do we go from there?

Detractors, one of them at least, argue that Einstein's equations are the ones that really applying in evaluating the CERN experiment. Einstein's field equations predicted that in a black hole scenario, an infinity of energy would be the result. (This would be a big explosion.) DisCerning readers will recall this harkens back to the famous black box radiation experiments which Einstein and Planck sought to discredit, experiments which also predicted "infinite" radiation as a possibility from ordinary matter. (This is allied to the idea which ultimately gave us E=Mc2.

So CERN is a threat, in this view, because it becomes a gigantic atom-splitting machine, the power of which has not been seen since the Big Bang itself.

So what do we do here? It don't look all that good, no matter which point of view you adopt, and in either case, proof one way or another is not forth-coming.

What to do?

I am trying to get more detailed info and will get back soon.

If anyone out there has anything to add to this story please contact me at Lonnie@lonniehicks.com

Oct 30, 2010
I am getting emails from individuals asking if I have any information on whether last week any tests were made at the LHC, the point being that we have had a Tsunami and an volcano eruption. Any connection? Not sure am email a few people to get information.

 I read on the CERN twitter page that an experiment ran on October 25th and another before than. Related. Don't know. Have to dig deeper.

Nov 23, 2010
Meantime see this you tube video on the CERN issues. It is view of Dr. Walter Wagner ho gives more details on the CERN situation.

http://www.youtube.com/watch?v=YZAQn-KxW_k&feature=related

Title: The Summary Goes on About Physics Theory

Updated 0/23. 2010

Summary: This is the never-ending blog which began with Einstein and examines many of ideas extent on how the Universe works. This one examines TEW which is the theory that Elementary Waves fill the universe everywhere at all quantum states and at all frequencies. See other blogs on this site for background and to pick up the story. I will begin the summary today after reviewing TEW theory.
Updated 9/23/10

The originator of Elementary Wave theory is generally conceded to be Lewis Little. Below a colleague, Stephen Speicher, gives a description of the theory.
See his website at http://physics.prodos.org/stephenspeicherexplains/

"The elementary wave cannot be understood by appealing to anything more basic to explain it-here is nothing more basic. The elementary waves have a structure and the effects of the changes in that structure are all we can know about them. So the ghost-like packets of waves in the standard theory have been replaced by a real existent, and the behavior of that wave is contrary to standard interpretation - the wave moves in reverse, from the target, or more generally from the detector, towards the source. In a way, Lytle's elementary wave is less like a traditional wave and closer to the idea of the elusive ether, in that it is like a flow, or a flux of material, while realizing that it makes no sense to talk about what kind of material it is -it just is.
Twenty-five hundred years ago Parmenides said (and more recently, as Leonard Peikoff is fond of saying) the universe is a "plenum". That is, there are no gaps, no voids, no place where there is nothing. That is what Lytle's theory has identified, the elementary waves are what fill the universe - they are omnipresent. According to Lytle's theory the waves exist for every possible quantum state, for every variable parameter that is possible."
This means that all of the universe is connected at every point in the universe by an invisible ether of the kind we have discussed above in the

---

295

Einstein blogs. Here we go again on the ether--which keeps popping up in Physics theory.
More on tomorrow.

Sept 15, 2010
Now, TEW ideas have not gained much currency but for our purposes we can give a few examples of how the theory works and the reader can make up h/her own mind.
Examples:
1-When we look at the sun what is actually occurring is that waves (yes waves) project directly from our eyes to the sun where photons are excited and shoot back along this wave path to our eyes and we see the sun.
2-Second example: when we blow into a bottle with our lips a sound is created. In EW theory pre-existing waves inside the bottle move toward our lips where the sound is then created moving back into the bottle at a particular frequency determined by the same wave configurations in the bottle. Different sized bottles, therefore, create different sound pitches.
3-In the famous double-slit experiment (look this up on the internet) the explanation is that waves move from the background board through the slits and then to the electron or photon source and a photon is then emitted back to the background board. It is a two-way exchange. This is a principle, the TEW people say televisions operate upon. They argue that a TEW does not supplant relativity and quantum theory but merely completes and explains these ideas.
Now TEW people explain that their theory can be proven by having one slit be transparent and then opaque alternatively in nanoseconds. This will show the actual direction of the transactions involved and can prove, thereby, the wave electron paths involved.
The problem with the theory is that these waves are hypothetical, like ether itself. But this critique can be made of many presuppositions in Physics. The basic nature of space its self, ether or no ether, is what is at issue. At this point no one seems to know for sure although there are certainly empirical data which suggest which descriptions of "empty space" are promising. This aspect is what we propose to examine next.
So there you have dear reader, a journey through modern physics and the ideas these folks are currently propounding and/or debating. Now lets see who has good data to back up claims because we see there are some pretty bizarre sounding ideas out there. But we ask, are they true?
Can they all be true?

Are some partially true?
Are all merely a measure of our lack of understanding of how things

———

actually work?

And last, does all this mean that we lack the mental capacity to understand the real fundamentals because we are merely human?

But, what is most striking to this observer is the startling consensus these various theories agree upon, and even more so, when we relate this consensus in physics to the religious themes which are often counterpoised against them, this consensus holds. This is the old science versus religion theme.

We can't do all of the consensus items in one blog so we will go through them one by in the coming days. But here is a pre-look.

The first consensus items:

1-Most people on the planet religious or scientist now agree:

There is an unseen world all around us; some of it comprehensible, some of it beyond our comprehension and, perhaps, we will never comprehend all of it. We humans simply lack to brain power to do so.

This unseen world in some theories include dark matter and dark energy ideas which state that 75% of what constitutes the universe we can not detect nor understand yet we know it exists.

This includes religious folks who claim all around us exists an unseen world including angels, gods, demons, spirits, heaven, hell and the like.

This includes membrane theories in science which state other dimensions may exist and we are a part of a muliti-verse where there might be millions of other universes and indeed millions of copies of our selves, perhaps existing, with slight variation in many of those worlds or universes.

This includes Einstein who argues that time-space--past present and future all exist simultaneously. That the universe is malleable and that space-time itself expands and contracts given one's speed and vantage point and so does matter itself.

This includes many who, by various names, indicate there is an yet undetected ether out there and we like fish have not discovered it. This is true of many of the theories of physics, even as they might call this ether by different names.

This includes ideas about God on both sides which simply state "we don't know if God exists but creation certainly does and we are limited in our ability to comp rend it.

We have seen plasma and Superwave theories which imply the universe is electric in nature and perhaps dangerous and the earth itself shows evidence of Superwave cosmic rays striking the earth at regular intervals, and, in the past, destroying much of life here.

We have seen ideas that much of the universe we perceive is really a product of the functioning of our brains and that, in effect, the moon doesn't exist, until and unless we observe it; that in between these observations the moon is a probability. This is what some quantum theorists say.

We see the argument that electrons can be in many different places at the same time and every electron in the universe is in contact with a partner electron else where in the universe at the same time and these pairs can instantly effect one another irrespective of the distance between them.

We see that some fear attempts to pierce the veil between dimensions and this great unseen at CERN can destroy the planet; that seeking to create the big bang has too many dangers to risk moving forward with the experiment. Too much is at stake, the critics say, and the earth can be destroyed, or that huge magnetic storms and earthquakes can occur.

Some religious people, argue that the end of the world is at hand, citing everything from the second coming to the prophecies of the Mayan calendar to ancient texts they say actually record in mythological terms previous cosmic ray bombardments, and that 2012 is a reasonable date for such a return.

Well as you can see this is quite a list. What are we to make of it? What is true here?

Well, I always leave the difficult questions until tomorrow. Then, I will blab and talk about what I think. We will start with the question which of the theories have actual evidence and verifiable proofs.

Sept 16th 2010

Above we saw that these various science theories and religious theories of the universe had some surprising similarities. Now we want to examine the issue of how can one evaluate the theories presented.

I propose to make the first level of examination based upon what evidence exists for each to merit closer examination.

First, let's do Einstein.

Do Einstein's theories bear out empirically?

Well much of it actually does, although there are some critical areas where it does not. For example, Einstein's theories and calculations do not account for critical processes in the context of black holes. Secondly, Einstein does not actually give us evidence of gravity. Gravity is the product of space-time being warped by mass in bodies, like planets but Einstein never tells us what gravity is, especially how it behaves in a black hole.

Third, Einstein himself, doubted his theory had adequately accounted for the issue of ether or the nature of space itself which gives the universe it's other characteristics.

Of course in his time he did not contemplate dark matter and dark energy and an expanding universe. He favored the notion of a steady state

---

universe. Finally, he did not believe in quantum mechanics although he helped create it. And, in fact, he ridiculed quantum pairing notions as "spooky action from a distance."

So there is Einstein.

Quantum mechanics is, perhaps, is one of the strangest theories. Reality becomes all math, all the time. We are given a theory where matter itself and its behavior is reduced to probabilities and all of nature only exists in a quantum world where the cat is alive and the cat is dead on a probabilistic basis; where an electron can be in two more places at the same time, where electrons are paired or "entangled" even though separated by distances light years apart. I am not of the view that these ideas have an empirical basis. They seem more math oriented than empirical. That does not mean quantum mechanics is incorrect. Rather, it feels incomplete. What it does not explain is a subject for another blog. (I know. Do not toss those rocks my way just yet.)

Plasma theories seem to have a solid empirical basis in two respects. It is clear that huge galaxy-sized magnetic clouds exist across many galaxies and do, in fact, form huge moving electric currents across immense distances. The role of magnetism is clearly at work in the universe at both the macro and the macro level. At issue is how does one interpret these phenomena?

A second level of data which seem to support plasma theories include ice-core data which show clearly that huge magnetic and cosmic impacts have affected the earth and its history. Moreover, binary star system behaviors do seem to lend support to plasma theories of star formation and dynamics. But work here needs to be done.

Plasma ideas are also generally recognized as part of a new branch of physics which has given new insights on the galaxy level as well as into the nature of Superfluids and wave behavior at the micro level, the subatomic. Few dispute plasma findings. Rather how those findings are interpreted seem to be the issue--central to the functioning of the universe or incidental?

The truths of plasma theories and magnetic and cosmic wave theories, however, have pretty gloomy outcomes in that their truth may imperil the entire planet. Moreover, some of the conclusions of plasma theorists seem to disagree with everything in the standard model, Einstein, astronomy and quantum mechanics as well.

The latter points of disagreement seem to be far-reaching and many, including myself, are not willing to go quite that far, while agreeing that

plasma theory is backed by some very strong data to support parts of the theory. To see the points of disagreement with the standard model see my blog above "Everything You Heard About the Universe is Wrong."
Religious ideas of how the world of the unseen works actually dove-tail with much of membrane theory where dimensions and multiple universes are posited. After all, if one cannot know the unknowable, the mysterious is permanent and that can be called God or the unknowable. Much is ultimately beyond our comprehension.
The point here is that if you argue that the whole universe is a construct beyond our ultimate knowledge then so-called empirical data, by definition, will not be forth-coming, even if it were available, it might not be comprehendible to us humans.
It becomes the height of assumption-ego to assume we can, in these theoretical constructs know everything or even a small part of what we call the universe. After all 95% of the universe is composed of stuff about which we know virtually nothing.
That leaves us to examine, string theory, membrane theory, and holographic theories for tomorrow. Until then let's do some head-scratching about it all.

Sept 17, 2010
Now holographic ideas sound Kantian and something like "the world is only perceived through our senses and therefore effected by those same senses."
In the words of one wag "The world is the story we tell ourselves about ourselves." And interestingly some quantum mechanic theorists might agree with that idea.
Others, in what I call the holographic view, state that all of what we perceive might exist only in the mind of God, ourselves included.
One interesting line of research is trying to produce the experience of "God" in experimental subjects by subjecting parts of the brain to electrical stimulation. There have been results where subjects have claimed a sense of contact with "another" with "God." This not so strange, many religious conversions claim similar contact.
The problem with this view is that such experiences are personal and not replicable upon demand or even sharable with others, and therefore, remain private views or visions.
Allied, but not the same, is the notion of different dimensions, of three four five or up to even eleven dimensions. See above for my discussion of string theory and eleven dimension postulations.
Examples of the possibility of a multi-dimensional universe or universes can be pretty convincing. After all, are do fish ever actually discover water? Maybe CERN can help in this regard if we are around to debate these issues, say the critics.

So where are we in this journey through the minds of those who think about the big questions?

Well, we have some pretty good ideas and goodness knows there are many dishes on the table to munch upon, but what in the end have we gained by this mental effort at comprehension?

Well on tomorrow I will begin a discussion of two next-step areas:

1-What are the next-in-line events or experiments which can decide these issues or at least move the debate forward?

2-And, in the case of some of these ideas, which if true, do they mean danger for us; and what can or should be done?

After all, as in the case of Plasma theory, solar flares SME"s (solar mass ejections) pose a threat to the planet and what should we be doing about it? What are we doing about it?

I would say let's sleep on it but who among us can sleep after all this?

Sept 23rd 2010

Now on the "possible immediate danger chart" there are two that stand out:

The first is the experiment at CERN where this month and next, I believe, the gigantic magnets are to be fired up once again. The scientists are doing so at much reduced capacity and plan to ramp up to full capacity in two to three years. The two colliders each have about 7 million TEV capacity so fired together they would equal 14 million electron volts.

This exceeds by far any thing that has been done in the past and will result in billions of photon-electron collisions a second at these almost light speeds.

The troubling aspect about the drivers in all this which could easily overcome caution is that hundreds of physicists and are running hundreds of experiments in all this which could determine careers, promotions, Nobel prizes and reputations.

That is a bad combination. The drive toward doing this thing is driven by human considerations rather than scientific ones and that is a bad mix of motivations..

Moreover, if one experiment does not produce the desired results then momentum builds to do it over and over again, such that the project has an endless momentum to continue.

Meantime, the military stands in the background, silently mouthing the question "Can we get a new weapon out of this?"

I stand ready to be corrected about all of this and would welcome data which show that the danger is not there or exists at acceptably low levels-- or even a credible environmental report. All I have seen is reference to Stephen Hawking's opinion/ work that any black holes which develop would quickly dissipate.

But, as you dear reader would know, in reading the blog on Einstein, the Hawking thesis on black holes has , excuse me, some very large holes. No reassurance lies there.

But since we must rely upon ideas about basic physics here (that is what the experiments are all about) we can ask the question what would some of the major ideas/theories in physics say about the danger here?

Lets take plasma theory first. Yes, the plasma theorists might say (I don't know anyone specifically) there is a danger here. Here is how I imagine their argument might go.

1- The gigantic magnets at play at CERN exactly match the electon-magnetic fields in the universe at large and the magnetic field which currently shields the earth from deadly cosmic rays.

These fields, both around the earth, the sun and the galaxies themselves are huge dynamos in effect and are tremendously explosive. In space we see that effect in the form of supernovas. Yes, we could trigger a supernova here on earth and the earth would, of course be destroyed.

2-They might argue that the disruption of the magnetic field of the earth could occur and this could trigger earthquakes, expose us to cosmic ray bombardments, floods--all of which could happen very quickly.

The forces of the universe are very delicate indeed, they would say, and we ought not tamper with what we cannot control if things get out of hand.

Well, my mouth is dry after these thoughts. Need something to drink.

Back tomorrow.

Title: The Problem of the Idea

The Philosopher:

"The Problem of the 21st century

is the problem of the Origins of the Idea."

The Idea has driven much

of human history-

a major motivator

many taken together are

Articulators;

Ideas compose all Human Dreams.

But ask what is this Idea

and silence ensues;

ask where is it

in the human mind

and we'll get charts of its activity centers

but nothing about what it is

or where it comes from.

The Scientist:

Well, we don't have to know what a thing is

to utilize it.

We can identify behaviors and integrate

them-harness them to purpose.

Philosopher:

Sure like the Atomic Bomb. It was built because

we could integrate various disciplines

and make things go bang

without thinking of Consequence.

technical Ideas-too have consequences.

Scientist:

So you would hold up all human progress

until the over-arching Idea comes along

before we act?

Philosopher:

Ah, but note that progress that destroys

the planet is not

progress at all

but only a blind mistake;

one I might add,

that did not have

an Idea or Clue

of what lesser ideas about tinkering

could and might signal or include.

So here my point and drift

good ideas are hard to find;

cleaver ideas

like a bomb

are easier to advance.

Cosmologist:

Well here is my notion-

I hesitate to say Idea-

but there is only a little drift

between you and

the neo-Kantians

who claim Plato's Ideation.

may have an empirical base.

I know, "heavens" such an outcome;

but contemplate

Astronomy's "Inflation Theory", Quantum Theory;

Cosmology's dark matter and energy,

ideas that every electron

is "aware" of the charge

of it's matching

opposite charge

and "reacts" to changes

across all our known universe;

and you will have lot of "I told you soy's"

coming from the ancients.

So if human history has been driven

by Grand Ideas political, social, and scientific,

we have a need know then

what is an Idea and where

does it comes from;

and even if a great new idea

does surface

and is entirely new

how is that an entirely new idea

can be understood and acted upon

by others who did not share in its generation?

If only two people in the world can understand an

Idea, what does that mean for History?

So Idea Generation and Transmission are therefore

of one cloth and shall we say comprehendible

only by Cosmology's "Inflation"?

Muse:

Well, if all Ideas generate in the mind

and assuming mind has a physical base

in generating mental things,

the assumption, too, must be that

the electrons of the mind are, too,

"popping in and out of the universe

in that same mind

as all Quantum things do.

So are we here

dealing with the " Mind As Portal"

between multi-existences and universes

and Ideas then are merely transmission

artifacts of that activity?

"Humm, said the Scientist

how would you study that?

Muse:

We are all becoming Poets are we not?

Poets of the Electron Dream.

Poet:

All knowledge comes from dreaming

and math, this is Einstein

but how are dreams possible

is yet

to be answered.

Yet we do dream

and we need to also ask

what is the archeology of these dreams?

"The Muse said

And too,

"who is doing the Dreaming? "

Kant smiles.

So, what is the dictionary definition of "Idea"?
i☐ de☐ a

/a☐ ☐ diǝ , a☐ ☐ diǝ / Show Spelled Pronunciation [ahy-dee-uh, ahy-deeuh] Show IPA

—noun

1.   any conception existing in the mind as a result of mental understanding, awareness, or activity.

2.   a thought, conception, or notion: That is an excellent idea.

3.   an impression: He gave me a general idea of how he plans to run the department.

4.   an opinion, view, or belief: His ideas on raising children are certainly strange.

5.   a plan of action; an intention: the idea of becoming an engineer.

6. a groundless supposition; fantasy.

7. Philosophy.

a. a concept developed by the mind.

b. a conception of what is desirable or ought to be; ideal.

c. (initial capital letter)   Platonism. Also called form. an archetype or pattern of which the individual objects in any natural class are imperfect copies and from which they derive their being.

d. Kantianism. idea of pure reason.

8. Music. a theme, phrase, or figure.

9. Obsolete.

a. a likeness.

b. a mental image.

Origin:
1400–50; < LL < Gk idéā form, pattern, equiv. to ide- (s. of ideîn to see) + -ā fem. n. ending; r. late ME idee < MF < LL, as above; akin to wit 1

Related forms:
i⬚ de⬚ a⬚ less, adjective

Synonyms:
1,2. Idea, thought, conception, notion refer to a product of mental activity. Idea, although it may refer to thoughts of any degree of seriousness or triviality, is commonly used for mental concepts considered more important or elaborate: We pondered the idea of the fourth dimension. The idea of his arrival frightened me. Thought, which reflects its primary emphasis on the mental process, may denote any concept except the more weighty and elaborate ones: I welcomed his thoughts on the subject. A thought came to him. Conception suggests a thought that seems complete, individual, recent, or somewhat intricate: The architect"s conception delighted them. Notion suggests a fleeting, vague, or imperfect thought: a bare notion of how to proceed.4. sentiment, judgment.
Dictionary.com Unabridged

Title: Indefinite Pronouns and the Universe

He said;

his arm flowing outward;

"The problem of the 21st Century

is the Indefinite Pronoun.

We're all everyone and no one

indefinite;

pronoun, but not a noun

the universal vagueness

of time, meaning, and identity,

rather like the cloud of electrons

flying around the nucleus of the atom

there and not there;

but capable of being anywhere

or in two places at the same time;

holding many beliefs constantly shifting,

feeling fervently one thing and its opposites

the next minute,

being who am I this minute

and not who I am the next minute;

in a world changing fast

speeding up

and speeding up faster

and faster;

indistinct;

shadowy

flashing lights

spark

racing by

approaching

and not approaching the speed of light.

There I'm me, us

none of us; we,

have said it;

both me?

The Indefinite Pronoun Defined

"Singular: another, anybody, anyone, anything, each, either, everybody, everyone, everything, little, much, neither, nobody, no one, nothing, one, other, somebody, someone, something

Plural: both, few, many, others, several.

Singular or Plural: all, any, more, most, none, some"

Is this a bizarre definition or what?

More bizarre, if this definition is literally true.

Modern Physics says this definition is literally true;

an accurate description of us and the universe

in which we live,

things popping in and out of existence.

We live in this universe and most likely have to come to

understand, like the indefinite pronoun,

we too, as individuals

and as collectives,

pop in and out of existence.

Not duality,

but multiplicities.

How else to explain

how we can harbor contradictory

———

beliefs;

sometime many

in a single day?

And feelings too.

Am I changed in all of this

or merely your view of me?

Devil or Saint?

Depends apparently

upon what

time it is.

Title: A Dreamer's Poet

Dreamers dream
dreaming that
all their dreams are dreams;
and is reality then multiple-shaped
or itself a dream?

If dreams are things not real or true
or don't yet exist
then what does it mean for dreamer to
act upon the dream and bring it forth
into reality?

Was the dream just reality
not yet existent;
in waiting so to speak?

Or was it live
always there
waiting to be discovered?

Seems to me
this is much like a poem;
how the poem comes to be-

unless, of course,
the poet
is a dream too,
outside reality
paradoxical conundrum
don't you think?

And more:
could it be the Dreamer's Poet
in dreaming thus
creates the Poet
and the Poetry

———

both of which
become Reality;
Thus

Note: In this section we have several goals:

1. We want to allow the reader to participate in the writing process, centered on the short-short story. I have developed the habit of starting a story or novel and then inviting the reader to participate in completing it, either in their own imagination, or in fact, on paper. I have no authors pride or copyright interest in retaining "rights." It is a way of working I have grown accustomed to in working with others on the internet.

2. A second goal achieved here is that readers in participating were asked to take these "beginnings" and relate them to their real life concerns and interests. In this way I was able to get a sense of how some American's feel in this Age of Obama and unprecedented anxiety.
    The reactions and the participation is on-going and will be the subject of a later book-which has a working title:
    "Participatory Novel Writing"
    Finally, I chose each story as an illustration of the over-all themes in this book.

Short Stories: The Complete and The To-Be-Imagined

Vignettes, Story-Poems and Real Life

Title: Time Sits With Me

Updated: 11/2/10

 She sat with Time at her elbow. He was there when she took out the old photographs looking them over, the faces shinning from the page, still new and fresh in her mind like yesterday; Time had not erased that. She looked over at him and he acknowledged her gratitude as she stood to go to the stove to put the pot on for tea, a pot given her by her daughter, now gone, first college and now beyond to a small apartment in a bad part of town with a boyfriend she had never bothered to introduce, with phone calls which offered strained reassurance that she was alright and that things were going great, but she knew they weren't; but she knew she wasn't supposed to pry, now that Katie was all grown up now. She wished they weren't "going well." At least she would call when she needed money, liked she used to do when she was in college.

The pot boiled and she turned to her window box to inspect the flowers and the garden beyond, full of herbs, rosemary, tomatoes. cilantro, not just a garden but a new crop of babies she sheared into the world each spring. Perhaps she would grow more Marijuana this year. The money was needed and the law said that she could grow 12 plants, Last year she had six, this year twelve.

She kept her eye on them the first month. A male plant could appear and kill all the female plants. She aimed to be an alert gardener this year.

Turning, she checked the phone and the answering machine just in case she had missed a call, the mailbox to see if there was mail she had missed, her email and her neighbors--all these the rhythms of grandmotherhood. Small town chatter grows with the years; and she didn't really like it.

She got up one more time. Time to watch her program.

She sighed as he sat down beside her to watch too. Her life-long companion.

He gave a her a long look after the show saying: "Take your time."

She nodded.

Chapter Two

"You have been good to me," she said "always there, always patient and many times it was just you and I, and again, it is now just you and I."

I often wonder why you have done it. Why you have stuck with me. Is it that you have no choice?"

She examined his face looking for a response which never came. She could never see that face clearly, she could not, despite thousands of times looking, see his age, really read his emotions. He was more like a spirit which actually lived inside her rather than outside her. But he was always there with her, no matter what.

Through kids and a husband she often ignored his presence but knew he was there. At times she thought he might be her soul-mate and that all else was illusion and people and things were just passing through, while he remained.

He and she, she thought, had become particularly close after Howard left. He stood at the door and protected her from that loneliness which can close in and suffocate in an empty house with just the light of night-time TV to keep the shadows away.

She looked at him, this time full in the face, wondering if he would be there after, after she went on, Would he be there then too?

He seemed to read her thoughts but merely smiled.

Chapter Three

But today he was different. He can across the room that day and stooped above her and with two hands took her knitting away, placing it on the lamp table beside her, smiling close to her face as he did so. Mildly surprised she look into his gray eyes questioningly and rose at his gentle urging.

She thought she knew what he was doing but she wasn't sure. She had imagined that he had thought of it too and she wasn't sure if this was it, the time he would say it. So she rose as his arms drew around her and he

———

offered her the slowing engulfing hug, one she realized she had longed for, needed.

His breath was upon her cheek and swept pass to her neck. She felt her arms rise around his shoulders and life flower petals close and join behind his neck settling there like a gentle rain. That is how she was imagining it. He felt like her garden to her in that moment, one of her prize roses opening up to her after a long, long time.

He had been there before Howard she suddenly thought and he was here now after Howard. She was coming home to someone familiar, someone whose companionship, who had all along been taken for granted; some now whose patience was seeing the light of day. Someone she knew intended to roll back the years in his embrace and make love to her.

———

Title: The Night Before

He walked, Streamers of his Youth trailing behind him frayed from the
punishing winds stretching back to his youth, sweet howls and howling
howls, too many strangers, not enough friends; too few precious loves.
His hands dug deeper into his pockets looking for lost treasures there
which time, the pirate, had stolen; who stood on the prow of his departing
ship yelling, "good bye me hearty" while he kept moving because there is
little else to do except accept being pushed ahead when there is no behind
left, no taut abs, no sideways devastating glance, no new photo or book,
no shots, no gig, no popping eyes and double-take, caught breathy stares,
when
he walked by; that replaced now by the bemused indifference of those with
barely twenty candles on their cake, whose mumbled muffled compliments
like "old lion" without a roar, "used to be" references, and "I think he was"
allusions, calculating stances in your path, asking for autographs,
references and jobs, beseeches and telephone numbers the scribbled on
business cards, of the those just learning to put on the clown paint while
you write your name bemoaning how art and hard work is strangled in the
crib by these unknowingly seeking their futures, each claiming they didn't
have the price of dues, and saw no need.
He stops before the office mirror for a last look before having to stand
before the humiliation desk, before the twenty-five year old, whose perfect
stand up collar shirt was only slightly younger than he was, would take up
paper to avoid looking at him, shocked as all the young are by any age five
more than their own, who had already practiced the mime of saying no to
those who had not gotten the word they had passed and were now gone;
his, the impatience of the young, who think that the old never know when it
is time to go who linger past their prime time and like stick people in the
drawing speak but have no torsos.
He unsheathed his photo which had been taken prior to his conception
placing it on the desk and took his preying mantis stance while youth sat
languidly sure that this outcome was not in doubt and courtesy was the
only thing here at risk and in twenty minutes New York time he would be
able to take the hot text message from Camilla of Last Night and then be
free to stare outside his corner window leisurely wondering how high is
high and how difficult it is to find the perfect place for lunch with one's The
Night Before.

Title: Radio On

"You used to tickle me" she said "and I could not resist,"

the most fun I can remember from my child hood. You tormented me

over the homework that never got done, while the TV blared,

while the music played and you were teaching me my first dance steps,

held me my first hold and embrace,

brought me close to my first almost kiss

my first hot breath

my first stick-straight eye contact

and whispered bedroom window laments

as you pretended to love the girl which ignored you

and I pretended to offer you advice

while my own breasts pounded

almost hurting from the effort

alleviated only by my gurgling giggles

at the 11pm hour

because to stay up past midnight

might bring out the goblins beneath the bed

and the monster in the closet

who, if I slipped, and stayed awake too long

my only protection then was my goo-goo doll

because she and I had a kid bubble all around

within which no monster could survive;

and sleep always saved us, didn't it?

In my gauzy dreams the wide world grew at night

to gigantic size and I lay on my bed of dreams

sleepy-eyed fixed on how big things were and how small

my size anchored only by the sounds of crickets outside,

muffled noises from Mom and Dad down the hall

in their room

and I lay often wondering if these nightly separations made any sense

at all, especially if I lay there in bed scared.

All I wanted was to feel safe and I really couldn't alone

so I would turn the radio on

and let the music fill in the gaps between me and the wide-wide world.
outside, my bated breathing, my only guide, my only safety clutch.

Title: The Easy Life

Life came so easy to her. Everyone remarked upon it. Beautiful she was and she had the essence of the grace that exists within without it's owner seemingly aware of it.

Kind and gentle she floats through rooms within an ether no one had but her, but all could see.

Anger put her way was never even seen or acknowledged; therefore never returned. Her hand was always the offering one.

People would meet her and not believe; and then test her with sharp words, verbal knives and jabbing eyes. But she never noticed and did not return what was never noticed.

Each and every one could see over time and ultimately perceived that she was what she seemed.

How incredible for all to come to perceive this was true, this was her truth, her gift, this something special about her was real; and each and every one of them sought over time, and some became, her very best friend and she never acknowledged prior slights from any.

Animals seemed hypnotized by her quiet administrations and she always acknowledged the children, never requiring that they be unseen.

That voice of heir's was bell-like clear.

Often new people would whisper "Is she for real?"

I was reassured she was.

But one day I, being a newcomer, visited her and sat observing the spirit that the whole town so much observed. She sat across from me quiet, observant. I filled the silence above the tea talking incessantly of me and finally i realized i had done so because she was really interested in my views.

323

I finally asked what was her secret to life. She looked up thoughtful and turned her head toward her bay window and in a whisper I could barely hear. I thought I heard her say:

"People say life is easy on me. I think it is that way because I am easy on life."

Title: Secrets

I told her all my secrets.

Once started they came out almost by themselves and she acted so enchanted it was easy to just keep going on and on.

I told her about my first kiss, about my stealing grapes from the grocery store, one grape, is all it was, but I never forgot taking it. I told her about the time I told a lie to make myself seem more important than I was.

I had never been to Russia. But I said I did to impress my friends. I told her of times I had been quiet when I should have spoken up, of that moment of cowardice when I should have helped my friend when the gang caught us. I didn't help. I ran and they caught him. I didn't go back to help.

I revealed what I think about at night when I am going to sleep, my little vanities and self-deceptions because they seem harmless. I told her about the little mean things I've done and the day I learned that you could lie if it was small one and it kept someone from feeling hurt; of the secret anxieties i felt and the loves I lost and never knew why, of how I worry about being in shape all the time and the times in my twenties when I looked everywhere in faces on the street, in magazines, among strangers asking myself are you The One? I told her that quest never ended--I simply shortened the voyage because long quests can be tiring.

I told her of my secret desire to impress her by telling her my secrets; no pretending to tell her secrets so as to get her to tell me her secrets and this was my ultimate secret which, of course was no secret at all, since I told.

She laughed saying "I know but the gesture, I thought was sweet."

So, I said, "Do you have pretend secrets for me?" "Sure," she said, "but I will mix in the telling some real ones, like you did, and we can then both guess which ones were true. A little mystery never hurt anyone."

So she began to reciprocate telling me her first kiss was through a screen door and her mother asked what was wrong with her lips, about never realizing until she was ten that it went in... there.. About the shock of all of it. About the time she saw her mother and dad doing it. She told me about the first time which was very short, and the boy who was afraid and fumbly.

325

About her first push-em-bra and lace underthings she bought at Victoria's Secret and the party where some one felt her up in the dark and she let him. About her belief that she had lived in some previous life and remembered bits and pieces of it.

About how she thought when getting her period that she was dying and didn't tell anyone until her mother discovered the blood. Her first boy friend who was sweet and a virgin and so was she. She thought you could get pregnant from tonguing when kissing; about her first O and how it scared her; how she looked in the mirror afterwards to she if she had changed; about how scared she was when it came time to deliver the baby.

We talked for hours, mostly about the secrets but ultimately we started to share dreams. She wanted to be a ballerina but had to give it up. I wanted to be a sports star, but too short. We share dreams gains and lost, mostly lost, given up for a good job or the quest for one or for family and kids.

From that first "she called my number by mistake call" we call once a year, in secret of course, and share some more. We've never met. Don't need to. I already know all her secrets and she knows mine.

———

Title: Immortality

Eterna, Grantor of Immortality, sat the Silver Throne her Judgment Stick tapping One's and Two's--one for "Yes" and Two for "No" while assembled below the thrones" height were the petitioning hordes--those who came seeking Eternal Life and Immortality; the religionists, the fame-seekers, the parents, the writers, poets, and novelists, the politicians and the evil seekers.

There were all the animal species the vegetation and the microbial and those seeking to become immortal in the memory of those they loved and those that admired them.

"I" said the Politician "pursued the War and won the Peace none more than I deserve Immortality," he exclaimed.

In a gnat-second the Judgment Stick pounded down twice for "No" and he was gone.

The Parent Two quietly pursued their story line which was it was only through the love of their children would their memory remain and asked the Queen to imbue that in all the children and the grandchildren.

"We are humble people," they said "and our lives have meaning only through the ones who love us when we are gone. Who will come each year to mind the flowers at our graves; who will tells the stories, and save the photographs?"

Sterna's eyes grew dim and gave them a quiet, single tap which resounded in the great hall and other parents there took heart.

"Who's next?" she exclaimed.

Moving forward were a group of entertainers whose leader stated simply "We want people to remember our names; we want fame."

One said "Yes, I came from no-where, from a small town, where people there had the view I would amount to nothing at all. But, if I become famous, it would put the lie to that assessment and I would become somebody, not a nobody."

327

Eterna, surveyed the entertainers and saying:

"Some of you gave joy to the shut-ins and the masses and overcame obstacles from your own backgrounds and these are no mean deeds. Making the world a better place for some has to be weighed in the general mix of things. But all are not the same."

"My judgment is: for some your fame is given but for only fifteen minutes. You there on the end, hour's shall be more enduring but none for more than a generation."

"Fame for fames sake shall not endure forever, especially when it is case that most in a generation will be gone and forgotten.

Beyond this I grant to you entertainers nothing."

A gasp flew up from the group who had sought something more eternal.

But, Eterna would not relent saying, "Let's move on, the line is long."

On the right flank were the evil doers, those whose leader frankly stated:

"We all recognized early on that we would never be remembered for any good deeds so we chose instead to seek our infamy in evil deeds. Great villains," he said "have populated history as much as saints and heroes."

"The precedence is set." he said, "What say you Eterna?

Trembling, Eterna rose to her full height, six feet and more, setting aside her Judgment Stick and moved straight toward the Evil Doers, intoning:

"True your fame shall endure, despite my wish to deter it but each of you shall die an early death and horrible to set the contrast for the children. More, I shall this day decree a fiery fate for some of you forthwith."

With that, her Judgment Stick rose transforming itself into a giant Serpent while Eterna gave it voice commands.

"For this one the hottest pyre," and the Serpent's tongue leapted forth and consumed the Hitler one whose agonized cries rang throughout the chamber.

"And you Eterna said, shall be condemned to come back again each year for all Eternity and we shall repeat this scene."

One by one the Evil Ones seeking Immortality took the fire from the Serpents" tongue and Sterna's Judgment Stick, crackled again as it took its place by her side as she sat again, to view other petitioners.

Thrill-Seeking serial killers, bombers and terrorists all met similar fates as the room grew smoky with the smell of sulfur and remorse.

The writer, novelists and poets were next. Some certain their judgment would not repeat that they had just seen, and they would get a single tap for "Yes" from Sterna's Judgment stick.

First the novelists, their book jackets and reviews in hand, and one by one stated "I want my work to be read in a hundred years and my fame to rise way above my grave. We want to be known as artists, as betterers of humanity. Let us Eterna" they said" "plead our case."

Eterna grasped the Judgment Stick and and nodded silently as one of these stepped forth with script in hand.

"True some of you have bent the arc and made this earth a better place with the written word, brought to the fore injustices, championed freedoms made clear the virtues of love, kindness, God, and spirituality. None can gainsay these deeds and I tap you thus."

With one gigantic tap some of the writers expressed great relief and thanked Eterna for her graciousness.

But the remaining ones looked up asking their fate.

Eterna turned and spoke: "Some of you are in between and while having done no great good have also done no great harm either. To you I grant one tap as well. These celebrated and joined the first group in leaving the room.

A remaining set of the writer's group, seemed to shrink under Sterna's gaze and shrank even more as she began to speak.

She said "You remaining ones have no such positive virtues. Your writings reek of hate and purvey smut to the young and old alike. You, I find, undeserving. a double tap, and moreover, you'll join the evil group for the

---

same regimen to repeat and appear here once a year. But mercy here beckons and I spare you this time the flames. This will convene in your case next time.

Eterna sat her throne once more and looked around. "We will pause today and all will return tomorrow. We then examine more of you writers in detail."

Title: Cold-Stroke Realities

Am I to fill this page with truth or fantasy
seized of the writer's dilemma which is
whether to indulge the need for entertainment
or present the unvarnished truth to audiences
which themselves contain both enthusiasts.

The novel, the poem, the blog
blurs these lines
and create thereby
mimicries of reality
in which author and reader
painfully subsist--co-conspirators
who don the mutual cloak
which says truth matters not sometimes
in the interest of creativity,
blurring more the line between
the two; or the reverse; imagination is smothered in the crib
in the service of some bleak notion of what's real;

out of this then is seductive, pseudo- realities
which author and reader mutually inhabit,

preferring sometimes this to Cold Stroke Reality.

What then the price we pay
for human kind's obsessive
need for stories' divertments
whose campfire origins
have given us not only hearth
and entertainment itself, but
civilization too.
Stories most often precede reality as a dream.

What then to sacrifice
if we cruel-stroke and strike away
one or the other;

---

will it be imagination's need for divertments and future visions
or Cold-Stroke Reality?
Each day, each stroke of the author's pen
yields the answer and reveals
each author's sense of responsibility, vision
or joy;

or is it that we must stroke Reality first before we can dream
because if we build too many imaginary castles, we'll be tempted
to pack up and live within them;

and risk that one day we may find
we cannot find our way back or desire to.

And what good would that be; because in the end this tack becomes
castles in the air which can be shattered by sure coming ,hulking Reality
and we'll find ourselves strung out on first one,
and then the other-and worse, we conceive that one is the enemy of the
other.

Neither sings alone.
Bedrock in all this is when we prefer the fantasy version of our own self
and delusion sets in.

Bedrock is when the fantasy of those we love replaces the real, flawed
people there or the reverse-or worse reject flesh and blood, in favor of the
dream.

Bedrock is when we cannot conceive any difference between the two.

This is no small thing, this.

What then is the true nature of this; mixed reality-or is it mixed fantasy?
I sit now with my frozen reality pen, awaiting inspiration.

Title: Katie

She is the Chalk Outline at the Murder Scene,
the shadow which precedes you and me.

She's the sea's retreat before the Tsunami,
the Silence before the Crash,
the Still before Mayhem,
the earthquake weather
before the shaking begins;
the Eye of the Hurricane.

She lives in moments
where Time is Hushed;
at the brink;
the interstices;
the river's rush,

the blue part of the flame;
the Single Hand
holding the Universe back.

And she gets away with it.

She is the one pulling
the curtain
back
at Oz,

she is the one
backing up
the one-way zone,

who seems to live
without money
because people
simply give her what she wants.

She goes to funerals of people
she doesn't know

and cries reading obituaries.

She is the uninvited wedding guest
that no one knows,
goes to hotels, uses the sauna
and the swimming pool
and never registers
or pays;

sits down
on the curb on city streets
to rest her feet;

goes to Poetry meetings
and reads
the Phone Book;
says
"I can be anyone I want to be
and then acts out that part
saying its just as satisfying
to act and dream who you want to be
at least it is the first step"

She walks against the light
if no cars are coming
leaving others at the curb,

talks in restaurants to strangers
asking them what dishes are good
and they'll give her a taste
to see what she'll like.

Laughs out loud
anywhere

Runs up and down stairs;

wears stripped socks
and short black boots

calls her mother
by her first name
always goes home for the holidays,

———

helps her male friends find girl friends
helps her girl friends find true love.

Sits wide legged;
reads novels out loud
on the subway;

asks strangers
to take photographs of her;

loves little children;
men gather round-
she waves
and moves on.

She once held
a Dumped Party
where everyone
got a chance
to tell
their story.

Holds pot lucks
every month
in her apartment building;
watches soap operas;

Got a good education
by attending big lecture
classes without ever registering.

Bought a cheap microphone
pretending to be a journalist
and interviewed the rich and famous
for the contacts.

Started a club for women over sixty
to help them find boyfriends;

She and her best friend read the steamy
parts of novels to each other over the phone;

flirts with ugly boys because they need love too.

Doormen love her, men love her, everyone does.

That's Katie;

Wrong all the time
Right all the time
but it doesn't seem to matter.

Title: Economy and Superficiality

"You don't," she said "understand. I live in a world in which every day I'm reminded is ephemeral, and my looks will not last.

I live in world where a tiny line on my face can change my life indeed determine for me love and how I am regarded, and my own sense of my self.

I live in a world where the inner me I may offer but all that matters among strangers is how I look. I can offer personality as a substitute but that implies contact, but first attraction, as we all know, is how you look walking down the street, your face, your body shape; that is what they see first, that is what they judge you by. Let's face it. This is what is happening at least in the city.

And I can choose to ignore these realities or I can pander to them increasing my own sense of betrayal to my self. I comfort myself and say I can always go back to where they love me, but even that is a me that was the me of my youth; not the me all grown up.

Am I to, therefore, find the love of others only in the me of my youth or shall I take the verdict of the city streets as the real me, or worse shall I look at the older ones who, even to me, look old, out of shape and are for me a source of fear and I make my silent vow, that I shall not allow myself to let my self go like that. I shall take care of myself, eat right, and exercise.

That's what I say to my self. But this is difficult ground but even in my short years I have seen that I can be dropped for a younger model and fickle are the affections of the other when all is based on how you look.

The trap is snapped often and does not relent at the employers table where too, looks matter it seems.

So here I am encased in the real me while outside what shows is a mirror reflecting only others financiers.

He said:
"I have a different burden to bear where all I am is judged on my future prospects and indeed, I too, must have the look, although not as much as you to bare. I too, get dropped, when the girl I'm dating is offered a better future and security. And I, am chained my entire life to a job and career,

sixty hour weeks and a bleak job future. I can offer only unattached romance and can't afford to marry. So some other guy has some nest egg of resources is preferred over me as you resolve that though you love me, a girl has to think of her future."

Heartache for each; a function of economy and superficiality.

Title: Belly Dancing

Updated Chapter Four 11-2-10

Summary: Moving On
Updated: 10/4/10 Meeting Antonio
Updated: 10/25/10. So Close
Updated: Chapter Four 11/2/10 This Is Crazy's Last Chance

At forty, she learned belly dancing because she wanted to get back in touch with her body after two kids. It felt dead to her and she wanted to see if the young girl inside could come alive again. It was, too, that she wanted to see if the belly dance instructors young lover would find her attractive, if her allure, too, could be re-captured, if life could seem like that first date again, if romance could happen after forty.

It was also, exercise, but the kind that she needed since moving her body, was reminicent of the days when she dreamed of being a ballerina. It was a revisiting.

The last of the kids were almost through college and it felt like it was her time. Now she could put down sacrifice, maybe even quit her job and look to recapture some years lost in rowing the boat for everyone else.

And, it had been that way all through the marriage and even through the divorce and now she would look to see what she had missed from her "mom" days. It was a halting beginning, but a beginning.

She made the drive, over fifty miles because she didn't want word to get around, didn't want to run into anyone where there would be polite nods and days later made up stories about what she was doing. She liked not knowing who the people were and they not knowing who she was. She liked not having a dull dry history that everyone she knew shared. She liked the idea of being able to re-invent the her she knew long ago before she was somebody's mom, somebody's husband, somebody's friend who was always there and supportive, the one who could always be relied upon to be dependable, bake the cakes, organize the parties, make sure the kids had what they needed. Who was that anyway.

———

She was sick to death of being reliable. Over time it sucked the life out of you.

And one day her friend described quietly and secretly her "toys" which helped with the lonely nights. It grabbed her and she thought about it never daring to ask, but it did not take much to guess and she would never do that, too shy, but she did think about it, it started her to think about her body and it's needs for the first time in a long time.

Did she have the right to be loved, to be made love to at her age? Should she put these things behind her and get on with being divorced, even if no longer needed by those who had depended upon her for so long.

She cooked for months after the divorce, even though there was no longer anyone to cook for other than herself; she knitted little sweaters for children who were practically grown, all this out of habit, and yes needed because these things made her feel connected. And doesn't every one need to feel connected, needed, loved?

Those needs don't go away just because the kids go away and there is a divorce.

Yes she would take belly dancing lessons. That now made sense. The pregnancy didn't matter.

Oct 4, 2010
The drive that first week to Hearldsburg was relaxing, the autumn leaves swirled roadside and she felt she was leaving, getting away, not only from the house, (she had taken to spending too much time alone in that house) but, instead, she felt she was leaving behind an old life, getting on with it, and moving, even, toward being a new person. No, maybe an older new person, her young girl might yet have a chance yet to dance, recapture a little of the excitement she once knew.

Or maybe she was just an middle-aged woman driving along making up a fantasy life that was never to be.
She thought about her high school boyfriends, besides John, whom she married (it was expected) Roger and James. Roger was divorced and living about a hundred miles away and James was married, but as everyone knew, not necessarily happily.

Her mind wandered to the belly-dance instructors lover, she was sure they were lovers. He was from Argentina, and my god she thought to her self, he looked like he was from Argentina.

She caught a glimpse of him when she came to Hearldsburg to sign up for the class. She had walked toward him in the corridor. (the class was in a school) and he watched her approach down that long corridor, leaning against the student lockers, never looking away, watching her every approaching step, dark eyes fixed upon her like dark moonbeams. It was like she was back in school the way he looked at her, every fiber in her body started to quiver, a feeling she used to have back then when the boys looked at you, naked looks, not-looking away looks. She did attract some attention then.

And now he was doing it. She was feeling it, the same old feeling as she drew closer to him and the classroom where the belly-dancing class sign-ups were proceeding. No one, no one but just the two of them in that corridor. Nervously, she glanced at her watch. She was early, she was always early. That was her.

She slowed as she approached him and he fixed her with his eyes, those unrelenting eyes, and she could not, did not look away as she normally would. His eyes would not allow that. The closer she came to him the slower she walked. Time seemed to slow down.

She caught herself not breathing and finally took a gulp of air, more like a gasp because as she came closer and closer she became devastated by how handsome he was. "My, my" she thought "now that is a man."

Maybe that moment was the moment. Maybe that moment was the moment of no return. Maybe at that first shock she was gone. Gone over. No turning back.

Chapter Three

The voice was quietly booming, polite, soft, sensual and it bore into her.

"Hello." He said

That was all but it was enough. She had heard that a woman knows if she is interested in a man in the first fifteen seconds. She didn't need that long. Her body knew in the corridor and her mind only confirmed what her body had already knew and responded to.

She had to move past him to get to the door of the classroom but he didn't more very much. He just slightly adjusted position; slightly such that she had to come very close to him to get by, very close. She hesitated and thought to her self "Am I crazy?"

She liked being that close to him. She could smell him. He had a smell. It was like a manly kind of odor mixed with a very light cologne and he was tall with massive shoulders. She attempted to glide by, pretending to peer into the class room but her hesitating brought her squarely beside him, inches away. She feigned preoccupation with seeing into the class room. In reality she wanted to stay near, explore, maybe even relish being close to him.

After all it was innocent. She was not actually flirting. He was flirting with her but she was not flirting with him. At least she didn't appear to be flirting with him.

But then he touched her arm. He touched her arm. It startled her.
e touched her arm guiding her as he opened the door for her.

"Here you go he said, in an accent which reverberated in the corridor like thick molasses pouring on toast. Everything seemed to slow down while it made it's way down the corridor. She fell in love with the voice.

And, she could feel her nipples tighten.

Chapter Four

She moved past him, hoping to conceal from him that she was trembling, her hand extended toward the door know which was there. He had opened the door for her and in doing so shrouded her with his sheer size, his manly, yes manly, trite but true; his presence was so strong. She felt little a little girl, no swept up, or about be swept up by the energy which seem to swirl out from him and engulf her.

Can this happen she thought feverishly. Can a person's mere physical presence overwhelm a person, overwhelm a person's senses? It could. It did.

She didn't dare look up. To look up would be to risk being taken up, physically engulfed, swept away, reveal his impact on her. To look up would be to never be able to go back to who she was or had been. She didn't look up. She didn't want to be taken away. She wanted that to be her choice. But maybe that was illusion. Maybe she had already been taken away and was refusing to look up, look into his eyes and see the truth of it.

But there was something more. It was not just that that she was trembling, disoriented and astounded. It was too, there was something else. He wanted her. Just that simple. He projected, silly sounding, he projected a hunger, which reached out and pounded into her chest and wrapped itself around her heart, caressed her breasts, made her tingle down there.

That need was powerful. Powerful because she liked it, was mesmerized by it. Who doesn't what to be needed, needed that way? Who can resist?

She couldn't. All this is an instant. Yet he made no advance. All he was doing was opening a door for a lady. Was all this in her mind, she was thinking but the thought shattered.

In the open door his full frame standing sideways faced her frontally as she turned sideways to go inside the room. She faced him and she he and the sliding by so close in the tipple-the-nipple space made a jumble of her mind.

She was losing it. This was crazy, but it was also, probably, Crazy's Last Chance.

Title: Quasi

Behind his back they called him "Quasi" marking the common belief
that he never gave fully of himself or anything to anyone; never understood
or felt he needed to understand anything or anyone because there was the
expectation that all this would come to him--both people and things; and he
was correct , they did.

The withholding, the silences, the numbing lack of words from him made
people uncomfortable so they talked to fill in the spaces where he was
supposed to speak but he didn't and they did ,and assumed he was not
only listening but was smarter than he actually was.

He had the gift of not trying.

Girls and women loved him because he never came on to them. He would
sit at the diner table and listen and listen. Many came into the diner when
they saw him and sat down with him special and just started to talk. He
never turned them away and he would make eye contact with them and
they looked back directly in his eyes, feeling comfortable in doing so.

No one thought he would ever marry and he didn't. But every woman in
town liked talking to him. He never had a girl-friend but many offered.

He would go fishing with those who asked him and they reported he could
make the fish jump up on the shore and hop into the fishing pail.

But one day that all changed. She came to town. A librarian from St. Louis
who took Mrs. Limet"s job because she was retiring and went to California
to live with her son.

There was a going away party and a welcoming party for the two of them
and Quasi came and parked his huge frame against the wall, staring ahead
as people took turns spending time with him. It was like he had a receiving
line where people stood beside him and talked to him and then another
one, each having a turn.

The men weren't jealous and didn't seem to mind because Quasi never
said much just stood there and gave out that small smile of his and nodded
in all the right places.

Well the new Librarian, Amy, stood back for a while and finally came over after a time and right there in front of everyone she stood behind one lady and gestured to Quasi to head for the door. To everyone's astonishment he stood up a little taller and nodded and started to make his way to the door, leaving behind the receiving line merging with Miss Amy at the door frame and both went out into the night.

Astonishment would not be the word for the reaction of those in the room. Had these two even met and yet she crooked her finger and Quasi walked right out with her like they were old time friends and buddies.

Mary Riley peeked out the side window and made reports: "They are just sitting out by the Gazebo talking. Talking is all they is doing. Strange, so strange" she said. "just sitting there." People took turns verifying the scene for themselves and having a look out of the window on their own.

The next day the whole thing was the talk of the town. Who was she to Quasi? What was he doing? Did they know one another?

Neither was talking.

Title: After All

He Said:

She was not the prettiest one, but, she had the aspect
of really loving me--no, not love, that is an overstatement--reality is more
complicated.

Rather, she saw me as someone she could not have hoped for
and that made her happy, which I think she morphed over into
into some kind of love, no, maybe she developed that into a sense
of devotion to me, under grid with a layer of gratitude mixed in.

I always sensed she couldn't believe her luck. And, that created a sense
of vulnerability in her and I noticed this and it made me like her even more.
That vulnerability even though I could not, and did not, see its origins
nonetheless, made me want to protect her and I felt that, in me, it could
easily grow into love. But, she saw it slightly differently because part of her
always felt that luck might change, that I might find someone else. Luck is,
after all, not the best of bases for a long-term relationship. That is why, I
suspect, she added to this circumstance that additional factor of devotion;
because luck does not require reward but devotion does, in her thinking.

She Said:

"He doesn't really understand me and I can see him looking at me
wondering what I really feel and why; but he seems content to consider
those answers a mystery and to content himself with appreciating whatever
that mysterious something was; he liked how it presented especially when I
presented to him my vulnerable self and proved to him that I was devoted
to him and needed him,. He needed to feel that I was sure."

So she gave that to him as her understanding of what she needed to do to
make the relationship stable and for it to grow. She gave him what he
responded to and seemed to need.

Simple.

And for a time that seemed to work just fine.

But it changed. No, rather she changed. After some time she began to feel
new pulls in new directions and a new self was getting born out of her

---

346

experiences and that while he loved her old self, she sensed he was not and did not like the new feelings and thoughts surging through her. Besides it was boring doing and being the same old person all the time. Why shouldn't she take belly-dancing lessons?

She found her self getting more insecure as these thoughts grew, the more she allowed herself to think about new ways of being and doing life, the more insecure she became.

But she couldn't show him all this. She wasn't sure of how he would react. No she was sure of how he would react. It was that she was not sure of how she would react to how he would react.

See. Its complicated.

Her real underneath fear was that the whole circumstance was beginning feel like an emotional trap and that had a component of ingratitude to it because she had devoted herself to him but, also, a fear of that because, after all, it was luck that he had chosen her in the first place. He could have had a lot of other girls. But by luck and some mysterious reasoning, he chose her. So why wasn't she content with that?

He Said:

He could see her, in his mind holding his hand, but her mind was on other things. Rote answers and silent nods made him feel she was drifting away in odd moments and even during those intimate ones. And that rode up in his throat and he thought she was losing her sense of how lucky she really was.

But that thought made him feel bad because he could see how hard she worked at things, how devoted she was to everything, him included. She was trying, really trying.

But underneath he could see despite all that trying it wasn't really working for her anymore, it was getting to be more and more work for her to be the cheery one, to anticipate his needs and moods.

That was the scary part. It didn't matter that it didn't work for him, after all, he had not asked for her devotion. That was what she had chosen to give. No, the scary part was that aspect, he could see, was no longer working for her.

The more he saw it was not working for her the more resentful he felt himself becoming because of that. It felt like she was foisting upon him

———

some emotional lie, one she no longer herself believed in, and one he had never even asked for. But, for it to go away, nonetheless, felt like a loss.

After all, if she was no longer interested in what she had to give, and what he had not asked for but had gotten used to getting--what now was he to do?

She Said:

It was devastating for her to realize that he was drifting away, no longer interested in her needing him, wanting to be close to him, in her doing little things for him. This was beginning to feel like despair. No, despair mixed with betrayal. She had worked so hard in the relationship. Why would he now reject what she had to give. It made no sense.

Unless there was another woman.

He:

He was sure of it. She was changing and he had no clue, no clue about how to go about getting back that which he had never asked for in the first place, and now, it was becoming clear, something she was less and less interested in giving.

She:

After all, she was thinking, maybe her luck was running out and some other woman now had the luck.

He:

Maybe he could get back to what he wanted, whatever that used to be. But he couldn't remember what that was. He was now all focused on what she was no longer offering.

After all what man would not want a woman who seemed very willing to be devoted to him?

What is our story here?" he thought to himself.

She:

"What is going on here?" she thought to herself.

Title: Death Bed Revealing

She was at her mother's bedside in the hospital looking at eyes which blinked incomprehensively at one moment and then recognition flickered and she said, "Hi, dear, when did you come in?"

It was that way what with the drugs and the cancer. Mary had gotten used to it and she played along with her mother's renderings of reality-Mary had been there all day.

But she did have her questions to ask especially now when she sensed things were at an end; mother would die, there was little hope and even now she slipped in and out of consciousness. But when awake and talking, Mary noticed that mother was more honest and open than she had ever been. Maybe the drugs made her so. Maybe it was mother's way of making amends, a hospital confession.

But, Mary knew that her own life and her understanding of her own life would not be complete unless she had a better understanding of her mother's life; and that would only come from asking her questions while she was lucid or between her drug treatments.

"Ma," she began, "how did you and dad meet, really?" she said. She had heard the story before, but in the last few weeks her mother had made allusions to how they met which made Mary wonder what the real story was. And now was her opportunity.

"Ma, she repeated, how did you and Dad meet?"

"Oh, that", her mother, Lavinia, slowly opened her eyes staring straight ahead, not looking at her, stirred.

"Oh he was so handsome. There was that spark from the very first, the very first time we laid eyes on one another. He was so handsome, like to take my breath away. I swooned like the young girl I was. And he liked me too, I could tell. He was married, of course, at the time, and I was engaged to someone else. But that was no mind, we knew that we were going to be together no matter what."

Mary was shocked. This was completely different version of the story her mother had told over the years about how they met. She wanted to hear more.

"So, Ma, you and Dad were with someone else when you met?"

Her mother smiled, saying "Yep, that was the way it was."

She said it as though she was repeating some familiar story often told, not realizing it was completely new to Mary.

"So, did the two of you run away together? Did Dad divorce his wife and you broke off your engagement. Is that the way it happened?" Mary said urgently.

"Oh, sorta," Livinia said, "I broke off my engagement. But your father was triffling and never bothered with no divorce. We just set up housekeeping and you were born, a few months later."

Mary's shock deepened. She caught herself saying to herself, "Don't jump to conclusions here, Lavinia was taking an awful lot of drugs."

"We made you together, our little angel. Didn't take no preacher and paper work when two people love one another."

For the first time Lavinia looked at her daughter, sighed and said

"I thought you should know these things now that I will be gone. I be with your Dad soon."

She looked at Mary's face and gave her a sad smile.

"I know these things can be shocking, a little to you. But now you know, and I will tell you anything you want to know."

Mary sat back in her chair realizing she did not know who she was, did not know herself because so much of who she really was lay on that bed.

She determined she would find out as much as her mother was willing to tell.

To be continued.

Title: A Box of Hearts

You have my heart in a silver box

wrapped in a sly smile

and you creep in my corner eye

stealthily.

You make no effort to acknowledge this

or even to open it

to take a peek

at what was given you long ago

by mistake.

The key is hidden in some secret place

and I search for it

even while unsure if my goal is to soothe

or retrieve;

yet I cannot be content; keyless.

I approach you at times

search your eyes

silently asking

where is my

missing soul?

You smile

that beautiful smile

flip your hair the way you do

engorged as you are with

numerous hearts in that silver box.

In the bad time nights

I wonder if you'd be soulless

without that silver box

like a collector with no quivering specimens.

I think probably;

and that helps me sleep

vowing relentlessly to seek

that hidden key

you have nonchantly

swallowed

preventing me

from moving on

or to stay and get what I need.

Title: A Flask of Time

There is a single leaf flying

in this my autumn gloaming,

a leaf fluttering light

as if being orchestrated

by your words in flight

rushing to my inner ear;

"I have fallen in love

with another" you said.

My leaf stammered,

swaying in its downward flight

unable to remount the tree,

terrified to crash the ground

suspended forever there

as was also true of your words;

better to not reach my inner ear

better to not have my leaf touch down dead.

Between us all these years

neither war, nor peace;

we existed in the troubled middle ground

purgatoried, unsensed, fluttering, leaf bound

frozen between tree and ground.

Now you have burned our tree down-

lit the leaf and made it flame-

and pulled from under us the very ground.

No matter the dead leaves, the burning tree

no matter the absent ground

these things will

in turn return

for the seasons never-end.

Therefore, I shall take my sip of sorrow

sipped slowly from my Flask of Time

and await

the Spring's return.

Title: A Gingham Dress-Beth's Memories

He told me that
he had seen me
on the cover of a dime store novel;
and that I looked a lot prettier in person.

On our first date
he brought my mother
a box of cigars
and my father
a dozen used golf balls.

The trunk of his car had no lid
and you could see the road
on the passenger side beneath your feet.

He had charm.

He stood under my bedroom window
and tied a note to a brick;
it broke the window
set off burglar alarms;
the police came
and he apologized.

We went to dinner and he smelled like chicken poop
from putting barb wire around the chicken coop.

I told him pigs would fly before I married him
and he showed up the next day
at the hardware store
where I worked
with a pig in the flatbed of a pick-up truck.

He called me out
strapping wings on the pig
yelling:
"Pig to fly on runway nine
Pig to fly on runway niner."

———

He had charm.

Showed up one Saturday
wearing a gingham dress
over his jeans
saving he was saving up
to buy it for me.
"How does it look? "
he said, "wanted to be sure."

I was sure.

Married him.

Oh, he still has charm;
lots of it still rubs off on me.

Title: A Grandma's Treasure Box

Each of us
when we reached 14
would make the Visit to

Grandmothers house
to see what was inside
her Treasure Box;

the Family Treasure Box
where each year
one of us
got to see
what she had
hidden there...

My Dad had been;
my older brother
had been
and now it was my turn
to see that part of
Family History.

No one who'd seen
could talk of it.

No one could reveal to anyone
what was in Grandma's secret box.

No one did.
No one would risk
Grandmother's upset.

She lived beneath
the "L" in Chicago
refusing to move
and they built

the tracks
right over her house;
each time one passed
it rocked her house
like rolling thunder;
Varoom, clacky clack
another one
going by.

Stubborn was not the word
for Grandmother.

She still wrote letters
30 years later
to every Mayor
complaining about the
tracks and the trains
saying she wanted them torn down.

Every month a letter.

Grandmother never
gave up;
never forgot;
fierce in her loves
fierce about her neighborhood
fierce about things which displeasured her
fierce about family
fierce about everything.

I sat with her,
apron on:
she served me pie.
"Sonny" she said
now you at the age
where you need to
learn grown-up things.

Like your Dad and brother
your turn now come
to see what drives
this family;
our family heirloom so to speak.

You'll see now.

As you grow up
you hear people talking about it
but we are the only family that
has it in our treasure box.
Lot's want it
but we the only one's
that has it.

She walked me up her tiny
narrow stair case to the attic
my head spinning,
wondering what it could be.

What did we have in our family
that the whole world wanted?

The treasure box was small;
a faded gold color
with a hand-carved lid
covered by Grandma's
liver-spotted hand
which shook in the dim
light.

She shifted the box,
opening it with a tiny key
smiling faintly
her eyes moistening
as a sliver of sunlight
reflected into the opening box
and I could just begin to
see what was inside.
"There it is"
she said
"What is it? " I said,
staring at a piece of cloth;
satin sheen
with a lace border.

"Every since your great
grandmother got

it has been the luck of this family
and so people's all over the
world hear about but
we the only one's who got it.
"What is it?
Your great great grandmother's;
cut from her mother's wedding dress
and from that day
this families" luck changed.

I looked at her eyes
looking for an answer there.
"Grandma what is it?
You heard of the Silver Lining"
Yes, I said.
Well this family has the only one.
It is the Silver Lining from your great, great,
grandmothers wedding dress.
Grandma had it
and she believed it had saved our family
all these years.
"I took it out when
your mother had her cancer
and she got better
and it took away her pain.

I took it out when your younger brother
had his accident, and he lived.

I took it out when your grandfather went to war
and he came home safe.

I take it out when ever this family needs things.
It is our Silver Lining.

Now you must never speak
or tell what is in the treasure box
or it will break the spell.

I never did to this day.

Today I have the Treasure Box
waiting for my child

to have a chance to see.

Grandma's gone
leaving behind her Silver Lining
for the rest of us.
And on some days
I do take it out
when things look
like they might go bad.
Just for luck.

Everyone
is always
looking for a Silver Lining
and some luck.

All the Grandmothers
gave us ours.

Title: A Grandmother

For her heart was pounding such

I thought it would leap from her chest

and fall flat onto the cold floor

to slide there to quivering extinction.

Her soul was shriveling such

that it twined and twisted upon a single thread-

its catchment snapping for the plunge into the river Styx.

 She lay down in her cool night,

misted with early dew in her eyes

she grieved cold, cold upon cold;

her body shivering.

Vulture claws and talons reached

her Spiritual Keep

and sank their meanness deep

wounding the marrow

of where she lived-

all her treasures now exposed

and her Will raw-tested near impoverishment.

Grandmother cried.

Yet I saw her over time repose

and recompose and thrust away

these encumberments;

the dreadful sight of a dead child-our mother,

birthed, she said from 72 hours labor-

and followed thereafter in days a husband dead

in cancer's clutch-

she sat alone, comfortless

as we children drew near in our bewilderment-

this sense of total demolishment shrouding all.

Our eyes drew near; we could see

she had began to shunt aside fear

transforming herself

from the Pity-Pyre to new resolve to live again

for the sake and betterment of us-the children.

Clear as the book and the page we read

Grandmother began repairing heart and sinew,

face and spirit and like the phoenix bird

rose before us-new mission ensconced upon her clear.

Steel Purpose all in her she said:

"I shall be here children, no need to be afraid."

This is what Grandmothers are for."

Title: A Pirate Hooked

My cravings land like a pirate horde
grappling to my fleeing ship
swinging on ropes
till they board
in critical numbers
large enough
to overwhelm
my resistance.

They all have the same face
and while my sword is sharp and swift
I'm soon overcome by desires mixed
as pirate laughter rings
throughout my ship
reminding me of what
I like about pirates
and their lust.

For pirates
live on the edge,
laugh low in the guttural throat
shivering my timbers;
making my attractions burst.

They make me love the pirate life;
unsafe
and a little rough;
but trading off there
smothering boredom
and life freed from correct complacencies.

Humm.Who has not inside
a secret pirate heart?
Who would not like to swoop down
and grapple life from stilled ships
drifting hulks, and frozen faces?

Who would not choose
life over death?
My Hearty?

Title: A Spring Bud

She was without her Spring
seemingly born from childhood to only Winter Cold
and I was drawn to her for that reason, it seemed.

I'd hoped for a manufactured Autumn in her
from my own intense desire of it and that
could, by mere exposure, melt her glacial-ness
and she would then be unable to resist
the Fire I had in-born for her;
that mere proximity would set her breasts afire
glaze her glassy eyes, make her breath in-drawn
by-passing her stony regard
over-coming the challenge she took for anyone to reach
her inside ice-berg which floated on what must
have been the Arctic Seas her Soul sailed.

I drew near, more confused as to my being
prey or preyed and she watched me in her mind's eye
advance my hand slightly to feign to touch heir's by mistake,
ready to embrace or retreat and pretend it was all accident-
yet hoping, even if there was retreat, that a spark would ignite and breach
the contour between the hand offered and the frozen finger-tip, if only in
repose.

These moments, I think-- a hand's touch, given or received
rejected or accepted-- can reel the curtain back on a promise
of more or reveal the door to slam and nothing gained.

I moved my finger close, not ready yet to risk the touch
looking for a sign to see if Affection's Beast would purr or pounce;
but it did neither and from my sense of her, she too had that
nervousness first encounter's make, entreaties in the yawl between
offered or given, smile or scowl, push away or grateful reach,
or better reciprocity.
We both were extended at the finger-tip; I then began to sense her cold
ship

———

had a willingness to sail to warmer climes; softly bold, I lay my hand
atop hers
measuring pitchful signs of a ship; softly anchoring or a ship ready to cast
moorings
for the comfort of the open Arctic sea again?

But overlapping warmth, mine to heir's, she allowed-not withdrawing
and I took this from her, her first Spring bud; all this blooming from a
finger's touch.

Title: A Tale of Two Breasts-Anna's Story

Whatever you call them

breasts or twins

they precede us

and divert looks

or maybe attract none.

All life suckles there

heads lay there

babies drink.

I remember at 13,

their nurturance

and that single wish

they'd grow.

Push-ups I admit,

I tried to hurry along the process,

but such mixed feelings there.

Mine grew

My sisters didn't.

They got the attention

I didn't;

my sister got interest

in her

and not them.

They hang

a little more now

than I like;

sister and I

hug

and they

bow-

between us.

she has one less

cancer-stricken;

and I have the love

she needs;

sister bonds;

us;

one is not missed.

Title: A Treasure Box

So soon this time
melts away
like you;

my common sense
sometimes
leaves me too
like you.

Often I am blind
and cannot see
the You before me;

many times I need
help to see
desperately
from you.

I lay down with you
to make peace
but cannot speak
the words;

I want to say I love you
but can only buy a present
which only signals how I feel
but is not what I feel.

Chocolates are not
a human heart.

Many times I want to reach
out you
but feel I cannot spare the hug

you need.

I'm always on the edge of hesitancy
feeling I cannot spare the Me
locked away in my small
meager
treasure box.

Nary a coin there
I feel
can leave,

and I guard even small
leavings
jealously.

The wonder is
I think,
such meager treasure box pickings
I have,
I think
I have to protect;

because it is always closed
it does not easily release
scarce
feeling coin;
or experience

new feeling coin bequeathed.

A treasure box I am with

no treasure within

and locked to new

treasure from without.

Title: A Tub of Potatoes

My grandmother used to say
don't marry for money
but stay open-minded.

She could squeeze a nickel
and make the buffalo feel light-headed;
she could make a dollar out of 15 cent.

Now she was a big woman;
ruled the family roost
with a simple look
and an iron skillet.

Many times I heard that skillet
go thunk!
Another suitor educated.
Another boyfriend righted.

She always took us kids aside
and whispered things like
"now see that"
I don't want you kids to grow up
and do things like that."

There was the woman or man who did not
take care of the family;
the Boyfriend Rogue;
or the Gallivant,
who tipped behind his ladies back;
the dandy who dressed so well
but did not have two dimes to rub together
and slept in the park in a tent.

These were depression days
when traveling men
rode the rails
not sure of where they came from
not sure of where they went
and the women who

longed for them;
who waited
for them
listening
for train whistles
and stock yard
freights
hauling
into Chicago
from the mid-west.

Grandmother
would sit
above a tub of water
peeling potatoes
like the layers of her life
each skin
would fall into the tub
of water
and go plop;
another chapter in Grandmother's life
told to us kids
sitting
wide-eyed.
"Time was" she would say
that this was a woman and man's country
now everything gone to hell."
They danced in the gin joints
till then the money ran out
and the party was over
and the big depression gave them all
a big headache.
Party she said but dig down deep because
there will be a piper to pay.
Plop. Plop
Time was.

Title: Autumn's Surcease

I gave you hurtings so that you might feel Winter in your Soul.

I sometimes placed upon my heart virgin olive oil to heal the scars you've caused.

I piled high in your eyes Love and its Laments as your cool wind blew down even the summer Solstice.

I carried your leaden comments to the cemetery where I buried them with the other
dead things and I blew you my last Summer Kiss for the luck I knew you'd need.

Your last leaf fell from your waterless tree revealing that Summer Kisses have no truck
or need for rusty dead leaves carpeting a Winter Soul; twice dead now skipping even
Autumn's surcease before your Winter blows.

Title: Bar Fly Queen

I've polished up my hard heart and now it gleams, diamond-studded seating itself

in its setting

at the bar

where all the cowboys

come

and chip away

at its facets-

word chisels flash-

crack on its face

and fade away

with yet another on the way

none making a scratch

because this heart was forged

in the whirlwind,

in the maw of a volcano

heat-sealed,

and it was spewed out from a thousand

white hot lava-cuts and mishandlings,

misunderstandings and purloined shiny babbles

which went dark like concert sing-a-long wands in two minutes from come-ons pronounced at five minutes before

the closing bell,

five minutes before last call,

and desperate Hope-Not-Coming

kidnapped love

lies in chains

at the bottom of those meaningless words

"what's your name, honey?"

But I am the bar-fly in the ointment;

Lady Chatterley who never rode nude

the cowgirl who'd kiss her horse

before she'd kiss you,

who sits impassively

draining admiration and false flatteries

from rodeo men

fresh from the last town

looking for circuit queens

and good night kisses and hugs

and bed room squeaks

from the not-really a honey-moon bed.

I am the bar-fly in the ointment

queen of my own bar-stool realm

all glittery made up

with a seven year old at home;

who's dug deep into my hope chest

took my place here

with lip-stick lips

knowing most nights

I don't pay for drinks

and wring from my smoky-room subjects

their last false compliments

their last strivings for youth

like me;

most times just like me

going through the motions

of a ghostly recapturing

of what might have been

or maybe even used to be

if only

someone or something

hadn't took my real heart

and replaced it with

a rock-hard diamond

which gleams

but is immovable

yet irresistible.

Title: Breaking Dawn

In the hush I hear you;
faint footsteps downstairs:

refrigerator opening
in the dead of night.

In the hush
I hear milk pour
and I wait;
my face to the wall;
my mind there too.

Double Doubts
and Triple Hurts
align the staircase
and I hear them
treading up.

Where were you?

I feign sleep
to the running water
and the sound of clothes rustling
in the quiet dark.

I am still;
the stillness
of time frozen.

Your weight hits the bed
and sinks.

"I got the job, worked tonight.
Sorry didn't call.
It's not much
but it's better than no job at all."

Outside dawn was breaking.

Title: Carried Water

I have carried water in buckets for many,

a bucket that leaked.

I have caught tears

before they fell to dead ground.

I've held hands,

cut my own hand reaching out;

felled those who would harm

and saved many who knew nothing of me;

helped the foolish,

shielded the innocents

and never gave on that it was me,

or even that I cared.

There are, too,

a few I have buried

in the dark ground

turned away and carried on--

because of the needs of the living--

who all looked at me--

soon as the first dirt fell

on the casket lid.

I may never die,

that would be letting too many others down;

and I couldn't do that.

My silent face

does not reveal all this

and this is as it should be

I can't step up to demand credit.

That is not like me.

And now I stand at store counters

count my change and my memories

knowing full well that while some know

most don't and never will

nor could they

understand the silent gnawing sacrifice

that much of life

is for many of us:

wives, husbands, grandfathers and grand mothers

yellow photos on the fireplace mantel

yester years" phantoms

who built the very ground the young ones walk on

and yet they don't know.

And I am not the one to tell

because all my audiences,

the ones who might appreciate,

have all gone.

So lonely is the peaceful silence I allow my self

knowing that gratitude in the later years

means you had to have been there

and most now were not there

so it is unreasonable to expect they'd understand

those long agos

when I was young

and, of course, knew everything.

To them I sit in the rocking chair

a fixture on the porch

symbol of a long ago

still here

but soon to be gone.

But no, that is not the way it really is.

I am their own yesterday

which I spent

making sure

they would have a tomorrow

and a silent witness to their Now

which even if unacknowledged

makes me proud.

Title: Cheating Her Story

He had strong arms
and I felt them
wrapping around my soul;
and his voice
soft
beautiful
penetrating me.

He listened to me
he talked to me
and the sex
was
really my thank you
to him for
caring about my being lonely.

At least this was
the reason for the sex
the first time
But the shock of it
was it felt different
creating
a dilemma.

I was looking for
a cure for lonely
and he
introduced me
me to sexual need.
That was not
supposed to be
in the equation.

Cheating for me
had been propelled
by a lacking
in my current relationship
and stumbling forward

I realized lonely
has more dimensions
than I counted on

To continue
now is to rent my soul
between my needs
and the marriage I've built
and the children
who are my everything.

So my soul
sits the fence
torn between
eternity,
heaven,
love,
marriage,
sex
need
and shattering
consequences.

Title: Cheating His Story

I know you are lonely,

I see you twisting slowly

in that ill wind

unable really to resist

his soft words.

I see how you look at him

the times you've disappeared,

your time unaccounted for.

I see it in your

new makeup

and dress

in the extra care

you take in the mirror.

I see changes in you

and know they

do not come from me.

I see her

because she is convenient

and asks little or nothing from me.

The sex is rough,

wild at times

more about release

than tenderness.

I know you're cheating

and worse

know

I can't soften now;

the anger blocks

the things you need.

So I perch here

on this abyss

going

no where

compass-less

Title: Come the Dark

Come the Dark again
I will be steel this time,
my Heart
Ready-Strength,
and toned.

Come the Dark
my Hope's Re-enforced
my Faith's Renewed"
and I shall toss aside
Diminishments
and Negativities
and Seething Flutterings.

I will wave
that Wand
which is Hearth and Kin;
tall Stance make
against dark Blandishments,
strike low
Fear-ments,
Afraid-ness,
Rage-ments,
Cynicalness
Devil-ments
and Tricks
which diminish
Human-ness
and the Light.

I will,
as I have
in the past,
do it
Again
and Again

as often as I Need to
and Should.

I will this time flip Fear
and wring from it Hope.
I will taffy stretch Time
to what I need to rehabilitate Negativities.
I will take Rage and make it to lie down with Peace
and make the Harming Ones weep Atonement Tears.
I'll not veer from my path, nor falter
and if need be
you find me on the other side
yet alive
still struggling if need be;
and if there, and there is no need
then my story will have ended well.

Title: Cupid's Arrow

The scab where Cupid's arrow had entered
had barely healed, leaving just a wisp of a scar
evident there; but the inner pain remained.

The sounds of its shaft, its purple burning shaft
still present
to my muffled memory
which flinches from its approaching sound
 its whoosh, its dull thud
piercing a heart valve,
denying blood to my feverished brain
which sounded the alarm that love
seen by many as Cupids blessing
but for me it was an arrow emptying out
my life's blood
outside and down, plunging
drawn by gravity
falling onto the maroon carpeting
invisible almost
while all around me urged that I celebrate
but I knew too
that heart valves burst too in love's first
volley
and that Cupid
is too, a mixed blessing.

But how to remove an embedded shaft
 without causing the wound to shed one's very blood life,
or is it best to leave it in place, count the bliss
and ignore the tremendous event
many saw as unvarnished and good?

Why must Cupid's arrow steal from me my identify
in favor of a new merging one?

Why must Cupid's arrow involve blood?
And who is to explain the scab and pain
the wound brings

---

when love leaves
that hollow,
 now bleeding vacuum,
which grows a scab
sometimes leaves a scar
plastered over with
urgings of "you must move on."

It is not that love is bad. It is not.

It is that it is transforming and the transforming
sometimes leaves me without a me I had known all my life
and the new me is merged with another
if they leave
I wonder what then what will I be left with?

Who has not pondered this?

Life then is the road traveled
strewn with Cupid's discarded arrows
and pained souls marching.

Yet, If i hear yet again

the shaft's approach
 that whooshing sound
that Cupid's arrow makes
I know, I once again
will bare my chest
and take its plunge full on
because that is how Love is Made.

I remind myself of all of this as I prepare for the date.

Title: Hard Scrabble Bubble Gum

Her face was hard and it had marks on it and she was smoking her
cigarette when I walked in to use the John she yelled out at me
"You, going up to the casinos "are ya? "

I said "Yes have to use the john."
"You probably rich, buy me a drink why don't ya? "

I said "sure, when I come back"

I came back to stand up cowboy style along side her at the bar and she
started talking to me like I was her best friend.

"These gents in here don't don't appreciate a lady like your self and they
sure as hell
don't by drinks."
Her voice was hard as below-the-seat bubble-gum with a hard scrabble
tone above a hacking cough.

"I was married once but he couldn't handle the ride; needed me a real man
and he got all upset-started to hit me.

It was plain to see he wasn't right in the head; wanted all the time to be
lovey dovey after. Hell a man I always say have to be 6 feet tall to take a
ride on me.

He wasn't and ran off with the carnivals that come through town.
How about another one?

Will, come on over here the lady is buying drinks."
Willie smiled a single tooth..

 "Thanks" he said.
She kept the conversation going.
"People look at me and they think what happened to her?

———

390

Life is what happened to me. Life is what happened to me.
Made bad decisions never got out of this town stayed too long and now I aim's fit to live
no where else "ceptin" here. A misfit living among all the other misfits around here.

 We all misfittin" together."
"Gotta go" I said.
"One more? "she said.

I drove away thinking how much of life is random luck good and bad choices and circumstance.

Title: Her Laugh

Her laugh
was the smell
of newly washed linens;

fresh cut grass

child smiles

gypsy dances

the green spot when the sun sets over water

how Niagara Falls sounds
when you get close on the bus

crunchy snow

good molasses pouring

a special touch
from one you love

joy ringing in certain church songs

happy eyes from babies,
giggles too,

the sigh, that special sigh
after love-making

an unexpected compliment
that makes you glow

quiet nights

really really good chocolate

music in your bedroom late at night

A look from someone you want that look from.

But most of all
she laughs
like she
likes you
and she does.

Like that.

That is her laugh

Title: Human Beings

Uncle Dan said
"now listen
There's right and there's wrong
and there two kinds of people:

those that can't be trusted to be right
and those that cannot be trusted with being wrong.

Take out the microscope and lets" see
what that person does when they
have you in the wrong.

If they treat you like you aim's" human
anymore
then that is the face of evil.

I worry more about those who
think they'd absolutely right more
than those that knot's they'd wrong.

Find out who is convinced they'd
absolutely right about anything
and run the other way
that is a dangerous woman,
or man.

Now if you find a person who
sees that you is wrong and
don't judge,
that is a human being-.
that includes you judging others
too.
Avoid people trying to prove
they is right
sure sign that they is wrong.
Avoid the person constantly
talking about how they have
been wronged

———

just means they are waiting their
chance to get even on somebody,
anybody,
anybody close will do.

Talk to people who say
I may be right or I may be wrong
but proving right or wrong is not important
only how you treat people and yourself
inside
is important.
Leave the rest.

Title: I Am The Pretty Girl

I am the pretty one,

the one the girls hate

and the boys pant for

and I stand aloof because

there is no room for me to be

who I am.

All I get is people reacting

to how I look

and I see them whisper

"She's so stuck up."

I am not.

I am lonely and superior to them

that make these kinds of comments.

So all day I have to take the stares

and the mini-hatreds

just because I am pretty.

I like being pretty

it comes easy to me;

takes no effort.

My hair is beautiful and I don't have to do anything to it.

My skin is good. Thank God, no zits

My figure is good

but I get the comments when I walk through-

the Neanderthals always make comments-

and I cannot help it if my parents are rich.

So I am trapped behind this wall.

I don't have to study hard to get good grades;

this school is easy.

I don't have to work hard for anything.

Things just come to me.

But it has made a prison for me

and because I don't have to get smart

or work hard-

I can get by on my looks.

My teachers like me-

one too much,

so in the end I am doing what I hate

others do-

seeing me only in terms of how I look

and I realize I am doing the same thing to myself.

I am my looks. I am trapped.

So when boys try to talk to me I clam up

because I think there is only one thing they want.

And most of the time I am right. They do-just want

one thing.

Other's of them just want to say I am their girl friend

even if that is not true just so they can brag to their friends.

Some of them lie and claim they had you, or you

are lesbian just because you don't like them.

I am the pretty girl and most times that is pretty sad.

So I don't talk to anyone except other pretty girls.

They understand. They have the pretty girl thing too.

So we stand around sometimes and think we are superior

but we also think secretly we might be inferior and lonely too

and who is going to feel sorry for the pretty girl? Nobody that's who.

So I dated the football guy who was pretty too. It seemed he would

understand-handsome and pretty, the same thing I thought.

Boy was I wrong. He was his mothers" boy and only liked me

because he thought there was prestige in it. And I did it for

the same reason. We both were boring when alone and tried to look like the super couple when people were around.

I was bored and truth be told I was also boring.

I had nothing to say and all's he wanted to talk about was football and sex.

I told him no.

And then he latched onto my best friend, well I called her my best friend, but

we were not really friends. We just sorta hung out together.

My real best friend was Alma for a while. She was the ugly sidekick

pretty girls seem to attract. All she wanted to do was be with me. She did

everything I asked her to, sometimes without me even asking. I began to think that just maybe being pretty was being superior. People like Alma

made it easy to think that. She seemed to think I was superior.

I used to lie to her about all the boys coming on to me and things they said and she believed those lies. I felt I had to tell the stories because the stories seemed to mean so much to her. Besides telling her the phony stories gave me a fantasy life to make up for my real one.

We were a good pair of friends for a while until Alma told me one day about her love. Her love for me. And I realized she was not talking about friend love.

That's another thing, you get come ons from both genders and some like Alma turn into stalkers. She lied and told her friend that we had been together. A total lie.

That is why high school is prison camp for the pretty girl.

I broke down one day while talking to Geek Billy who came over to my house to fix my computer. He was rad-geek and shorter than me and I never really considered him a real person or anything so I was talking like he was not even there. I was saying why me, why does everyone hate me?

He started yammering that he didn't hate me, and put his arm around me. I looked up and saw that he was not trying to jump my bones, he really was trying to comfort me like he understood and all that. It was laughable you know. I was so above him and everything but he seemed that day like a real person to me for just a tiny minute.

He left and I lay on my bed and wrote into my diary-"Geek boy loves me."

I wrote: "I am the pretty girl no one likes because I am above them."

Title: I Do

He said "I do," but I was not standing beside him;

it was a bottle of liquor he was talking to.

He said I do, to every floozy in the cowboy bar

while I was at home saying "don't."

He needed to learn how to say "I don't."

What do you say to a man who

is polymorphous perverse;

who has a need to share beyond what he needs to

with the lonely and the needy?

And I am the burning moth

which flaps its wings and hovers close

because that is what moths do.

I do;

never minding the heat

or flaming wings;

I guess I don't

and I should.

Title: Individual Thus?

It could be that I am Perfection's Love
and all that you need.

It could be that you will brim with satiation
from all I seem;

I could be in error though,
and therefore cannot be Me
if all of above were true.

But Being Me should not lie down at
Needs Door
and be external to the Me
I was born with
and the Me I am.

So perhaps I should be the Am I already Am
and need not Be for you
the All you need,

understanding however that tack
is mere self-contained self-sufficiency
which in the end is isolating and lonely.

Surely self-containment is not the perfection we all should seek.
It must thus
that the individualistic suppositions we all assume
are clearly not true
because I am not truly the individual Am
and never was and cannot become individual
without the support of the many and their love down the years.

If, therefore, I am indeed a collective Me,
then how can I be the perfect match-
singularly- for thee?

The only way I think this could be
is that I and you
become Singularities and Multiplicities simultaneously.

But is this Schizophrenia
both individually and culturally?
There is that word Individual again.
Yet it seems obvious in the end
we are individual and ,too, partake of multiplicities;
both in the mix.
No wonder we are confused--creatures who crave individualism
yet are totally dependent upon the many.
So who are we?
Down one road is the loneliness of perfection and total self-sufficiency
and down the other is smothering conformity.
And we bounce back and forth in the in-between.

Title: Lumpy Lumps-Mary and John

He presses his hand
on my breast
and increases the pressure
exploring
moving slowing
rotating his finger tips
to that adjacency
where index finger
takes a turn
on my gentle breast rise
and probes
the gentle probe
which mixes
exigency,
and anxiety.

'Do you feel a lump I said'
'No nothing yet' he says.

He strokes with his finger tip
moving across the mounting rise
centering on the nipple tip
pressing down
breast deep
centering with
smooth
rollings
and I say
'Do you feel anything'
'Nothing yet'

He presses both
slowly upward
till
"There" he says "I feels I small bumps.

404

I say "They are glands
not growths."

Every week he feels my breasts
to see if lumpy lumps
have appeared.

We both share
this tense time
mixed
with intimacy.

Title: Me-Me

I am the Me-Me Princess;

surrounded as I am by all of me

I hold fast to the idea

that nothing around me is very interesting, except me.

Absorbed as I am with my own thoughts

I contend that the charm of this self-obsession

is more fascinating

than the mere complacency I see everywhere else.

If I cannot espy my Hero Man

then I will have to suffice with me

and perhaps

marry myself

and spare myself

the agonies of love

and the agonies of childbirth;

perhaps skip it all

and go straight to my imaginary divorce

while congratulating myself

on my sagacity.

———

Did I mention that to me

I am the thing most interesting?

Don't scold me

because you know this might be true;

tell me who or what is more fascinating--

me or you?

I am choosing myself because I am close at hand

and I can be my own best supplicant

who will admire me, love me, and never betray

Me knowingly.

So I cross-leggedly languish,

do my nails

watch my programs

on my quilted throne

in my bedroom realm

watching the screen

filled up with all the other Me-Em's

who are the only one's

who really understand Me

even if they are not real

Me-Em's;

You see I am the only one who is real.

A real Me-Me Princess, that is.

Title: More Me

I am what they call plain pretty, an in-betweener not really pretty not really plain and I attract guys who see me as a compromise from what they really what--the cheer leader blond with the hot bod.

I am the bland personality with pretty eyes a weak chin; cautious with an intense gaze reflecting my need to have more than what I am ever offered by guys who are plain-pretty too or too too nice or have the slow uptake of the often rejected.

My world offers me only the boring. I could do something I suppose but I missed the ring; I was the also ran, the next to the last chosen the bridesmaid; the sidekick; the not-as-pretty friend and what I did was to break free of my old world and soar with plastic surgery.

Last year I took the knife and now I am strangely pretty but I still know who I am inside
and that is disturbing; and more disturbing is that I want to reject the guys seeking pretty
for the times the rejected me as almost pretty and that makes me feel pretty-strange; angry and not lovable; not an airhead now--but the trophy. I thought last night how almost-pretty might have been easier and more me.

The Environment Speaks

Title: I am the Aquifer

I am the Aquifer
in the deep gorge.

I'm rain.

I was water for the many herds
who drank from me.
I'm shelter from the deluge;
treasure house of oxygen
and minerals
which seep
into my rooms
in deep soils replenishing.

I'm life's ecology.
The water source
of all chemistry
and you are my children.

Hear my sad tears.

I taste dirty waterings
and poisonings.

Plentiful I was in the
early years,
under deserts I was salvation for the caravans,
well source for the Egyptians
reservoir for villagers,
beast bird and fowl;
insect and amoebae
all drank from me.
I was the culture source for all life.
My rivers spawned civilization.

Now, I am retreated.
A mixed drink,
consumed
with a steel straw,
nonrenewable;
sipped with too much
over-confidence
and greed.

My table is thin.
My offerings slim.
My purity waned.

I seep below my own level
scattering precious tear-drops
vulcanized to bloody steam
and sometimes I explode
up up
to the blasting cone
and I am deposited amid the ruin,
into the gorge again.

I am slower;
my cycle recedes,
my dry tears howl.

I see Harmony's Crown
crashing down.

I see the End of Plenty
and Horsemen moving
looming, looming, looming;
climate backing up,
bent down eyes,
reeling waterfalls
receding times,
calm resignations,
generations lined up,
against the wall,
whole cities caterwaul,
lakes pirouette,
swirling times sweep up,

all regrets,
all maybes,
all lost,
all gone.

I was the Aquifer
life sustaining;
now, a shadowy voice
dumbfounded
drilled down
in weeping earth.

Title: I Am The Wind

I am the Southern Breeze;
bearer of the Wisteria;

The North Wind
from where the ice blows.

I am the lover's caress
on sandy beach,

The Wind-Mill Corn Grinder
and the Water Wheel;

I am invisible
yet everywhere
I blow all over
this globe.

I've billowed your sails
propelled your ships
carried you
to far lands;
opened to you
new worlds.

True, too,
I have blown your houses down
tornadoed the things you love.

I am too
the wind of Bad Luck
and Ill Fate.

I am the wind in your lungs.

I carry the oxygen you breathe
first life's halting blush
and likely the last to leave
your body's chest.

Now my clear air
is grey

smoky
smoke-stacked
and my once proud
life of this planet
is near extinct.

Sixty miles;
just an hour's drive
of me and my oxygen
are your only shield;
against the void of outer space;
the cosmic rays,
the deadly magnetic fields
meteors and asteroids
all crash down were it
not for me;
the sun's infrared rays
would burn if I did not block.
for you and provide a cloak.

Indeed,
I am the life you breathe
from birth's first
to death's last.

You've felt me
on your face
riding the plains,
while walking the meadows;

remember I am
the Invisible Sea
you sail
and your final
Destiny.
I am the wind;
your oxygen.

Title: Robin Suicide

A robin committed suicide today-
dead against my living room window pane;
flying fast in chilly mid-November;
perhaps heading south.

The sound; wings blurred; a thump!
he went straight to ground.

He should have missed the house,
it's large, the window is below the roof,
he was not flying blind
or forgot to look.

Like a jet with no flaps down,
he hit the window full-throttle;
probably cracked his crown;

I got up, took a look
expecting him to fly or stir
but he didn't move below; lay quiet.

I went down to see.
Robin, older, neck awry
didn't stir, didn't move.
I touched him.

Neck broken.
Instant Death.
Instant Oblivion,

I looked for mourners.
There were none.

This Robin was solo in Death as we all are;
on his own.

It didn't seem fitting
to conduct a garbage-can burial,
I said a few words, cursed,
and decided to bury him in dirt.

414

Picked him up by his tail plumage
took him to the back yard;

dug a shallow grave, mumbled something;
lay him down in there;
patted the top of his dirt pyre-
my good deed done.

A dead robin in my yard,
by my window undone.
But, I was thinking was he really a deliberate suicide?

There were clues.
How can a Robin miss
a big house,
there must be more hints
to this dead Robin mystery.

Perhaps he was an old Robin, diseased,
disoriented by Alzheimer's, or a bird pandemic;

could have been a bird fight
he fled,
The Crows around here are criminals and rough;
the Robin could have been bested in a West Side Story Bird Fight.

I rose to look for myself;
to look for clues to Robins" death,
not content for the time being
to dismiss it lightly
as dumb bird lost.

So... from Robin's height my window pane looks straight
on through the house, out through the back windows and
out into the trees in my backyard.

Ah ha; Robin's keen eyes
could have been looking at
my backyard trees,
flying straight and hard, not seeing
the window pane. Blam and there you are-

an explanation which made some sense
Robin in seeing his destination could not see what was right before him;
Death with painful irony--

his grave lay beneath those trees
he was so intent
to reach.
Dead Robin flying fast,
gaze fixed upon his own death.
How Shakespearean.

I think final destinations,
as in where we will die:
inside hospitals, on the road,
in a plane. For most of us
this is unknown.

My robin could see his own demise;
the means to him were clear and unclear;
my window, both opaque
and transparent
was right there before him.

Ah, again how Shakespearean.
A Robin causality;

wonder if he had kids.

Title: The Earth Speaks

I am the Earth, your mother
and you are my children.

I am from
the cosmic dust
of a thousand, billion, trillion stars;
I was conceived in tumult;
I've endured millions asteroid hits
I have felt cataclysmic comet shots,
hot lava flows over my face,
volcanic steam;
titanic explosions-
my insides
blown up;
where time and time again,
asteroids destroyed all my life;
but I started again;
renewed it
and I gave birth to you,
to all life.

I have created
beautiful blue oceans
continents, and woods
greens, and life, life
I have given life everywhere.

I took from the seas
my tiniest amino
bits
and created the smallest creatures;
one cell first,
then colonies
and then whole beings,
you;

I nurtured beautiful and ugly creatures alike,
your brothers and sisters.

I also gave you the moon
for silver nights,
the stars for inspiration,
a magnetic shield
to protect your from the burning rays of the sun;
I gave you food, trees and animals
so that you might thrive.
I taught you fire.

You are all my children
whom I have reared in paradise;
in a world of plenty.

I took you from the caves
and showed you how to grow large brains,
sacrificed my own wood trees
so that you might eat your food;
gave you animal skins
of my own creation
to shelter you from winter;
gave you water.

I showed you the beauty of the stars;
and too, alas, too
a brain big enough to study war.

And you did discover war;
you discovered hate;

you took my abundance
and transformed it
into destruction.

My forests now burn
ignited by your hand;
you have rent my face with mining scars
and quarries;
polluted my rivers and oceans
for beads and baubles;
and fleeting shiny things
for your amusements,
and, then you threw them away;
whole pollution mountains created.

There seems no retreat from you
and the relentlessness
with which you pursue
all this
for reasons
I do not fathom;
my canopy ages.

Hear me my children;
my fate is entrapped
with yours,
whether you live
is whether I live,

what you do
can destroy me
and life itself.

I will return to being a cold, rocky world
in the rushing void;
my blues
will become gray
and then black.

Hear me my children
for we are family.

Note: The American Cultural Landscape is, of course, nonetheless displays that characteristic American sensibility to romance, humor, love and optimism.

Romance, Family, Humor

And The Light Touch:

American Style

Title: What Is Love?

The synonyms below for what is Love
only illustrate how complex the thing is.

Is Love affection, sex, brotherly, motherly
or infatuation?

Is it strong attraction,
Mysterious Intensity
which cannot be defined?

And what of Love of God
which of these below
fits best that loving style?

Forced to look at this
in detail
I had not noticed before,
I now need to decide
which is best in my regard-
the passionate soul-mated-ness Love,
the Hungry Style,
the Affection Model
the Devoted Lover
stable but less exciting fare?

Should Love-
the kind I give
and prefer-

be the dangerous kind,
heart leaping,
or the more adult
view of love
as Foundation Building?

Perhaps we love in different ways
which vary throughout the years;
so no one loving style fits all.

But, forced to choose, my choice
is clear;
I will take Devotion as my best way
of Love
given and received.

Here's why:
Devotion is Focused Beam
steady and unrelenting
and implies a certain Unconditionally.

My Love is devoted to me and I to her
seems a good basis for Eternity.

Devotion never veers,
in storm or adversity
and that gives comfort
in treacherous times as these.

I'll trade the flaming kind,
for while it burns brightly,
soon flickers
makes apologies
and leaves
never to return.

No, give me the long-haul comfort
of a Love that's there when these hands
wrinkle,
for then and there
is when I will need the most
steadfast loving care.

Others may take the photos out
of flaming loves
gained and lost.
I for one
am playing for keeps
I want my love
here beside me
always

And you know,
she is
for keeps
I mean.

WHAT IS LOVE?

Synonyms: These nouns denote feelings of warm personal attachment or strong attraction to another person. Love is the most intense: marrying for love.

Affection is a less ardent and more unvarying feeling of tender regard: parental affection.

Devotion is earnest, affectionate dedication and implies selflessness: teachers admired for their devotion to children.

Fondness is strong liking or affection: a fondness for small animals.

Infatuation is foolish or extravagant attraction, often of short duration: lovers blinded to their differences by their mutual infatuation

The American Way of Seduction

Title: The Seduction Of Ada

It was his hand

as we sat side by side;

he waved it

as a flag

waves in a breeze.

The fingers arched

and flowed

up

down

and up again;

pausing at one time

then moving again.

I looked into his eyes

and his eyes slanted

to his hand

saying "Look again."

I looked to notice that hand

was spelling a word

each finger

making a letter;

I could see

an "I"

and a crooked L

and O

a V

an E

a U.

He was so close I could

feel his body move

with each letter formed.

Enraptured, he took my hand

and he guided it

lettering:

first the M

A

R

R

Y

M

E

and the crooked finger

question mark.

How could you not

love a man like this?

I did:

and I spelled it out

for him too

Y

E

S

My fingers swayed

in that loving breeze

and do still today.

He seduced

me,

fingering

the air.

We still finger the air

saying each day

hello and goodbye

our secret code

for remembering.

Title: Small Space Photo Seduction

We were at your mother's house
in the early autumn chill
rummaging the attic
looking at photographs;
close
in the small space,
turning pages

You leaned into me
to get a better look
and I let you.

A murmur
over a blurred baby photo
and the hairs on my neck
curled from the
warmth of your breath,

I tried to hide the fact
that I was shuddering.

"Are you cold" you said.
putting your arm around
offering warmth.

I took that cuddle
and let it settle
into my heart space.

That was all
that was needed then
a simple hug and touch
your warm breath
and I eased back
relaxed
feeling at home;
and I was.
I was thinking we were looking at family
and I was imagining you there in photos

———

and our kids might be look like years from now.

And you were too:
you said it:
"Wonder what our kids would look like."
you said

You seduced me with that question
and I you when I said:
"I wonder too."

We started with a hug
above those photographs.

Title: Stick People Kissing

It was the working late,

hours in that office together

the comfortableness;

the small talk

and the glancing looks.

You held my arm

to trace along the blackboard

the picture of the stick-people

we drew in the crowd.

So close.

You began to trace

two stick people

one kneeling

and the bubble over his head

said,

"I love you."

I said:

"What are you doing? "

You said: "Don't talk to me

say it with the stick people."

I drew my stick lady with a bubble

saying,

"Are you talking to me? "

You drew and bubbled:

"Must be, you the only

beautiful stick-lady in this drawing."

"Humm, " I said,

"need a little more than that.

Who's talking; stick-man or you? "
"Oh if you must know

stick-man is my wing-man

It is you

I love."

I bubbled back

my stick-lady saying

"xxxx

hearts and kisses"

The next day in the conference room

on that blackboard

were two stick-people

arms wrapped around each other

kissing;

bubbling exclamations.

Title: The Kiss

She slipped into her smiling stance
so easily.

Her lips parted showing her teeth
alabaster white and gleaming

as she sat on the couch
in dim light
bathing in the self-confident light

women sometimes have that says

"whatever happens in this encounter

with him:

it

will not matter

and will be only a ripple made by a rock thrown in the pond

with no consequence

because in her dry dock, she was thinking,

her emotional ship

had already sailed;

while she had only to move slightly or whisper-speak

and my dingy boat of disappointment and rejection would start to sink

as sure as white teeth part

and then

clamp down swallowing.

Transfixed at her mouth's opening

I only too late realized that alabaster,

shiny smiles

form the emotional bite

where something is bit off

and then swallowed down.

One sided complacency

married to desperate attraction

ends badly

if one of the party

is blinded by bright smiling teeth

which rise in the darkened night

offering the promise of a kiss

but delivering only the fatal bites

the cat delivers

to the hypnotized mouse.

Such to me is irrestible.

Danger's erotic quiverings

place my hand in fire

to see how close heat can be

without singeing the soul

which lingers close by

but not too close

and I fix my gaze on that oraficed opened mouth

and my butter-fly breathing

lent to the event

one soft breath

rising to meet those panting lips

like the sirens offering

but never giving;

promising neither solace or need fulfilled;

silently demanding that she cross my

river Styx.

I watch as she stiffens from the shock

realizing, she herself, had been denied

what she had always felt

was her birth-right;

a kiss proffered; a kiss received,

but here for the first time

she experienced denial

a kiss in abeyance

close but willfully

withheld;

coming, but never came;

siren songs

which are near but stay outside

the closing circle;

out of reach

leaving her mouth

dry and bereft;

stunned that the moth

could come so close yet

resist the flame;

eyes now wide

she stares at me

seeking soul-level knowledge

of how and who could approach her crimson mouth

and yet resist..

She stared at my lips hovering.

I said

"Come close

step over the line more than halfway;

I need the surrender

of your mouth to mine

and in doing so

know you have abandoned that complacency

___

which shrouds you.

Don't hesitate, or it will be too late

your mouth is mine

even if we never touch

because it is the on-coming need

I see in its quivering, hesitancy

and your breathing

tells me you are done;

warmth exudes

and retreats;

I see your breasts rising

determinedly seeking

what had been denied;

yet the denial act

ignites both our needings

now mixed with curiosity

engorged lips, and

erstwhile somnambulant

needs.

At the marker point it is now

for each of us advance or retreat;

two breathings now indistinguishable;

pouty mouth

and hungry lips

meet

and meld;

fire-breathing

soul-fusing tremblings.

Title: Body Mine

This solar system mobile
slowly rotates
moved by a tiny breeze
I imagined just might
come from me below
breathing.

This was the silence of me.

The blank day was still
as the inside of a vault
no sound outside
no sound from within.

I sank into the moment;
my breathing muting
wanting to see
how comfortable
I was with the me
lying there.

Stillness is a severe test.

Then a quiet shudder
as I allowed an exhale longer
and deeper than usual,
this first shudder then
followed by another.
And another.

Breathing seemed to direct
my very being to another space
and my Body Being
in this circumstance
roused itself
came out
and displayed

---

its secret existence
which I
I realized
I ignore most of my life.

Startling to feel
Startling to realize
my thoughts leapt
to the idea
that this body was alive
separate from my mind
and had it own needs
goals and direction.

Startling to realize
that this my body
is alive in its own right,

separate from
me or mind
having a separate Being.

I'd always thought that
aliveness was somehow
seated in my mind.

It and I talked.
It and I conversed
but what I thought
in that moment
did my body have to say?

What language does it speak?

I realized I
had regarded it as a machine
to be feed or fueled
but not an entity
with its own Ideas and feelings.

For example,
does insecurity
lie in the mind,
in the brain
or in the body?

What is a body idea
anyway, separate from
my mind?

Can a body dream?

All of this was startling
and to this day
I'm still seeking answers
to questions

with more questions still.

Where does my mind start
and my body end?
Not sure.
but one thing is clear
bodies domain
is sexual;
and it wants to live.

Title: The Used To Be Possible-Charlene Testifies

I carefully explained to him that women
don't fall in love--
that is a luxury for teens.
The twenties are for fun
but after that it is serious business
to find a mate.

When you are a woman among boys
your vision changes;
fun are toys to be put away
which guys never leave
but us girls feel more responsibility,
feel more,
have more at stake;
we are the ones who get pregnant
have the babies
balance the budgets
have a dream of the future
and the boy-men
only dream of womanizing
and giggling about it to their
boy friends.

We have more at stake;
love after thirty
is far more serious;

and second place

to the long term needs
of a child and a homestead
and if that is not to be
we have a career to think of
with a man
or man-free.

This mind-set is alien
to the man-child
who understandably
can't afford romance
or marriage
who retreats to his video games;
girl-chasing, bar-drinking and in-ward things.

So what is a girl to conclude;
one on one, or solitude,
adoption; or man-child on the week-end
for one's needs?

Well, that is the state of things;
things reduced to the affordable,
the minimum, and the possible.

We girls are the barometers
of what is going on in society
and the one's first
asked to make the sacrifice
to What Is
and to forego
the Used To Be Possible.

Title: Touching

She has a four inch scar-vertical-
from above her navel,
to her almost there.

Slightly raised
it has it's smooth parts
and bumpy edges
which I stroke most nights;

each time wondering if
the bumpy will get smooth
or the smooth bumpier.

It at times seems to signify
her good half
and her better half.

She doesn't notice
since I touch it so often;
a nightly ritual.

It must be soothing to her;
she doesn't protest.

"Thanks Dear" she most often says.
I imagine
she imagines
this is our way
of staying in touch
and I feel her
in this way

knowing if I sooth

long enough

the scar will melt away.

Title: Woman Talk-Man Talk -Lisa and Jody

"Why do I

she said

 always have to carry the torch

 be the one who illuminates

while you bask

in the hidden shadows

making no effort;

the one dog

on the dog

sled team

 not really pulling?

Why do I have to answer the phone,

talk to the neighbors

organize the birthday parties

talk to the in-laws

and then get all dressed up

after cooking dinner

and make you feel wanted?

Why do I have to do the dishes

dress the kids

empty the trash

while you watch the ball game?

You're right he said,

Why do I have to be the one

to always tell you I'm right

and you never have to discover

that out yourself?

You're right he said.

 "Are you mocking me"

"No, " he said

"that would be wrong"

"You're right."

"Talk to me" she said.

"Well, " he said "this is how it feels to me.

I come home and while I'm working

you have stolen the kids.

I know you work too

but you tell them that if they

do wrong when I come home

I will discipline them.

 So they don't have any real feel

for me

———

except that you can protect them

from me

if you keep their wrong doing from me.

If I am too close to the girls you get jealous

and tell me to empty the trash.

If I really do the dishes and take over

he household with that teenager

we talked about coming in to help-

you oppose.

I'm not to be Household King

but House hold Helper.

If I talk to the in-laws I find out that you

have sabotaged

having told them that behind closed doors

you are suffering

and they think I am mean.

You talk to them more than you talk to me.

If I watch a game

it is a man thing

but if you do lunch with the girls

I'm told I am jealous of girl things.

If I am strong in standing up for my self

I am a chauvinistic;

if you do

you are Warrior Woman.

If I can't sit for hours on the phone

you can

and say I am anti-social.

All the things you do now

and hate

you want me to do

and I think

you would like to see me

in an apron.

And by the way,

sometimes I like to

see you put me before

your friends, the dog

the kids and your mother.

I am in fifth place.

"So "she said

"is this all there is

to our relationship? "

"No, " he said I have been meaning

to talk to you about the sex.

You seem to think that most men

are bad in bed

but a woman can't be

bad in bed"

Flash bulletin

that is not true.

So she said

is that all?

No he said

I love you.

And she said

"I love you too."

Neither

was bad

that night.

Note: We could not end this work without taking into account some of the aspects of American humor. I have taken some of these from my own family history, and from my readers, always display the fact that, no matter how hard times get, Americans seem not to lose their sense of humor.

The American Way of Humor Title:

What Men Need To Know About Women

She will not be looking at you when the food arrives

She will not be looking at you in the midst of children

She will not be aware of you if there is a cat, or dog

She does not love you past three years but loves the idea of you.

She is not romantic past 25.

She does not care as much about how you look past 25. Other things come to matter more.

She talks to her friends more than you.

You like doing it, she likes foreplay.

Your choice is just for now, she is thinking, after 30, about forever

She is thinking she has allowed you to capture her.

Women choose you, not the other way around.

You are not as handsome as Ben Franklin past 45.

If she is not the star you are the villain

Learn to go blind after 45

Young women don't know how to make love, but do.
Older women know how but don't.

———

There is no truth that can't be clouded by memory.

She remembers everything. You don't.

You fear losing your hair, women fear losing their beauty and their bodies.

The way to a woman's heart is through the restaurant menu and the beautiful house.

Women talk, you don't

Women are smarter than you outside the office

Women are smarter than you in the home

Ok, you are smarter at work-sometimes

The secret of romance is her being attracted to you and you doing nothing to mess that up.

If you think sex is the key to making women fall in love with you, you'd be better off betting on chocolate--the odds are better.

Learn to like women, things work out better that way.

Title: What Women Need to Know About Men

He is as uncomplicated as he seems; sex, food and sports.

If he is choosing work over sex, give more sex.

If he is still choosing work over sex, find out who she is.

Men want to be in high-school shape but love beer more.

He is not trying to please you, he is trying to please him.

If he goes to sleep, nature made things that way-stop complaining.

If you go to sleep, you are fantasizing about some other man.

For you sex is closeness and love, for him it is release.

A truly romantic man is under 25.

A truly romantic woman is 16 and 45

If you don't like men soon you will not like him

Don't make love, be love

You want tender and dangerous, he wants Madonna and the other thing, both don't really work.

If you marry him and divorce him, in the marriage, for the kids, there will be trouble

In the list of priorities, friends, family, kids, pets, work, your looks, if he is number seven there will be trouble.

The way to a man's heart in not through his stomach--lower.

A sense of male-humor is sexy to a man

Flirt, kiss slow and run fast; and be sure to get caught.

If you wonder "why can't a man be more like a woman" there will be trouble.

If you wonder why a man can't be more like a man there will be trouble

If you like your man being a man, you are lucky- and there will be no trouble.

Note: This piece tries to sum up much of this book.

Title: The Sayings of Uncle Dan

Don't think too much;
that not the way to smartness;
day-dream more,
that makes you
smarter, if you believe in it.
Einstein did.

Don't be too obsequiously humble
it implies you are great enough to need
to be.

Don't be too wise;
it upsets people
hold back a little
you seem smarter that way.

Don't try to look too good
people will see you only
as good for looking good.

Make one or two good
friends;
too many and you
will acquire enemies posing
as friends.

Don't think too much
about the Future
you'll stumble over Right Now
won't get to the Future at all.

Love your parents
even if they don't deserve it
because you have to have
some love
to give some love.

Remember is Karma is Karma
is Karma

Don't get all hung up
on bad and good
pretty soon you won't
have any friends.

Kiss and hug
all the children
all the time.

People are not a movie.
People are real
and they are not in your movie.

Don't watch television--
interrogate television

Open the blinds;
it'll prove you don't have
secret powers

You can't be cute
past 16.

Don't kiss in the dark
if you are not willing
to kiss in the light.

Wonder why and why
at all times.

Smile at someone
for no reason;
remember how
much it meant
when it happened to you?

Don't try to be sexy;
be sexy.

Get low with animals
and children;
get on the floor.

Let someone else
shine sometimes.

Be quiet sometimes,
You don't have to talk
just because you can.

Don't eat anything
bigger than your head.

Don't eat without chewing good.

Don't eat just to be nice.
.
Control what goes into your body
you are going to need it a long time.

Nobody is better than you
even if they think so;
and you are no better than
anyone else
even if you think so.

Want what you need;
it works out best that way
and need, too,
what you want.

Kiss slow
run fast
and play for keeps.

If someone
makes you laugh till you pee
marry "um.

The rich are children;
they are really attached
to their lattes.

You can't go home
if you never come back.

You can get along with people
if you can be alone with people;
quietly.

Your life is going to be
engraved on the inside lid
of your casket.
Don't have it be blank.

You can get over yourself
if you get naked
face a full-length mirror
turn around,
bend over
and look through your legs.

If Jesus came back
he'd go to some churches
and take his money back
and the collection plate too.

If someone calls you a name
ask for details;
what kind of cow?
Do you mean Jersey,
Holstein?
"Oh you don't know you say?
Then you are not only mean
but dumb too;
and ugly."

You are old if you
don't want to get out of bed

in the morning-and depressed too.
If you do then you are young
no matter what your age.

The perfect woman wears
a gingham dress.
The perfect man
wears only a smile.

Babies come naked
kids like to be naked
Grown ups have their most fun naked;
In the grave you will soon get naked.
There is something going on with naked.

When you come home
give a hug and a smile;
don't be a coward.

Kissing a pig
don't make bacon
and kissing rear-ends
don't make friends

Catch up;
I am so far behind you
I am ahead.

Wearing a watch
don't mean
you know what time it is.

If being smart made you happy
happy people would be smart
but they aim's
but they do know something
you don't.

I had an uncle Dan
who always said that a man
had to be taught
how to please a lady

by learning to say "yes dear"
just like she means it.

I had an Auntie Sal
who always said that a woman
had to be taught how to please
a man
by learning to say "yes dear"
just like he means it.

Remember
nothing happens
in life until somebody
falls in love
with something,
or somebody.

Every time someone says
"Now I am not bragging on my self"
expect some self-bragging is going to be happening soon.

You can win every argument
by calling your opponent a do-do head.

I walked past the plate glass window
on the street
and a demon had taken over my body-a plump one.

"Really, really smart people are always ugly." he said
"It's a rule."
"You must be very very smart." she said.

She asked me where babies come from.
I told her LA; they also whine a lot there.

"He was beautiful" she said
but not as beautiful as Ben Franklin
on the 100 dollar bill.

"I used my rapier wit on him," he said "but left out the wit."

Always choose the happy meal at the restaurant and over-tip

Don't tell the truth if it will be used to murder someone else.

Be nice to people-
it don't cost nothing.

Growing up is about
more than just getting taller.

You can have anything you want in the world
if you are willing to let others have what they want too.

Always give credit to others more than yourself
even if this is not true.

The most important phrase in the world is
"I am not sure. Let's go find out."

You can get any woman to fall in love with you
if you really love women. If you don't like women
the woman you end up with will return the favor

If you don't like men, see above.

Gossip is the refuge
of those who lack skills

Don't spend your life protecting
what didn't deserve protecting in the first place

It is hard to find a good woman
so get a hard woman to help you look

Women want a man who understands
what women want without having to be told.
A man wants a woman who gives him what
he wants without asking

You can't find your princess
without being a prince yourself

Act like a loving person
and soon you don't have to act no more

Being happy only comes to the happy being.
Happy being is the willingness to be without demands

Joy is a happy smile
Best be yours.

Scheme, plot, and calculate at all times
to tell the exact truth.

Hit a man when he is down
make an enemy for life

Never eat what you can't digest.

Animals are people too.

Money is the root of all evil;
jealousy is the tree upon which it grows.

Past 40, just stop looking in the mirror
you'll be happier

Big lips kiss better

Don't hold on to the illusion
that you can hold on to what you never had
 to begin with.

"You never understood me," she said
"Huh? he said

"I don't like sex" she said
too many noises, too many smells and grunts
and the position is ridiculous."
"Good thing" he said "it only lasts a coupla minutes."

When I was a young man I liked thin girls and after I went to sleep.
When I was an older man I liked thick girls because they provided the
pillow.

Enjoy life," Uncle Dan said
"just not too much."

Ask "Were those gunshots?"
five blocks away.

Love starts when you stop being all hung up about love.

Peace is the ability to get along with others.

Cowardice is the inability to tolerate peace.

Always, always, be the first to reach out;
from there you have the choice to shake a hand
or slap a face.

Communism is the exploitation of man by man:
with Capitalism, it is just the other way around.

With Dictatorship the people get the leadership they don't deserve
With Democracy the people get the leadership they do deserve.

A Six-foot goose standing beside a man on a corner:
  "Embarrassed to be seen talking to an imaginary goose huh?"

The End